I0754519

1.

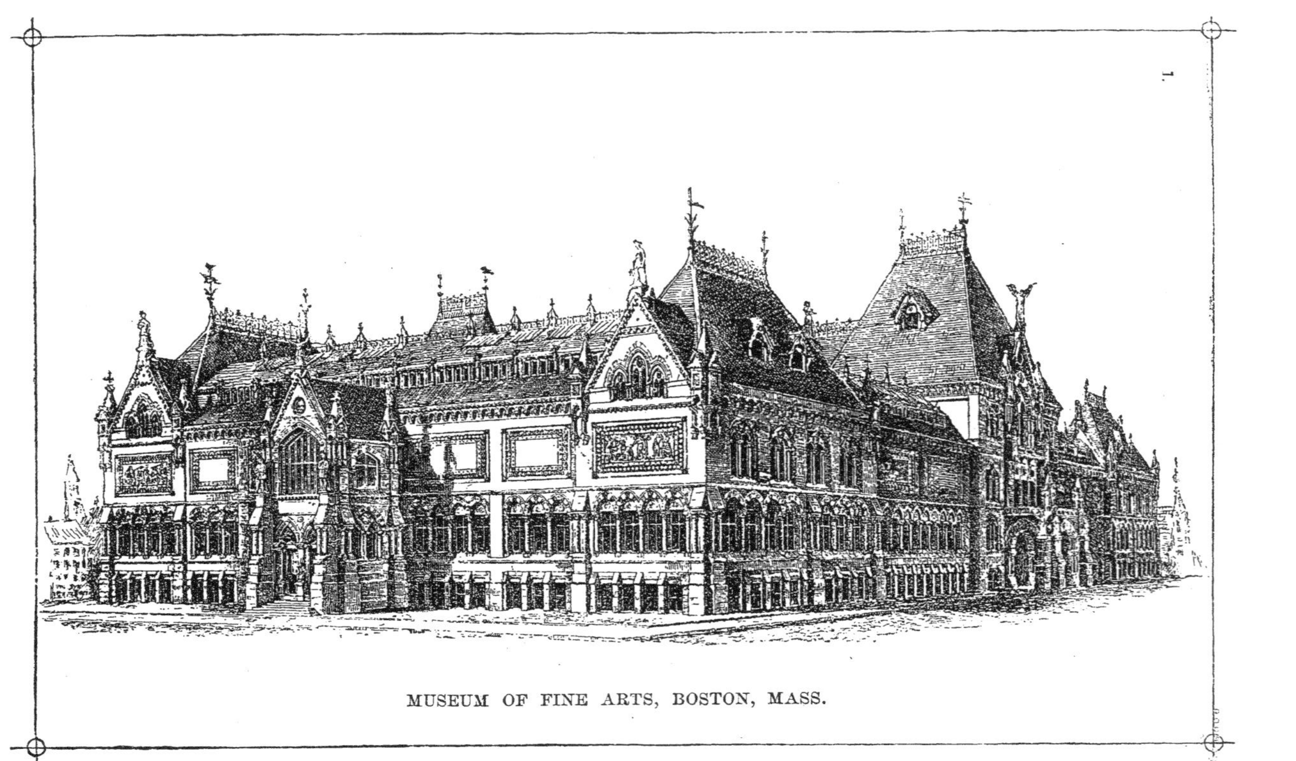

MUSEUM OF FINE ARTS, BOSTON, MASS.

ART EDUCATION,

SCHOLASTIC AND INDUSTRIAL.

BY

WALTER SMITH,

ART MASTER, LONDON; LATE HEAD MASTER OF THE LEEDS SCHOOL OF ART AND SCIENCE AND TRAINING SCHOOL FOR ART TEACHERS; NOW PROFESSOR OF ART EDUCATION IN THE CITY OF BOSTON NORMAL SCHOOL OF ART, AND STATE DIRECTOR OF ART EDUCATION, MASSACHUSETTS.

WITH ILLUSTRATIONS.

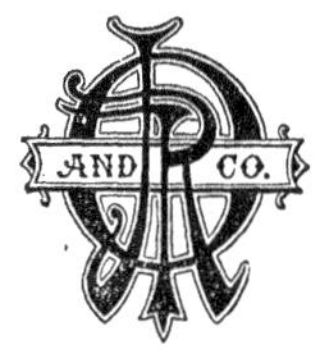

BOSTON:
JAMES R. OSGOOD AND COMPANY,
(LATE TICKNOR & FIELDS, AND FIELDS, OSGOOD, & CO.)
1873.

Entered according to Act of Congress, in the year 1872,

By JAMES R. OSGOOD & CO.,

In the Office of the Librarian of Congress, at Washington.

Boston:
Stereotyped and Printed by Rand, Avery, & Co.

TO

THE HON. JOHN A. LOWELL,

OF BOSTON,

THIS BOOK,

WHICH RESULTED FROM A COURSE OF LECTURES INITIATED BY HIM,

IS RESPECTFULLLY DEDICATED.

INTRODUCTION.

THOUGH introductions have long since come to be regarded as impertinences, and prefaces abandoned as unnecessary, I feel that some sort of general statement is due from me, when offering to the public a work of such a distinctly two-fold character as this, in one volume.

The time has come, which has been so long looked for, when this country, prosperous, and developing beyond all precedent, has sought in art the enjoyment and refinement which trade and commerce alone cannot give. The movement in favor of art education in Massachusetts is distinctly traceable to the influence of a few men, who, from European experience, saw that their country and State were behind the times in the promotion of art; that this materially affected the commercial prosperity of the nation, and its character as an educated people; whilst the natural progress of manufactures, and the accumulation of wealth by the people, required increased skill in the workmen, and the varied opportunities of art education generally. The effect of delaying practical movements to insure instruction in art for so long a time has been, that, now it is being taken up, the demand for information concerning all phases of the subject is great and continuous. In the first section of this work, I have endeavored to give such practical information about schools of art and art teaching as I have learnt by experience is now required. In the second part, on the more general question of industrial art education, I have tried to enunciate general principles, which, when made possible by the development of art skill, may control the motive or character of the manufactures of the country. Public opinion directs the workshop; and it is to that I have appealed: the unskilled workman seeks skill in art schools; and I have aimed to make them practicable, and adapted to the wants and circumstances of this country.

I have to acknowledge the help received from the pages of "The London Builder" and Mr. Eastlake's book on "Household Taste" in the matter of illustrations, and hope at some future time to increase their number, so that every distinct branch of industrial art may be represented.

CITY POINT, BOSTON, August, 1872.

CONTENTS.

CHAPTER I.

CHAPTER II.

CHAPTER III.

CHAPTER IV.

CHAPTER V.

CHAPTER VI.

CHAPTER VII.

CHAPTER VIII.

CHAPTER IX.

CHAPTER X.

CHAPTER XI.

CHAPTER XII.

APPENDIX I.

APPENDIX II.

APPENDIX III.

APPENDIX IV.

LIST OF ILLUSTRATIONS.

[*For Mechanical reasons the Plates are placed at regular intervals throughout the work; but the figures given herewith will guide in referring to them.*]

NOTE.

The colored plates numbered XIV. and XV. should read 29 and 30, and those numbered VI., VII., VIII., and IX. should be 37, 38, 39, and 40 respectively.

Classified List of Illustrations.

SCHOOLS OF ART, — ENGLISH.

SCHOOLS OF ART, — AMERICAN.

DESIGNS FOR SCHOOLS OF ART.

FURNITURE, POTTERY, &c.

COLORED PLATES.

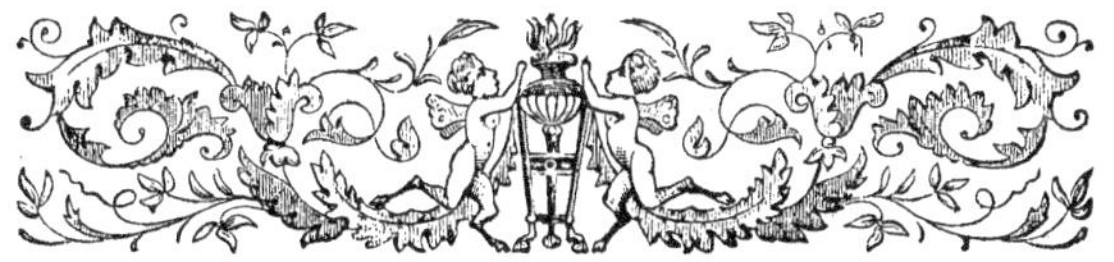

ART EDUCATION.

CHAPTER I.

GENERAL REVIEW.

THE subject of Art Education has, during the last quarter of a century, become a question of some importance,—both because its neglect, or imperfect realization, previously had allowed valuable human faculties to remain undeveloped, whilst the improvement of general education produced a consciousness of the deficiency; and because the fruitfulness of modern discoveries in science, by which the happiness and prosperity of the human race have been advanced, has drawn attention to the possibility of deriving corresponding benefits from its sister subject, Art. Education of the past is open to the charge of having concerned itself very much about what men in distant ages, and with limited perceptions, have said and written and done with reference to the earth they inhabited, the beliefs they held, and the passing circumstances which surrounded them; and to have concerned itself very little with unfolding to living men the practical value of physical laws which affect them day by day, or endeavored to open up the capabilities we have for "conquering the earth, and subduing it;" to have accepted as an all-important mission the display of the literature, or explanation of the precise theological dogmas or political creeds, of eminently respectable persons who arrayed themselves in togas, wore sandals, and believed in mythological creations called gods, and that the sun moved round the earth every four and twenty hours; whilst it might have been more profitably engaged in furnishing means for discovering the application of natural laws, by which living men might live acceptably, tearing from their minds the fables and puerilities that kept them under mental subjection, and which limited their intellectual and moral growth, as well as their conquest and subjection of the earth and its hidden forces. What may be described as practical education, which fits a man to be self-possessed and master of the situation twelve working hours of the twenty-four that he lives each day, has, to state it moderately, not been the prime object in universities or schools in their production of working-men, of all ranks; so that, whilst the pious bequests and patriotic endowments of centuries have been used educationally to produce generations, and thousands of men who have "sung the same sad song" as their predecessors, it is to others, outside the universities, who have been brought violently into contact with ever-present necessities, that we owe most of the advantages of existence in this century, and many of its most cherished privileges.

Far be it from me to express one word of disrespect towards any branch of intellectual education: it would be a misrepresentation of the love I bear to every kind of mental culture if that impression were conveyed by my words; but looking back at the world's history for many centuries, during which time polite literature in the dead languages, heathen mythology, and polemical theology have held undisputed educational possession of the mental field, I cannot but be impressed by the fact, that they have, as schoolboys would express it, had a very considerably long innings, and made a poor score: and, if we look to what has been accomplished by men who have not benefited by that kind of education, still more if we consider what has been the result of modern scientific education, in many a field both intellectual and social, we must acknowledge, that in a very short innings there has been registered a winning score, in a contest wherein human liberty and happiness have been the victors, — a liberty which we possess because of our deliverance from ignorance of some of God's laws, and a happiness which arises from their more perfected knowledge.

It is not to be wondered at, therefore, that now, when the majority of human beings in countries where so marked a progress has occurred are to be educated, and that they are to be educated for the practical business of life rather than its contemplation, instruction should at least include subjects which have reference to the arts of daily life, and the occupations of a vast majority of the people. It is undoubtedly right that the mind should be cultivated, and that the intellectual faculties, developed by study of the wisdom of past ages, be enabled to profit by experience, and grasp the spiritual laws which govern us; but it cannot be wrong, so long as our physical frames vitally connect us with the earth we are upon, that our bodies should, by training, be made the ready servants of our minds, and be enabled to express completely, without interception or distortion, the ideas or conceptions we mentally create. Education is not the accumulation of facts and formulæ, as dry goods are stored in a warehouse, any more than the Church is composed of the conveniently-arranged heaps of stones in which men worship their Creator: it is the clothing of men's minds with a shield from igno rance, whilst full play is allowed for the exercise of their trained wills; and it is the training of those wills to do what the trained mind and the skilful hand shall find to do, and do it with all their *might*, — might being power of knowledge and power of execution, expressed in one strong word, — that constitutes a real and practical education, in which the known and the possible unite to form the practically-educated man. A passage from an address by Dr. Lyon Playfair embodies in an example a fair representation of the value of the two kinds of education: —

"The German States, towards the end of the last century and the first part of the present one, fully perceived the necessity of educating their population; and schools were liberally spread over the country, both for the poor and for the middle classes. Classical education, which operates on the truth that man's moral nature is always the same, and that, therefore, the human passions may be governed by a knowledge of past experience, was made the groundwork upon which the German schools were taught. The schools succeeded admirably; and their pupils were worthy of the excellent instruction they received. But, after being educated, they naturally looked for employment in the direction of their education. They said to the Government which had established those schools, 'You have taught us how to understand the nature of our fellow-men by the experience of the past; we can now aid you to govern them: give us employment.' It was in vain for Government to say, 'We have given you a good education: go and work for yourselves.' The natural answer was, 'The sort of education you have given does not at all adapt us for an industrial life. We know much about history, logic, and philosophy, but nothing about manufactures and commerce.' Accordingly, the Government had gradually to enlarge their bureau for the reception of their well-educated men, until, finally, one in sixty of the population entered into State employment." At that time Germany, though a classically-educated country, was neither rich nor strong. "Then the Trade or Industrial Schools were opened, which, giving an education in the direction of production, drew off men's minds from looking to the State as the only source of respectable employment; relieving the old pressure, while it increased the resources of the country."

Germany, which is now half a century ahead of other European countries in schools of practical industry, is the acknowledged leader in many other ways, and may be quoted as an example of modern industrial education affecting the circumstances and character of a whole people. A nation of dreamers has been transformed into the most intensely-practical workers, who enter every vocation with knowledge, and pursue it with success.

Now, I do not wish to attempt to prove too much, nor to fall into the error of the advocates of classical education simply, by asserting that industrial education is all-sufficient. My plea is, that a mistake has been made by ignoring it, and is still being made by those who regard it as of less importance than classical education; and I say, that the evidence of the last fifty years goes to show, that, of the two, technical or industrial education, carried on in the laboratory, studio, and workshop, has been the most fruitful in its influence and effects on the happiness of mankind.

What I have advocated has, with remarkable foresight, long since been anticipated by the keen, practical instincts of the men of Massachusetts; and in the Boston Technological Institute, now in the full career of its beneficent operations, the State possesses an invaluable agency for the development of industrial education; whilst its existence is the most complete evidence that could be given of belief in the value attached to such agencies. What is here being done for science, covering half the ground of the subject, I want to see done for art also, that the whole field of the industrial arts pertaining to our daily lives may be thoroughly cultivated. Science has attracted to its enticing embraces the brilliant master minds of this practical age, who have, by the greatness and the fruitfulness of their discoveries, placed the claims of their mistress beyond the needs of advocacy. Scientific education, though yet in its infancy, has had such excellent nurses, being in itself a precocious child, that it can now run alone without the aid of sponsors or guardians.

The same can hardly be said for art education. It is only very recently, that, driven by necessity, the English-speaking race has recognized in art education any practical value at all; and at the present time men who regard all art as a plaything are unhappily not yet to be classed with the dodo, the fish-lizards of the mud period, and other extinct animals.

It has been this senseless estimate of art which, ignoring its capabilities for ministering to the highest requirements and capacities of men, and looking upon it as an exceptional characteristic of a few eccentric persons, — this false judgment has alone been responsible for the absence of opportunities for its development into usefulness, and its elevation into the position of an element in all education. Men's capacities lie buried within them, like precious stones in the mine, or minerals on the hillside; to discover which we must search long in many places, or dig deeply over the whole field, if we are to find what there is beneath the surface.

Unless more than one trial be made to discover the hidden treasure, it may lie forever useless to those who most need it, and are its unconscious possessors. The iron ore and the coal lying uselessly beneath the earth require first to be found, and their value tested; and then comes a Newcastle pitman, with a mine of natural science yet undiscovered within him, who combines the properties and capacities of these two materials into the locomotive engine, — an instrument of civilization which has done more for every person in this century than any one other material agency for human happiness.

The stupid boy at school, to whom tenses and cases are an abomination, and who finally, given up by his teachers, is turned adrift on the world as a lout, may be compared to a waste field showing evidences of unskilful trials to find iron or silver ore, ending in blind mines and abandoned workings. It might have been, that, had a wider range been taken, the mine would have been discovered; the boy would have found the work his hands had to do in the world, and been strengthened to accomplish it; the vein would have been hit, the well tapped; but, unfound, he has to grope his dispirited way through the world, leading a valueless life, or stumbling late in life, if ever, by what we will term a providential accident, into his natural vocation. In broadening the basis of education by the addition of the elements of science and art to the subjects of instruction in schools, we give opportunities not yet obtainable for reaching the faculties of peculiarly-constituted minds, and place within the reach of all the first steps of many useful careers; and thus we guard against a waste of human power, and a misdirection of human life, and at the same time pave the way for greater intelligence and refinement generally. A child who cannot draw the forms of objects which his eye sees, as readily as he can write or repeat the words his ear hears, is only half educated; for only half his natural powers have been EDUCED, or brought out. A child who is brought up ignorant of physical laws and the elements of scientific knowledge has to buy his experience at a costly rate in all his after life, often at the price of life itself.

There is one difference between the claims of science and art to a recognition in general elementary education, which is, that, though a certain advance must have been made on the other subjects of education before the child is capable of receiving scientific axioms, in art, whose first exercises are in imitation only, the child cannot begin too young; because the reasoning powers are not brought into play so much as the purely sensual, — the sense of vision and the sense of touch. It is a matter of question in my mind, whether drawing ought not to precede writing in education, as a more natural and simpler style of writing, less complicated, and employing less of the reasoning powers than the practice of making arbitrary signs, which conventionally represent thoughts, and often thoughts the child never had, and would not believe if they occurred to him and he understood them, such as "Correction is good for the unruly." Writing is, in fact, only drawing from memory; and the page I am now covering, if you will allow me to meditate, is nothing more nor less than a drawing from memory of signs which visibly imitate the thoughts passing through my mind.

A convention of schoolmasters in London, who had made instruction in drawing general in their schools for a year, as an experiment, passed this resolution: "That half of the time previously given to writing had been given to drawing, with the result, that the writing had

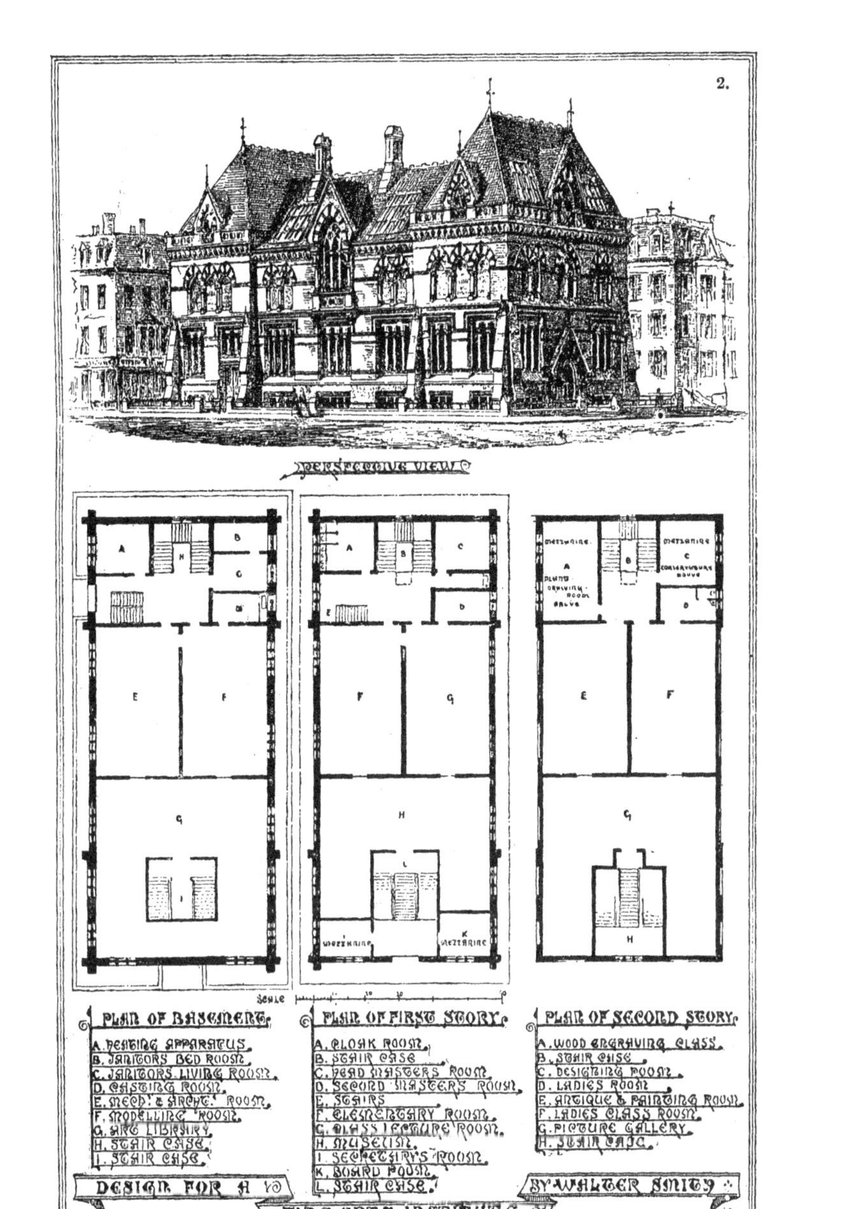
2.
PERSPECTIVE VIEW
SCALE
PLAN OF BASEMENT.
A. HEATING APPARATUS.
B. JANITORS BED ROOM.
C. JANITORS LIVING ROOM.
D. CASTING ROOM.
E. MECH.L & ARCHT.L ROOM.
F. MODELLING ROOM.
G. ART LIBRARY.
H. STAIR CASE.
I. STAIR CASE.
PLAN OF FIRST STORY.
A. CLOAK ROOM.
B. STAIR CASE.
C. HEAD MASTERS ROOM.
D. SECOND MASTERS ROOM.
E. STAIRS.
F. ELEMENTARY ROOM.
G. CLASS LECTURE ROOM.
H. MUSEUM.
I. SECRETARY'S ROOM.
K. BOARD ROOM.
L. STAIR CASE.
PLAN OF SECOND STORY.
A. WOOD ENGRAVING CLASS.
B. STAIR CASE.
C. DESIGNING ROOM.
D. LADIES ROOM.
E. ANTIQUE & PAINTING ROOM.
F. LADIES CLASS ROOM.
G. PICTURE GALLERY.
H. STAIR CASE.
DESIGN FOR A
FINE ARTS INSTITUTE
BY WALTER SMITH

been better, and the power of drawing was a clear gain." That was in about the year 1852, since which time very little has been said in that country of the difficulties in teaching children to draw. It was demonstrated by fair experiment, that about a hundred per cent of school children could be taught to draw well, and that demonstration shattered the ancient notion of genius monopolizing art powers. Indeed, not only is this true of children, but experience in the city of Boston shows that adults of nearly all ages can be taught also; the evening classes and the Normal School having pupils varying between the ages of fifteen and sixty, who are, without an exception, steadily acquiring skill in drawing. There are but four classes of human beings whom it is not found practicable to instruct in drawing. They are the blind, the idiotic, the lunatic, and the paralytic. Of the rest of mankind and womankind, exactly a hundred per cent can be taught to draw. The only real difficulty in teaching drawing to adults is found in the settled conviction in some people's minds, that they are incapable of learning. It is the only fatal hinderance; for, until that is removed, little progress can be made. And the delusion usually occupies a well-fortified stronghold, and will not easily surrender. I have often retreated in discomfiture before an enemy of that kind; and my only consolation has been the soliloquy of the henpecked husband:—

> "If she says she *will*, she *will*, you may depend on't:
> If she says she *won't*, she *won't*; and there's an end on't."

If we consider the place of drawing in general education, it may be said, that, commencing with the child upon first entry to school life, it should, under various developments, suitable to change of age and increase of powers, be practised through the whole school course. The ability to represent the forms of all objects with accuracy and readiness must inevitably result from including drawing in the education of every child; and that is a very useful power to all. What we want is, that all kinds of elementary drawing shall be taught as a language, not as an art, and be used as an instrument, not as a plaything. Drawing treated as a language is a criticism made by ourselves upon our own knowledge, in which we either discover the depths of our ignorance, or express intelligibly the knowledge and ideas we have. Especially will drawing be found a ready handmaid to scientific study, illustrating its axioms, recording its phenomena, and explaining its laws. In the schoolroom, the danger is strenuously to be guarded against of allowing drawing to be practised for the mere purpose of producing pretty things. It should be regarded as a servant, or vehicle, to assist expression in the study of other subjects, as it is in geography, by means of map-drawing. Thus, I would not teach a class the art of flower-drawing as an accomplishment, but give it lessons in botany, and require the illustrations to be drawn to fix the principles of growth on the memory. By that means we should get accurate drawings, and the botanical knowledge would be an additional gain.

In teaching drawing, from the very first, objectless and meaningless forms ought to be avoided as copies; for they make no appeal to other knowledge possessed by the pupil, or which can be communicated. Thus it is as easy to give a class information about the historical details of architecture, by selecting type-forms of the different periods as drawing-copies, as to give mere exercises in drawing, embodying neither history nor architecture. Fitting subjects of study in drawing and painting may be thus adapted to all the school ages, beginning with the lowest class in the primary school and ending with graduation at the university: during all of which time the study is to be regarded as the means to an end, and not the end itself; the end being to see, to know, to remember, to reproduce, and finally to create: in other words, education. The time spent in practising drawing weekly need be no longer, and should not be shorter, than that given to other elementary subjects, such as reading, writing, and arithmetic; and great economy of time in after life will be insured by the possession of a means of expression as ready as the tongue and more descriptive than the pen.

The use of drawing in the workshop and office needs but little demonstration; seeing that, without its skilful practice, many trades and manufactures and several professions cannot get on at all. And when we come to the practical business of every-day life in the shop, factory, and studio, we must substitute the more general word of art education, including drawing, painting, modelling, and designing, as the extent of art instruction required.

The same act of the Massachusetts State Legislature which made elementary drawing a compulsory subject of instruction in every public school in the State, so that every school-teacher neglecting or refusing to teach it to the best of his or her ability is breaking the law, or setting it at defiance, — the same act imposed on all cities and towns which had a population of above ten thousand, the additional duty of providing free instruction for adults in evening classes in the subject of industrial drawing.

This industrial drawing, a term variously interpreted, may be taken to include instruction in such branches of drawing as will make all those engaged in industrial occupations better workmen, through the improvement of their knowledge, and elevation of their taste; which instruction has not been furnished them at school, and cannot be obtained in the workshop. The phrase is well chosen and comprehensive; indeed, the whole act is a model of composition, both in what it says and in what it does. Two words, however, require to be added to it; and I hope will be added at some future time, — the words "and modelling" after the words "industrial drawing;" and then it would embrace practice in industrial art such as is most required by carvers, modellers, plasterers, chasers, and moulders, and all who work in solid materials. Two words also should be erased from the act, — the words "or mechanical" after the word "industrial," referring to drawing: for the word "industrial" includes the section of it, mechanical; and their use in the act suggests that the two words are synonymous, which is not the case; and that interpretation has misled many.

Among the ways in which art knowledge may be of use in the workshop, is in the economy of labor arising from the workman having definite objects in view, and having to make no experiments in carrying out work which must be executed to scale, plan, and design. I venture to say, that in every workshop or factory where no knowledge of drawing is possessed by the workmen, there is a waste of material, a waste of time, and an inferior article produced in the end, — evils which are a loss to the employer, through sacrificing of his material, and inferiority of work; a loss to the workman, by his time having to be wasted in experiments; and a loss to the public of tasteful objects to be obtained at a moderate cost.

It is known how important a part the foreman in every workshop or factory has to perform; yet often the only difference between him and the average artisan is, that the foreman has more technical and artistic or scientific knowledge than those under him. There is no reason why every man should not be raised to the foreman's standard, and the foreman himself many degrees higher than he now stands; and that will occur when, in the common schools and in the municipal art schools, workmen are taught to draw and design. Art education in the form of industrial drawing, whatever it may cost the country, will be repaid to it in the increased value of industrial products: it will develop the intellect of the people in an eminently practical direction; and there will be no workshops standing still, because the one man who understands working drawings happens to be away (as is not unfrequently the case now), if every man in the shop can as easily make the working drawing as he can work from it, and is prepared to do both if required. It is not unusual for English tradesmen to insert in the indentures of their apprentices, that the youth shall attend a school of art or science for two or three nights per week, forty weeks in the year; for which the employer or master pays the fees. That clause recognizes the increased worth in the work of the apprentice likely to arise from his improvement by means of technical study.

It will be a source of comfort to architects and engineers when their offices can command skilful draughtsmen from schools of art in this country; and, though that is a work of some difficulty now, by the help of art institutions it cannot long remain so. The advanced classes of the free evening schools, necessitated by the law of the State of Massachusetts, will probably attract many students, whose studies in light and shade of the human figure and historical sculpture must be a source of great improvement to them professionally. When architecture is taking so great a hold on the desires of the moneyed classes as it is in the cities and elsewhere in the whole country, a great demand will necessarily arise for the highest skill in draughtsmanship and design before very long. It will be well, therefore, that architectural students should lay hold of the opportunities which will freely be given to them to prepare for the advancement in taste to be expected from a general education in art of the people, and the consequent elevation in character of the demand for architectural art.

Perhaps the most practically important view of the subject of art education is its value commercially. In an essentially utilitarian age, things are judged by the standard of usefulness, rather than sentiment; and wherever we find great success following the experiment of introducing art education, it is where business men have forwarded and developed it as a question of dollars and cents. If any apology were required why the State of Massachusetts is expending some few thousand dollars a year in fostering art education, it would be found in the statement, that the leading manufacturers and merchants in the State had petitioned it to move in the matter, and that, in answer to inquiries made of practical men to discover whether drawing was of any use, every respondent said, "Yes." There can be no misunderstanding such evidence as the following, published in a pamphlet called "Papers on Drawing," by the State Board of Education of Massachusetts, and written in reply to a series of questions as to the value and practicability of instruction in drawing, printed in 1870. Prof. Thompson of the Worcester Technical School says, "A boy who spends two hours a week in drawing, and the rest of the time in working at the bench, learns his business faster, and becomes more skilful in it, than one who works all the time." Again, "It is calculated that the productive efficiency of every machine shop would be increased thirty-three per cent if every journeyman could read any common working drawing and work by it."

Prof. Ware, Professor of Architecture in the Boston Institute of Technology, replied, "Drawing is an invaluable element in general education. To the workman it is of the greatest practical use: it makes him a more intelligent and serviceable workman. If he attains to real skill in the use of his pencil, and develops the tastes and talents that cannot without this training be either discovered or made use of, he becomes a valuable person at once. Every branch of our manufactures is suffering from the want of just this intelligence and skill." With a courage born of true patriotism, which does not shrink from telling the truth to his fellow-countrymen, even though it be unpalatable, Prof. Ware concludes his reply thus: —

"At the Universal Exhibition of 1851, England found herself, by general consent, almost at the bottom of the list, among all the countries of the world, in respect of her art manufactures. Only the United States, among the great nations, stood below her. The first result of this discovery was the establishment of Schools of Art in every large town. At the Paris Exhibition of 1867, England stood among the foremost, and in some branches of manufacture distanced the most artistic nations. It was the Schools of Art and the great collection of works of Industrial Art at the South Kensington Museum that accomplished this result. The United States still held her place at the foot of the column."

Another witness, Prof. Bail of Yale College, testifies thus: —

"Such instruction will make our nation richer, by

making our artisans more tasteful and skilful, and by developing the latent talent of the industrial classes. Without this cultivation, no people can aspire to become a first-class manufacturing nation, nor will they be able to compete successfully with the products of skilled industry in the great markets of the world.

"Mechanics are the sinew of our commonwealth, and deserve the highest consideration of educators. At the conclusion of a lesson, gray-haired mechanics have often almost overpowered me with thanks, saying to me, 'This lesson is worth hundreds of dollars to me;' or, 'I shall work better all my life for this.' I have often found some pupil repeating the lessons to others poorer than himself.

"The whole nation is deploring the lack of good ornamental designers. We are becoming tired of sending so many millions to Europe for articles that we might produce cheaper at home if we had skilful designers. This branch of industry affects articles for the homeliest use."

Mr. Bartholomew, late Professor of Drawing in the Boston Public Schools, and whose efforts to popularize art education have been lifelong, deserving of the best thanks of the community, relates the following incident in support of the commercial value of drawing: —

"A few days since, I chanced to meet E. P. Morgan, Esq., mechanical engineer of the Saco Water-Power Machine Shop; and, in the course of our conversation, he said, that, through the inability of their workmen to understand a drawing, hundreds of dollars were lost every year. Now, what is true in this case is true of our manufacturing establishments all over the land. The time lost in doing that which must be done again because of error; the loss of material, the use of power, and the wear and tear of tools to no good purpose; the

NOTTINGHAM SCHOOL OF ART.

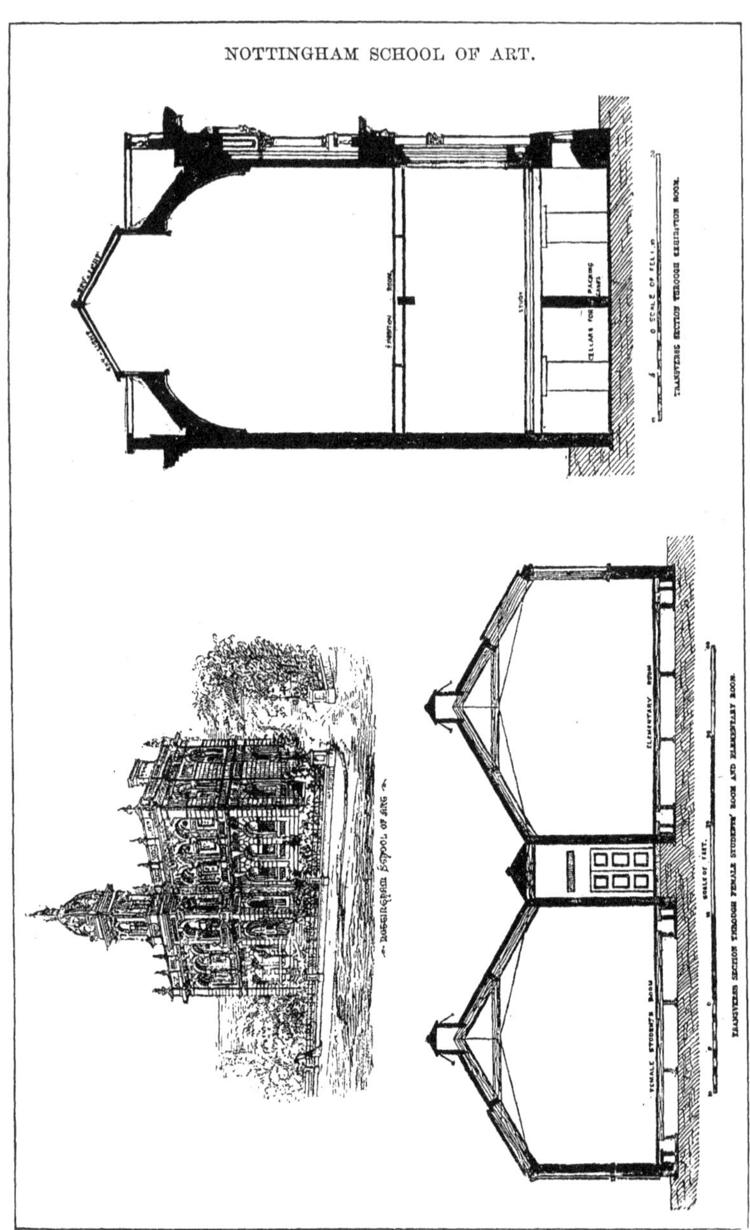

time of engineers and foremen spent in explaining drawings which would have been understood at a glance, had the workmen been instructed in drawing, and the time consumed in listening to these explanations, — costs the country, it is safe to say, millions of dollars annually. This, certainly, is an argument in favor of doing something towards giving our mechanics some knowledge of drawing."

With such evidence as this in its possession, and much more of a similar kind, the State was justified in doing something; and perhaps the consciousness that every other civilized country besides America had already recognized the needs of trade, and provided art education for its people, did not delay the movement. In my visits as State Director of Art Education to various cities in the Commonwealth, I have heard many remarkable statements made concerning the money value of a knowledge of drawing. At Worcester a manager of an important branch of local industry said, that when a lad he was one of a class of thirteen who spent all their leisure time in studying drawing. At the present time every one then in the class had attained to important positions, either as manufacturers or managers; and each had owed his power to seize the opportunity of advancement to his knowledge of drawing. That is testimony such as requires no comment. Within the last five and twenty years, we have seen a wonderful change take place in the money value of the manufactures of England. Whilst the cost of producing most of the products of industrial art has decreased by about one-half, through the invention of various machines and the discovery of labor-saving processes, the actual value of the manufactured article, taking one branch of manufacture with another, is nearly doubled; and this difference is not to be accounted for by any alteration in the value of money. How, then, is it to be explained? Simply thus: A manufactured article, whether a garment, a piece of porcelain, an article of furniture, or even a golden chalice, may be said to possess three elements of value: 1st, the raw material; 2d, the labor of production; 3d, the art character. The two first in some few cases are a large proportion of the value of the whole; and, where no art whatever is displayed, it forms the whole value. But in a vast majority of the manufacturing products of every country, the elements of cost of material and cost of labor are insignificant in comparison with the third element; viz., art character. It is that which makes the object attractive and pleasing, or repulsive or uninteresting, to the purchaser, and is consequently of commercial value. In many objects, where the material is of little or no intrinsic worth, the taste displayed in their design forms the sole value, or the principal; and it has been the general elevation of that element which has nearly doubled the commercial value of English manufactures. I am not aware of any great improvement of material or of demand, but have seen with my own eyes an advance in the artistic element in many branches of British industry from a condition closely bordering upon the barbarism of savage races to the refinement of the greatest art epochs. And it has not been an exceptional case, or a development in one direction owing to peculiar circumstances. If we take pottery, glass, porcelain, terracotta, metal work in wrought iron, brass, bronze, silver plate, goldsmith's work, jewellery, paper-hanging, carpets, parquetry, encaustic tiles, furniture, cabinet-making, upholstery, stained glass, mural decoration, wood and stone carving, chasing, enamelling, lace-making, embroidery, — all show that infusion of taste which has in all cases increased, and in many cases doubled their value in the market in five and twenty years. Now, just as drawing is the only universal language, so art is an almost universal currency, and amongst civilized races *is* universal; with this remarkable characteristic that let the art in a thing be good art, based upon natural laws, and treated with consistency and purity of feeling, and it shall consecrate the material which it ennobles, so that lapse of time will add to its value until antiquity enshrines it.

As long as civilization is allowed to pursue its course, however tastes may change, and whatever developments may be wrought, the stamp of good, honest, skilful, and cultured art industry will not only preserve its value, but pay compound interest as well. The best example I know of this is that of the South-Kensington Museum and its contents. In 1851 the English schools of design were put under the control of a hard-headed business man, who grasped the whole subject of art education, and saw its relationship to industrial art. He saw that two things were needed, — a museum of industrial art, and art masters to give instruction. Beginning with a grant of fifty thousand dollars to purchase works from the Exhibition of 1851, and an annual appropriation, which has increased every year, Mr. Cole has created a museum of industrial art which is one of the joys of the whole earth. Of course, economists would sometimes start up in the House of Commons and oppose the grants to art, as a waste of public money, and oppose the appropriation to the museum, as extravagant outlay which would bear no return. I say it with shame, also, that others opposed the expenditure upon the museum. Mr. Cole's answer to his critics was unique; and, since it was given, no one has yet had the temerity to find fault. It was this: "Gentlemen, the nation has expended a certain amount of money in buying up

Majolica plates and Cellini vases, cabinets and examples of art workmanship in every material and style and period. If it repents of its bargain, I am prepared to find a responsible committee to take the collection off the nation's hands at the price given for it, and pay interest, and compound interest, for the money which has been sunk." This set the economists a-thinking and inquiring; and they found, that so well had purchases been made, and so greatly had masterpieces of industrial art increased in value, that, if the collections were brought to the hammer, the nation would be unnumbered thousands of pounds in pocket, besides having increased the value of its own industrial manufacturing products by about fifty per cent, through the influence of art culture and the examples displayed in the museum. Since then little has been heard of waste of public money by investing in objects of art for public purposes.

This much may be said of the commercial value of art education nationally, that it both increases the estimation of ancient works, and the quality of contemporary productions; whilst individuals who become proficient in art become simultaneously, as Prof. Ware says, "valuable persons" both to themselves and society.

We will now consider how the several advantages to be derived from art education in its broadest interpretation are to be secured for this country. The division of the general government into sovereign States will probably prevent for a considerable time national action in the matter, even if the enormous geographical area of the country does not wholly prevent it. This, in my opinion, is an advantage, because it will necessitate decentralization. The capitals of the several American States are farther apart than London, Brussels, and Paris; and many of them at a greater distance from each other than Berlin, Vienna, St. Petersburg, Madrid, and Rome. Supposing, therefore, departments of science and art of the State governments to be in existence in every metropolitan city, they will be spread over America as the capitals of the European nations are distributed over Europe. I have no doubt but that eventually, whilst the bond of a common tongue, the interests of trade, and the facilities of intercommunication, will forever unite the sovereign States of America in one nation, having capacities for becoming the greatest and grandest that has ever existed upon the earth, there will yet be independent departments of science and art in every metropolitan city, from which will emanate the art education of each State. But just as Harvard and Yale, through the results of private or local action, may be said to be the national universities of America; so I believe it will be found, that in one or two intellectual centres there will arise national schools of design, which will be to industrial education what Harvard and Yale have been to professional education. Technical education in art and science may be described as the liberal education of the working classes, who have not found a home in the universities, yet who require secondary instruction of a practical character in the industrial direction, as much as the theologian needs his Greek and Hebrew, the engineer his mathematics, the physician his chemistry and anatomy, and the statesman his philosophy and logic. The evidence is strongly in favor of the city of Boston being the first city in the Union to establish a national school of design. The existence of Harvard College in close proximity to the city gives it the advantage of a phalanx of eminent men in the professors, which forms its thought, and shapes its aspirations. That a large proportion of men of culture and European travellers and students reside in Boston has also had its effect upon the desire for progress in the arts which has recently been developed.

The establishment of a museum of fine and industrial art in Boston, which is now in the process of construction, has committed the city to the project which forms an important part of any national system of art education. Yet valuable as will be the aid of the art museum in its effects on the public taste, and impossible as it would be to have a system of art education without it, it must not be forgotten that a museum is only a part of a scheme, which must be supplemented by many other parts if the whole result is ever to be attained. A museum, however rich in its contents, and perfect in its arrangements for exhibition, is but a show, unless it combines with its wealth of art the active educational agencies in the class-room which are to transmute this wealth into currency. The absence of this is the fault of the British Museum, the Louvre, and many other priceless collections of art and antiquities which exist simply as museums, and not as training-schools. The opposite of this is the virtue of the South-Kensington Museum, where above a thousand students annually obtain education, fitting them for every branch of art work, whether as designers, public instructors, painters, sculptors, architects, engravers, lithographers, or as connoisseurs. And the glorious collections which form a holiday sight for sight-seers stand as faithful witnesses, giving evidence to the inquiring art student, and, through his education, becoming general in their influence upon the national taste. Thus both ends are attained: the public has its show, and the student his instruction; for, when principles have been inculcated in the class-room and lecture-theatre, he adjourns to the museum to see the historical application of those principles in specimens of the best periods of art and art workmanship.

I am aware that this matter is receiving the best attention of those engaged upon the construction of the museum, and desire to place on record, and bring before the public, suggestions concerning a development of the scheme. The drawing-classes now established in Boston and many other cities of the Commonwealth are not schools of design nor schools of art: the fine arts museum of itself will not be a school of art or design. It is the union of the two for the same purpose, in the same place, which will constitute a *real* school of design; and the absence of either half of the programme deprives the scheme of art education of considerably more than half of its efficiency. The peculiar character of my duties as State Director of Art Education, in conference with public committees and boards of education, in discussing the means and difficulties of establishing schools of art and drawing classes, securing teachers, providing examples of study, and other work incidental to the cultivation of art, — these duties give me special opportunities of knowing what is wanted in this country in the form of a national school of art; whilst a somewhat long and wide experience in other countries of how such institutions are constructed and managed, together with their successes and failures, have given me the means of judging, and have impressed me with a sense of responsibility in expressing the result of my present observations here, and knowledge of the past elsewhere.

It seems to me, then, that the one thing needful for making art education more successful here than it has been or than it can be otherwise, is a central institution, which shall be to the diffusion of art instruction in this country what the heart is to the human body, — a centre of vitality, and the source of circulation of the life-blood of the individual. And no one of the objects sought for in the various organizations which attempt only a phase of the subject will be so readily or efficiently attained, as when all are attempted in one grand scheme, because the parts both rest upon and support each other. Above all, there is immediate and pressing need for the creation of a class of public art instructors; for I do not spend a week without receiving applications from different parts of the State of Massachusetts, and from other States as well, requesting me to nominate a public instructor in art for the locality making the application. On the other hand, I have been consulted by many individuals, and am being consulted every day, by those who want to become teachers of art, and to be put into the way of getting the necessary professional instruction. Here, then, face to face, are the actual need of the community, and the people who are anxious to minister to that need, but who are not yet qualified to do so. Several persons who have thus sought counsel of me have proceeded to Europe to get their art training, in despair of immediately securing it here; and that is a loss to themselves and to art education at home. Seeing thus daily the wants both of the community and of individuals, it cannot be thought unpractical if I most strongly express my conviction, that what we want in Massachusetts, and indeed in all America, is a professional art training-school, which will supply us both with accomplished art masters as instructors, and give art culture of the highest order to painters, sculptors, and architects. What has been provided for the city of Boston in the form of a Normal Drawing School for the teachers of the common schools, should be established in Boston by the State, for the art instructors of the Commonwealth, just as the State supports four normal schools for general education. And, until that is done here, we shall only be going through the same unsatisfactory state of experimenting as England went

4.

NOTTINGHAM SCHOOL OF ART.

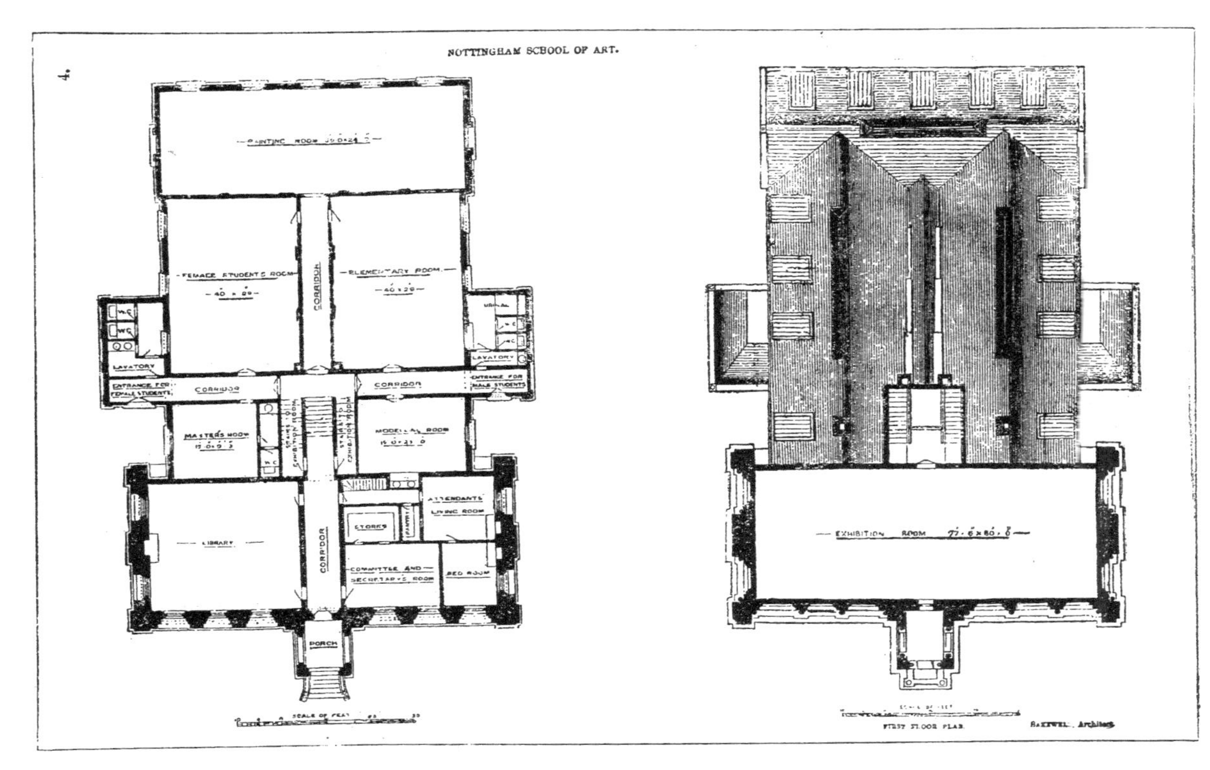

through between the years 1836 and 1851. During that period any artist or draughtsman who had sufficient interest could be appointed as master of a school of design, without passing through any test of his professional knowledge, or giving evidence of possessing any educational experience. And the result was, that very little good was done; for the artist frequently lacked the power to teach, and the draughtsman knew no more of the broad field of art education than the one specialty he practised in his daily work. Thus fifteen years of progress were thrown away; and then the Government, by establishing an art museum and a professional training-school for art masters and instructors, supplied the proved deficiencies, and began that system of public art education, the progress and development of which has no parallel in any country.

Now, in an essentially-practical country like this, where old fashions and slow progress are not worshipped, where the general diffusion of education and development of keen intelligence enable the people to estimate the value of time, I see no reason why we also should throw away fifteen years before we discover what is wanted.

In the cities I have visited, I have found the men of wealth and progress listening most attentively to proposals for establishing schools of art and science; and so great is the interest awakened, that resolutions have been passed for immediate action to supply the deficiency. In a short time, in a goodly number of cities, there will be such schools in operation, lacking nothing but accomplished instructors. And I hope to see Boston not lagging behind in the movement; but rather, remembering her ancient and acknowledged capacity of leader, her bright and universal reputation in the field of education, her practical wisdom in business and commerce, and her wholesome ambition to be at once the Athens and Venice of the New World, — remembering all this, I anticipate that we shall soon see here an institution which shall have the same relationship to similar institutions in other places, that Boston, as a metropolis, has to the provincial cities of the Commonwealth, and, as a seat of learning, she has to all America.

Having thus indicated the need for so important an institution as a national school of design, I will endeavor to describe the character and means of usefulness such an institution should have. In the first place, the Boston Art Museum stands first in its importance, as it will probably be the first feature provided in realization of the plan. What that museum should be is, happily, almost secured already, by the character of the men who are engaged in its organization. The experience, the proved knowledge, and the extensive acquaintance with similar museums in the Old World, which are represented on the Board of Trustees, are the best possible guaranties that their work and arrangement will be all that can be desirable. The public confidence, thus inspired, will doubtless lead to magnificent gifts and bequests, with which to supply the museum with objects of art: for be it remembered that the building is but the casket, not the gem; and before it ceases to be only a building, and becomes, through its contents, an actual museum, the trustees will want half a million of dollars to expend in reproductions of works of art, just to make a beginning. Here is an opportunity for some wealthy and public-spirited citizens to enrich the whole community by substantial gifts in furnishing this museum. It will be an enviable distinction and a well-earned immortality for the man who, having both the means and inclination, employs them in thus identifying himself, by a noble liberality, with the foundation of art culture in

America, — a worthy ambition for some of the millionnaires and merchant-princes of Boston. And that it will be done I have no doubt; for a museum of this kind has always been a gathering-ground for donations, bequests, and loans. The many inventions by which works of art can be reproduced will enable the trustees to become possessed of every class of art work, except original pictures; and even these may come when collections in Europe change hands, and wealthy Americans are in the market ready to purchase pictures of the highest class. How this will affect the general taste need hardly be described. For the painter and the sculptor, the galleries and collections of casts will provide the opportunity of professional study of schools and styles: the historical periods, shown in architectural carvings, will enable the architect to avail himself of the wealth of past ages in originating new combinations for the present age. Choice examples of industrial masterpieces will display to the artisan and manufacturer the skill which comes of art power, and the value resulting therefrom; and the library of art and scientific works will assist students in every rank and profession to enter into and possess, as if by birthright inheritance, the accumulated thoughts and conceptions of the wisest men and most skilful men the world has yet produced.

To change these relics of the past into the living reality of the present and germinating seeds of the future; to translate this as yet unknown tongue into the vernacular language, so that all men shall read it with ease and profit, there will need to be an interpreting medium, — the *education* of the class-room and lecture-theatre. This museum will be the granary, and Education is the husbandman.

In the city of Boston and elsewhere, where lectures on general topics are so attractive and frequent, and are made so much a means of public education, it would be an addition to the culture and enjoyment of society if courses of lectures upon art were delivered by the professors of the art school, open alike both to the student in training and the public; upon which courses the students would be examined for their degrees, and the public attend simply as auditors. I believe, that if two-thirds of a public lecture-hall in the future art museums were open free to the public, and the remaining third in front of the platform were allotted to professional students, both ladies and gentlemen, who were pupils in the schools, and who would be engaged with note-books and sketch-books taking down the materials for their examination as received from the professor's hands; and that if these courses were delivered at night instead of, as usual, in the daytime, — the public would attend them, and find them good intellectual food, worthy of the serious attention of men and women, contrasting somewhat favorably with those courses which apparently exist here, and I have known in the old country, and which are merely intellectual dissipation, frivolous amusements to please grown-up boys and girls who have nothing better to do.

There is an unworked mine of untold wealth among us in the art education of women. In the field of general education here I am informed that nine-tenths of the teachers are women; and some explanation of its excellence may be found in that fact. I have discovered in my experience, and from my own continued observations, that the peculiar phases of mind and disposition which are absolutely necessary for the possession of teaching-power are more frequently to be found in women than in men. This would point in the direction of utilizing much human life now not profitably occupied, by educating and employing ladies as teachers of

THE BIRKENHEAD SCHOOL OF ART.

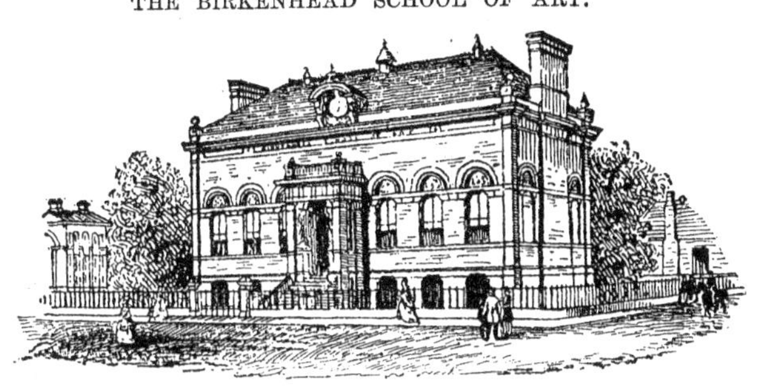

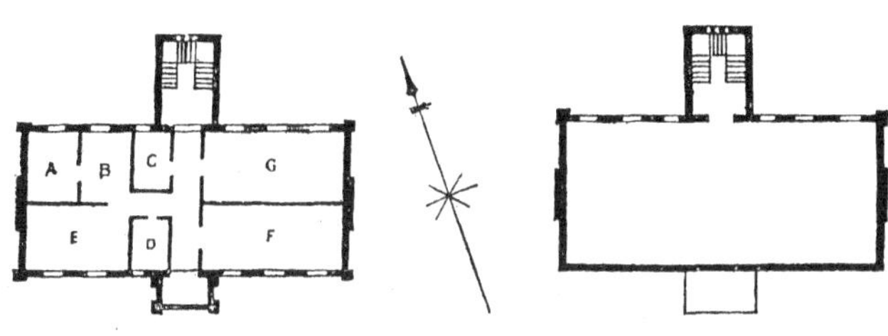

BASEMENT FLOOR. UPPER FLOOR.

Basement Floor.

A and B. Keeper's Apartments.
C. Heating Apparatus-Room.
D. Lavatory.
E, F. Class-Rooms.
G. Modelling-Room.

Ground Floor.

H. Open Portico.
I. Lavatory for Ladies.
J. Class-Room, say for Ladies.
K, L. Head Master's Rooms.
M M. Room for Life Class.

Upper Floor.

Consisting of one large room, 70 x 30 feet, for elementary classes, with the painting-room at one end, capable of being enlarged or diminished at pleasure by means of movable screens.

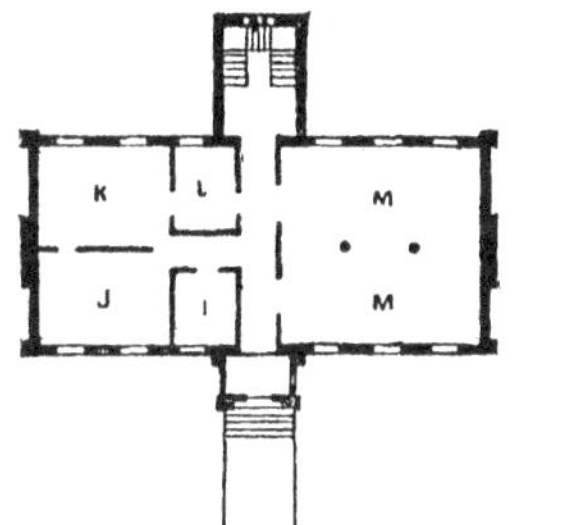

GROUND FLOOR.

art. There are also many branches of art workmanship, requiring delicate fingers and native readiness of taste, which could be better performed by women than men. It seems to me that an infinite amount of good would be done by opening up the whole field of art instruction and art workmanship to the gentler sex; and I do hope, that whenever a great scheme of art education is founded, either here or elsewhere, there shall be absolutely no distinction made concerning the eligibility or disqualification of sex in the students. It is only fair and honest that both should have the identically same training and the same opportunities for becoming "valuable persons," as Prof. Ware expresses it; and then we shall attain to one great result at any rate: we shall double both the agency and area of art culture, and provide employment for a large number of excellent persons who suffer from the lack of it now.

At South Kensington, where there are more lady pupils than men, each sex has its separate class and practising rooms; whilst the lecture-room, examination-room, library, and museum are common to both. In all the examinations, the tests are the same, except that ladies are not required to take the papers in architectural and machine drawing. The success of the lady pupils, to put it in the very mildest form, is greater than that of the male students; and this in face of infinitely greater difficulties, arising from limitation of subjects of study, and other distinctions, which need not be referred to by me. The mention of examinations leads me to the subject of graduation and degrees. If the course of study in the national school of design be systematized and regulated by experience in other branches of education, the course must last at least three years, with distinctive groups of study for each year, at the end of which would be a special examination upon the year's work, and, at the termination of the three years, the graduating examination for a degree.

I regard this professional examination for a degree in art as one of the safeguards of society from mere quacks and charlatans. The bulk of people who have the responsibility of choosing teachers, or of employing skilled labor, have no means of judging, before they buy their experience practically, whether a candidate for employment is qualified or not for the work proposed to be done. Now, although a degree is not an all-sufficient proof of the required capacity for every office, it is at least a guaranty that one of the essential conditions of qualifications has been complied with, and that the candidate is educated, tried, and stamped by a competent and impartial authority. The fact that this means of testing men's powers is accepted as a convenience in almost all professions in almost all countries in the world whose civilization is recognized, is perhaps sufficient evidence of its value. And that especially in education some definite proof is required of training and testing before important charges are given with confidence to school-teachers, is an acknowledgment that such a method of assaying is a protection to society, and a merited distinction for proficiency. I think, that, to meet the requirements of this country, three degrees are essential. The first, that which is awarded by the senate of the national school of design after the three years' course, upon examination and proved competence, and which should describe the art attainments of the candidate, by some such designation as S.A. (*Student of Art*). The second, referring either to the practice of a branch of art — as painting, sculpture, or architecture — successfully, for which the degree of M.A. (*Master of Arts*), might be conferred; or, for successful experience in art instruction, the second degree, D.A. (*Doctor of

Arts), might be substituted; and the third degree of P.A. (*Professor of Art*) should be reserved as a great distinction, for either marked success in the practice of one of the three branches of art, — painting, sculpture, or architecture, — or the very highest attainments of the teacher who has given proof of his abilities to cover successfully the whole field of art education by practical educational experience. Now, I know that liveries and uniforms are not popular in this country, and that men are judged by their acts rather than by their titles. Yet I also know that here, as elsewhere, every bale of goods has been sampled, labelled, and is invoiced to the customer, so that he knows what is purchased and the market-price at which the article is quoted; and this very simple arrangement is as useful in professions as it is in trade, and as much to be relied on in one case as it is in the other. It may not be complete proof of the quality of the article supplied; but it is legal evidence of what it professes to be, and furnishes a standard by which it may fairly be judged.

Concerning the curriculum of study for such a school, I need say little, except that, supposing scientific departments of it to exist, the first year's work of the science students and the arts students should be identical. The two subjects are so intimately related, that it is impossible to fix any line of division between them; each having sections vital to itself which are clearly in the domain of the other. Thus descriptive geometry, botany, sciagraphy (or the science of shadows), mathematical and engineering drawing, chemistry, anatomy, radial and parallel and isometric projection, — none of these can be described as art studies; yet the art knowledge which does not embrace at least all these is imperfect, shallow, and treacherous. Again, free-hand drawing, coloring, drawing from objects, knowledge of many processes of art manufacture, and many more which might be named, are not usually regarded as purely scientific subjects; yet I venture to say, that the governing body of any scientific college would affirm, that, without considerable proficiency in all of these art studies, the scientific man has been very imperfectly educated.

And thus art and science seem indissolubly united, the one being the ready servant of man's necessities, the other ministering to his enjoyment of the beautiful; and their relationship to each other is that of the body and the soul, which constitute the man created in the image of God. In Boston we are proud to own the Institute of Technology; and a few yards to the right of it is the Museum of Natural History. Perhaps a hundred yards away is the site of the Fine Arts Museum; and, either as part of it or as an adjunct to it, will be undoubtedly, sooner or later, a national school of design, and training-school for artists and art masters. There needs to be added a geological museum and horticultural gardens, a school of naval science and architecture, and of anatomy and medicine; and then there would be associated the various agencies which form a technical university, each of which, as a separate college, would have its special students, and all of which would undertake a part of the education of every graduate of the university. Such institutions as this are rising up in other countries, or already exist there in separate organizations; but to none do they seem to me so important as in this; to no part of this country are they of such vital necessity as the New-England manufacturing States: and if it has fallen to the lot of one State to provide them, it is clear to me the lot has fallen upon Massachusetts; and the site of the Boston Art Museum is within a stone's-throw of where the lot fell.

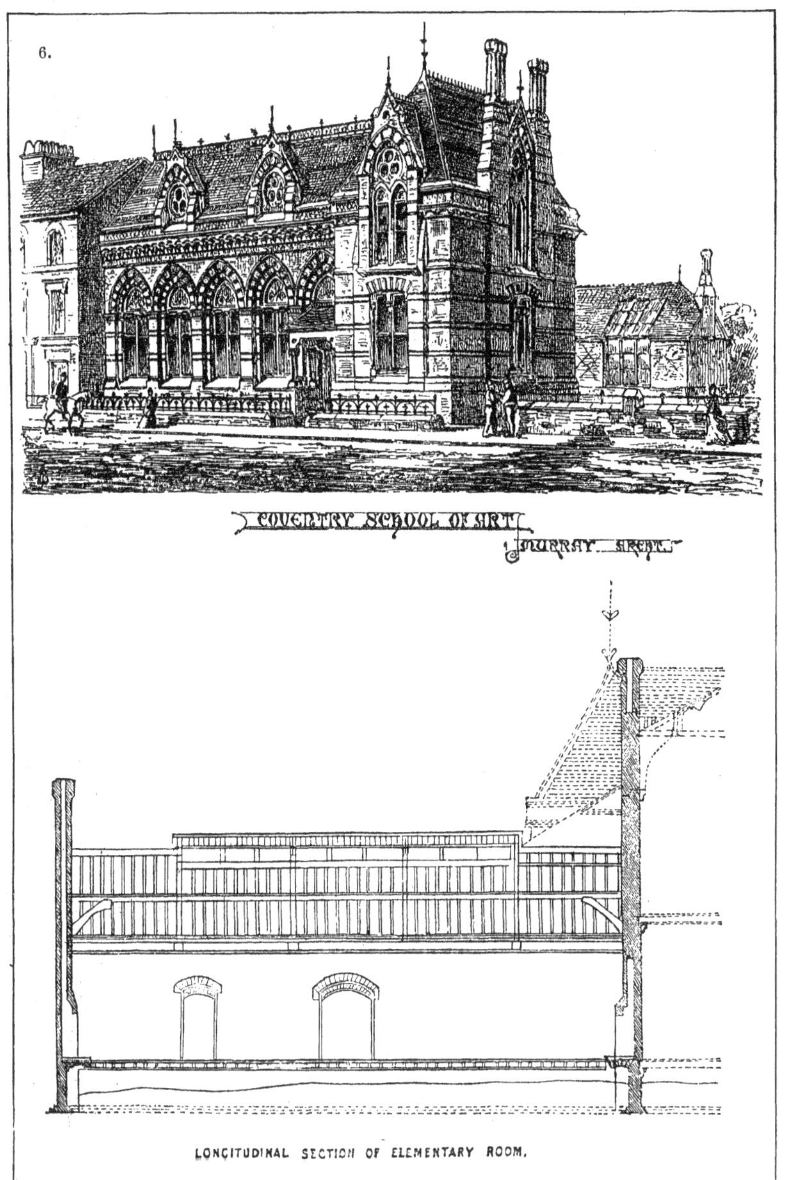

LONGITUDINAL SECTION OF ELEMENTARY ROOM.

It is no mere fanciful assertion to say that the time has come for some such development of education, which will fit men for their work in this world, and not interfere with their prospects in the next. Look at the extent of the country to be subdued and conquered, and tell me whether it is to be done by Latin and Greek, or by the arts and sciences. Turn out a thousand graduates from this modern industrial university every year, and you would soon double the producing power of the land and the people.

The country is hungering and thirsting for this knowledge; and the mere offer of it by the act of the Massachusetts Legislature has been seized upon generally throughout the State, though the means do not as yet exist here for complying with the law, and ministering to the hunger and thirst which is felt. I quoted what Prof. Bail said about a gray-haired mechanic's overpowering him with thanks for a drawing-lesson, and saying, "This lesson is worth hundreds of dollars to me." What would it have been worth to that gray-haired man if it had been given to him forty years ago? I see in the class-rooms of the various cities, where drawing is being taught, more old men who have felt the lack of some technical instruction than of young men who have not yet discovered its value. Ancient mechanics, whose hands are stiffening with decay, and whose vision is getting dimmed by age, requiring to be assisted by little lamps on each desk in addition to the gaslight, are very frequent among the students: that tells a tale to those who are able to see and understand its meaning. In one room, where I saw an actual preponderance of old men, who were studying the same subject from the same book which I have taught to children of eight years old and upwards, a manufacturer made the statement, that their designs cost them forty thousand dollars a year, every dollar of which went to England, France, and Germany. If a school of art had been in operation in that city for ten years, the designs would have cost that manufacturer perhaps five thousand dollars; and the dollars would have been kept within a mile of the mill, — a clear gain of forty thousand dollars a year to the country in one city alone. That forty thousand dollars a year is one of the self-imposed taxes upon our ignorance we pay to other countries, and is a sign of our bondage and slavery to them. Having emancipated black slaves, it seems to me time to emancipate ourselves from this particular form of white slavery. And now it devolves upon me to say what we are doing to remedy all these evils, and provide facilities for study of art.

Here a tribute must be paid to Massachusetts and to Boston for what has been already done by them. The legislative trumpet has given forth no uncertain sound; and Boston has clothed itself with that glorious armor with which a city is arrayed when it rises up in response to the trumpet-call to obey the law. And there can be no surer sign of its capacity to lead and command than its own ready and instant submission to the law, — its power to obey.

No sooner had the act of the Legislature been passed than drawing was made more general in the common schools of Boston; and the first winter saw evening schools established to teach industrial drawing to working-men. For the instruction of masters and teachers, a normal school of drawing was opened, and is now in what I consider most successful operation, and will improve in its efficiency every week. For the evening classes, an excellent assortment of examples has been provided, which are the beginning, I hope, of a collection as complete as is to be found in every European school of art.

This has been an honest commencement, and will rapidly develop into successful operation in every department of its action. With patience and the public confidence, great results will be achieved in Boston. And to inspire confidence, let me say that the Drawing Committee of the School Board are not trying theoretical experiments, concerning the issue of which there may be a doubt: they are working upon an already well-tried system, that has yet to make its first failure. Whatever difficulties the Committee may experience, and the limitations it will be bound by, will arise from not having sufficient means to work with, and highly-qualified men to do the work. Both of these hinderances will speedily pass away, let us hope; for not until they do, will our way be clear, the road straight, the rate of travel satisfactory.

I cannot leave this part of this subject without expressing an opinion, that to individuals society owes much; and that to the active and energetic members of the Drawing Committee the City of Boston owes its gratitude for their unparalleled labors and generosity in the promotion of art education. In other parts of the State of Massachusetts, drawing-classes are being rapidly established, and the introduction of drawing in the public schools is becoming general. The State Board of Education of Massachusetts has purchased, and is now in possession of, a small travelling collection of examples for art study, which is being exhibited every week in some provincial city; and during this exhibition the teachers are instructed in drawing, public meetings are held, at which the subject of establishing art schools is discussed and considered, and the ways and means are pointed out.

One of the means of ascertaining what has been done, and the equally-important information of what has not been done, will be an annual exhibition of works produced by different drawing-classes in all parts of the State, as soon as possible after the termination of their sessions, probably in May or June; and I would propose to every State Board of Education to petition the Legislature for an appropriation to meet the necessary expenses of exhibition, and also for the awarding of some recognition of merit, both to successful students and successful teachers. This will be national action at a very trifling expense, which will be a powerful stimulus towards excellence. To make it permanent and satisfactory, will require the cordial co-operation of local school committees; and as it is intended for the common advantage of all who are helping forward the general movement, I do not doubt, for an instant, but that the co-operation will be heartily tendered.

The practicability of this proposition, and the good that may be done by carrying it out, has already been demonstrated in Massachusetts by a State's exhibition of the works produced by students in the free industrial drawing-classes of the State; which was held in Boston on May 16, 17, and 18, 1872, in conjunction with that of the pupils in the Boston public schools. The exhibition attracted many thousands of visitors, and elicited very general approval. A report was made by a Board of Honorary Examiners upon the works displayed; and this being perhaps the first recognition by any American State of efforts in the direction of exhibiting and judging industrial drawings, I quote the report in full: —

To J. D. Philbrick, Esq., *Chairman of the Exhibition Committee of the State Board of Education, Massachusetts.*

Dear Sir, — Having been appointed to examine the drawings displayed in the exhibition of the works of the free industrial drawing-classes of the State of Massachusetts, and to award marks of distinction to the most deserving, we have great pleasure in submitting the following report.

7.

TRANSVERSE SECTION OF ELEMENTARY ROOM.
MODELLING ROOM
PAINTING ROOM
GENERAL
STORES
CORRIDOR
SCHOOL OF ART.
COVENTRY.
JAMES MURRAY
LAVATORY
CLASS ROOM
W.C.
W.C.
LAVATORY W.C.
SIDE ENTRANCE
CLOSET
LOBBY
KEEPER
PASSAGE
SCALE OF FEET
MASTER
LADIES ROOM
HALL
GROUND PLAN

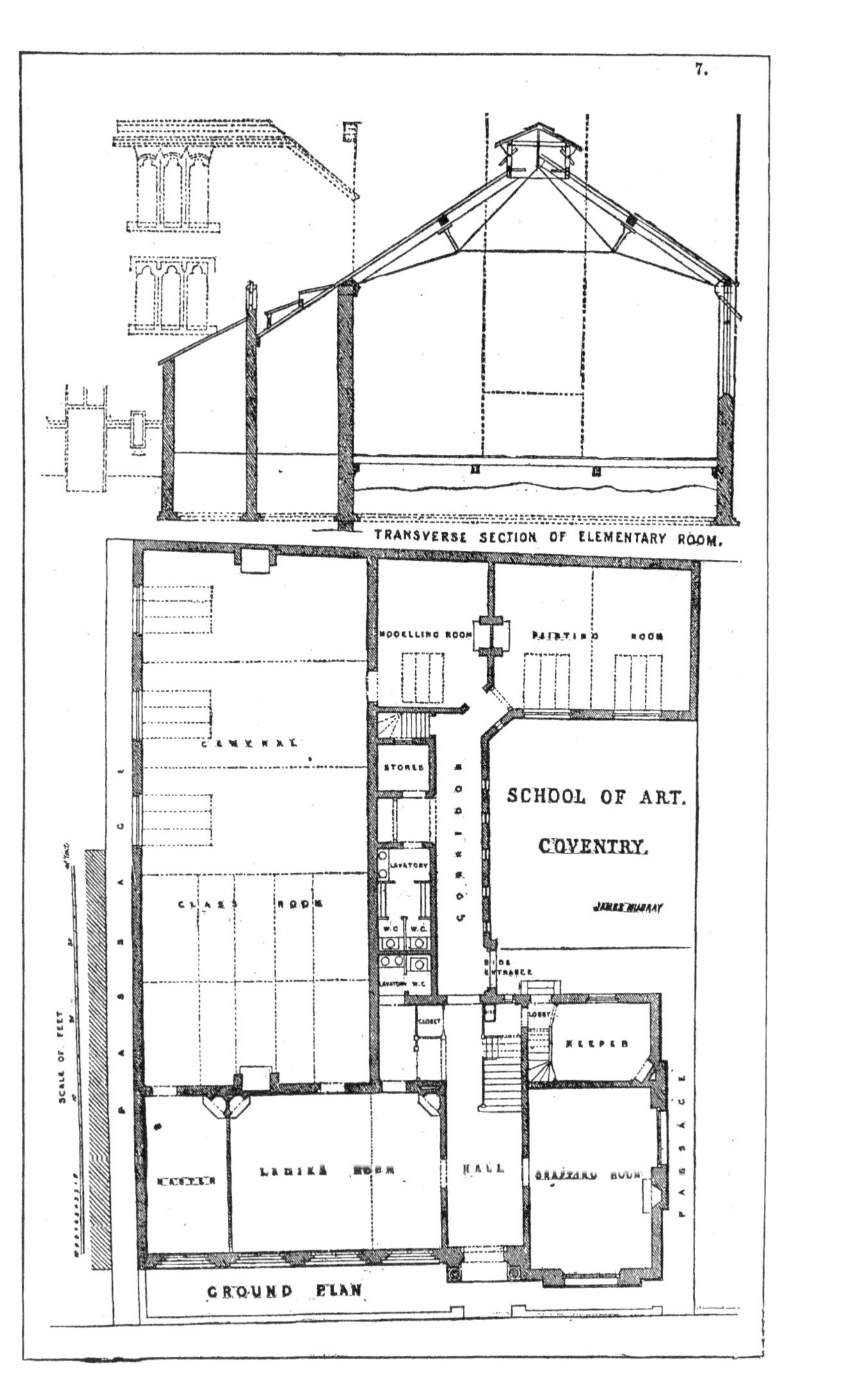

The exhibition represents the results obtained in the free evening drawing-schools held during the past winter in Haverhill, Lawrence, Lowell, Lynn, New Bedford, Newton, Northampton, Springfield, Taunton, Worcester, and Boston. There are no works of the classes in Cambridge, Charlestown, Fall River, Fitchburg, Newburyport, Pittsfield, Salem, and Somerville. We understand that no classes have as yet been organized in the other towns included within the scope of the statute, — Chelsea, Gloucester, Holyoke, and North Adams. The exhibition consists of about six hundred drawings; comprising exercises from the blackboard of free-hand, geometrical, mechanical, isometrical, and constructional drawing, in outline and tinted; drawing in light and shade, and color of foliage; figures, animal forms, machine-drawing, and architectural tinting; designs for buildings, for carpets, &c.; natural objects, geometric solids in shadow and color, and many other branches of industrial art-study.

The difficulty of selecting the works most deserving of commendation, where the general range of merit was so uniform as we found it, and the excellence in some respects so great, rendered our task by no means an easy one. We found, however, drawings which seemed to us to deserve a mark of Excellence, and some to which we have given an Honorable Mention.

The Lynn school is represented by eight drawings, chiefly of instrumental work. The mark of excellence was given to two, and an honorable mention to three. The school at Lawrence sends thirteen drawings, chiefly mechanical drawings and projections. We gave the mark of excellence to one, and an honorable mention to four. Both schools show evidence of good and careful instruction, although within a limited field. The works specially distinguished by marks of approval deserve high praise. The Lowell school, though organized only in March, exhibits a large amount of excellent work. Free-hand drawing is included, and has been carefully taught. The application of free-hand drawing to the details of machinery deserves special notice and commendation. Men are naturally most easily interested in the representation of objects which they understand. The rest of the work consisted of a design for a carpet, projections of details of machinery, architectural outlines, &c., making seventy drawings in all. Of these, three were marked excellent, and six had an honorable mention. At New Bedford, the instruction has been apparently limited to instrumental drawing, and most of the work shown is of an elementary character. But there are some excellent specimens of machine drawing in color. Out of twenty-four drawings, we gave the mark of excellence to two, and an honorable mention to three. The work exhibited from the Worcester school is large in amount, and embraces an unusual range of subjects, in which the free-hand work bears a large proportion to the mechanical and geometrical drawings, and is itself more than usually varied, consisting of outlines of ornament, shaded drawings from solid models, and drawings from groups of natural objects. The evident want of success in some of this work is to be attributed to the absence of proper models, without which it is useless to expect satisfactory results, however capable the pupils, and however skilful the teachers. We have the less hesitation in expressing our sense of these defects, as this deficiency, which is the only obstacle to success, is removable at will. Out of eighty drawings from this school, one received the mark of excellent, and eleven an honorable mention.

The work from Springfield, though limited in range, consisting entirely of drawings of machinery, is remarkably good in quality, exhibiting also an unusual uniformity of standard, — one of the surest marks of good discipline. But the total result would have been much more satisfactory, if free-hand work, though only of the kind of which we have spoken as distinguishing the Lowell school, had been added. Out of twenty drawings, we found two to be excellent, and gave an honorable mention to three.

The school at Taunton is distinguished by the number and the excellence of the drawings, in both which respects it stands next to the Boston school. Out of a hundred and thirty drawings, room could be afforded in the exhibition for only seventy-nine; but of these, five received the mark excellent, and fourteen an honorable mention. Though the absence of free-hand work is here again to be regretted, the drawings exhibit much uniformity of excellence and great variety of subject. A large portion, moreover, of the best work is drawn from blackboard instruction, evincing a high degree of faithfulness and competency in the teaching. The works of the classes in Haverhill and Northampton, though showing diligence and fidelity, are so limited, both in number and range of subject, as not to call for special remark. This is doubtless in great part due to the fact, that the exhibition was not announced until the drawings of the year had already been dispersed, so that it was difficult to get together a fair representation of the year's work. Eight drawings are shown from each town, Haverhill receiving two honorable mentions, and Northampton one excellent, and two honorable mentions. The Newton class appears to have been well taught in elementary work, the students not being required to finish their drawings. We awarded one honorable mention to this class.

The Boston school stands first, both in the number of the drawings — furnishing two hundred and eighty-two altogether, or nearly one-half of the whole collection — and in the variety and excellence of the work, especially the free-hand work. The mark of excellent was given to six, and an honorable mention to thirty-five. The examples of ornamental figure work, both from the flat copy and from models, are quite beyond what any of the other schools have to show. The architectural and engineering work is also to be noticed. This excellence is to be mainly imputed, it seems to us, to the very superior advantages these classes have enjoyed in the respect of casts, — solid models and flat copies. It is not that the instruction has been better here than elsewhere, but that proper appliances have rendered it more efficient.

This is, in our judgment, the key to the whole question. It is perfectly plain that there is in the State no lack of ability on the part either of pupils or teachers, and no want of support on the part of the public. The results already achieved are excellent, — remarkably so, if we consider, that in most of these towns there was no proper preparation for the work, and no applicances whatever, except what the teachers could bring in their hands. There is no reason why any of the schools here repesented should not, in future, present work equal to the best. A moderate outlay of money upon proper models, suited to the special wants of each place, would put all these schools upon an absolutely equal footing. The marked superiority in almost every department of the work of the Boston school is one that ought to disappear entirely in future years. The exhibition must convince every visitor that this is the point upon which the whole movement hangs. Nothing but the want of suitable models can prevent a great and permanent success.

We are, very respectfully,

Your obedient servants,

Charles C. Perkins,
William R. Ware, — *Board of Examiners.*
Walter Smith,

May 16, 1872.

CHAPTER II.

ART TEACHING IN PUBLIC SCHOOLS.

TEACHING OF ELEMENTARY DRAWING.

THE act of the Massachusetts State Legislature, which has paved the way for a general recognition of the value of drawing as an educational subject in America, is short enough and important enough to be here quoted. It is as follows: —

CHAPTER 248, ACTS OF 1870.

SECTION 1. The first section of chapter thirty-eight of the General Statutes is hereby amended so as to include Drawing among the branches of learning which are by said section required to be taught in the public schools.

SECT. 2. Any city or town may, and every city and town having more than ten thousand inhabitants shall, annually make provision for giving free instruction in industrial or mechanical drawing to persons over fifteen years of age, either in day or evening schools, under the direction of the school committee.

SECT. 3. This Act shall take effect upon its passage.

[*Approved May* 16, 1870.

By this law of Massachusetts, art education has been ingrafted upon its far-famed system of public instruction, and henceforward will form a part, and, I hope and believe, no unimportant section, of its excellent organization. Provision for the instruction in drawing of

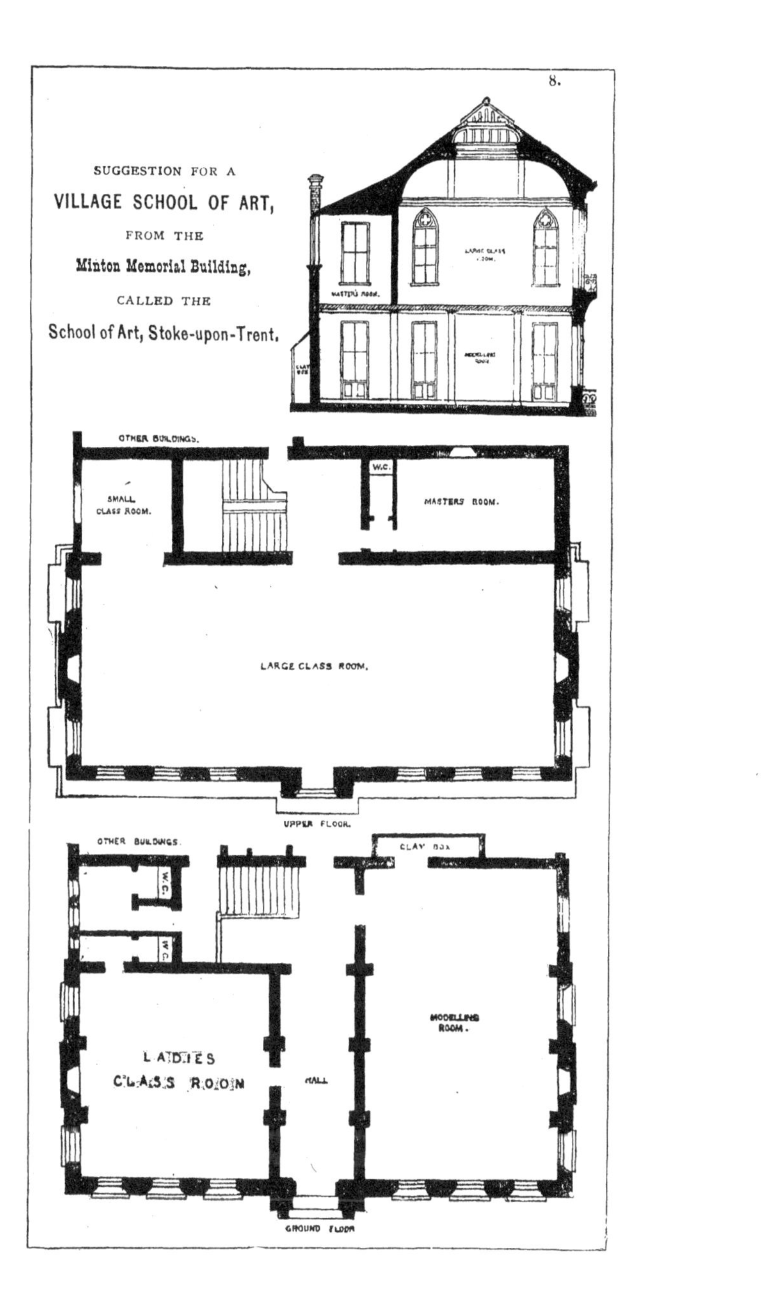
8.
SUGGESTION FOR A
VILLAGE SCHOOL OF ART,
FROM THE
Minton Memorial Building,
CALLED THE
School of Art, Stoke-upon-Trent.
OTHER BUILDINGS.
W.C.
SMALL CLASS ROOM.
MASTERS ROOM.
LARGE CLASS ROOM.
UPPER FLOOR.
OTHER BUILDINGS.
CLAY BOX
W.C.
W.C.
MODELLING ROOM.
LADIES CLASS ROOM
HALL
GROUND FLOOR

teachers and children in the public schools, and of adults in the night classes, will be arranged for, as opportunities occur and teachers can be found. The passing of this law, and the efforts made to comply with it, will, it is supposed, create a desire for information concerning art education, of especial interest just now; and, having been appointed by the City of Boston and the State of Massachusetts to assist in their development of art education. I would take the opportunity of stating that I believe the choice of the art authorities of the United Kingdom, upon the request of the Boston school-board, fell upon me for recommendation to the appointments I now hold because, though acquainted with the national system of my own country and of other European States, I am not committed to, nor do I wholly approve of, any one of them, but believe, that, in the construction of a system in a country where the subject is new, we can adapt the good parts of all the old methods to the requirements of this country, and omit all the bad parts. And there can be no reason why the thoroughness which characterizes the general education of America should not influence and give tone to any instruction in technical subjects which may be added to it. Whilst we may thus profit by the experience of other nations, having greater experience than our own, there will be many features of this country and of society so superior to theirs, and so much more favorable to the development and advancement of education, that I look forward to a future in which our field of art education shall in no prominent part be a reflex of others, but be a combination of excellences that will offer a model for their imitation.

So much of a general introduction I conceived to be necessary before speaking practically on the subject we are about to consider.

4*

That subject briefly described is *Art Education in Public Schools.*

The kind of drawing which the State of Massachusetts requires that its citizens shall have an opportunity of studying, is called "industrial drawing;" and wisely so called, for in that lies a justification of its public action in the matter.

It is so described, I apprehend, to distinguish it from those more ornamental or professional branches of art which people study rather as an amusement or gratification, or as a lucrative profession, than as an important element in the success of trades and manufactures. Economists are agreed that it fairly falls within the scope of government in any civilized country to initiate movements by which the trades or manufactures carried on by its subjects shall be improved in character and increased in value, and thus, through a higher appreciation, find a wider market for their consumption. The prosperity of the many is the argument upon which this agreement is founded. The principle thus acknowledged has led some of the most far-seeing and enlightened of modern governments to establish systems of art education, with a view of improving all branches of industrial trades and manufactures, having regard to the ultimate influence on production and sale, as well as increased value of exports and articles of home consumption. The success of these experiments has been so great, that several European States at the present time owe their prosperity in no slight degree to the artistic excellence of their manufactures, brought about mainly by their cultivation of art education.

The time has arrived when the government of the State of Massachusetts has viewed the matter in the same light; and thus we are upon the threshold of a new fabric, — a system of art education for the State, which will undoubtedly foreshadow a national system of secondary education.

The means whereby such a system would be best organized to meet the requirements of all classes of society, and keep supply and demand in their true relationship, has been a great problem to the educationists of this locality, as it has been previously to the educationists of the Old World. There are three sections of the public to be educated, — children, adult artisans, and the public generally, who come under neither of the first two divisions. How this has been provided for in most of the European States I may here shortly describe. For children, elementary drawing is taught as a part of general education in most of the public schools; for adult artisans, night schools and classes have been established in almost all towns or populous villages; and for the general public, museums, galleries of art, and courses of public lectures on art subjects, are becoming general. Upon the comparative value of these several means there may be and is much difference of opinion; but upon one point there is a general agreement, viz., that *to make national art education possible, it must commence with the children in public schools.*

After several unsuccessful experiments, that is the conclusion at which, twenty years ago, the educationists of Great Britain arrived; and the progress which has since been made in art education, and the consequent improvement of industrial art, is evidence enough that the problem had been solved, and that they were on the right track. To establish schools of art and art galleries before the mass of the *community* were taught to draw was like opening a university before people knew the alphabet; but to provide both of these agencies in conjunction with, or as a continuation of, the instruction in drawing in public schools, was like a logical sequence, going in rational order from strength to strength of an unbroken chain; from bud to branch, and from branch to flower of natural educational growth.

Whilst England has appropriated, in Mr. Foster's scheme, all the features of the Massachusetts system of general education that are worth any thing, we are borrowing from Great Britain, as well as from other countries, the most valuable portions of their experience in technical education; and I venture to prophesy, that, upon a better general basis, we shall erect an infinitely better superstructure, so soon as the development of public opinion in this country will furnish us with the means for its accomplishment.

What has been done here in the way of instruction in night classes for adults is sufficient to demonstrate the need of additional efforts, and has shown the extent of the field awaiting culture at our hands; and the fact that already a Boston museum of fine and industrial art is on the way, and its foundations laid on a broad and comprehensive plan, is a final proof that eventually no feature of a perfect scheme will be wanting to complete the fabric of art education.

Though these secondary agencies are matter of interest in a consideration of the whole subject, it is not they especially that we have now to consider.

The teaching of drawing in public schools is that phase of the question concerning which I wish to speak now. How, with our present means, and in a reasonable time, is it to be brought about? and what can be done to make the teaching general?

Here, at this point, we are brought face to face with the same difficulty that has confronted the pioneers of art education elsewhere; viz., Who is to teach drawing in the public schools? and the question must be answered in the same way. To this there can be but one reply; which is, There can be no special teachers of drawing as a separate subject, any more than of writing or arithmetic as separate subjects; but the general teachers themselves must learn and teach elementary drawing to the children, in the same way they learn and teach other subjects. It will only be by having a teacher of drawing in every class-room in every school in the country, that all the children can be taught to draw; and this can only be accomplished by making the general teachers include drawing among their subjects of instruction. That is how the difficulty has been met in other countries, and it is the only way possible of meeting it here. Now, if elementary drawing were either an abstruse subject, or as difficult of acquisition as a new language, it would seem something like a hardship, that teachers, whose daily labor is so great, and whose leisure is so scarce, should be expected to increase their labors and sacrifice their leisure to learn this new subject. But it has been found in Europe, that a valuable and sufficient power of drawing can be acquired by teachers who have the desire to learn in a comparatively short time, and without any very great sacrifice either of their leisure or their patience. At the present time, in the Boston Normal Art School, the teachers of the city are receiving one lesson of one hour on alternate weeks, which, if they work out the exercises on each lesson, is in my opinion sufficient time to give; and I calculate that they will have passed through a course of instruction in two subjects, — free-hand and model drawing, — qualifying them to give their pupils lessons in the same, after one year's course of study.

Another year the subjects of geometrical and perspective drawing will be taken up; and, though these subjects will entail a little more home-work, they will be got through in the sessions of one year.

I can hardly suppose that any teacher would consider such an amount of attendance on two courses of lessons as too great a price to pay for the qualification to teach elementary drawing; and I would desire to inspire teachers with confidence in their own art powers, even if yet undeveloped, by saying, that, to those who are intimately acquainted with educational processes, as teachers must be, the labor of acquiring skill in drawing is reduced to a minimum, whilst the result is a practical certainty. As they have great experience in teaching other subjects, I have always found school-teachers, even with a very limited power of drawing, to make by far the best teachers of drawing; and what they themselves acquire without difficulty, they teach most successfully.

Drawing is in many respects like a language, — a visible language, the language of form; having but two letters in its alphabet, — the straight line and the curve; in this respect like our own written words, made up of combinations of straight and curved lines, — with this difference, that, whilst a word suggests the name and thought, drawing suggests the thing itself. Both drawing and writing depend for attainment on the same faculty, — the faculty of imitation; though drawing, being simpler in its elements than writing, is the more easy of acquirement. It has been amply demonstrated that every person who can be taught to write can be taught to draw; and where both are taught simultaneously, they assist each other, — success in one being a certain indication of success in both.

Imitative power is common to the human race, and exists in children before they can either walk or speak: it is developed so early, that, from the moment a child can hold a pencil, it may be taught to imitate by drawing the forms it sees. Those children whom it is found impossible to teach to write, it would be waste of time to attempt to teach to draw; for want of capacity in the first must proceed from some physical deficiency which would prove fatal also to success in drawing. But for the rest, — and experience convinces us they are a somewhat considerable majority, — as soon as they begin to go to school, so soon should they begin learning to draw; and they will be found to take to and acquire it best who commence it earliest, and pursue it the most systematically through the whole school course. Neither is any special gift of more than usual taste required to enable persons to become excellent draughtsmen. It is a matter of mere conjecture whether such gifts exist at all; and it is certain, if they do exist, their possession is of no account whatever when compared with perseverance and a determination to succeed. The best draughtsmen I have known began to draw at about five years old or earlier; and it is a singular commentary on genius, which is supposed to be heaven-born, that those men who are most universally acknowledged to be geniuses have spent their industrious lives in self-improvement, ignoring their supposed endowments, and working patiently like journeymen whilst learning a trade.

Much undoubtedly depends upon the way in which teaching is carried on; that definite objects should be sought for, and the various steps be graduated in difficulty, though well defined in purpose. My own experience leads me to think there are good points in even very opposite methods, and failings in all. It is impossible, so long as human nature is varied in individuals, that any method of instruction should apply equally well to a number of different characters, or develop the faculties of all. A cast-iron method or system presupposes such a similarity of disposition and faculties in pupils as never existed nor is likely to exist; and unless a system, whilst adhering closely to principles, is at the same time elastic in practice, it will probably cramp and destroy the faculties it was intended to develop. In this matter much depends upon the teacher, — a good, kind, and sympathetic teacher producing better results upon a bad system than a bad teacher upon the best of methods.

There are, however, some schemes of art instruction which have been more widely tried than others, and experiments in them more perfected by long practice.

The old drawing-master's method of giving shaded copies to beginners, without any arrangement of examples or sequence in subjects, is followed no longer in any national schools in Europe, or in any public schools under government inspection. The use of flat examples only, without extensive illustration on and explanation from the blackboard, is also becoming a thing of the past. What is now commonly described as the English blackboard system of teaching elementary drawing is perhaps the most elastic and efficient of methods for class-teaching; but it should not supersede individual instruction, simultaneously given; nor can it be used successfully without the concurrent use of text-books in the hands of each pupil to supply accurate illustrations of the course of study, and to encourage home-work in support of school-work. Unless a pupil can be induced to work sometimes wholly by himself, he never attains to self-reliance, nor learns how to master an entirely new difficulty without resorting to assistance from other people.

The group of art instruction in elementary drawing which is considered suitable to the powers of the pupils in day schools comprises five subjects, and includes: 1. Free-hand Drawing. 2. Model or Object Drawing. 3. Memory Drawing. 4. Geometrical Drawing. 5. Perspective. A thorough grounding in these subjects is one of the best preparations for any further study of the

BURSLEM SCHOOL OF ART.

(WEDGEWOOD MEMORIAL.)

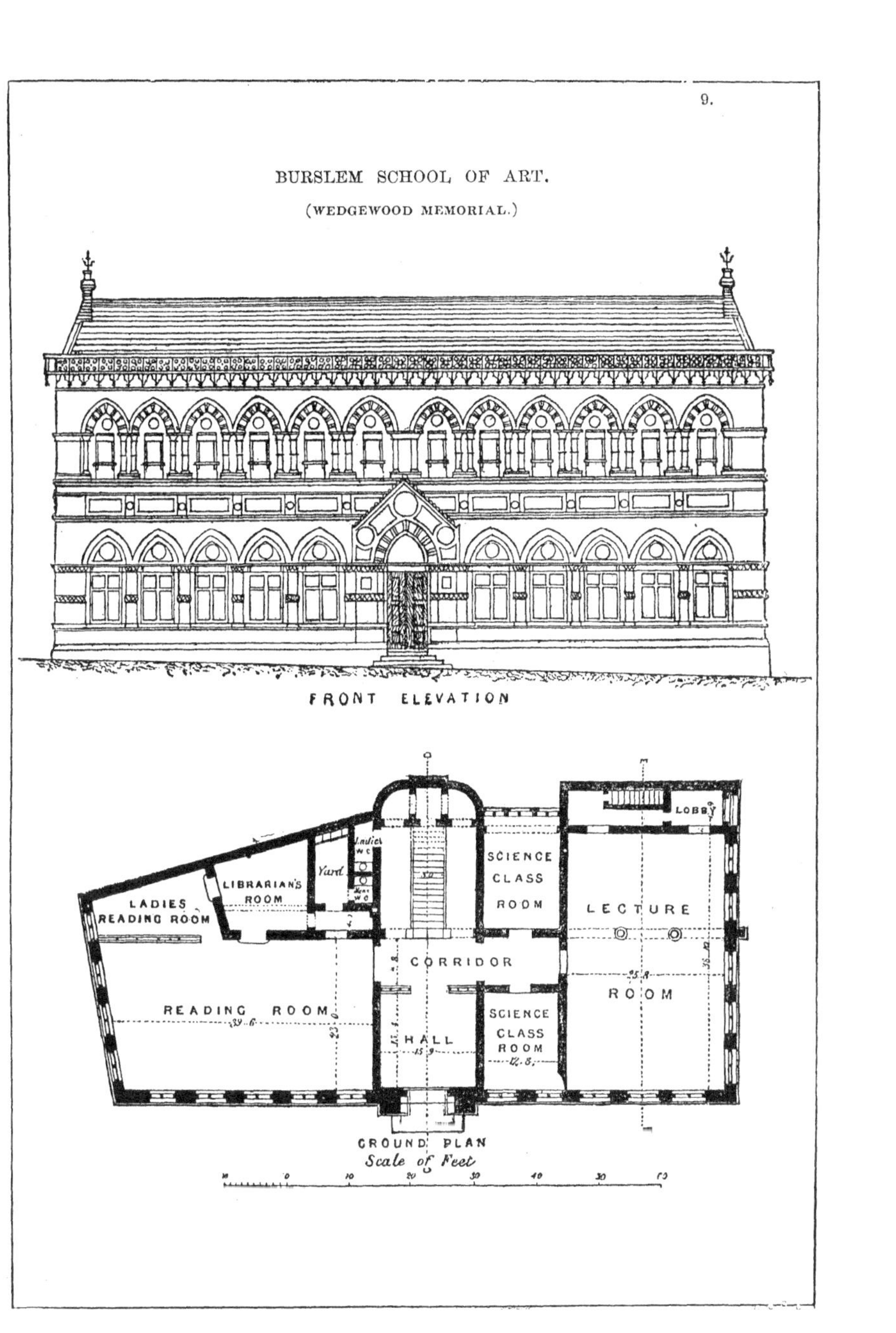

higher branches of art education. A pupil, having passed examination in such, would be ready to take hold of the instruction in schools of art, or even to continue his studies by himself in more advanced subjects. The group of five subjects named is that in which the public school-teachers of England have to become proficient, and for a successful examination in which the government grants a drawing certificate, stating that the holder is competent to give instruction in drawing in public schools.

The adaptation of this course of study to the graded schools of this country is not a difficult matter, the moment the corps of teachers become qualified to teach drawing; and it can be commenced at once in those subjects which the teachers themselves are practising, or have already become proficient in. The order in which the subjects are usually taken will decide the suitability of each to the different schools.

A simple arrangement would be as follows, giving progressive subjects in each grade of school:—

IN PRIMARY SCHOOLS.—*Free-hand, Model, and Memory Drawing,* from the blackboard and from copies in books, the objects to be geometrically drawn; i.e., having no perspective effects in them.

IN GRAMMAR SCHOOLS.—*Model Drawing* from the blackboard, and from copies showing the principles of perspective, and from real objects; *Memory Drawing; Geometrical Drawing* of plane geometrical problems with instruments; Free-hand enlargements and reductions from flat copies of historical and other ornament, in outline, to teach styles of art.

IN HIGH AND NORMAL SCHOOLS.—Memory, Model, and Perspective Drawing; shading, coloring; drawing from casts, from natural plants and elementary designs.

I propose to describe in what manner and to what degree these subjects may be taught in the three grades of schools.

I. — *Primary Schools.*

FREE-HAND OUTLINE DRAWING.

In the very earliest lessons to the youngest children, drawings on the blackboard by the teacher are the only examples used; the illustrations being vertical, horizontal, and oblique lines, singly and in simple combinations, such as angles, squares, triangles, and the division of straight lines into equal or proportionate parts; curved lines associated with straight lines on the simplest symmetrical arrangement. That is the commencement of free-hand drawing, the pupils drawing on their slates until the first difficulties are over. A moderate use of Roman capital letters is not objectionable for copies; but too frequent use is wearisome. Monograms and initial letters are also interesting subjects; and if the teacher takes his own initials, and makes an ornamental monogram of them, and asks his pupils to do the same with their initials, he will set them all drawing at home enthusiastically. Very young children will draw best those forms in which there are the fewest possible lines, and those lines expressing the forms of objects they are most familiar with, — apples and pears, common crockery-ware, leaves of trees and flowers, and suchlike. The older pupils who are drawing free-hand outline from the board upon paper should have their subjects alternated with flat copies, to be drawn either the same size as the originals, or enlarged a definite proportion, — either a third or a fourth, or by measure, as an inch or two inches in height and proportionately in width. As all the blackboard lessons are exercises in the reduction of forms, it is well to vary the lessons by practice of the identical size and by enlargements. I have found it not to be a good custom to keep children drawing on slates longer than the time when they attain the power of fairly balancing the forms given them to copy. It is so easy to rub out errors upon slates that carelessness often results from too long practice on them.

In the choice of examples, it should be remembered that diagrams from objects should be represented geometrically, not by views of the objects as seen in perspective, until the pupils have arrived at drawing from objects. The principal use of free-hand outline drawing is to teach pupils the proper use of materials, the names of lines and forms, and to educate the eye in judging of proportion; also to inculcate perception of the beautiful in curves and forms of objects.

The time given per week to drawing should not be less than two hours. With the youngest children, the length of each lesson should not be more than half an hour, i.e., four *short* lessons per week; with those a little older, three lessons of forty minutes each; and with the oldest pupils who draw upon paper, two lessons of an hour each.

It is of some importance, in maintaining interest in the lessons, that each should be complete in itself, — the exercise be begun and finished in the allotted time; and, if this be found difficult, it is better to take simpler examples, with less work in them, than either to lengthen the time given, or leave the exercise unfinished. In the same class, if some pupils draw better than others, the best may be allowed to draw in books, and the more backward on slates. Each exercise should be criticised by the teacher during the lesson, in addition to the general criticism from the blackboard, thus combining individual with class instruction.

The object given as a lesson should be well drawn on the blackboard before the lesson begins; and the teacher, in giving the lesson, should commence by explaining its proportions and general character, and then draw it again, step by step, during the process of the lesson, being followed by the class, line for line, as the form develops on the board.

The standard of quality in outline varies in different countries; but whether a thick or thin line be allowed, it must be the same thickness or thinness everywhere; and the best line, in my opinion, is a thin, gray, unbroken line, without the slightest variation in a whole drawing, either in color or breadth.

MODEL-DRAWING IN OUTLINE.

The model drawing in primary schools should be of an exceedingly simple character; for into the proper practice of it perspective must more or less enter. Only the older children ought to attempt it, and the objects used to be as much as possible those which appear of the same form on all sides. These may be defined as such objects as are turned in a lathe, or made upon a potter's wheel: thus a cylinder, a sphere, a cone, in geometric shapes; a vase without a handle, a goblet or a wine-glass, a basin, a saucer, a round bottle; or wooden vessels, such as a bucket or a round box. These have the double advantage of being symmetrical, enabling the teacher and pupils to use a central line in drawing them; and they will be seen alike by all the pupils, so that the explanations and demonstrations given on the blackboard will apply to all the drawings made.

The models used should be painted white, which displays the form better than any color. If rectangular solids be used, such as cubes, oblong blocks, prisms, square boxes, chairs, or such-like, the teacher will find himself plunged at once into all the difficulties of linear perspective, beyond the understanding of children so young as those in primary schools.

With regard to the method of teaching, and implements used, what I have said with reference to free-hand drawing from flat examples on the blackboard applies similarly to object drawing. Care must be taken in setting a model for the class, that it is not placed so near to any pupil as to give him a distorted view, or so far away as to be seen with difficulty. The best position with regard to height is, that the top of the object should be at least six inches below the level of the pupil's eye. A set of three or four dozen objects should be kept in each school, in a cupboard or cabinet reserved for the purpose; and teachers might occasionally exchange models of equal value with each other, so as to give freshness and variety to the subjects: otherwise the pupils may get wearied of drawing the same objects over and over again. The models should include common forms such as are frequently seen by the pupils, as pitchers, teacups and saucers, and other objects before-named.

Combined with free-hand and model drawing, the definitions of plane geometric figures should be taught, and are best taught, by being drawn as exercises, as well as learned by heart. This will be preparation for geometrical drawing, to be afterwards learned in the grammar schools, as well as being of great value in imparting correct knowledge of common forms.

DRAWING FROM MEMORY.

The third subject for the primary schools is drawing from memory.

I attach the very highest importance to the systematic development of memory-drawing as an element of education; and art education is incomplete without it. Beginning with geometric forms of a given size, it will be found possible to lead even the children in primary schools to reproduce entirely from memory the copies which they have already drawn, however elaborate and full of detail they may be. The memory exercises will consist of special examples or of recently-finished drawings, the proportions of which will be easily remembered; though at first it may be necessary that the teacher should describe to the class some of the leading characters of the example given, or sketch it freely on the blackboard, to refresh the memory before the pupils proceed to draw it. At the conclusion of the exercise, the best and worst efforts should be taken to the board, and their good and bad qualities pointed out and criticised, and an accurate drawing of the example be put on the board for each pupil to contrast and compare with his own work. He should then be allowed to correct and revise his drawing from the teacher's example upon the board. For this purpose charts of drawing examples are valuable, enabling the teacher to suspend a good illustration of a lesson on the board, for the pupils to correct their work by. Home exercises in memory-drawing may also occasionally be required of the pupils with much advantage.

II. — *Grammar Schools.*

The group of subjects, model, memory, and geometrical drawing, suitable for the pupils in grammar schools, introduces one new subject only, — that of geometrical drawing, which takes the place of free-hand outline from the blackboard, practised sufficiently in drawing from objects and memory.

MODEL-DRAWING.

The model-drawing may now be made to include such geometric forms as can be used to convey the first elementary rules of perspective, such as the convergence of parallel lines retreating from the eye, the foreshortening of lines and planes according to the angle they make with the direction in which the student is looking at the object, and other elementary rules. More difficult models being used, every pupil will have a different view of the same object; and though general principles may and should be explained by diagrams on the blackboard, the teaching will be more individual than before. The measuring of heights and widths proportionately, and of vanishing planes, by means of the pencil held in the hand at the full extent of the outstretched arm, must be explained to and practised by the pupils; for that is the only practical and accurate method of model-drawing. This way of measuring, which every draughtsman and artist adopts, does not come under the head or description of mechanical measurement, being only the means of ascertaining the proportion of the various parts, as affected by the laws of perspective. Instead of single objects being given, as in the primary schools, groups of objects may profitably be placed before the pupils, some of which they will have already drawn, and others which will be fresh to them. Geometric solids, such as the cube, oblong block, triangular, square, pentagonal, and hexagonal prisms and pyramids, as well as the cylinder, cone, and sphere, are very usefully employed, each or more than one at a time in conjunction with some familiar object, together composing a group of forms. The great difficulty at present, which the friends of art education in America will have to meet, is the provision of suitable examples for study; so that I see no other way of forwarding the cause, or of removing the difficulty, than by establishing an agency, either by the State government of each Commonwealth, or through private enterprise where all the most approved models and copies may always be attainable at a moderate cost. At present, models which a professionally-educated art master could conscientiously use do not apparently exist on sale in the United States.

In England, nearly forty years ago, when the nation was awakened to the necessity of at once giving an art education to its people, the two difficulties were, the want of teachers and of copies. That will be our want; but it will exist no longer than people feel apathetic about the matter. When once a real, earnest demand shall exist, the want can be supplied, in as many months as it has taken years to produce them in the old country.

MEMORY-DRAWING.

Just as the groups of subjects in model-drawing will be more difficult than those used in primary schools, so, of course, the memory exercises will be more advanced also. Sometimes a whole class may be required to draw any given example which has been practised months before, or perhaps formed part of a course in the primary schools. Every pupil should have one lesson per week in drawing on the blackboard, in chalk, on a large scale. It would be well to let a third of the class draw either their models or memory exercises upon the board, each lesson; so that during the week, if three lessons be given, all will have drawn upon the board, which is one of the most valuable of all methods of teaching drawing by the *free* hand.

GEOMETRICAL DRAWING.

The pupils, having been previously taught the definitions of terms used in plane geometry, may be passed on to the construction of figures. Each pupil requires

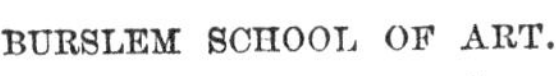

BURSLEM SCHOOL OF ART.

(WEDGWOOD MEMORIAL.)

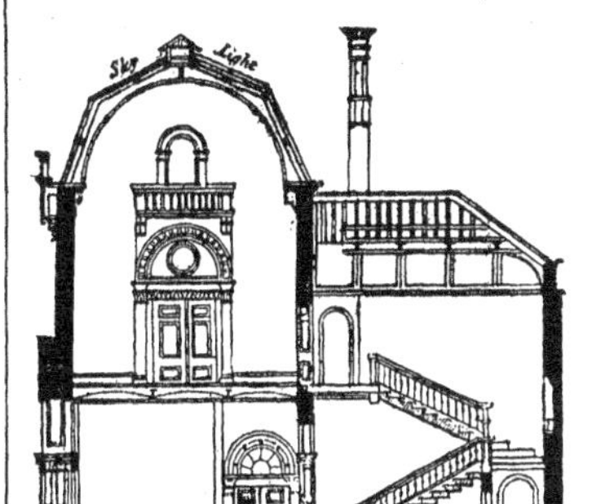

SECTION ON THE LINE C.D.

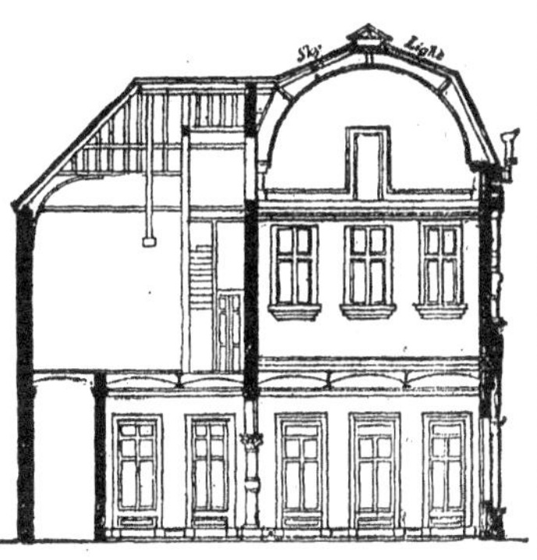

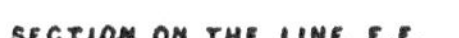

SECTION ON THE LINE E.F.

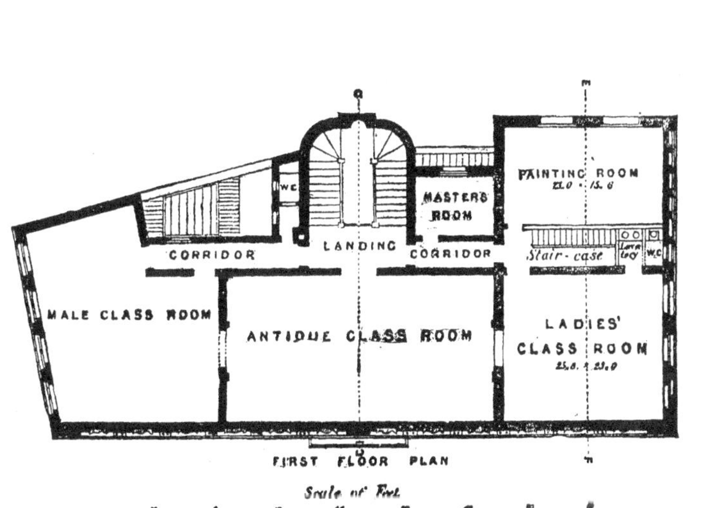

FIRST FLOOR PLAN

Scale of Feet

a good pair of pencil compasses, a ruler with inches marked upon it, and a ruled book of smooth paper to work his problems in. The teacher enunciates the problem to the class, who writes the enunciation from his dictation. He then works out the problem on the board, the class following, step by step. Six elementary problems are an hour's work, and four of the more intricate problems will take the same time. Every third or fourth lesson in geometrical drawing should be a *résumé* from memory of previous lessons. There is one consideration, with reference to this subject, teachers should strongly impress upon the minds of pupils : as demonstrations of the results are not required, their own accuracy must be the demonstration. If a geometrical drawing is not accurate, it is nothing, or worse than nothing. It does not pretend to be beautiful, and, unless intensely true in its result, is not useful, but a piece of delusive and worthless ugliness. I mention this because pupils will sometimes apologize for inaccurate results, by stating that they *do* know how to work the problem, which always seems to me an aggravation of the original offence rather than an excuse for it. It is like a man caught in the act of telling a lie, who tries to excuse himself on the grounds that he knew it was a lie, and did not himself believe the statement he was making. Accuracy and inaccuracy are merely habits which are formed either by good training or bad and careless instruction.

III. — *High and Normal Schools.*

In the high and normal schools, a wider range of study is permissible, because the capacities of the students are more developed. Still, it seems to me that there is some danger in attempting too much. In future years it will be desirable that the students in the normal schools should, during their period of training, complete an advanced course of lessons in the five subjects of free-hand, model, memory, geometrical, and perspective drawing, and by passing examinations in them receive diplomas or certificates of competency to give instruction; the examinations being conducted and diplomas awarded by the responsible officers of the State governments. This, however, must be a matter of growth.

MODEL-DRAWING.

The model-drawing of the high and normal schools should be made a most instructive course, and, besides illustrating the use of different materials, as chalk, monochrome, and color, be very comprehensive in subject. Drawing from plaster casts in crayon and sepia; from groups of natural objects, as fruits and flowers; from still life and objects of art in water-colors, — will give a wider scope and a greater interest to the object drawing than was possible in the elementary schools.

Drawing ought to be so familiar to the pupils who have previously passed through the primary and grammar schools, that in the high and normal schools it should be used generally in the study of other subjects, and exercises in botany, geology, natural history, anatomy, or mechanics be readily illustrated by drawings and sketches in the preparation of which instruction should be given to the students in shading and coloring.

In these exercises high finish or pretty ornamental painting are not to be sought after, — good drawing, having a round effect, and fairly tinted like nature, being more educational, besides being more economical of time, than finished painting.

In time I hope the neglected subject of art education may become of so much value educationally, that we shall use it freely in acquiring knowledge of history, of the social life of other ages and peoples, of the glorious art epochs of the Old World, and the still glorious natural phenomena which surround us every day in the New World. A refined perception of the beautiful in nature and art, and the enjoyment arising therefrom, will be ample compensation for time spent in art study by those who derive no pecuniary or social advantages from it.

PERSPECTIVE.

The additional subject of *Perspective* is put down for study in the high and normal schools. It is, of course, of the very highest importance to the proper understanding of all kinds of drawing, and has the same relationship to linear representation that grammar has to language. It would be possible to speak grammatically without a knowledge of grammar, and to draw accurately, as Turner did, without a technical knowledge of perspective; but these things are possible only to the few whose enormous experience compensates for their want of education. Perspective studied systematically gives the teacher of drawing such a grasp of the whole subject of linear representation, that, combined with model and memory drawing, he need never be at a loss for examples, nor fear to reproduce them.

In this subject, which is taught entirely on the blackboard, the teacher requires much power of illustration by sketches, and great clearness of verbal explanation, to make the problems intelligible to the student. Great experience in teaching the subject has enabled us to reduce its main principles to a plain system; and, when we secure the assistance of a good text-book, it will be found comparatively easy of attainment. Geometrical drawing must necessarily precede the study of perspective, which is dependent on it for the construction of forms used, as well as for experience in handling the instruments by which it is worked out.

DRAWING FROM FLOWERS AND FOLIAGE, AND ELEMENTARY DESIGN.

Drawing from natural foliage in outline is both instructive as an exercise, and may be utilized by making it a preliminary study to original design. Thus a class should be one day required to draw a given plant (1) as it appears naturally; (2) to make diagrams on the margin of the paper of its structure, showing front, back, and side views of the leaves, and buds and flowers, if any, geometric plans of its principle of growth, and the color of all suggested by tints washed over the outlines. The following lesson might then be an exercise, and had better be a home exercise to use this material in the design for a pattern of ornament, to fill a given space. A geometrical form as a square, oblong, triangle, hexagon, pentagon, or circle of sufficient size, the teacher being careful that the form to be ornamented shall be such as the subject may properly be applied to. If the pupils be instructed generally how to use their sketches, they will find the designing of original ornament from them a most interesting and valuable study; and then, at a subsequent lesson, the exercises of the whole class should be brought in and delivered up to the teacher, and openly criticised before all.

Upon a just recognition of the good features in the systems of nations where the subject is not a new one, and a deliberate consideration of our own circumstances and requirements, let us hope in time to establish a system of art education in this country. It is not a branch of education capable of a very rapid growth; for we know that "art is long:" but the same wisdom that has built up the magnificent educational system of

America will, I feel confident, be as capable of perfecting and completing each phase and feature that it may be considered desirable to add to that system; and, having begun well, will be in no disposition to look back, or be impatient and lose heart if the highest results do not immediately manifest themselves.

We have the satisfaction of knowing, that, in beginning with the public schools, we are beginning at the right end; and we have the prospect of possessing before very long a central institute of art in the Boston Museum of Art, which will be like the head-quarters of fine art for the State of Massachusetts: and what is done in the modern Athens will be copied elsewhere. The education of teachers will be provided for by the normal art schools, which will in due time arise in every State; and before very long there will be hardly a common school in which satisfactory instruction is not given. The supply of examples to carry on an efficient course of art education will follow upon the demand for them, without unnecessary delay; and thus I maintain that the prospects of naturalizing the subject, and providing for its development, are of the most encouraging character.

SUGGESTIONS TO THE TEACHER, AND USE OF BLACKBOARD ILLUSTRATIONS.

The greatest obstacle to the progress of drawing, as a subject of general education in the common schools of America, appears to be a want of confidence on the part of the regular school-teachers in their own ability to learn drawing themselves and teach it to their pupils. So much of the wonderful has been associated with the possession of great art powers, with which simple ability to draw has been confused, that perhaps this diffidence is reasonable: it becomes, however, unreasonable when it is associated with disinclination to learn, on the ground, that, to understand and succeed in mastering the elements of drawing, special gifts are required in art. The prevalence of this erroneous opinion is due mainly to the fact, that, until recently, only those children in schools were permitted to draw who had the inclination and showed proficiency. Had the same test been applied to other subjects of instruction, the schools would soon have been emptied, and the teachers' occupations gone. But the relationship of children to other subjects of instruction was understood, because the teachers themselves understood those subjects: the relationship of drawing to the education of children has been misunderstood, from the accident of the teachers being generally unacquainted with its practice. They are not responsible for this lack of experience in drawing: the misconception of its uses, and the delusive notion of its difficulty, have been much owing to want of proper gradation and method in the arrangement of the elementary exercises, and because, in many courses of drawing, the understanding has been too often ignored for appeals to the fancy or the taste, — very unreliable guides at first.

A reasonable and trustworthy power of drawing, which will enable the possessor to represent form with as much ease and certainty as to speak or write, — which power is possible of attainment to every human being who is neither mentally nor physically incapable, either by lunacy, idiotcy, blindness, or paralysis, — such a power must be based upon a thorough understanding of each step in and element of drawing, known by name and sight, from the dot to the most subtle compound curve, from the geometric form to the last problem in perspective; and if from the first the hand is made the agent of the mind in acquiring and testing and displaying its knowledge, then understanding will guide execution, and the two associated, acting and re-acting upon each other, will develop inevitable ability to draw. Methods and systems of instruction designed to suit unusual faculties, either great or small, are not practical for general use; and this is the error into which artists have fallen, who without long and extensive experience in art education, or such experience only as is limited to a few subjects, have designed special methods of instruction. It is the gaps between one step and another which frighten people of ordinary capacity, and hinder feeble footsteps. There should be no one point in a series of consecutive lessons in drawing which could be described as the place where the subject begins to be difficult. Instruction should proceed as though it were the ascent of an inclined plane, possible to all; not the climbing-up of a mountain-side, uneven in gradation, and interrupted by crevasses and precipices, requiring extraordinary faculties to surmount; and System should be the engineer, who, when the road has to be made and travelled, fixes the gradients, lays down the lines, and reduces or fills up inequalities to make the gradients safe and economic to average power.

For this reason it would appear to be the duty of those who have, by much experience, become acquainted with the best methods of instruction, to endeavor to make them the common property of educationists, who know by their own experience, that, in the long run, the best road is the safest, but not always the shortest.

Form is the language of nature, and drawing the speech of the eye, expressed by the hand. The alphabet of this language is the series of signs by which form can be represented, color being the local, inherent, or transient circumstance. The letters in this alphabet are straight lines and curves, equal, proportionate, or various, in the ratio of their simplicity or subtlety. It is necessary, therefore, that, if we are to understand this language, we must first learn its alphabet, then spell its short words, and afterwards construct the sentences which delineate natural phenomena, or record our own perceptions of them. Lastly, if our natural qualities be receptive, — capable of taking in the wealth of natural phenomena, — and our tastes be cultivated into refinement, comes the faculty of originality in art, which is the result of educating all our faculties, not the spontaneous generation of passing fancy or of sudden caprice.

That is the experience of education generally, and art education supplies us with no new developments. The greatest men in all vocations are neither produced nor hindered by a system of education: they will come with our help or without it; but the average men can only be produced by systematic training and education, and those beneath the average require both. So that it comes to this: systematic education is necessary for many, requisite for most of us, and not without value even to the few who are destined to stand foremost and highest.

A sign of educational experience is when we fairly divide the labor of acquiring knowledge into proper stages, — neither requiring the work of developed skill from the inexperienced, nor withholding the most advanced exercises from matured practice. It is not a sign of wisdom in the teacher when intense accuracy is expected from the young child, who knows not wherein it consists; nor is it merciful to insist on the manipulative craft, which comes by long practice, from those who are taking the first faltering steps. If the understanding is displayed and proved, manipulative dexterity will come, as surely as the mind is master of the body, in due time. It has been the fashion with some to say,

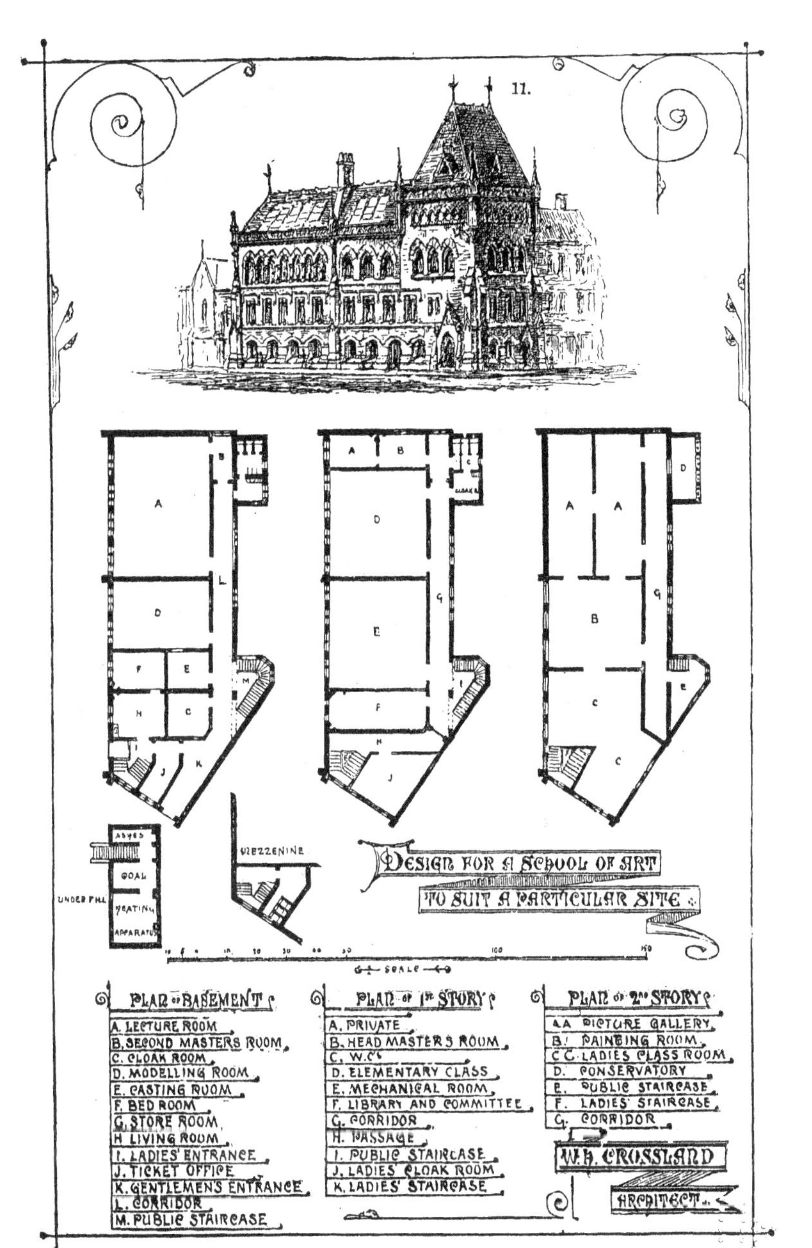
11.
ASHES
COAL
UNDER THE
HEATING
APPARATUS
MEZZENINE
DESIGN FOR A SCHOOL OF ART
TO SUIT A PARTICULAR SITE
SCALE
PLAN OF BASEMENT
A. LECTURE ROOM
B. SECOND MASTERS ROOM
C. CLOAK ROOM
D. MODELLING ROOM
E. CASTING ROOM
F. BED ROOM
G. STORE ROOM
H LIVING ROOM
I. LADIES' ENTRANCE
J. TICKET OFFICE
K. GENTLEMEN'S ENTRANCE
L. CORRIDOR
M. PUBLIC STAIRCASE
PLAN OF 1ST STORY
A. PRIVATE
B. HEAD MASTERS ROOM
C. W.C's
D. ELEMENTARY CLASS
E. MECHANICAL ROOM
F. LIBRARY AND COMMITTEE
G. CORRIDOR
H. PASSAGE
I. PUBLIC STAIRCASE
J. LADIES' CLOAK ROOM
K. LADIES' STAIRCASE
PLAN OF 2ND STORY
A.A PICTURE GALLERY
B. PAINTING ROOM
C.C. LADIES CLASS ROOM
D. CONSERVATORY
E. PUBLIC STAIRCASE
F. LADIES' STAIRCASE
G. CORRIDOR
W.H. CROSSLAND
ARCHITECT.

that no mechanical means of assisting the young beginners to draw should be allowed for an instant, for fear of crippling the young faculties; and that the drawing-book must be kept in one position always, regardless of the line to be drawn, or whether the anatomy of the human body was capable of drawing a certain line in a fixed position; nor must mechanical means of correction be allowed. Yet, if we observe the habits of experienced artists in their studios, we find they resort to every resource of mechanical assistance, reserving their skill and power for the parts where mechanical means are useless, and human skill is absolutely required. So that, to judge by the rules laid down by theorists, the tests of geometric accuracy are to be forbidden to babes, whilst they are invariably resorted to as necessary and economical by strong men in their ripest development! That is a delusion and mere pedagogism. Drawing is easy enough to be capable of human attainment generally; but it is difficult enough to enlist all our powers, whether of scientific invention or artistic skill: and the time when mechanical means of correction are most required and most possible of usefulness is, when the artistic powers are the least developed in beginners, and can be most easily corrected and disciplined by scientific tests and criticism. The teacher who insists on the exactness of 90° in a right-angle drawn by a child of tender age, or who gives, as a preliminary exercise, the circle which it was Giotto's pride in his maturity to have drawn with a stroke, is imposing burdens grievous to be borne on the shoulders of the weak and unprotected, and crushing a faculty he is employed to cultivate. That is holding on by the horns of the altar, whilst the altar itself is dishonored, and desecrated by the misinterpretation of its precepts. Approximate accuracy, such as may be expected of the individual in his particular stage of practice and development, is all that should be expected, as it is all that can be gotten from him. With this the teacher should be content, trusting to growth, development, and industry to do the rest. Those who learn with the most difficulty, and honestly express all the ignorance that is in them, sometimes come out right in the end, and know best the special forms of ignorance and truth by their own disciplined experience. But it is killing to such to apply the highest standard of exactness at once: it must be applied by degrees, and with a kindly manner which recognizes every advancement, while it impresses the pupil with a feeling that something else is yet to be attained. This is so well known, and so very generally practised in all other subjects, that I ought to apologize for referring to it as equally true of drawing as a subject of instruction; and I should do so, were it not for the fact, that I am conscious of tests being usually applied to first efforts in drawing by inexperienced teachers, which are unusual, as they are unnecessary, in it as in other branches of education.

Measuring the accuracy of length in straight lines, or the altitude of curves, should be resorted to, not to save the exercise of the judgment, but to correct the inaccuracy of the eye. Beginners will be unable to divide lines truly; and therefore every drawing-lesson should include that exercise as part of its progress, as in the division of the central line in symmetrical figures; but, before proceeding to draw the more important parts of an exercise, the accuracy of the proportions should be tested, and faults corrected, either by the experienced hand of the teacher, or by mechanical means, it matters little which, if the error be proved and put right. But to allow errors in the first steps to make all subsequent steps equally erroneous, from a sentimental objection to the use of measuring as a corrective agent, is a mistake which perpetuates what it professes to remove. The eye will not be trained into truthful perception by letting it get accustomed to its own imperfection; but it will be educated by the substitution of right for wrong, every time the wrong is committed. Mechanical means alone furnish us with absolute accuracy in geometric forms, and are therefore the only tests to be relied on; and in proportion as they are judiciously resorted to at first will the need for them gradually cease. People speak of this as the use of crutches, which hinder the power of walking alone. If we look at the simile closely, we shall see that a crutch has sometimes protected and preserved an injured or undeveloped limb, until its powers have been restored or developed, and the crutch thrown away; whilst a sentimental prejudice against its use might have led to permanent injury of the weak part, that would have necessitated the use of the crutch for all after life. We need not fear that sound people will use such a support after the necessity has passed away; and to deny it to them when they want it, is dangerous cruelty.

A species of idolatry exists in the minds of some concerning the value attached to the drawing of straight lines and circles. It may therefore be as well to state, that to draw either, except by accident or mechanical assistance, is an impossibility: though to draw lines approximately straight and circular is not difficult of attainment, nor of extraordinary value when acquired; the result being so far inferior to the lines of the ruler or the compasses as to be universally discarded for the mechanically-made lines, when straightness or roundness has to be relied upon. What we want in art education is to develop the power of doing that which to mechanical means is unattainable; viz., original and tasteful and learned work, scholarlike and artistic: and the steps towards this are only the means, not the end, which end may be hindered by exaltation of straight lines and circles, as subjects of adoration, unto a miserable god.

Drawing is also made needlessly difficult by arbitrary regulations in its practice, such as insisting that the book or board should always be kept in one position. It would be as well to recognize that our hand and arm are only a complex instrument, like a machine or compound pair of compasses, and that the movements of which they are capable are limited by the construction of the skeleton and the action of the muscles. Thus a curve of short radius may be struck by the movement of the fingers on the second joint from their ends, a longer curve from the movement of the hand on the wrist-joint, longer still by the fore-arm on the elbow-joint, and the longest and most perfect of all by the whole arm moving from the ball-and-socket joint of the shoulder; the head of the *humerus* working in the concavity of the *scapula*. But from neither is it possible to strike a curve inwards towards the joint which is used as its centre, any more than it is possible to strike a curve with a pair of compasses which shall tend towards the centre from which it is struck. So that, in drawing curves which tend inwards towards the hand or the body, we must either shift our hands, arm, or body, to get at the centres of such curves, or we must shift the book or paper upon which we are drawing, to bring the centres into our hand or arm. Of the two, it will be found more convenient and orderly to allow pupils to change the positions of their books than to change the positions of their bodies, or to walk round the tables they are drawing upon in search of the centres of each curve they have to draw.

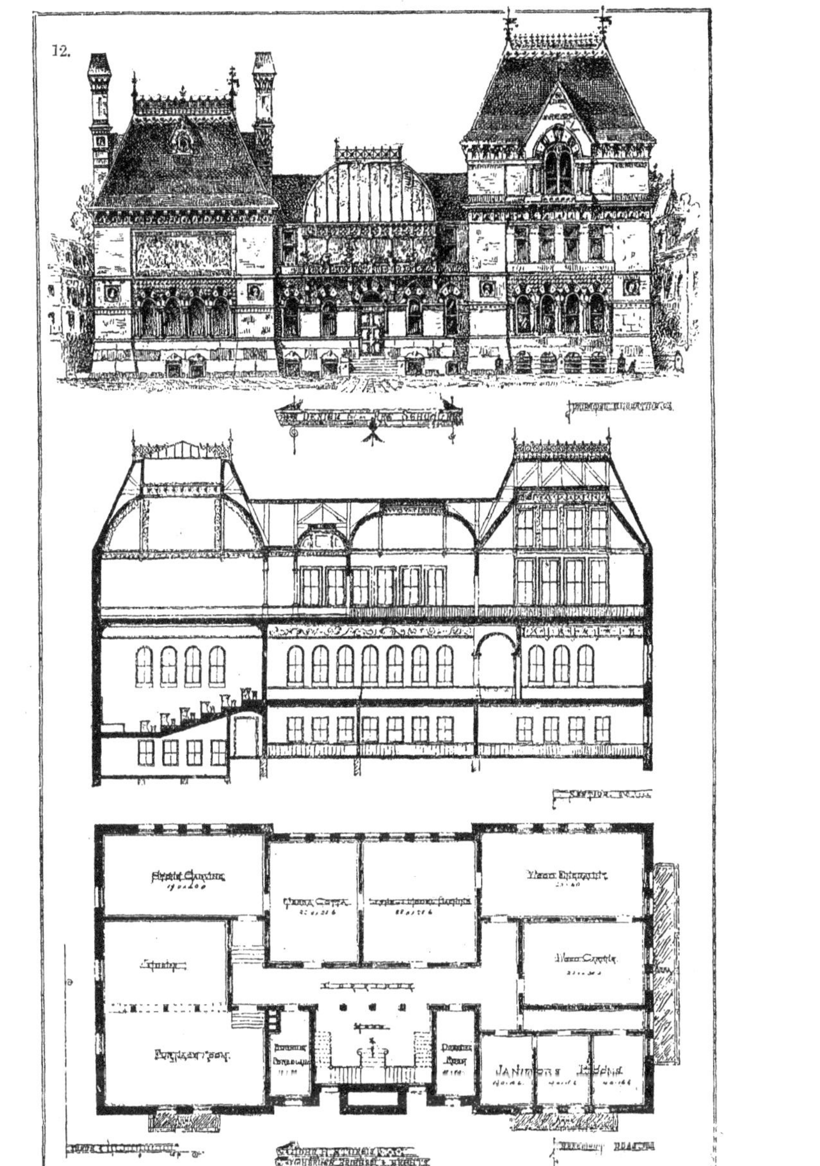
12.

Methods of testing the accuracy of geometric forms should be taught to pupils from the earliest lessons. When the definitions of plane geometry are given as exercises in drawing, preceding all other exercises, the test of the true construction of each shape should be shown to all pupils, and its application to the work of each be required. Thus in drawing a square, not only the length of each side must be the same as in a rhombus, but the length of the two diagonals be identical, or its form will be rhomboidal. Individual analyses for each form will be familiar to the teacher, and must be made equally familiar to the pupil, that the understanding may assist and support the hand and eye.

Having said thus much upon the proper value of the geometric exercises in drawing, and deprecated too stringent and arbitrary regulations concerning its practice, perhaps it would be right I should say that the opposite mistake of undue laxity is as much to be avoided. In many points the teacher cannot be too strict in details which have an important share in successful work, however indirectly they seem to bear upon it. Thus sharp points to pencils, and clean hands and rubber, and a book neither dog's-eared, defiled, nor crumpled, should be absolutely insisted on; and incorrigibles should be made to draw upon slates only until they can be trusted in contact with white paper without defiling it. It requires no great art genius in a teacher to insure that; yet the ability to command it is half-way towards getting the best results from his instruction. The excellent order and method common in American schools make this an easy matter; and it requires only that the accomplished teachers in the schools should turn their attention seriously to the subject of teaching drawing, to guarantee as good results in this as in any other branch of a common school education already attained to by them.

There is a satisfaction to the student in mastering any subject, whether it be purely intellectual or experimental; but there is a keen delight, a sensuous enjoyment, in acquiring skill in art. The first time a student succeeds in realizing some natural effect, or expresses an idea of the mind which had previously existed only in thought, is a moment of inexpressible joy: it is beyond explanation to those who have not felt it, and worth all the pains and discipline it costs to obtain the sensation.

Happily, this enjoyment, pure in its character and godlike in its creativeness, is within the reach and appreciation of all who care to possess it; but, like some other excellent inventions, it must be wooed, and will "not unsought be won." It does not drop like a ripe apple from the tree of knowledge into the mouth of a lazy Adam below, but needs well-directed climbing to be secured.

DRAWING ON THE BLACKBOARD.

The use of the blackboard for instruction in all subjects of elementary drawing is highly essential. It may be well, therefore, to suggest its capabilities and the best means of acquiring command over it.

The chalk used should be square in section; so that, when it is advisable, a line of uniform thickness can be obtained, — which is difficult, if not impossible, with conical-shaped pieces of chalk. A short stick of wood about eight inches long, having a cone of four inches altitude and two inches base, its apex at one end of the stick, and its axis the stick itself, — the cone to be covered with wash-leather, chamois-skin, or soft cloth with a good staple, — is the best implement with which to erase lines not wanted; the pointed end of the cone enabling the draughtsman to take out constructional or other lines without destroying the curves which are near them.

Vertical lines are drawn from above downwards, the weight of the hand and arm, allowed to fall naturally, assisting the eye. The draughtsman should stand with his right shoulder opposite the vertical line to be drawn. Horizontal lines are made with the greatest facility when a fixed and firm point has been made to the left, and the arm and body moved with the hand firmly pressed from left to right, thus steadying the hand and keeping its position relative to the body the same. In drawing curved lines, it is well, unless the draughtsman has great experience, to make a few dots in the path the curve has to traverse; not more than four or six for any curve, but enough to guide the eye and give confidence to the hand. Passing the chalk-point over the place where the intended curve is to be, without marking, is also useful, as it accustoms the hand and arm to the motion and change of joint required in the curve. Very rapid drawing upon the board is not recommended, because, until the teacher has had great experience, it will not be likely to be accurate enough: on the other hand, the whole amount of time spent in drawing an hour's lesson for pupils ought not to be more than five minutes. The left curves should be drawn first; and, when drawing the balancing forms on the right hand, the eye should take in, not only the curve in process of formation, but that already made, to which it is symmetrical. That suggests standing far enough from the board, and the teacher will find it is better to draw with the whole arm from the shoulder-joint than from the elbow or wrist, the face not being nearer the board than a distance of two feet in a perpendicular line to its surface.

The diagram should not extend much above the

draughtsman's head, for above that his hand will lose power; nor below his elbow when the arm hangs at the side, for to draw then brings the head close to the board, and prevents a clear view. If it be necessary that lines be made both above and below these points, the position of the body and head must be raised or lowered, so as to avoid stooping or straining, which is fatal to good work. Drawing on the board is the most perfect illustration of the expression, "free-hand drawing;" and unless the hand be quite free and supple in its motion, and the arm as well, sweet curves or refined lines are impossible.

The best preparation for blackboard work is to draw the diagrams with pen and ink on a small scale, which forms the habit of slow, deliberate, and thoughtful execution, besides familiarizing the eye and hand with the character and nature of the forms to be reproduced. Very good drawing on the board is easily acquired; but it must have a basis of the power to draw pretty well to begin with. After all, valuable as the ability is to teachers, as a means of instruction, it can only be regarded as a rough process to illustrate principles, and has the same sort of relation to actual representation as the foundation of a building has to the whole and the parts of its superstructure. There is danger in thinking too little or too much of the power of drawing on the board: to the teacher it is, perhaps, above all other agencies in elementary instruction, and of less value than other processes in advanced instruction, being useless in conveying information concerning light and shade or color. Skill and readiness to draw forms on the board are sometimes confounded with the ability to explain the nature and character of the forms which are illustrated: but, of the two, the latter is the more valuable; for, with intelligent descriptions and critical acumen, even rough

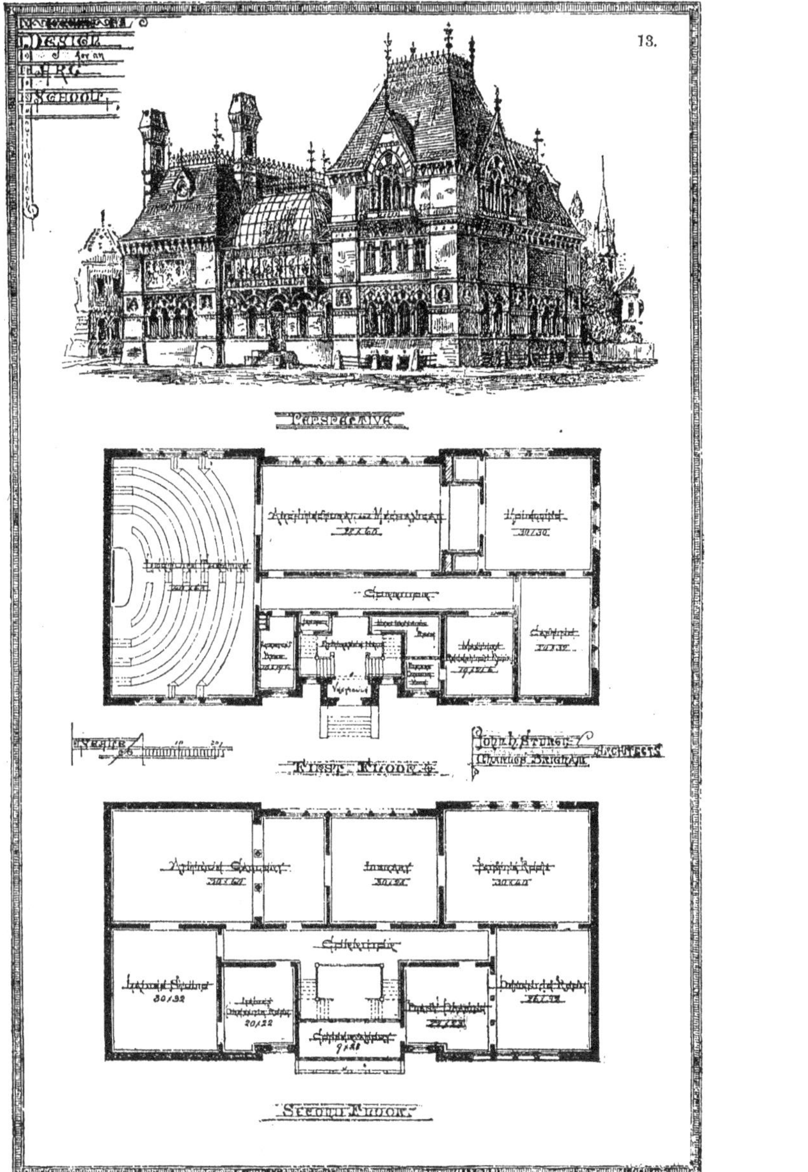
13.
Design
for an
School
Perspective
First Floor
Scale
Architects
Second Floor

diagrams may be made to serve all practical purposes of instruction; whilst the best drawings in so rude a material as white chalk will not teach of themselves, unless accompanied by clear and intelligent explanation. It is only the most simple and rudimentary forms which can be illustrated on the board: a draughtsman who wishes to illustrate subtle forms or refined gradation in curvature would not think of employing such a rough vehicle as white chalk, or so violently contrasted degrees of line and background as black and white.

The power to draw on the board is so easily acquired, that it is somewhat surprising to find such a degree of importance and value attached to its possession. It is the very cheapest way of securing a reputation for ability to draw, usually valued more than it deserves to be, and not valued at all, except as a rough expedient, by those who have a much better and more costly article, which includes in its comprehensiveness the power of using all mediums upon any material, applied to every subject capable of representation. So that, whilst to the teacher it is of the highest instructional use, as the alphabet is, it is easy of attainment to all, and nothing to be very proud about when acquired.

It is said that a drawing will convey a truthful idea when words fail. To do this, the drawing must be either very good and the words very feeble, or the audience very ignorant. There are very few drawings which convey completely any idea which could not be more fully expressed with the assistance of language added to visible forms. At the same time, the understanding can be appealed to through the eye, as well as through the ear; and it is either bad economy which prefers one medium to the exclusion of others, or inefficient educational powers which cannot resort to all or any one as the need arises. The scale in music is perfectly illustrated by a ladder with half-steps between E and F and B and C; and the major and minor keys are as well demonstrated by the circle and elliptic curves. There is hardly any educational process which may not draw its similes from subjects outside of its own resources, for development is very similar in all things: the growth of a plant, the progress of a day, the education of a child, the history of a nation, the comprehension of a religious or political principle, — all have stages almost precisely alike, which can be explained and understood by comparison. It is the mark of a teacher, that he detects these resemblances, and uses them to illustrate principles, just as it is a sign of his power to grasp all means within his reach to make his explanations plain. Amongst these means is drawing, — of no more importance than others, and of no less; and a teacher who can illustrate a lesson in physical geography by sketches of the natural products of the country, and character of the people and their habits, or who accompanies his historical exercises by drawings of the costume, architecture, portraits of eminent men, weapons and implements used in war and agriculture, or maps of contested ground, or charts of geographical distinctions, is twice as powerful a teacher as he who appeals only through the ears to the understanding, without illustration of forms or display of visible peculiarities.

CHAPTER III.

SCHOOLS OF ART AND INDUSTRIAL DRAWING.

THE very general desire to establish agencies by which to secure a development of general in the form of secondary or technical education, as well as the movement in favor of what is somewhat vaguely termed industrial education, suggests that information of a practical character concerning what has already been done in the same direction in European countries, may be of value in America just now. The study of art in its elementary, advanced, or technical stages requires accommodation of a special kind, — in buildings, their arrangement as to lighting, &c., and the apparatus and examples to illustrate varied subjects of study. To furnish suggestions concerning these requirements is my aim in this chapter, with the hope that those who have not yet had opportunities of obtaining such information may find it of some use to them when provision for art study has to be made.

It will be well to recognize the distinction between elementary instruction in drawing, such as ought to be given in the common schools, and advanced scientific or technical instruction, which more properly belongs to the special schools, called schools of art. There is no necessity for providing in a permanent manner the means of elementary instruction in these special schools; for eventually it will be furnished as a part of general education: though, until that becomes an accomplished fact, temporary provision should be made for those adults who desire such instruction, and were not able to obtain it during their school terms.

A school of art, then, should be designed upon the assumption that the knowledge of elementary drawing in such subjects as free-hand, model, geometric, and simple linear perspective drawing has already been acquired; and its mission is to take up the student upon his leaving the day-school, and carry on his general art education to a higher level firstly, and guide it in a special direction afterwards. The school should be to artisans what the university is to the professional man; and to such professions as those of the architect and engineer it should be a professional school also. The best arrangements for study, the best examples to study from, and the best instruction which can be obtained, are alone worth the outlay of providing them: makeshifts of badly-lighted and ill-adapted rooms, poor or bad examples, and feeble or incompetent instruction, may possibly be better than nothing; and, if that be allowed, a generous estimate has exhausted the whole value of such provision. It is useless to delude ourselves into believing that we are practising economy by establishing drawing-classes in rooms used for other purposes than art study, and furnished with desks and a blackboard only, and taught by a teacher whose sole qualification is, that he can himself draw: that may do for a single term, until elementary principles have been acquired; but, unless it be followed by something more complete in its character as a provision for art instruction, we are only increasing a demand for which we provide no supply. The most economical way of commencing classes is to begin upon a plan requiring little or no modification, nor to be without any means for instruction suitable to the end sought, which are procurable by a reasonable outlay. The courses of study should be determined upon for each school by competent persons deliberating on the special wants of a locality. The premises to be occupied for the pursuit of these studies should be designed by an architect who understands the requirements of art education, in conference with the professional art master who is to be intrusted with the task of carrying on the school; and the examples and apparatus for instruction should be obtained at first, so that there may be no difficulties in the way of administering the system adopted. A great waste of money usually results from premises being adapted for drawing-classes or art schools by persons who know nothing of the special requirements of study in each of the rooms; and the efficiency of the schools and classes is thus sacrificed until further alterations are made, adapting the rooms for each specialty, upon experienced advice. I have been made so painfully aware in many instances of the wastefulness of such proceedings, and the disappointments and discouragements they have occasioned on all sides, — to students, teachers, school committee, and the public, — that I would seriously warn all to whom is intrusted the provision of facilities for art study not to be misled in that manner, on the false cry of economy, which is really extravagance. It has come under my observation, that schools miserably prepared and equipped for their work have done miserably; and that when the same schools have had fair play, in new premises built specially for them, the whole character of the students' work has been improved, its quantity increased, and all connected with the new administration have been gratified with the changes effected. The time spent in working under difficulties and drawbacks which were accidental or removable was time wasted, in so far as the results fell short of what they might have been with only natural difficulties to encounter. For these and many other reasons which could be given, it is better to begin right: the result will justify the outlay incurred, and prove it to be the most economical way of expending public money.

RANGE OF STUDY.

In order to consider this matter methodically, we should first see what is proposed to be done in schools of art and industrial drawing-classes. This may be described as the cultivation of the understanding and increase of knowledge of the students in the field of art generally, supplemented by the acquisition of manipulative and technical skill in some branch of art practice. Thus for a time all the students will study a common course, intended to prepare them for the special courses they will follow afterwards. Then they branch off into advanced work, either (1) scientific instrumental drawing, (2) artistic work in light and shade, color and design, (3) modelling.

The common course ought to include drawing in pencil, crayon, and one color, from ornamental casts, models and objects grouped, natural foliage, flowers and objects of natural history, details of the human and animal figures, in outline and light and shade. Where it has not been previously studied, the course should include the common-school course of (*a*) free-hand drawing from flat examples in outline, (*b*) model drawing from geometric solids, (*c*) geometric drawing, (*d*) perspective projection, (*e*) orthographic projection. When this has been gone through, the student should then be allowed to commence practice in the special subjects: carpenters and others connected with the building trades, in building, construction and planning of houses, drawing and designing of architectural details; machinists and engineers should take up mechanical drawing of details of machinery and mechanical motions, drawing from measurement of actual machines and tools in use, and isometric and parallel projection applied to machinery; and both carpenters and machinists should learn the art of making scale drawings to work from, laying out work from written specifications, and making the specifications themselves from original designs.

The draughtsman, lithographer, and art student require instruction in light and shade, color and design, historical study, drawing from the antique and the living model, from natural foliage and still life. The modeller not only needs the same instruction in drawing as the painter, but the additional practice of work in the round, modelling his subjects to scale from the originals; and should know how to reproduce them in a hard material, as plaster, by casting his own productions.

Thus, though the basis of all successful art is good drawing, which should be never lost sight of, industrial art education must be discursive enough to meet the wants of all industries, and in those particular directions which the varied occupations of the students suggest. The method of study adopted will necessarily affect the disposition and arrangement of the rooms to be used; but there can hardly be much difference in the way rooms are fitted up for study of the same subject, whatever be the method of instruction adopted. The most important considerations which must be decided before a school of art be carried out to completion are, 1*st*, *The building and its accommodation;* 2*d*, *Fitting and lighting;* 3*d*, *The examples for study*. Taking these in order, I propose to make some suggestions concerning each of these subjects.

THE BUILDING AND ITS ACCOMMODATION.

The size of the building, and character of the instruction most generally required in any locality, will determine the proportion of many parts of the building to each other. Thus, the seat of a particular manufacture may wisely require that special and considerable accommodation be allotted to that kind of industrial drawing which will most assist the trade of the district. When that is the case, an addition should be made to the average proportions of the school, or special class-rooms be built for the technical study requiring to be developed. The proportion of students to population, which it would be judicious to provide room for, will vary according to the character of the trade carried on in each locality, whether it be one in which art knowledge is valuable, or the reverse ; and though it would be difficult to discover any industrial calling in which art skill would be of no value, yet its pecuniary and marketable worth is greater in some manufactures than in others. But when it is remembered that the usual trades carried on in every city or town ought to supply a large number of students, irrespective of particular manufactures, it will not be advisable to provide for less than five per cent of the population as students. Taking a city of ten thousand inhabitants, five hundred, at least, ought to be found in schools of art or branch drawing-classes. If one school only be built in a city, it should provide for that number of students, not necessarily at one time, but at twice; and the attendances might be on two evenings per week for each class, thus allowing a building accommodating five hundred to provide for a thousand pupils, or one to hold two hundred and fifty at a time to provide for five hundred.

The following is an estimate of a school for five hun-

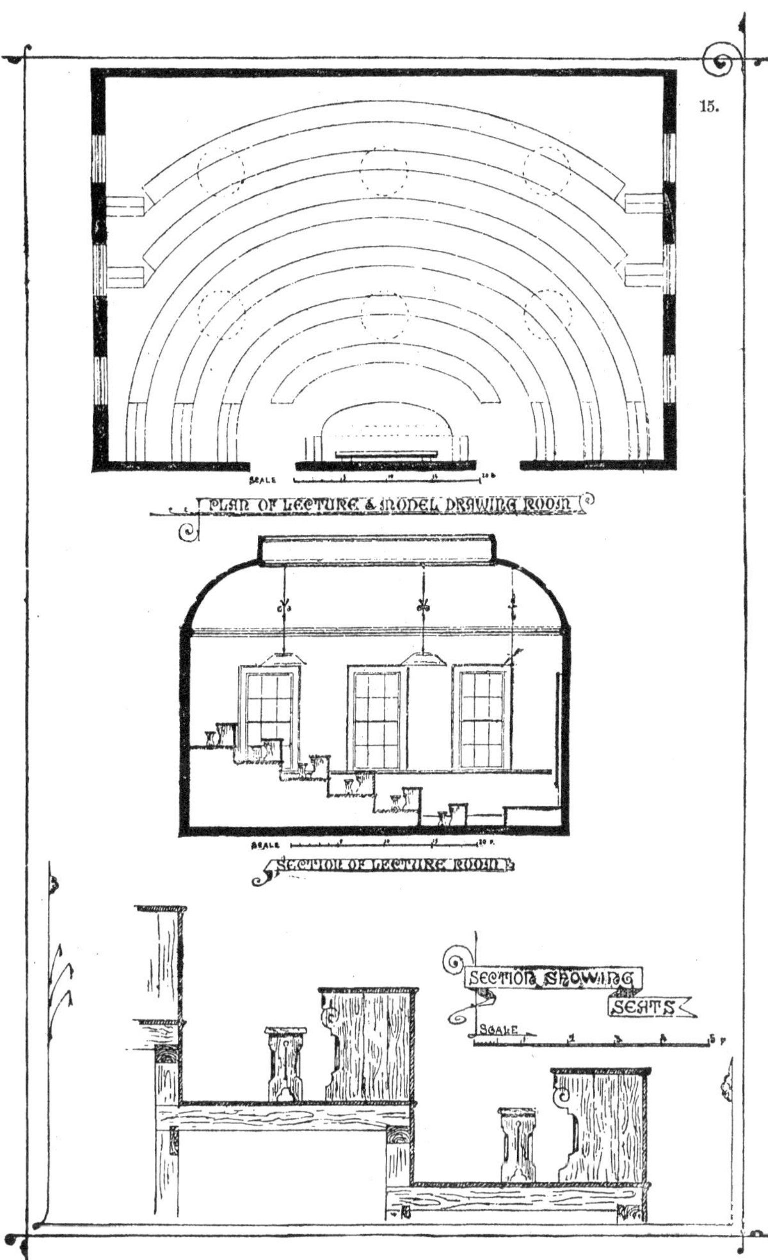
15.
SCALE
PLAN OF LECTURE & MODEL DRAWING ROOM
SCALE
SECTION OF LECTURE ROOM
SECTION SHOWING
SEATS
SCALE

dred students at one time. The class-rooms are divided into two groups; viz., those requiring top-light, and those for which side-light is suitable, — if top-light be not available.

TOP-LIGHT.	Feet.	TOP OR SIDE LIGHT.	Feet.
Exhibition and antique rooms .	60x30	Entrance-hall	20x20
Painting-room	30x30	Lecture-theatre	60x40
Conservatory	10x30	Mechanical & architectural room	60x30
Ladies' class-room	30x30	Elementary and cast room . . .	60x30
Plant drawing-room	20x30	Modelling-room	30x30
		Casting-room	20x30
		Designing-room	20x20
		Library and museum	20x30
		Master's room	20x20
		Janitor's offices and living-rooms	
		Male and female cloak-rooms	
		Small private studios for advanced students, — if desirable.	

The larger rooms should not be less than sixteen feet high, and the smaller not less than twelve feet. The top-lighted rooms, with the exception of the conservatory for plants and flowers, may be any thing between twenty and thirty feet high, but not less than twenty feet. The painting-room should have windows at the side joined to the skylights, provided with blinds, capable of obtaining either a side or top light, as desirable. The entrance hall and staircase are valuable for the display of students' works from selected specimens of the school's production, and should, if possible, be excellently lighted. The best place for the dais and blackboard of the lecture-theatre is the centre of one of its long sides, the seats and desks for students being ranged elliptically about it. The modelling-room and casting-room to communicate with each other, and all the rooms to be accessible from a corridor as well as from each other: the exhibition, painting, and ladies' class rooms should be connected by large folding-doors, so as to be thrown into one gallery for exhibitions. As a well-considered scheme of arrangement is of great consequence to the satisfactory working of a school of art, I have given illustrations of several schools in England whose plans I am familiar with; each of them having some point of advantage, and being of very different dimensions, may suggest the scale upon which schools for larger or smaller towns might be planned. Perhaps no one plan may be said to embrace all that a school of art should be, nor are they extensive enough to meet the wants of all classes: but in England fees varying from a small to a large sum per month are required from the pupils; and that limits their numbers very considerably. Education is better understood in America than in England; and the people are wise enough to see that education, like light and air, should be enjoyed by every one, and be free to all. It would not be advisable, therefore, to copy any feature of the planning of the schools illustrated as to scale, except such as relate to provision for particular kinds of study, the lighting of galleries, &c.: the scale of a school of art in America must vary from that for a school in any European country, with the exception of those in the several capital cities.

In the instructions issued to committees of art schools who are about to build, the English department of Science and Art makes the following suggestions concerning the building of an art school: —

"THE SITE. — The site must be not unhealthy in situation, nor in a noisy locality. It must be within convenient distance of the homes of the students. In tenure, fee simple, without encumbrance of rights reserved over the surface, or reservation of minerals.

"THE PLANS. — The following dimensions are suggested as affording adequate provision for accommodation for a hundred students: Elementary-room, 40 feet × 30; painting-room, 20 × 30; modelling-room, 20 × 30; master's room, 24 × 15; cloak-room for females; closets, laboratories, and anterooms, and kitchen and bedroom for attendant. The elementary-room should be east and west: it should not be less than 16 feet high, and be lighted from above. The painting-room should be lighted from the north side, and should have a top-light in the roof over and in continuation of the side-light. The master's room should be lighted by a side-light from the north if possible. The rooms for study should be not less than 15 feet high to the wall-plate, if ceiled flat, or 12 feet high to the wall-plate, if ceiled to the collar-beams or common rafter. The rooms should be well ventilated by the admission of air at the floor level, with an ample outlet above. The external walls of the school, if of brick, should not be less than one brick and a half in thickness, and, if of stone, not less than 20 inches in thickness. All the roofs must be either tiled or slated; gutters and drains to carry away the roof-water being provided. If the roof be unceiled to the tie-beam or collar-beam, there must be ceiling to the rafters. Rooms which are top-lighted should, in all cases, be ceiled to the common rafters, in order to give increased height; and all tie-beams, or other heavy roof-timbering, should be avoided, and iron tie-rods used where practicable."

The most valuable light for art study is that direct from the north, because there is no sunlight in it of direct rays: it is steady and continuous, and does not alter its direction during the course of the day, as light from the south and west does. Next to the north light, east light is best; the sun being soon away from the east, and leaving, after it has gone, a steady light. The exhibition-room and gallery of antique statues should be lighted from above, through two windows, — an outside and a counter light; the second being of ground glass to soften the light. If sufficient lighting surface can be got from the north, it is best to exclude southern light altogether. All the general class-rooms should be lighted with gas, methods for which are suggested in the section on Fittings, with the exception of the conservatory and plant drawing-room; the latter, being off the former, ought either not to be lighted at all at night, or, if the plant drawing-room be lighted, it should be done with oil lamps, which are less destructive to the plants than gaslight. The amount of gas consumed in class-rooms should not be more than one medium-sized burner for two pupils, when the rooms are filled: if more is required, the arrangement is wasteful. So large a quantity of gas being consumed, together with the vitiation of the air caused by a large number of students, there should in all rooms be the means of a constant renewal of fresh, pure air, by escapement of exhausted and introduction of fresh air.

The school should not be designed on more than three floors for the larger rooms; though small rooms, such as those suggested for private studios, may, by needing less height, occur as mezzanines. The best-managed schools I know are upon one floor only, — the master having better control over the whole school in that way than any other; and, where land is available, the cheapest and best class-rooms can be obtained by making the whole of them on one story, with top-light for all, approached by a common corridor. Remembering, however, that one necessary condition of the site of a school of art is, that it shall be within reasonable distance of the homes of the students; which means, that it be within the city limits, neither in the best nor worst quarters: land enough to put either all or the principal rooms on one floor will be probably beyond the means of the school committees.

The style most adapted for a permanent building of several stories for a school of art, when the top story is used for a gallery, and therefore there will be a deep piece of wall at the top of the façade unlighted by side windows, will be that in which are the greatest resources for breaking up in a picturesque manner this same dead wall. It seems to me most possible in a fourteenth-century Gothic, with a liberal use of inlays and colored materials of all kinds. A building for a school of art should not itself be a libel upon the public taste, nor a satire externally upon its work internally. Those who wish to elevate the taste and skill of the community ought to teach by example as well as precept: whatever value it may have elsewhere, faith without works in this subject is a very blind creed, not likely to make many converts, nor to regenerate the world of art.

In the sketch I have given of dimensions for a school of art for a city having ten thousand inhabitants, a conservatory is mentioned. This provision for plants and flowers is as necessary as to provide casts and flat examples. It is found to be both economical and convenient to have a janitor residing upon the premises; there being ample work for a man and his wife in keeping the plants cared for, the registers of attendance, the rooms in order, and as clean as they should be. A male and female attendant on the classes are constantly required; and their time should be wholly given up to their duties under the direction of the master. A ladies' class-room is also mentioned. The object of that is, not to provide separate accommodation for males and females in the ordinary courses of instruction, but to give advanced pupils who are commencing professional work, either as artists or teachers, a special room for practising undisturbed their several exercises. I would in all other cases let no separation of the sexes whilst being taught be made: the course of instruction ought to be precisely the same for both, until they severally branch off into technical studies.

It may be sometimes advisable to unite the various agencies for secondary education in one building; and there are many advantages in it. Thus, there may be added to the school of art a museum of industrial art and processes of manufacture, a picture-gallery, and a reference art library, open to the public as well as the students. Such an association would necessitate a larger and more important building; but it would very much increase the efficiency of each department. In case of an institution having much and valuable property in it, as would be contained in a library, and an industrial and fine-art museum, it should be entirely detached from all other buildings, and be fire-proof as well. Iron staircases, concrete floors upon brick arches, between girders of iron, instead of wooden joists, would practically make the building fire-proof. There need not be a foot of wood used in the construction of an art museum; though its contents and the furniture of the class-rooms in connection with it would necessarily be inflammable. An institution to combine these objects, for a small town or city, it has long been my desire to see built; and I designed such a building before I left England, and now illustrate it (plate 2).

It is supposed to be on a rectangular plot, entirely detached, designed so, that, if necessary, the structure may be built in two sections, the school being entirely distinct from the block which forms the library, museum, and gallery, but so arranged, that, should the school be built first, when the other is added, it will form a complete plan. If it be advisable to secure more space for the library and rooms above, the vestibule and staircase could be brought forward and built outside, so as to leave the fifty feet square entirely clear. That would give three rooms, which would be best divided into two upon each floor, making six rooms of about fifty feet by twenty-five feet each; and when furnished in each department by choice books, industrial masterpieces, and pictures, would form a valuable adjunct to any school of art, and be useful as a public institution, irrespective of the classes. I suggest this plan to the consideration of those about to erect a serviceable institution, combining many agencies for good. No room is wasted in passages or corridors: all the large rooms may be made into one grand exhibition-gallery by the opening of folding-doors; and the administrative part of the school can be kept entirely free during such an exhibition by locking the class-room doors opening on to the school staircase. The exterior is intended to be of plain and moulded brick, string-courses in encaustic tiles, and all enrichments in terra-cotta; so that it would be burnt earth entirely, from top to bottom.

Plans of schools of art are not very familiar to the people of this country; and I therefore give illustrations of some that have been built in England, which are found to be well arranged, though in all cases having been the result of voluntary subscriptions by private individuals, they are, as a rule, contracted in accommodation.

The Nottingham School has the advantage of being on one floor, with the exception of the exhibition-gallery, and is a handsome building which cost very little money. Its lighting is not as good as it might be; but the painting-room has the right kind of window, half in the roof and half in the wall, and is to the north or north-east, which is nearly as good a light as due north. The gallery, or exhibition-room, is right in section, but has no counter-light of ground-glass to soften and diffuse the light, as in the Sheepshanks Gallery (plate 14), — a better arrangement in every way.

The Birkenhead School has the disadvantage of being on three floors; but as one is below, on the basement, the principal floor is only one flight of stairs above the middle floor, approached by an outer flight of steps. It is commodious and very well lighted, and not too large to be managed by one master and assistants. The upper floor is used as a general class-room, and for exhibitions when necessary. The building is wholly detached, and ample space is left in the rear for conservatory and garden, and probably a library and museum at some future time. The school is only recently erected, and is a gift from a private individual to the town of Birkenhead, and will be an instrument of great benefit to coming generations of skilled artisans who reside in the borough. The elevation is an example of the difficulty of providing height enough for a gallery to be top-lighted, without leaving a heavy mass of dead wall on the upper part of the structure. That difficulty is better met in the Nottingham School, the more plastic style of which allows the wall to be broken up in a picturesque manner. The furniture, fittings, and examples of this school are particularly excellent; and I recommend American visitors to England, who are interested in art education, when arriving at Liverpool, to pay a visit to the school, which is across the river at Birkenhead. They will find in Mr. John Bentley, the present head-master (1872), a genial gentleman, who has spent much time on this side of the Atlantic, and whose practical knowledge of art educational matters cannot fail to be instructive to his visitors.

The Coventry School is, like that at Nottingham, an example of building a front of two stories, the gallery occupying the upper floor of the front, and the class-rooms being on one floor only; viz., the ground floor. It is an arrangement of great convenience, which may possibly be only understood by those who have been responsible for the conduct of a school of art. The building was the work of a young architect (Mr. Murray), who unhappily was cut off before he had reached his prime; and it is remarkable for having cost only two thousand pounds, — say ten thousand dollars. The arrangement of having several classes in one large room (the general class-room) may have some advantages,

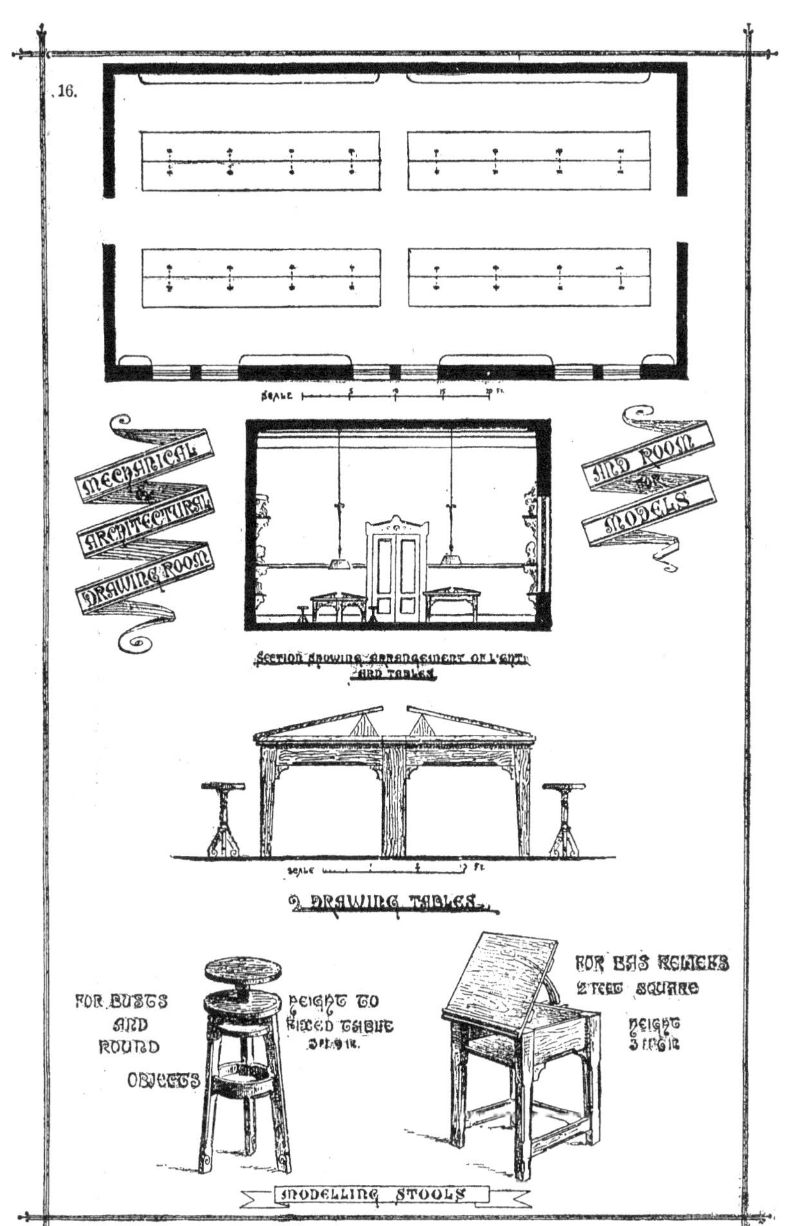
16.
SCALE 5 10 15 20 FT.
MECHANICAL & ARCHITECTURAL DRAWING ROOM
AND ROOM FOR MODELS
SECTION SHOWING ARRANGEMENT OF LIGHT AND TABLES
SCALE 1 2 3 FT.
2 DRAWING TABLES.
FOR BUSTS AND ROUND OBJECTS
HEIGHT TO FIXED TABLE 3 FT. 9 IN.
FOR BAS RELIEFS 2 FEET SQUARE
HEIGHT 3 FT. 6 IN.
MODELLING STOOLS

but it has many disadvantages; and I do not recommend its adoption here. It is resorted to as a means of decreasing the cost of conducting a school, by the employment of fewer teachers than are necessary; but in this country, where a proper value, social and economical, is attached to education, such expedients are not necessary; and as each class in the common schools has its own room and teacher, so I hope each separate branch of art study will have its distinct room and instructor.

The Minton memorial building at Stoke upon Trent is a good suggestion for a village school of art, where only a hundred students may be expected to be in attendance at one time. It has the demerit of being on two floors, arising probably from want of space in the site. The modelling-room, of great importance in the potteries (where the school is situated), could be used both for that purpose and drawing from the antique by night, though it should be loftier for day studies.

The Wedgewood memorial — the Burslem School of Art — is another example of a village school, having a façade whose ornamentation consists of very excellent terra-cotta work, though the scale of the engraving prevents its display. This design, as well as the Minton memorial, is planned to meet special requirements, — designing and modelling; but the ordinary classes are not neglected. Some rooms are adapted for work, not strictly speaking of an art character; yet it is so seldom that schools of art err on the side of comprehensiveness, that no exception ought to be taken to it on that account.

The two latter schools are testimonials to the valuable lives of two princely manufacturers, who strove hard, at much pecuniary sacrifice to themselves at first, for the elevation of industrial art. Their success and its appreciation have led to the founding of two excellent art schools; and I would suggest to those whom it may concern, whether, in the absence of any better opportunities, wealthy Americans might not erect such structures in their own lifetimes, and present them to the towns in which their wealth has been secured, or those to which they are attached by birth or family connection. It may be one way of preventing the good they do being interred with their bones, and making it live after them in future epochs.

As schools may sometimes be built which have to be accommodated to contracted sites, and may have to occupy several floors, I have engraved a plan by Mr. W. H. Crossland of London (who is rapidly rising into the most distinguished position as a Gothic architect), and which meets the difficulty of an uncomfortable site in a very able manner. Two entrances for males and females are obtained on each side of a janitor's office, — an arrangement which facilitates the taking of students' attendance on their entrance; and the janitor's living rooms are near the doors, — an advantage to both himself and visitors. The staircase for the public and for male students is thrown out behind, and thus secures much saving of space, and protects the class-rooms and corridors from noise. There is enough room in this building for two hundred students at once, distributing them fairly over the several classes; and the suite of rooms at the top can be thrown into a very large gallery for exhibitions. The positions of the classes with reference to each other are well chosen; and the arrangements generally are convenient, considering the space at disposal.

I owe to Messrs. J. H. Sturgis and C. Brigham, architects of the Boston Fine Arts Museum, the opportunity of illustrating a school of art designed by them to suit the requirements of a city of from twenty to forty thousand inhabitants. The size and proportion of the rooms have been arranged so as to comply very closely with the table given in the beginning of this chapter; and I do not think, that, for the size of the building, a better school could be planned. The building is supposed to front to the south; and thus the lighting of the suite of rooms at the top, requiring top-light, faces to the north. In the basement are rooms for technical or industrial study, anticipating a development in that direction which is very likely to take place. The lecture-room, in which so much of the real work of the school ought to be done, is arranged so as to be accessible from the corridor of the first story; and the rows of desks descend from the level of the corridor to the blackboard, which is nearly on the level of the basement. The introduction of the conservatory into the front elevation is a feature especially pleasing to me, suggesting as it does the important part that nature plays in the study of art. In the façade, tiles, terra-cotta, and colored brick are used to obtain an ornamental effect; and the building altogether, both in its design and arrangements, will commend itself to the favorable opinion of those who understand what is wanted in an art school, as well as to the lovers of architectural art generally. Such a building as this would be well adapted to form the nucleus of a fine-arts institute in any metropolitan city; the picture-gallery and industrial museum to be afterwards built in connection with it, in its rear. That some community, anxious for the distinction of establishing the first industrial art school on the continent of America, may adopt this plan, and carry it out in its entirety, is my fervent hope; for, not only would art education receive a powerful impulse thereby, but an element of architectural leaven would be introduced by its erection, that would probably influence in the right direction the artistic taste of any locality which adopted it.

The lighting of picture galleries and exhibition rooms is a matter of such consequence, that their construction results from the solution of this problem; and, as no school of art may be said to be complete without its gallery, information concerning the requirements of a satisfactory exhibition room may be serviceable. It is a mistake to suppose that much light is wanted to be able to see pictures, but rather the right sort of light, which will be the outer daylight toned and modified from its natural glare. On a cool, gray day, when the sun is not shining, light admitted into a room through clear glass gives the perfection of a light in which to see a picture or a drawing. But in the sunshine, when direct rays of sunlight find their way into the same room, the effect is not to illuminate, but to obscure, the greater part of the room, by the violent contrast in the eye between the brightness of objects the sunlight falls upon and the shady parts it does not reach. The problem, then, in lighting a picture gallery, is to maintain always the character of the light which we have through clear glass when the sun does not shine, — to put, in fact, between the sun and the pictures what a certain condition of the atmosphere puts when the sun is invisible but the sky clear. This can only be effected by the admission of sunlight through a semi-transparent medium, which diffuses the light and disperses direct rays; and, to accomplish this, in some of the best galleries two windows are employed in the skylight, — the outer one of clear glass or slightly obscured plate glass, with northern aspect, and the inner or counter light of ground glass. The Sheepshanks Gallery in London, designed by Capt. Fowke, is the best room I know for a clear, steady light, neither too much nor too little; and it is constructed on the principle described. The engraving opposite will explain its arrangement, the two lights being at an angle with each other. The vertical distance of the light from the picture is also of the greatest importance. We know how almost impossible it is to see pictures or engravings in rooms lighted from the side, like ordinary dwelling-house apartments, because of the shining and reflection upon their surfaces. The cause of this is explained by the two diagrams below the plan of the Sheepshanks Gallery; and Capt. Fowke's own words referring to this part of the subject are as follows: —

"Lighting by Day. — The upper rooms of the building (that is, those appropriated to the exhibition of the pictures of the Sheepshanks collection) are lighted from the roof. This is accomplished by means of a skylight, which extends along the entire length of the roof, and measures 14 feet in width; that is, 7 feet from the ridge on either side, the entire width of opening being 12 feet 6 inches, measured on a horizontal plane. As will be seen by reference to the section, each room is 20 feet wide; and at a height of 14 feet 6 inches from the floor, a cove, springing from a cornice on each side wall, reaches the height of the tie-beam of the principals (18 feet 8 inches above the floor), at a distance of 4 feet 6 inches from the wall, thus leaving a space of 11 feet between the coves: in this space a ground-glass internal skylight or ceiling is introduced; which, however, is raised 2 feet above the highest level of the cove, or 20 feet 8 inches from the floor, the ridge of this skylight being pitched 1 foot higher, thus giving a fall of 2 in 11 to each side, in order the more readily to carry off any moisture that may occur from condensation. The space between the highest point of the cove and the eave of the ground-glass light is filled in with perforated panels, for purposes of ventilation. One peculiarity in this coving requires notice; namely, that it is not returned at the end of the room, but cuts out on the end walls.

"By this arrangement, which militates somewhat with strict architectural precedent, the skylight is preserved in its integrity throughout the entire length of the room; and those parts of the side walls nearest to the ends receive an equal amount of light with that under the middle of the skylight. In the smaller rooms there is, by this means, a gain in amount of light of rather more than one-third over a similar room coved all round, and in the larger ones a little more than a fourth.

"These proportions have been adopted with a view of affording to the gallery as much light as possible, and at the same time of avoiding any reflection of light, or, as it is commonly called, 'glitter,' from the surface of the pictures; and, as regards the quantity of light admitted, it may be stated shortly, that the opening for the admission of light is exactly half the floor area of the gallery, the two areas being in the large rooms 920 feet and 460 feet respectively; thus, floor 46 feet × 20 feet = 920 feet; light 46 × 10 = 460 feet; and it is also precisely equal to the entire surface of either wall, which might be made use of for the hanging pictures. In dealing with the quantity of light, another important point must not be lost sight of; namely, the height of the opening from the floor, and its consequent distance from the pictures; and this will be found to be in this gallery reduced to the minimum, consistently with the avoidance of glitter, being only 20 feet 9½ inches from the floor, or less than 18 feet above the lowest point of the bottom pictures. The possibility of reflection or glitter is guarded against in the following manner: Supposing a mirror to be hung against the entire surface of the wall, it will be seen by referring to the diagram that a ray of light from the skylight, at its extremity (S) farthest from either wall, striking that wall at A, at a height of 11 feet 6 inches from the floor, will be reflected (the angles of incidence and reflection being equal) so as to reach the eye (E) of a beholder (say 5 feet above the floor), standing midway between the walls, or at a distance of 10 feet from the mirror; and consequently that all the rays striking the mirror below that point will fall below his eye; or, in other words, that he will not be able to see the image of the skylight at any point in the mirror below 11 feet 6 inches from the floor; and that, as a matter of course, there will be no glitter on the wall, or on pictures hung on the wall below that point, while the surface of the wall above the 11 feet 6-inch point will reflect the image of the skylight.*

* This principle of lighting with double glazing in the ceiling was successfully demonstrated in the gallery which Mr. Sheepshanks erected at Rutland Gate, and from which he helped to remove, with his own hands, his pictures into the vans, to bring them to the South Kensington Museum. Mr. Redgrave, R.A., called Capt. Fowke's attention to this gallery, and to the principle of lighting which it demonstrated; and, in all subsequent experiments, Capt. Fowke derived great benefit from his great practical experience on the subject. A good general rule for perfectly lighting a picture-gallery may thus be stated: given the width of the gallery, say 20 feet, the height should be the same to the ceiling, that is, 20 feet; and half this, that is, 10 feet, should be given to the skylight. Double glazing is indispensably necessary. This rule requires modification where rooms are square, or of special forms. — H. C.

"It will be seen from the diagram, that this point, which we may call the glitter-point, alters according to the position of the beholder; for instance, at E^2, 5 feet from the wall, the glitter-point is at B, 9 feet from the floor; while, on coming closer (that is, to F^3, or within 2 feet of the wall), it will be found to have descended to C, at a height of 7 feet: on the other hand, by receding to a distance of 15 feet, the wall may be seen without glitter to a height of 13 feet. Looking again to the same diagram, it will be seen, that, apart from all considerations of reflection, a person desiring to see a picture at a height of 11 feet 6 inches, would naturally retire to a distance of at least 10 feet from it; and the same may be said of the other heights and positions shown in the sectional diagram: so that, in any position in which a person can conveniently examine a picture in this gallery, he may be sure of having the surface of the picture free from glitter.

"Care has been taken, in fixing on these proportions, to avoid as much as possible the incidence of rays on the surface of pictures at very acute angles. This, which would not be of any consequence provided the pictures were smooth or plane surfaces, becomes of great importance when rough or thickly painted pictures have to be dealt with; and, as few pictures are perfectly smooth and even, it is a matter of some moment with all, as it produces an unpleasant, spotty appearance, by lighting up strongly one side of all inequalities, and throwing a corresponding shade on the opposite side.

"The lower or museum rooms are, of course, side-lighted; but, by keeping the centre supporting piers as thin as possible, and strengthening them by counterposts, the daylight is admitted in the proportion of two-thirds of window to one-third of wall measured on plan. The large rooms have 16 windows of 50 square feet each, giving a total lighting area of 800 feet to the large, and 600 feet to the small rooms, or nearly as much as in the picture-gallery above described.

"Lighting by Gas. — It has been thought desirable to try the experiment of lighting up the gallery with gas for evening exhibitions; and, in doing so, the gas is introduced so as to light the pictures as nearly as possible at the same angle as the daylight.

"For this purpose, a horizontal pipe is carried the entire length of the gallery, at a height of 18 feet from the floor, directly under the centre of the skylight; and from this pipe a number of fish-tail burners are projected on small brass elbows at each side of the pipe, and distant from it about 2 inches. On reference to the diagram, the rule for fixing the position of the line of gas-burners will become apparent, as it will be seen that its position at G exactly coincides with the intersection of the two rays from the extremities of the skylight, which strike the opposite walls respectively at the highest glitter-points above alluded to; and it is evident, that, by such an arrangement, all danger of glitter from the gaslight is avoided.

"The gas-burners are placed in such a position with regard to the horizontal pipe, that its shadow from each line of lights is projected into the cove on the opposite side. By placing the burners in this position, not only is the part of the wall devoted to the pictures kept in the brightest light and free from shadow, but the coved part is kept in shade, and is thus prevented from reflecting the light of the gas on the pictures, and thereby in another way causing the objectionable glitter."

Fittings and Lighting. — The fittings, furniture, and lighting by night and day, of an art school, have hardly less part in its successful conduct than the plan of the building; for they affect, not only the comfort, but the possibility of study in numerous cases. With the exception of the most elementary class-rooms, the lighting of every room in a school will require a different treatment; from which it will be seen that some experience is necessary before building and fitting premises for art study. The same may be said of the fittings. Desks and apparatus admirably fitted for one branch of study will be inconvenient and a hinderance to success in another; and this arises from difference of processes in the pursuit of art study. Thus, an easel for the painter, a flat table for the mechanical draughtsman, and a modelling-stool for the modeller, are all as different from each other as the works produced upon them, and are as necessary to the student as tools are to any other workman. With a desire to make this book as practically useful as I can to all engaged in providing for and administering art education, and hoping to answer numerous and lengthy applications for advice and information which are addressed to me from all parts of America, I propose to enter into the question of fittings rather fully; so that a considera-

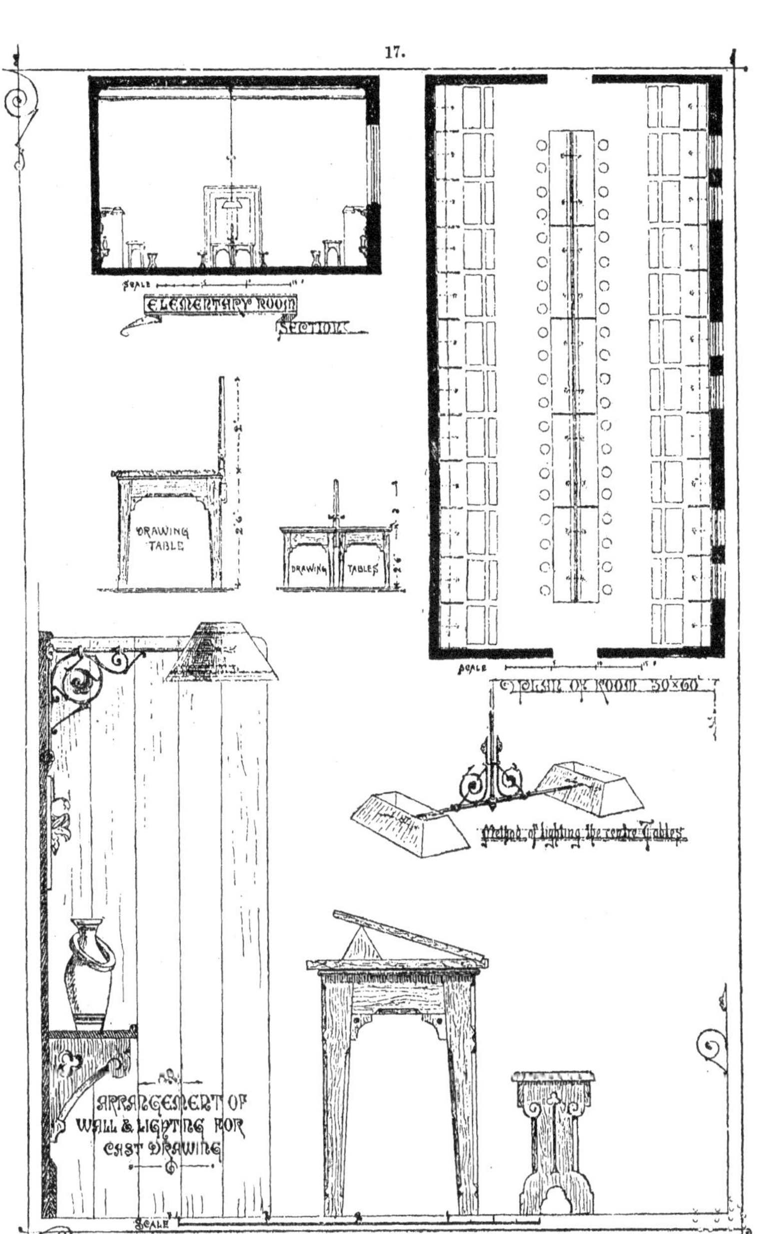

ELEMENTARY ROOM
SECTION
DRAWING TABLE
DRAWING TABLES
PLAN OF ROOM 50×60
Method of lighting the centre Tables
ARRANGEMENT OF WALL & LIGHTING FOR CAST DRAWING
SCALE

tion of what is said here may assist committees and teachers who have not yet had opportunities of observing what is done in European countries, or experience in testing the arrangements they propose to adopt. Taking each room separately, its use will be first described, and then the fitting and lighting suitable to it. The order in which the rooms are placed on the list of accommodation given on page 81, will be observed; so that reference may be made from that list to any one room it is necessary to consider.

THE LECTURE-THEATRE. — In this room, the subjects which are taught *in class* will be carried on. They are the general lectures on art, and the special lectures on geometrical, perspective, and mechanical or orthographic projection, building construction, and model drawing from geometric solids, vases, &c. The instruction is given in the form of practical lectures by the teacher, illustrated by diagrams, drawn in the presence of the pupils, on the blackboard, and copied by them. The first necessity, then, is, that the room be so arranged, that every pupil has an uninterrupted view of the blackboard, and of the stand upon which models or objects are placed; the second, that the teacher should have a large blackboard sliding up and down, so that he can make his diagrams large enough for all the students to see clearly, and get something like a similar view of objects to be drawn, with ample wall-space near the blackboard for the suspension of charts and diagrams. The best shape of room is a rectangular space of about 60 × 40, with the blackboard in the centre of one of the long sides; the platform in front projecting about eight feet into the room. The desks for pupils to be arranged in concentric semi-ellipses, the axis of the semi-ellipse to be coincident with the front line of the platform, as shown in the sketch, and placed upon a gallery rising from the platform, so that each row receding from the platform will be higher than that in front of it. The desks and benches to be continuous; the former large enough to allow of an imperial board 30 in. × 22 in. being used, with T square and instruments, by the student following the lecturer. If top-light be possible by day, it should come from as much as possible over the blackboard and in front of the students; if side-light, from the left and right of the students, never from behind them. The lighting at night should be from two or three sunlights in front of, and a sufficient distance above, the students, — say fifteen feet, — and the black-board be illuminated by a row of jets in a straight line coincident with its length, above its highest point, or where it can be placed by sliding upwards, the lights to be concealed from the eyes of the students by an ample reflector, throwing all the light out to the board. This room would give accommodation to a hundred students, allowing to each desk-room a yard wide, and leaving five feet from front to front of each desk, — two feet for desk-top, and three feet for seat and gangway. That will enable the lecturer or an assistant to examine the work of the students whilst the lecture is going on, if their inexperience should make it desirable.

In a school of art the lecture-room may be made the place of all others where the most work is done, or the least, according to the regulations adopted. If students merely sit as listeners, without being required to make notes and sketches, it will be accidental if good result to them from the lectures. If they be required to reproduce the main features of every lecture, in prepared sketch-books, both text and illustrations; to submit these regularly to the lecturer for examination, and be inevitably examined upon each course at its end, — then the lecture-room becomes the most important class-room in the art school.

MECHANICAL AND ARCHITECTURAL DRAWING-ROOM. — This room should be used for drawing from copies, and from models of machinery, details of drawing, of architectural specimens, flat and round, building construction, &c. It will be principally occupied at night by artisans and others. The teaching here is individual; so that every student will be engaged upon his own work, irrespective of others. The principal requirements will be, that the drawings in progress be well lighted, and the light kept out of the eyes of the pupils. It should never be forgotten, that, in drawing from flat copies or models, the light should be strong upon them and the drawing; but the eyes should not see the blaze of the light itself: so that sunlights, or any lights a long way from the pupils, are not suitable, giving only a poor light, and casting shadows where light is wanted.

A room 60 × 30 feet, arranged as in plan and section, would give two hundred feet of table, and, calculating three feet for each pupil, would accommodate sixty-six persons. The thirty feet divided by five will give two tables, each six feet wide, and three gangways of the same width. The walls on each side should be fitted with bracketed shelves to receive models. The lights down the centres of the tables will light both rows of students sitting face to face, — reflectors being employed to cast the light on the drawings. In working at mechanical and architectural drawing, many students prefer standing to their work rather than sitting to it, though the latter is, in my opinion, less fatiguing and injurious than the former. Half of the tables might be arranged for work whilst sitting, and half for standing, as the sketch shows, — the lights being higher over the standing table. Stools, fixed to the ground, are better than forms for this class; so that when drawing from models, which will be kept on the shelves at the side, the students can move easily to and from both drawing and model, without shaking the form or disturbing their fellow-students.

In the section of the table, there is shown a manner of preserving and storing the drawing-boards of the class, which is convenient and handy. In the centre of the six-feet table, there is a box covered by a hinged lid, 6 inches broad, 4 feet long, and 2 feet 2 inches deep; i.e., the depth of the table. When the student has finished his work, he puts his board and squares in this place; and they are preserved from dust and injury until he wants them again. Each groove will hold eight imperial boards (22 by 30 inches).

THE ELEMENTARY AND CAST DRAWING-ROOM. — The precise nature of studies carried on in the elementary-room will depend upon the previous preparation of the students; but, speaking generally, drawing from copies will be practised here as well as shading from the solid model of geometric forms, casts of ornament, and details of the human and animal figures.

The arrangements and lighting of this room must be on two principles; drawing from copies and from the cast being subjects requiring very different modes of light. Taking a room 60 × 30, the two largest walls should be devoted to drawing from the cast and model, and the middle part of the room to drawing from copies. Tables 2 feet wide and 2 feet 4 inches high, placed so that the edge nearest the wall is 3 feet from it, run the whole length of the room on both sides, will give 2 feet 6 inches of table for each pupil; and thus 48 students will be accommodated, there being 120 feet of table. At intervals of 5 feet on the side walls, there should be a projection, or wooden partition, of 2 feet 6 inches deep, to concentrate the light, and shield other casts from it; and in the centre of each compartment of five feet a gas-jet with reflector above it. The jet should be horizontal, and the bracket movable, so that it can be turned nearer or farther from the wall as required; the length from the wall being 1 foot 6 inches, the height of the light from the floor about 6 feet. The wall should be boarded to a height of 10 feet from the ground, to allow of casts being hung at any point upon it; and, at a distance of 2 feet from the floor, there should be a shelf projecting 1 foot from the wall, to display vases and such subjects as busts, feet, or flowers, which rest on a base, and cannot, therefore, be hung on a wall.

The tables for the centre of the room should be 2 feet 6 inches broad, standing together, making a table of 5 feet, or one table of 5 feet divided in the centre; the students sitting face to face, but not seeing each other. Suggestions for these tables are given in the diagrams. These would give 2 feet 6 inches of table for each pupil; and the tables, being together 100 feet long, would thus accommodate 40 students. Thus 88 students would be comfortably provided for in the elementary-room, leaving 6 feet 6 inches for gangway and seats on either side of the desks. The lighting of the central tables should be by 20 double horizontal jets over the centre of the tables, each jet projecting 6 inches from the centre, so that the light falls on the copy as well as the drawing on each side; and these lights must be so covered by reflectors that no direct rays can reach the side walls: for, if that occurs, the light and shade on the casts will be destroyed.

This method of lighting has one great advantage: it is both thoroughly efficient and very economical. Only as many jets are lighted as there are students in attendance to want them, so that there is no waste; yet every student who is at work will always get as much light as he requires. Forty-four jets to light eighty-eight students must be considered an economical arrangement; and the amount of gas consumed will always be in proportion to the students in attendance.

THE MODELLING-ROOM. — No special arrangements are required for this room, except in the form of modelling-stools, two specimens of which are sketched. The square stool is used for modelling relievos upon, subjects which require a background of clay, and are usually modelled upon a board or slate. The forms of these may be varied to suit different-sized works; but the proportions suggested will be found convenient. The top of the square stool is hinged on to the framework, and can be placed, therefore, at any angle with the ground. The frame is 2 feet square, and its height is 3 feet 6 inches. The support to the top should be in the form of a wrought-iron or brass arc perforated with holes, hinged on to the top of the stool, and working into a sheath on the framework at the back; a thumbscrew, fixing it by screwing through sheath and arc at the angle required for the model, securing it firmly. The circular stool is a tripod, the top being fixed to a screw, which should be brass, and capable both of being turned round to get different views of the work whilst in progress, and also of being elevated or lowered according to the subject to be modelled. This stool is the most suitable for busts, statuettes, and other objects in the round. The shelves shown are for modelling-tools, both in the square and round stool.

The lighting of the modelling-room should be by a powerful sunlight at a moderate distance from the floor, — about 14 or 15 feet, — a reflector of about 5 or 6 feet diameter diffusing the light throughout the room. A clay-bin, in size about 3 feet by 5 feet, made of wood and lined with lead, and covered by a hinged top, is required, in which to keep the modelling-clay damp and clean.

It should be in the coolest and darkest corner of the room. A sink with water laid on will also be necessary.

THE CASTING-ROOM. — An adjunct to the modelling-room, fitted with tables in height 2 feet 4 inches; a sink and water-tray, 2 feet deep and 4 feet long, to clean and soak moulds in. There should be a fireplace in the casting-room for wax and gelatine moulding, and to dry moulds when required. A stove, flat at the top, is the best form of fireplace, something like a small cooking-range; the wax or gelatine or sulphur, as the case may be, being heated in iron or tin vessels upon the top of it, or in the baking apparatus. No special kind of lighting is necessary in the casting-room: brackets or pendants without reflectors are sufficient, at convenient heights and places above the heads of the students, six or seven feet from the ground. The casting-room should be placed in such a part of the building as to be near a receptacle for dust and ashes, so that the waste moulds and other refuse can be frequently removed. With care and convenient arrangements, the modelling and casting rooms may be kept as orderly as other rooms; but if otherwise placed, and not kept scrupulously clean, they will be a nuisance to the whole building: the clay and waste plaster will be trodden about, and defile every passage and staircase near the two rooms.

The best way to secure cleanliness in the casting-room is to have a covered shoot, or wooden tube, running obliquely through the wall from the casting-room to a receptacle for studio refuse outside; and a rule of the school to be, that all students engaged in casting should remove the waste and plaster, when they have completed their casts, by throwing it down this shoot. Details of this sort may seem trivial; but they have considerable influence on the pleasant working of a school.

Cupboards and receptacles for stocks of plaster, wax,

and gelatine, basins, casting apparatus, &c., should be placed round the walls of the casting-room; and strong shelves also for moulds and casts in process of completion, at distances of three and five feet from the floor, projecting two feet, and supported by iron brackets: every thing connected with fittings in this room should be painted, or the damp and water used in casting will soon destroy them.

THE DESIGNING-ROOM requires no special fittings, unless it be considered advisable to make provision for growing plants, which may be used during the process of designing. That may be done by letting the lower part of the windows be converted into a miniature garden, protected from the gas by glass. Ordinary tables, such as are used for the mechanical room, are suitable for this room also,—about 10 feet long, 2 feet 6 inches high, and the same breadth at top. Cupboards and presses, in which to keep specimens of designs for the several subjects which are studied, should form a part of the furniture of the designing-room.

THE LIBRARY AND MUSEUM.—A small room, in which students may consult books of reference, make tracings or sketches of flat examples of industrial master-pieces, or study subjects connected with their own branch of workmanship, is a valuable adjunct to a school of art. Some tables should be arranged to hold large books in an upright position before the student, whilst he sketches the illustration, and others sloped at a convenient angle for tracing. A portion of the books may be usefully employed by being lent to advanced students; though indiscriminate lending to the younger pupils is neither advantageous to them nor the library. The museum portion of the school's outfit may also be conveniently kept in this room, in glass cases; for, otherwise, time and use will soon destroy delicate objects of art, especially if exposed to dust and rough handling.

The Exhibition and Antique Room. — It is in this room that the antique statues are usually displayed, on suitable pedestals round the walls, and about four feet from them. The students sit at easels or easel-stools, as shown in plate 19; so that no tables nor particular form of seats are required. The walls, colored a neutral sage green or warm gray, should be covered up to a height of ten feet with boarding, so as to allow the works of the student to be annually exhibited here. In some schools a convenient groove is formed by projecting ledges, into which the frames containing the drawings may be slipped without difficulty, and retain them safely. No drawings ought to be displayed in an exhibition without being mounted to a uniform size, and put in glazed frames. The top lighting of the antique-room should be so managed, that, instead of being in one continuous line of window, it can be broken up into two or more lights, at a distance apart which will localize the light. A counter light of ground glass should be provided, to protect the statues from direct sunlight, as in the Sheepshanks Gallery,(plate 14). A lofty room, with space enough for the students to get far enough away from the figures, is an essential for good figure-drawing; and it would be well to remember that no subject can be well seen, without distortion of effect, unless the spectator be at least three times the greatest length, width, or height of the object from it. That the eye may comprehend a statue of six feet in height, the student must be eighteen feet from it. Twelve feet of distance is sufficient to take in a view of the figure; but so near the perspective is violent, and the effect unpleasant. The lighting at night of the antique-room is successfully carried out by sunlights, assisted by large reflectors, the jets of gas being arranged in a circular ring, close together, so as to give as nearly as possible the effect of one light. Where two or more sunlights are necessary, there should be a division made between them by a curtain, which will isolate each light, and can be conveniently drawn by day, or when it is necessary to throw the divided parts into one room. Two sunlights should be sufficient to light a room sixty feet by thirty feet, placed fifteen feet from the floor. The pedestals upon which the figures are placed, colored a neutral tint, or covered with red cloth, should be made to run on strong, large casters, so that the statues may be altered in position or shifted from one part of the room to another, without danger or injury. This movement of figures is continually being required; and if the pedestals be merely stationary boxes, or placed on very small casters, every time the figure is moved, it is in imminent danger of being destroyed, and of killing the students who are shifting it. The best height for the pedestals is that which will bring the knees of a standing figure on the level of the eye.

THE PAINTING-ROOM. — The light required for this room is somewhat peculiar; being considered best when of two kinds in one window, side and top joined together, an example of which may be seen in the plan of the Nottingham School. This is obtained by letting the side window, which should always be to the north, continue into the roof as a skylight, no cornice or wall-plate intervening to break up the light. A blind which draws up from below will enable the side-light to be withheld when desirable; and another blind, drawn on cords and rollers from above, will control the top-light, if the side-light alone be required. The studies carried on in this room will be painting from copies and nature, groups of still-life, foliage, flowers, fruit, and the living model. Painting from flat copies of small subjects will require a desk similar to that in use in the centre of

14.

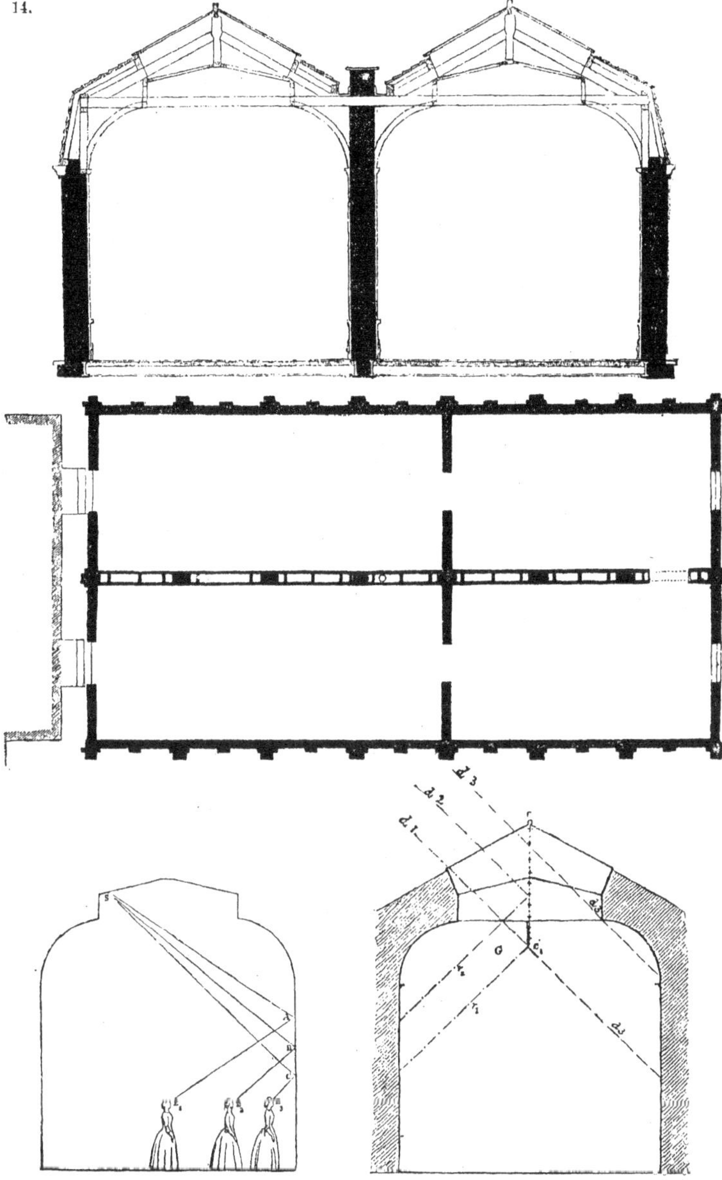

Building for the Sheepshanks Collection, Brompton.

the elementary and cast-room ; but other stages of study, such as painting from nature, are usually pursued by placing the canvas or drawing-board on an easel, near to the subject.

A peculiar shaped box, called in London an angle-box, is useful to contain small groups of fruit and still-life. It is sketched in plate 19, to show the shape and character, and is usually painted of any neutral color, or may be left rough, made with unplaned boards. The advantage of it is, that the light is shielded from all sides but the one required; and the group may be moved from place to place without disarrangement, and protected from dust when not in use by being covered.

THE CONSERVATORY should be fitted in the ordinary way; plants being kept in it for the use of students who are drawing from nature, and therefore grown in small pots, to be easily removable. Trays of the smaller flowers are useful also ; so that groups may be made from them, in compositions, which are the first efforts of the students pictorially. Shrubs and plants which have bold foliage, together with ferns, creeping and parasitical plants, form excellent subjects for outline drawing and design ; vegetable leaves, such as the potato and cabbage, are good forms also ; and casts made from such leaves are the best to use for chalk-drawing from the solid model, in the early stages of the study. Fruits which can be grown in the conservatory, and placed with the bloom still fresh upon them before the students, are among the best materials for painting; and a garden attached to a school of art would be of great value to supply subjects of study.

THE PLANT DRAWING-ROOM, attached to the conservatory for convenience, is also of use in a school; and the two rooms may be made from one apartment, divided from each other by a glass screen. If used at night, the plant drawing-room should not be lighted with gas, but with oil-lamps, so that the vitiated air may not destroy the plants; and special provision should be made to carry off the fumes of the oil-lamps.

Ordinary tables and chairs comprise the furniture of this room, supplemented by a press, in which leaves and flowers may be pressed, and preserved for future use, arranged in large books, and catalogued for the use of the students. Fine specimens, either in form or color, should be annually secured, so that the winter studies may not be interrupted for want of examples. It requires some skill so to press leaves and flowers that their peculiarities may be retained; yet if a branch which displays the chief features of a plant be selected, and the flowers so arranged that the front and side views of leaves and flowers and buds will be retained, it will be found possible to press them successfully, with practice; and if pencil and colored notes be made of the flower color, whilst still fresh, valuable information will be preserved for the designer. One of the teachers in every school of art should be a practical botanist, who is able to give courses of lectures upon artistic botany, illustrated by specimens from the conservatory and collection of pressed plants; the students writing out such lectures from notes taken at the time, and illustrating them by actual specimens of leaves and sketches of the flowers, diagrams being made to show principles of growth and arrangement.

THE LADIES' CLASS-ROOM. — Intended for the more advanced and technical work of the female students, this room should be fitted up like the painting-room, provision being also made, by means of a platform, for study from the living model. It should be a private studio for the students who have passed through the general elementary stages, and are entering upon professional work. The best class of pupils thus studying together will be found to assist each other very much. It is commonly said, in the great European schools, that students learn more from each other than from their teachers; and that is frequently true: for fellow-students are merciless critics of each other's productions, good-humoredly so; and a few skilful workers, by friendly criticism and a good style, will raise the standard of all the rest of the work. Angle-boxes, as used in the painting-room, and easels and easel-stools for the students to work upon, are convenient in this room also. The lighting at night should be by one large sunlight in the centre of the room, and by day ought to be the same as that of the painting-room, with a window in the wall to the north, running up into the skylight in one aperture. Above all sunlights, there should be a chimney to carry off the foul air and heat generated by the consumption of so much coal-gas. These chimneys materially assist ventilation, if ingress be allowed for pure air at the floor-level.

It may be quite possible, that, in the progress of art education in America, special wants will arise, and particular branches of study be required, of which we have no practical experience now. The application of art knowledge in every occupation will in the end be found valuable, and may result in a much more general demand for it than exists at present. Such a change may modify, or even entirely change, the character of buildings required for schools of art. The general study of drawing in the public schools will undoubtedly create a vast constituency of students for art schools; and more extensive buildings will be required for their accommodation than are suggested in this chapter. Meanwhile, for the next twenty years, many art schools and galleries will be built in America; and the hints and plans given may be of some use in their design.

American Schools.

A method of arrangement for drawing from objects adopted in the Cooper Institute School of Design for Women, New York, is shown in plate 20, which is different to that I have recommended, but may be made very efficient when a narrow room is to be adapted. A very similar method is in use in some French schools. In the New-York illustration, the figure of the student sketched is rather larger than it would be in proportion to the room; which looks as if only capable of holding two students, though four may be accommodated in each compartment. The munificence of Mr. Peter Cooper in providing a day school of design for females, and a night school for male students, is highly commendable and worthy of example. I have examined the work of the students and the premises of the school, and feel sure it is doing good service in New York. Nevertheless, the school reminds me of the time, twenty years ago, in England, when the first experiments were being tried, and art schools were so new that the studies had not been thoroughly arranged. Re-organized, refitted, and filled with an ample collection of casts and works of art, the school and the teaching, good as it may now be, would be twice as useful and thrice as efficient as they can be under present circumstances. The same care for the public good which established the institute will, I feel sure, cause this improvement to be made. Art education is now, happily, of sufficient importance to be studied and improved in its character and appliances continually; and the antique studio system is giving place to gradation of study, and sequence of subject, in class-work. The blackboard and the lecture-room must be the basis on which to found an intelligent appreciation of the many phases of knowledge that go to form a

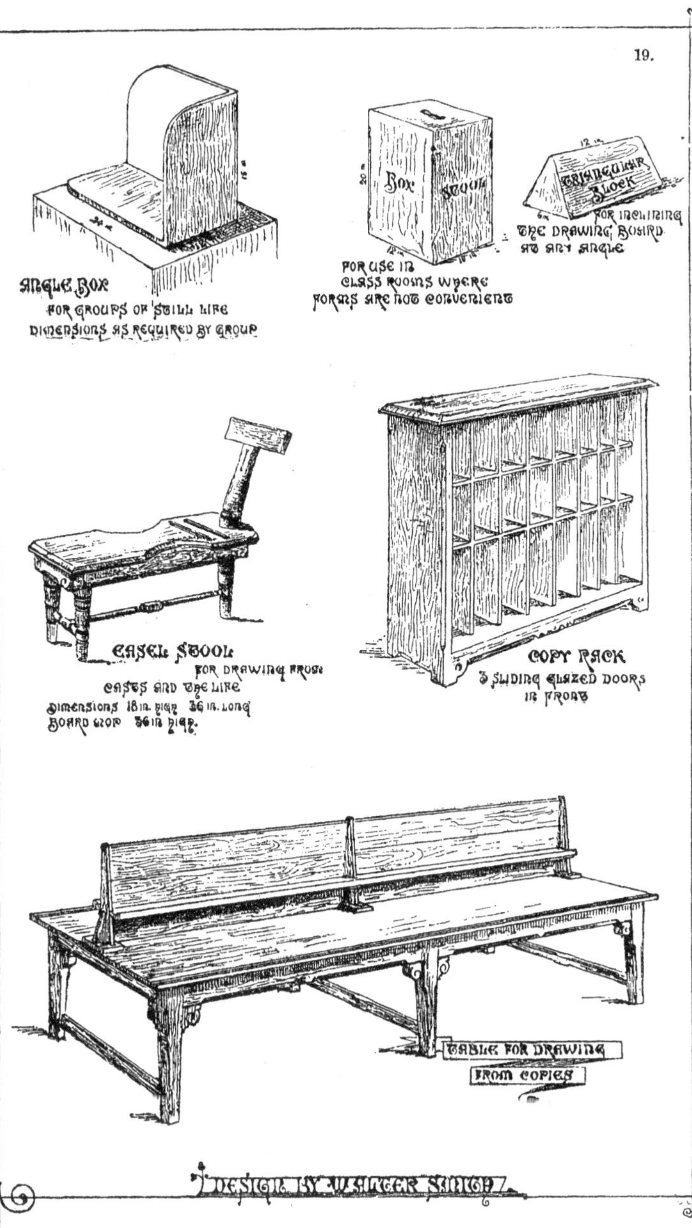
ANGLE BOX
FOR GROUPS OF STILL LIFE
DIMENSIONS AS REQUIRED BY GROUP
BOX STOOL
FOR USE IN
CLASS ROOMS WHERE
FORMS ARE NOT CONVENIENT
TRIANGULAR BLOCK
FOR INCLINING
THE DRAWING BOARD
AT ANY ANGLE
EASEL STOOL
FOR DRAWING FROM
CASTS AND THE LIFE
DIMENSIONS 18 IN. HIGH 36 IN. LONG
BOARD TOP 36 IN. HIGH.
COPY RACK
3 SLIDING GLAZED DOORS
IN FRONT
TABLE FOR DRAWING
FROM COPIES
DESIGN BY WALTER SMITH

FITTINGS FOR SCHOOLS OF ART.

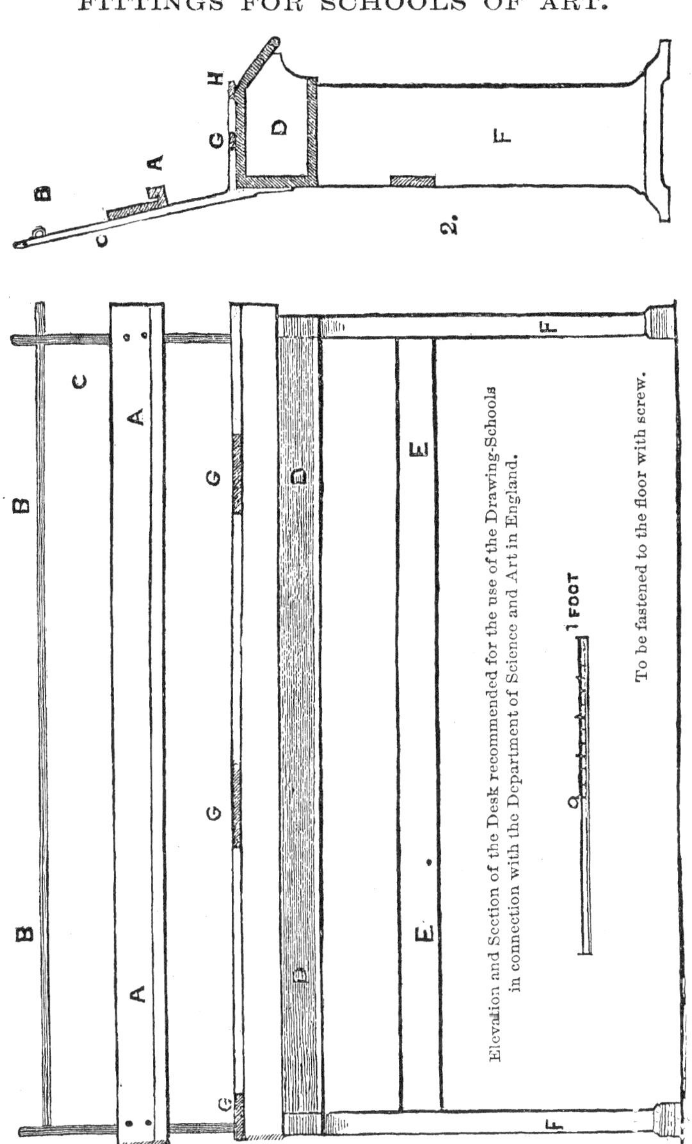

Elevation and Section of the Desk recommended for the use of the Drawing-Schools in connection with the Department of Science and Art in England.

broad plan of art education; and the lectures on perspective and other subjects, which have been made part of the course of study in the Cooper Institute, are indications that it is not to be considered stationary in its means of usefulness. The rules and regulations of the school will be found in Appendix IV.

The Philadelphia School of Design for Women is another institution which seeks to provide an art training of a high class for females, besides acting a sort of art missionary part towards other schools, by presentation of casts, &c. Its casts and examples are the same as those in use in English schools of art; and the course of instruction is very similar. A very good and terse description of this school appeared in "The Boston Daily Advertiser" of March, 1872; and I subjoin it:—

The Philadelphia School of Design for Women. Its location, collection, methods, and success.

I was delighted yesterday with what I saw and heard at the school of design for women in this city. This school was established in 1853, for "the systematic training of young women in the practice of art and in the knowledge of its scientific principles, with the view of qualifying them to impart to others a careful art education, and to develop its application to the common uses of life and its relation to the requirements of trade and manufactures." The object set forth in the act of incorporation is held steadily in view, and attained by a course of rigidly systematic instruction. Great difficulties were encountered in obtaining a suitable building, and such designs, models, appliances, and works of instruction, as are necessary to the full equipment of a school of art. These difficulties have been overcome in great measure by the efforts of the officers and directors, by public and private liberality, and by the personal exertions of T. W. Braidwood, the principal of the school and its chief instructor. The library, however, is still meagre; but it is hoped it will soon receive the attention which its possibilities of usefulness demand. I called two hours before the beginning of the daily session, and, introducing myself as a practical teacher, was received with great courtesy by Mr. Braidwood himself, who accompanied me to all parts of the building, assisted me in examining its contents, and explained clearly the methods of instruction.

The building, formerly a dwelling-house, is situated at the corner of Filbert Street and North-west Pennsylvania Square. It has a fair supply of light, and is as well adapted to the purposes of such an institution as one could expect. It is too small. A larger building of peculiar design, and exposed to the light and air on all sides, is necessary to the proper growth of the school. Great judgment has been displayed in the selection of casts, diagrams, and other models. In the entire building I found not a piece of useless furniture.

The course of instruction varies in time from two and a half to four and a half years, depending upon the industry of the student. "We desire no geniuses here," said Mr. Braidwood; "or, rather, industry is the genius which we respect." The growing interest in art education warrants me in giving the order of studies with some degree of practical detail. [See Appendix IV.]

During the two preceding stages (landscape-painting and drawing from casts), students are engaged on Mondays in drawing and painting in water-colors, plant-forms, mostly from nature. At the end of the advanced stages, pupils may enter any of the professional classes; viz., designing for printing calico, oil-cloth, wall-paper, &c.; wood-engraving, lithography, drawing, and painting in oil and water colors, and art teaching. In each of these, the work is accurately detailed.

By a careful perusal of the scheme given in the Appendix, it will be seen, in regard to models, that the use of real objects is kept parallel with that of flat diagrams, a decided preference being given to the former; and, in regard to method of execution, that the same is true of free-hand and mechanical drawing.

The simple method and accurate result of teaching the pupils to decide upon and reproduce any color, or any shade of color, from nature, was particularly interesting; and I regret that the technicalities involved, and the impossibility of illustrating by diagrams, prevent me from explaining here what, under favorable circumstances, may easily be made intelligible to any ordinary mind. Connected with the regular class-drill are lectures, which are open to the public.

Rule 10 is rigidly enforced; and the inspection of the finished productions of the pupils in every department makes a favorable impression. After a thorough explanation of the mechanical and intellectual means employed in the instruction of the pupils, I was convinced that the power of producing not merely creditable, but beautiful and valuable works of art may be developed, and trained to precision, by methods as exact and progressive as those applied to the purely intellectual or to the physical powers. W.

The National Academy of Design, New York, which is illustrated in plate 21, gives an art education of a professional character, rather than industrial; and its plan is well stated in the papers concerning the academy, obligingly furnished for me by its present secretary [See Appendix IV]. It does not enter into the scope of my subject so much as others of a purely industrial kind, being relatively to other institutions in America what the Royal Academy in London is to the English provincial art schools, or the *École des Beaux Arts* in Paris is to the municipal schools of France. The genuine love of art which foreign travel creates or develops, and which is now becoming so general in this country, will, I hope, by means of such schools as the New-York Academy, foster the initiation of a national school or style, and terminate the importation of inferior French pictures, by producing a race of professional artists who paint better works than those imported. The great promise of many young artists studying there is an indication that I do not prematurely anticipate such a result.

The Massachusetts Institute of Technology in Boston has already been referred to in these pages. It gives to drawing, both mechanical and free-hand, a prominent place in its studies and a large share of its building, as may be seen from the engraving. The students in chemistry, engineering, and mathematics are all alike obliged to acquire a certain skill and proficiency in the use of the pencil and crayon as well as of the drawing-pen and T square. But the architectural department is a true school of art as far as it goes; and Mr. Ware, the professor of architecture, whose testimony in favor of art education I have quoted in Chap. I., has able assistants, trained in both the French and German systems of drawing. This appreciation of what is excellent in both systems is equally displayed in the extensive collections, both of casts and of drawings, from distinct schools, and illustrating different styles, which are available for these students. There are few, if any, more thoroughly interesting museum studios in America than those of this department, supplemented as they are by the admirable collections of engineering models which the institute possesses.

Another valuable institution is the Worcester Free Technical Institute, the plans of which are also illustrated. A larger amount of time is given to instruction in drawing in it, by each student, than in any other American school probably, unless it be a professional art school; and when the Worcester school is satisfactorily furnished with the best examples of casts and copies, and its students come well prepared by elementary instruction in drawing from the public schools, we may look forward to this institute producing as valuable men in art as it already does in scientific subjects; whilst all its graduates will be qualified by their education to take an intelligent interest in the advancement of art, besides acquitting themselves creditably when their own art powers are called upon. This school has been a pioneer in more ways than one, and an especial honor to its founders and the city in which it is situated. The principal, Prof. C. O. Thompson, is an ardent friend of art education, which he has striven to advance both in his own school and in this country: and a great deal of the interest now felt in the subject is due to him, and his far-seeing advocacy of it as a commercial and social agent; showing how much good one really earnest man may do in a good cause, if actuated by public-spirited motives. The professor of drawing, Mr. G. E. Gladwin, has had the advantage of European training and study for many years, and is doing an excellent work in the school. Its system is based on that of South Kensington, with a liberal leaning towards French methods; and that is precisely what should be adopted in the education of adults. By the recognition of drawing as an educational agent in the studies of men preparing for an active life in business and trade, much good may be effected; and it seems to me quite as desirable to ingraft the subject upon the curriculum of existing institutions, such as that at Worcester, as to establish altogether new agencies for its development. When drawing exists as a department of an institute for scientific, industrial, or general education, there is created a constituency for the special schools of art which are sure to follow.

The Lowell Institute Free Drawing School, which has been in operation since 1850, furnishes instruction in drawing from objects, including geometric solids, the human figure, and ornament, to both male and female students, the latter in afternoon and former in evening classes, two lessons per week, each of two hours. The instruction is wholly gratuitous, being conducted as a section of the Lowell Institute, supported by a fund left in trust for the advancement of good objects, such as lectures by the best men of the day in all intellectual subjects, or practical education in the class-room, of the kind that is not supplied by any other agency. The administrator, the Hon. John Amory Lowell, to whom from a recognition of his zeal for the advancement of art education in America I have dedicated this book, has kept the school in active efficiency for above twenty years; during which time, some of the best artists now practising in this country have been students in its class-rooms. A life-class, for drawing from the nude living model, is carried on for the benefit of professional students; and the whole character of the school, though it has supplied a practical education in drawing to many workmen, is rather of the nature of a general than an industrial school. Its method of study is somewhat severe upon the beginner, but there is an entire absence of meretricious systems in the stages of study. I look forward to the development of this school, by increasing its range of study, the multiplying of its classes, and the adaptation of its *matériel* and class-rooms to modern requirements, as a most important feature in the future art educational institutions of Boston. A school that is entirely free from the trammels of being over-managed by public bodies (whose own hands are sometimes tied), and which can undertake the work that other agencies are either not allowed to engage in, or which does not appeal to their sympathies, may do excellent work for the profession of art and for its highest developments. Such a school is that of the Lowell Institute. In the session of 1871–2, a hundred and twenty-four male and a hundred and twenty-seven female students were instructed in the Lowell school, with an average attendance of fifty-five of the former and sixty-five of the latter. The rooms used have never been able to accommodate the numbers seeking admission; but it will be seen from the numbers in attendance how influential for good it must have been during the past twenty years.*

The fact that the universities of Oxford, Cambridge, and London, in England, have recently established professorships of fine art, under the Slade bequest, and that such distinguished art critics as Mr. Ruskin, Sir Matthew Digby Wyatt, and Mr. Poynter have been chosen respectively to fill the chairs of art in the three universities, suggests to us in America that the national universities here might not be entirely negligent of

* The annual advertisement of the opening of the school for 1871–2 will be found in Appendix IV.; and Dr. Cotting, its genial curator, directs the school for Mr. Lowell.

their interests in recognizing among the arts they study that art which is common to every great civilization, ancient or modern. A step in this direction has already been taken by Yale; and I give a statement of its aims, forwarded to me by one of the professors of the university.

After describing the opening lecture of the session of 1872, the account says, —

"The course itself begins the second term of a practical working art school here in New Haven, — a school wider in its plan, and intended to be more thorough and advanced in its instruction, than any school of fine arts in this country. There are now three professorships filled by men who are devoting their whole energies to the work. Prof. Weir holds the department of painting; and to him also falls the branches of the theory and philosophy of art. Prof. Henry Niemeyer is professor of drawing; but his training at the Paris *École des Beaux Arts* enables him to fill, as the growing needs of the school may demand, the place of teacher of perspective and design. Prof. D. Cady Eaton is engaged with the history of art. This faculty have elaborated a scheme of art study which shall be as comprehensive and as definite in its sphere as that of the academic department is in its own. Their idea, following out that of the founder of the school, Mr. A. R. Street, is to build up an art home. It is to be a place where all possible influences for the fostering of art knowledge and criticism and taste shall centre; which shall send out, in time, an art sentiment which shall be felt in the whole country. It will act with the university, and have all the fostering care, and the same effects of general culture, that the university gives to the learned professions. It is the great difficulty and obstacle to American artists, that they find in their own country no place where thorough and symmetrical art training can be had. There is no place from which are diffused the long collected treasures of art traditions, and in which may be found the influence of the presence of the monuments of art and of artists. For this they must go to Europe. This is the want this school is intended to supply. By pursuing the best European methods, the art faculty propose to make, if possible, a standard of art instruction higher and more effective than any thing yet tried in America. It is a bold hope; but yet it is cherished, that, with suitable encouragement, there can be established a centre of art culture which shall remove the necessity of study at foreign schools. Not that the necessity for foreign study of all kinds is to be withdrawn. The managers of the schools, artists themselves, know that no instruction can take the place of that thorough and careful study of the monuments of art themselves which only the galleries of Europe can furnish. But now a man cannot go from this country prepared to enter upon such study. He needs years of preliminary drill and training, which only European schools can give. This is the want the New Haven school of fine arts would supply. Success in this effort will have a double result. The home work of American artists will be greatly improved. If there appear no genius, and if originality be wanting, there will at least be that perfection of work, and something of that practised and informed judgment, which are now so uniformly absent, and which so clearly distinguish the foreign from the native painter. And though the influences of great works will be missed, such a full and symmetrical education as this scheme proposes must prune away crudities. Another effect will be to raise the standard of taste. The school is expected and intended to work not only upon artists as such, but upon all the educated men who are to go out from the University. No man will bear a degree from Yale henceforth who has not had ample opportunity to become familiar with the principles of art criticism, the canons of taste, and something of the history and development of art. This, which has been wanting hitherto in all university courses, cannot but have a wide influence. And in this union of influences, in this educating at once artists and critics, producers, and those who will create the demand, lies the peculiarity, and, it is hoped, the distinctive merit, of this plan. That it has been attempted is worthy of notice and remark; and though its success should be for a time but limited, and its progress slow, its existence is a proof of real art feeling and a desire for its most perfect development."

It is comforting to find, that, in so many centres, the same desire exists to establish not only *a* school, but *the* school of art, which is to fructify the incipient taste of America; and, from accounts which are daily reaching me from all parts of the country, I think that Boston and Harvard must be up and doing, if they cherish their ancient reputation in arts, or value their traditional character as leaders in education.

FITTINGS FOR SCHOOLS OF ART.

ARRANGEMENTS FOR DRAWING FROM MODELS AND OBJECTS.
COOPER INSTITUTE, NEW YORK.

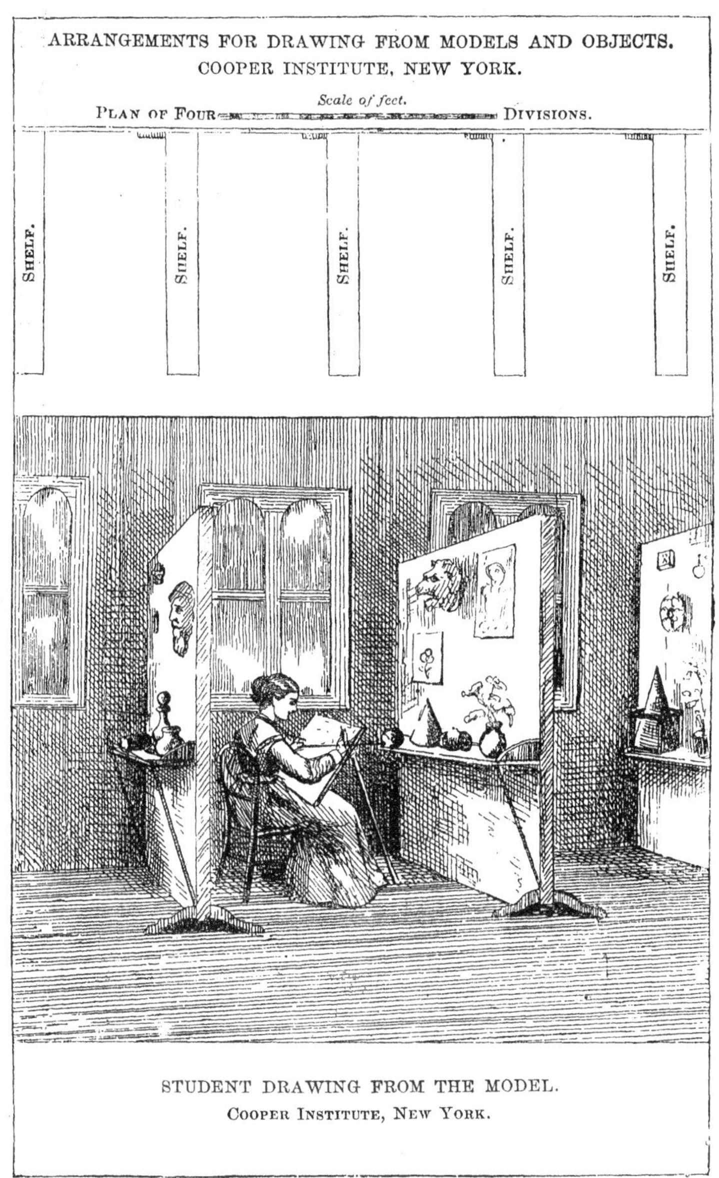

STUDENT DRAWING FROM THE MODEL.
COOPER INSTITUTE, NEW YORK.

That this is already felt in Boston, the beginning of a collection for the fine-arts museum, before it is built, is a sufficient proof. By a combination of fortunate accidents, and the keen watchfulness of vigilant eyes, several small collections of both ancient and mediæval objects have already been secured for public exhibition, of a character which is enough in itself to give tone to the museum when it is opened. How much depends upon this may be calculated by all who have seen the influence of national collections in other countries, and the untold effects on the industry of all countries where a tender care has been felt for the promotion of education through such collections. And though America will be wealthy enough, and before very long eager enough, to possess museums of art in all her great States, the supply even of antiquities and modern master-pieces is not unlimited; and therefore we can expect great collections in but one or two places on this continent. Whatever may be done elsewhere, it is certain that one of these collections will be in Boston; and the frontispiece of this book, an engraving of the building now in course of erection for the Boston Fine Arts Museum, will be ample testimony of the spirit of Massachusetts and her capital city to provide a fitting dwelling-place for the arts of the past and the present. What Athens was in ancient times, and Venice in the brilliant epoch of mediæval art, Boston, another city by the sea, may aspire to be in the modern civilization of the New World; and that such a character it is in her instinct and ambition to assume may be inferred by recent experience. It needs but that the princely gifts of her men of wealth shall be sometimes directed towards cherishing and sustaining the arts, and then the glory of other ages and peoples may be revived among us to-day, in the youth and with the vigor of a great nation; and, as America's national poet has sung in words which have been read in every modern language, "the artist never dies," so more truly may it be said of art, that it may be eclipsed but never destroyed, rising again from Egyptian tombs, or descending to us from Greek temples, or speaking to us from the buried Pompeian households, until the utterance of peaceful arts shall become the universal language, and, in the godlike faculty of creating the beautiful, men shall discover their greatest happiness and their universal brotherhood.

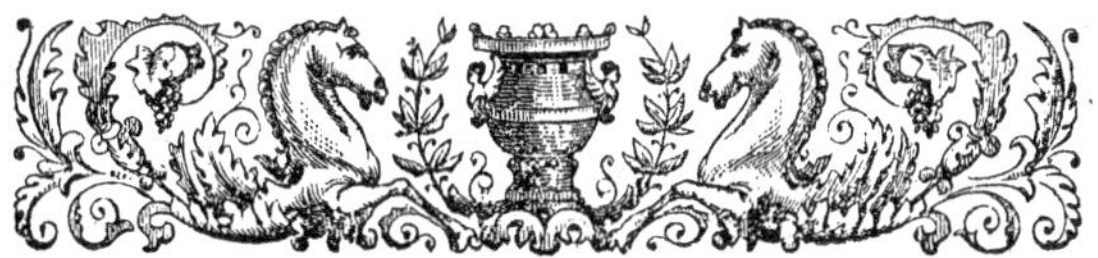

CHAPTER IV.

METHODS OF INDUSTRIAL ART STUDY, — FRENCH, ENGLISH, AND GERMAN.

IN a country like America, where, in the matter of art, educationists are not bound either by traditional formulæ or opposing schools, it might be well to consider the methods of study pursued in other countries before any be adopted in this. More than once in these pages, I have expressed the opinion, that no system of instruction developed elsewhere is wholly suited to the requirements of America; and that what is wanted here will grow, by the accumulation of experience, into a national system, indigenous to the soil, any feature of which being transplanted from other places must undergo a process of acclimation and transformation before it will become assimilated by our necessities.

The building-up of such a system must, however, be a work of time; and meanwhile, now as in the past, this country must rely very much on the experience of other countries for suggestions of methods, where experiments have passed into systems. To describe the three best known methods, so that opinions may be formed concerning them, is my aim in this chapter; and having, by practical and long connection with schools of art, had many opportunities of testing the efficiency of the several methods referred to, I may say, that the conclusions here expressed are derived from close observations in the class-room, where distinct systems have been put into operation. So little of serious consideration has ever been given to this phase of education by practical men, — whilst in many countries it is even now quite new, — that we may expect in any new system very great changes from either plan described, when the subject is thoroughly investigated and analyzed.

It is not my intention to consider the professional art education of the three countries, — that being another branch of the subject, — but to describe the nature of studies carried on in the schools for workmen supposed to be employed in industrial occupations. In France the municipal schools, in England the local schools of art, and in Germany the night drawing-classes, which are now almost general, are the places where, for artisans, industrial drawing is taught.

The French municipal schools vary in the character of their studies, much as their masters vary; there being no national organization or test which would assimilate them to a common standard, and require uniformity of study. But the points of difference are limited to details, and are comparatively unimportant: a description of one school would therefore, with slight modifications, apply to all. In the year 1863 I was commissioned by the Science and Art Department of the English Government to go to Paris, and examine and report upon an exhibition of the works of the municipal schools and drawing-classes then being displayed in the Palais de l'Industrie. The very general use of methods of study, — such as the ignoring of outline drawing, and the use of stump and leather in shading, — which were tabooed in England, made the examination of the works of especial interest to me; and I expressed, in my report, favorable opinions concerning the value of some processes and modes of work which were very unpopular with home authorities at that time. During the year 1867, that of the last Great International Exhibition, I spent a considerable time in Paris, examining, for literary purposes, the contents of the Exhibition: among which the most interesting portion to me was the display of drawings illustrating the various national methods of art education. Subsequent visits to the schools which had produced the best French drawings, and observation of works in progress in the several classes as carried on by the students, gave me ample opportunity of arriving at fair conclusions concerning the character of their productions, and of the system on which those works are produced. My impressions were favorable, and have since remained so; one ground of approval being, that the method of instruction, implements, and style of work adopted, are apparently as well suited to adult beginners as to the more experienced, and to the ignorant as to the well educated. To one of these schools in Paris, — that of M. Lequien *fils*, — I paid several visits; and, regarding it as a representative school, wrote a description of it, which appeared at the time in "The London Builder." I now give the programme, or prospectus, of the school, with the description referred to.*

The "École Municipale de Dessin et de Sculpture," of the 10th Arrondissement of Paris, situated in the Rue des Pétits Hotels, is conducted by M. Lequien *fils*, whose father has long been engaged as master of a municipal school in another part of Paris. M. Lequien *fils* is professionally a sculptor, and his school has a high reputation for drawing and modelling.

From information concerning the principal schools, we

* For programme, see Appendix.

are justified in regarding M. Lequien's as a good representative of its order, and especially so of the peculiarly characteristic method of teaching drawing, — alike in all the schools, — which was to be seen there in operation. The students varied in age from fifteen years to thirty, and seemed to be clad in the ordinary costume of the workman; no effort being made to appear in best clothes, as is usually the case in English schools of art.

Beginning with a pupil who had been but a few days in the school, and had not previously studied in an art school, and going on through the various stages until we came to the work of young men who were drawing from the living model, and who were employed in the daytime as designers for the French manufacturing firms, at large salaries, the whole of the students' drawings were carefully examined, in the presence and with the explanation of the professor.

Afterwards all the works produced during the past year, some of which were in the Exposition, and many others still in the school, were displayed by M. Lequien; and information concerning the ages, occupations, and length of time occupied in study and production of the drawings, was communicated by him also. It seems, then, that in teaching drawing but one medium is used, — carbon, chalk, or charcoal; and from first to last the drawings are made upon a coarse, cheap paper, of a gray color, very much like what grocers wrap their moist sugar in, only that the drawing-paper is not of quite so good a quality. There are three stages of study: —

1. From lithographed shaded copies or original drawings.
2. Shading, from the cast, of figure and ornament.
3. Shading from the living model.

The examples used by beginners were simple, bold details of ornament, drawn with thick lines, and having little more than half-tint shadows: perhaps there were as many as three degrees of shade, all being boldly expressed by lines.

The point used was such as a boy of fifteen would be able or willing to keep on a stick of charcoal, and the means of erasure was a piece of wash-leather.

The student is placed at a distance of perhaps a yard from his copy, which is hung on a screen or the wall in a glazed frame, and which he is not allowed to touch or measure from. Painful was the mess made by the first two or three boys, with their blunt points making such heavy black lines, and their still blunter eyesight, which betrayed them into such doleful errors. "But," said M. Lequien, "they soon tire of this black mess and these frivolous lines, and get to cleaner habits and more accurate observation of form. This boy, fifth up the line from the bottom of the school, has been here two months, and has done twenty drawings; and you see he is already using his charcoal in an economical manner, and putting shadow in only where he sees it in the copy."

The pupils attend five nights in the week for two hours; and it is commonly in the indentures of the young apprentice, that he attend a municipal school of art, for which his master pays the fee. At the first about two of these simple, rough drawings are made in a week, — imperfect many of them, but each showing some advance on the last. Thus the interest of the pupil is kept up by a change of examples, and he is never allowed to form a habit of slow or monotonous work. A little further on in the school the examples used are larger and more elaborate pieces of ornament, in which either the human or animal form is partially introduced.

This takes the students as many evenings as his earlier copies occupied hours, and some of them as many weeks as the more elementary examples took evenings to copy. But by this time his work has lost all traces of blackness and messiness, the shadows become delicate and transparent, the free outlines made by the soft and willing charcoal are firm and expressive, the white chalk begins to express light and direct reflection, and the workman appears to be getting master of his medium. The improvement appears to be startling, and M. Lequien says it is not exceptional. He objects to outline-drawing with lead-pencil as a commencement, and thinks more power is got by regarding drawing as the imitation of masses of light and shade from the first to the last. Judging from what we saw, there certainly appears to be a corrective influence in adding the shadow to the outline, which mere outline cannot have by itself. By adding shadow to bad form, you intensify the errors: mistakes of proportion become evident, and bad lines become uglier still.

The middle stage is drawing from the cast, the same medium being used: good specimens of drawings made by previous pupils are displayed for the student's guidance in his first efforts; and the casts are very simple in form, — sometimes a section of the echinus moulding; one acanthus leaf from an antique capital; a cast of the eye, mouth, or chin from heroic busts; or mask of a smooth face. By the time the student arrives at this stage, he has mastered his vehicle of expression partially, — not so completely as he will when he gets to the living model; but it no longer gives him trouble and vexation of spirit by doing in his hands just what he wishes not done. The process of drawing from the cast may thus be stated: the large forms are firstly indicated by faint outlines, and the lines dividing masses of light from shadow are touched in. The shapes of shadows are drawn, but shade is not at first

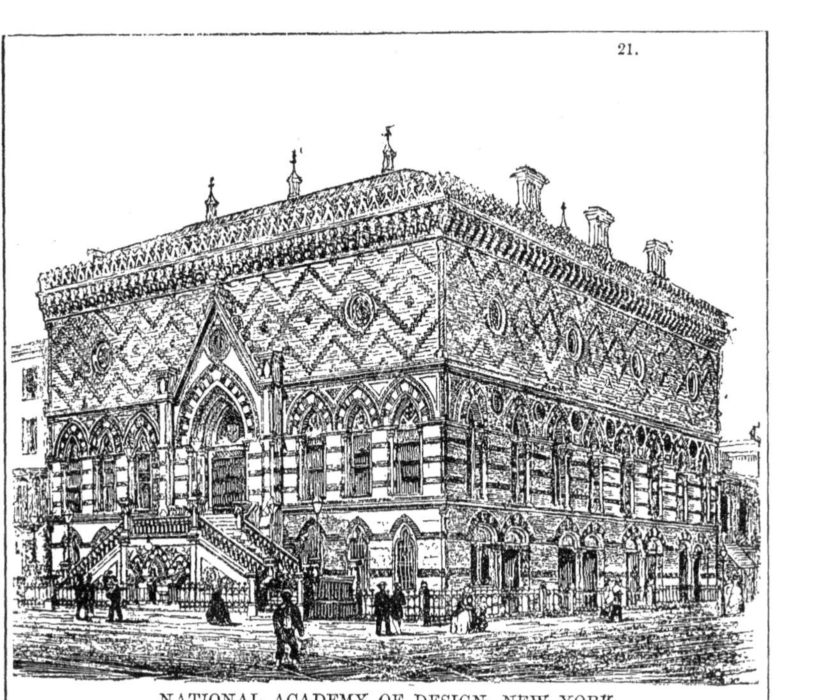

NATIONAL ACADEMY OF DESIGN, NEW YORK.

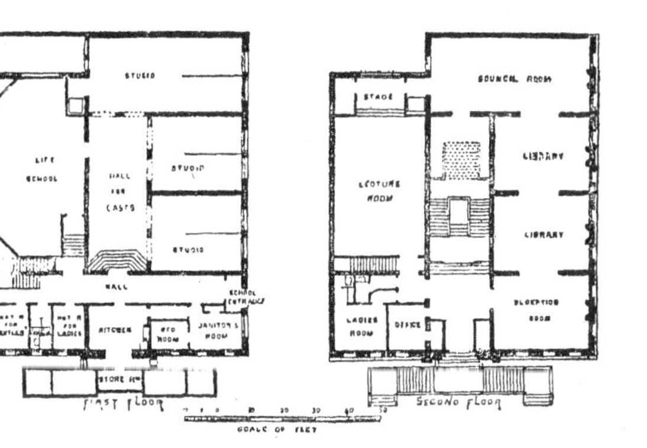

expressed: * when a sort of map of the form has been thus obtained, the cast shadows are rubbed in flatly with wash-leather and soft chalk, and deeper tints in these shadows drawn in with the blunt point of a leather stump. In this condition, the drawing looks exactly like a faintly-printed photograph; and it seems to me that is some recommendation of the system, which is natural, effective, and simple. Then the student, having obtained the general effect of his subject, proceeds to add the shades, whether faint or deep, of the half-tints, blending them into the shadows, and afterwards taking out, by means of a clean corner of his wash-leather, the reflected light in the shadows, and by the use of white chalk adding the high lights, used thickly or thinly according to the amount of brilliancy of the light. The gray paper stands for the natural color of the cast; or sometimes much white chalk is used, and the color of the paper then becomes a half-tint to express the lighter shades. This mode of drawing from the cast is a rapid one in comparison with the English method of stippling shadow with the chalk-point; and it is very much more effective. A week, or even a month, may be spent on a subject from the cast by M. Lequien's pupils, — seldom more; and the drawings made are varied in size according to the pupil's powers, — from a foot-square representation of a hand, or a leaf, to a cartoon on strained canvas, some five feet or six feet square, of the Apollo Belvedere, or the actual size of a section of the Panathenaic frieze. Very lovely in feeling, and truth of chiaroscuro, were many of these large drawings from the cast, — absolute imitation of natural effect being the aim of the student; and every detail of form was carefully rendered, either by the

* Shade is the partial absence of direct light on an object; shadow, the total absence.

sharp bits of forcible shadows occurring where the light was strongest, or by delicate modulations in the broad shadows, or in the play of reflected light on the prominent portions of the unilluminated parts of the cast. The subjects used for study are similar to those in use in the British Royal Academy and schools of art, with the addition of a few good modern French busts and figures.

The Greek and Roman antique and French Renaissance are the styles of ornament which exclusively supply the ornamental casts, no example of Gothic being apparently used. The final stage, after the practice of figure-drawing from the antique, is drawing from the living nude model.

In this stage, only the more advanced students study; and a very considerable power in drawing has been acquired previously to commencing from the living subject. A longer time is given to each model than we are prepared to expect, — three hours each evening for five nights a week being allotted to each study. A very great amount of care is expended on the form of the figure; and the degree of finish is expected to be higher, though even in this the effect and truth of drawing are considered of more importance than finish. Stump and leather are used also in drawing from the life: they may, in fact, be considered as universal in teaching drawing in France. Besides drawing, modelling is practised in the schools, in similar stages as already described for drawing, alto-relievo being the general method adopted for studying the antique and living figure. Ornament appears rarely to be copied, though original designs for special purposes of ornamental treatment were exhibited to us as the work of the students; and these were well designed and very spiritedly modelled. French art masters appear to believe that figure practice includes the study of all kinds of form, and that a good draughtsman of the human figure can draw ornament, or design decoration, in any style, as a matter of course. The evidence is rather in favor of this view, — at any rate, so far as drawing goes. In another class, a few students were drawing, from examples, architectural line drawings and projections of geometric solids; but there was nothing in this portion of the school studies in any way remarkable.

The drawings of the Toulouse School of Industrial Science are so excellent, that those who adhere entirely to the system of study described in the Paris school, and which is the same as at Toulouse, may do so with confidence for adult classes.* It must not, however, be supposed that this free and powerful mode of work can be resorted to without the aid of good examples and excellent instructors; so much depending on the process, that continued correction and supervision on the part of the teacher are required, — more so than in the English and German methods, where the pupils begin with practice in outline. Nor do I consider the French method adapted for children in day-schools, having myself fairly tried it, and having been compelled to return from it to the English method of blackboard work, from the impossibility of giving to each pupil the requisite amount of instruction to guide him, when in a large class. It may be said that drawing from the solid object necessitates individual rather than class instruction; and beginners who commence with models, or even shading, must have their steps guided and closely watched; for all the difficulties are upon them at once. Where I have found the French system most suc-

* See Appendix, for Toulouse Programme.

cessful has been with adults who have never learned to draw at all, but are capable of understanding and remembering concise explanations, and where the number of pupils to one teacher is small.

The one great defect of the *curriculum*, as displayed in the schools, though not in the prospectuses, is, that it ignores nature so far as drawing from foliage and flowers, or practice in color, goes. In free-hand drawing, casts and solid models of ornament, or the human figure, together with geometric solids, are the only round forms used; and thus French design of sculptured ornament is, as a rule, a repetition or modification of classic or Italian or French Renaissance ornament, such as the students have been educated from. That is a serious omission in any course of study; and though occasional mention of studies from natural foliage is made in the prospectuses of schools, yet in practice the work is nominal.

The virtue of the French method is its rapidity and effect, by which it is possible to arrive at power of hand, and knowledge of light and shade, within a reasonable time; and, considering the short average time spent by students in art schools, that is a great advantage. The wisest use which could be made in this country of the French system would be for adults in night classes, who come utterly unprepared by elementary instruction, and have more need for readiness of hand and eye than time for a thorough training of both. In time sketches, and studies of imaginary effects of light and shade, stump and leather work is excellent as a medium for shading; and it could be used for examinations with advantage.

In the subjects which form so large a proportion of the course in English schools of art, — instrumental drawing, — very little is done in the French art schools; but in the scientific classes of ordinary educational institutes, and in some special schools, great attention is given to both mechanical and architectural drawing. I remember that the school for adults in the Marchê St. Martin, Paris, and the Institution Rossat, at Charleville, used to give almost their whole attention to scientific drawing, and were very successful in it. Perspective and descriptive geometry was also studied, and admirably illustrated by models in glass and thread to show results, and mode of work.

The French schools, whether purely scientific or artistic, or a combination of both, have advantages over similar institutions in any other part of the world, in possessing the most complete examples for instruction that are to be found, whether in mechanical drawing, building construction, or in light and shade from casts; and their courses of lessons in many branches of art study, particularly that of the figure, are so good as to be in use all over the world. At the same time very many of the colored publications which are sometimes used in French drawing-classes are execrable; and it is quite unsafe to purchase any examples from Paris, choosing them on speculation from their titles in a bookseller's list. In the Appendix will be found a copy of the list of French examples purchased for the city of Boston, and selected by myself with some care. All are not equally good, but there are no bad works; and selections from that list may be made with confidence. The whole of these copies will be required for a drawing-class which is in its second year's work.

It will be seen from the description given of French art study, that the idea acted upon is to develop a power of drawing by study of effects of light and shade, leaving the student to apply this power to his own wants in industry. When instruction is required in special or technical studies, such as flower-painting or porcelain-painting, it is usually given in a school for that purpose. Thus, in the school of Mdlle. Henriette Lecluse in Paris, pupils are prepared for their work as industrial artists by practising drawing from flowers, designing ornament for fans, &c.; but it is seldom that this secondary education is included in the work of the drawing-schools. The programme of studies in this school will be found in the Appendix.

If we turn from the French system to examine the English or German methods of instruction, the difference between them at once appears very obvious; and the elaborate character of the two latter may be ascertained by an examination of their programmes of study. There is no fundamental difference between the English and German systems, except that the latter is the more scientific of the two. The programmes of the South Kensington School and the Industrial School at Nuremberg (both of which are printed in the Appendix), represent the courses of studies pursued in the national drawing-schools of England and Germany, limited only by local circumstances. In England the same stages of study are common to both the national training-school and the local schools of art; and, from the fact that the masters of the provincial schools are all trained and examined, and receive their diplomas upon the same course as they afterwards give instruction to their pupils in, only of a much more advanced grade, there is a general similarity in the works of all the schools, and harmony in the national system. This systematizing of art study is made more certain by the annual examinations of the schools in every grade of study, with the same tests for each grade in every school throughout the country; and this unification extends even to holding the annual examinations at the same hour in all the schools of the United Kingdom. The building up of this system has taken many years to accomplish; the schools of design dating from 1836, when the Government established the head school at Somerset House in London, and several provincial schools. The distinctive features, however, of the English scheme date only from the year 1851; and the details have been wrought out and consolidated by successful experiments since that time. The administration is in the hands of the Department of Science and Art of the Committee of Council on Education, a department of the government; and thus uniformity of plan is secured. The agencies for industrial art education employed are, (first), a museum of industrial masterpieces; and a large portion of the national collection of pictures in connection with, (secondly), a national training-school for art masters, both located in the same building, a plan of which, together with a view of one portion, is illustrated in plates 26 and 40; (thirdly), a travelling museum for exhibition in the provinces, which circulates good specimens of industrial art, and forms the nucleus for local exhibitions, and also the circulation of books and paintings, on loan, to provincial schools; (fourthly), examination and supervision of all grades of art instruction carried on in connection with the national system. Art instruction is divided into three grades, progressing in difficulty from the first, and called First, Second, and Third Grade. Teachers are trained and certificated to give instruction in each, according to their powers; and, thus qualified, the Government recognizes their qualifications by paying, on a published scale, a sum of money for each successful examination passed by the pupils of these certificated teachers.

The First Grade of instruction is that given in day schools to children by teachers holding the second-grade certificate. Examinations in this grade are conducted in three subjects, — free-hand, model, and geometrical drawing. I have illustrated this grade of instruction by specimens of the examination-papers, which will be found in the Appendix. The examinations are held annually in March.

The Second Grade comprises the elementary instruction given in schools of art and night drawing-classes, and is the grade in which teachers of the national or common schools become certificated. The subjects are free-hand, model, geometrical, and perspective drawing, — all in outline; to which is added, for teachers, blackboard drawing from memory. Orthographic projection, or solid geometry, used to be also included in this group; but it has recently been removed to the science subjects of examination.

The standard of second grade may be judged by looking at the group of papers printed in the Appendix. The examinations are held annually in each town or village in the month of May.

The Third Grade consists of the highest subjects of instruction in drawing, from copies, casts, nature, and original design, painting, modelling, architecture, drawing and design, and mechanical and machine drawing from copies and models, which form the studies in schools of art; and the masters or mistresses of such schools have to become certificated in this grade before the Government recognizes them as art masters or mistresses. The drawings annually produced in schools of art, not of the second grade as before described, are of the third grade, and are every year sent to London for examination, rewards, and exhibition. The stages of study are twenty-three in number, and are printed in the programme of the South Kensington School: the drawings, models, &c., being divided into two groups, — elementary

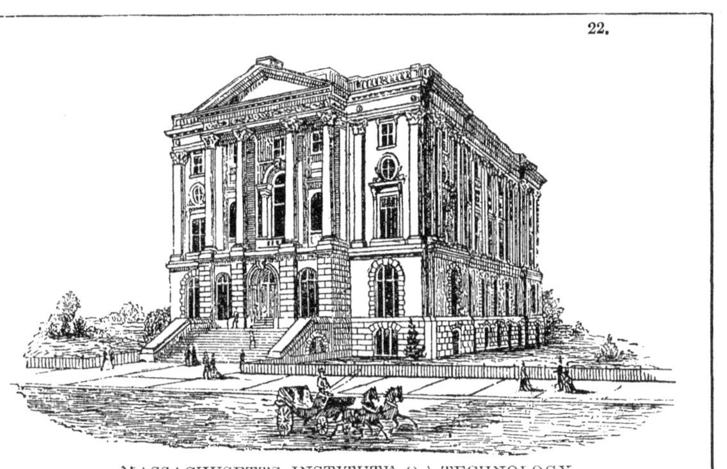

MASSACHUSETTS INSTITUTE OF TECHNOLOGY.

HALF STORY FLOOR.

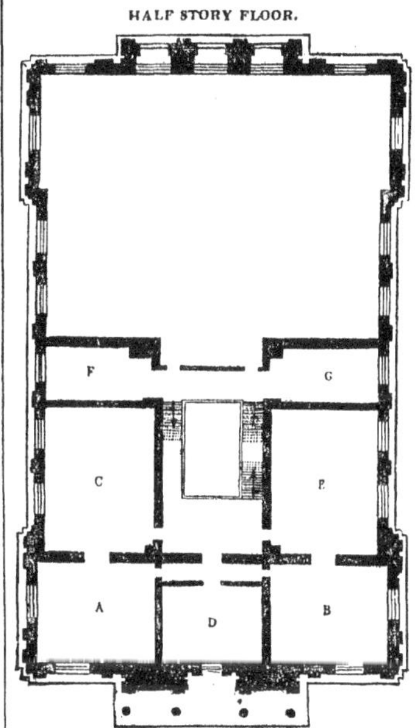

A, B, & C. Architectural Museum and Library.

D. Natural History Lecture Room.

E. Reading Room.

F & G. Professors' Studies.

THIRD STORY FLOOR.

A, B, C, D, & E. Drawing Rooms.

F. Mechanical Engineering Lecture Room.

G. Geometry Lecture Room.

H. Model Room.

and advanced; the latter being selected from the best works of all the schools of art, and examined together in what is termed the National Competition.

The teachers' certificates in this group are awarded after examination in London only, in the month of February, at the close of the winter session of the training-school. Full information concerning these professional examinations is given in the programme of the South Kensington School; and the examination-papers for the first certificate of third grade, for 1868, are printed also in the Appendix.

Having given a sketch of the grades of study, I propose to notice the effects of this system in operation.

The foundation of the system is outline drawing with pencil; and, until the pupil gets over this stage, there is no advancement. From the first efforts in the National Schools to the elementary work in schools of art, all is outline; and that is a net through which every pupil must pass. In this the method differs utterly from the French; which, as the description of M. Lequien's school shows, ignores outline drawing altogether, and looks on pencil-work as inferior in all ways to crayon and charcoal. Having passed this introduction, the subsequent practice is not unlike the French plan; only that, as a rule, shading is done with the point of the chalk, and no rubbing or stumping is permitted until the student has attained to considerable skill in point-work. Painting in all stages is also taught; and, disregarding the sequence of the stages in numerical order, study in light and shade in monochrome, sepia, or neutral tint is very soon among the vehicles used by the young student. Drawing in outline of flowers and foliage, and botanical analysis of plants, with original elementary design, are generally resorted to, and form some of the most agreeable subjects of study.

As a scheme of art education, comprehending all the necessities, whether of the child, the artisan, or the art student, the English system must be acknowledged to be more thoroughly adapted to the general wants of all grades of society than any other, because it has more scope, is progressive in its grades of instruction, and provides what no other national system does so thoroughly for the professional education and examination of the art masters who are to carry it out. The severity which used to characterize its early stages, and against which, in times past, I have waged a not wholly unsuccessful war, is now passing away, if it has not entirely disappeared. All the freedom of stump and leather work, and the boldness of large practice, are both allowed and encouraged in the English schools, when once the outline stage is passed, and the student can use the crayon point fairly. But a radical difference is still maintained between the art education of the child in the common schools, and the youth or adult in the schools of art, — and wisely so, as all who have had great experience in both fields of education will allow to be necessary.

Compared with the French plan, the English may be said to begin earlier with its pupils, and go on longer, and thus is necessarily a more extended course; but in its gradation of exercises and comprehension of practice with all mediums, and upon a wide variety of subjects, the latter seems to me more systematic and educational in its arrangement than the former.

I have spoken more fully on the scheme of art education originating in England than I should have done otherwise, because its recent success, both in common-school instruction, and influence upon manufacturing industry, has drawn the attention of the whole world to its organization and system; and also because I have noticed that theorists, who know little or nothing of either plan practically, are in the habit of comparing French and English methods to the great disadvantage of the latter. Now, I entirely disagree with that view, and hope that I can judge impartially of the two, not blinded by national prejudice, but as a practical educator, having already written, perhaps, more in favor of French art education than any other Englishman; and I contend, that, in this subject, as in all others, before any person is competent to discriminate the good points of both systems, he must be familiar with both in the class-room and lecture-room, — not for a day or a year, but for many years, and see the effects upon many students through a whole course of art instruction. This has been my experience; and the opinions formed by me are based upon that experience. When I say also, that a better scheme than either can, I believe, be developed in this country, it will be seen, that, whilst I have more faith in the English than the French system, I hope the American will be the best of them all. Still, it must be remembered that we are in this country only buckling on our art armor, and must not boast as those who are taking it off.

The German industrial art schools, which in the form either of important institutions, like that at Nuremberg, or as drawing-classes in the common schools, are now becoming as general as other agencies for instruction, have much the same method of study as the English, though they all require larger and bolder practice of outline drawing, and considerably less of it.

The system makes clearness of line, balance of form, and cleanliness of workmanship in the use of the medium, a required accomplishment in all pupils before advancing to more difficult studies. The sort of outline practised is very various as to thickness of line, sketchy and effective, and suggestive of light and shade and roundness, — a pleasant medium between the hardness and wiriness of English and utter absence of French outline practice. In the study of light and shade, which is begun at a very early stage from casts, the processes used are combinations both of point and stump work; but the exercises are more carefully wrought, with greater attention to workmanship, than in French stump drawings. A very complete collection of examples of study is used in the German schools, both of flat copies and casts, and, being accessible and cheap, may account for the great popularity of art study, and some of its excellence.

The best German exhibit of art schools in the Paris Exhibition of 1867 was that from Wurtemberg. Whilst examining this collection, I met and conversed with one of the royal commissioners of the kingdom, — Dr. Steinberg, — who told me, that, though the population of Wurtemberg was only about two millions, they had sixty-four successful schools of art in full operation; the Government appointing and paying the teachers, and the local authorities in each town or village provided the places for study.

In drawing from the cast, a set of conventional ornamental casts is used for the first exercises which appear to me very objectionable, being made for the purpose of displaying flat planes of light and shade, cutting harshly from their backgrounds, without modulation of line or losing of distinction in parts. This is intended to simplify the first exercises, and give breadth of effect in light and shade. But the principle of such relief is contrary to historical precedent in architectural ornament, and is totally different from the effects seen in nature, — two objections, which, in my opinion, quite overbalance the apparent advantages of breadth, and simplicity of subject, in the German casts. Great use is also made of casts from nature in study of light and shade; and these are so excellent, that one cannot help wondering why the wooden-looking ornamental casts are not dispensed with, and casts of historical ornament and natural foliage and figures entirely relied upon.

The schools are particularly successful in the scientific branches of art education, plane and solid geometry, perspective and projection; and this study is pursued to the extent of making models to illustrate problems worked on paper. The latter feature seems peculiar to the German art schools, though it is practised in the French scientific ones, and it is wholly unknown in England.

The good manifestly resulting from such a thorough analysis of form as must arise from its study, both in the solid and on a plane surface, would point this out as a feature to be adopted in American schools of the future. Given the power of drawing an object, the student would make it better than if he could not draw it; and, given the exercise of making it, he ought to know it better, and draw it more truly, than if his acquaintance with the subject was in making it only.

The industrial school at Nuremberg has a reputation for thoroughness not exceeded by that of any other German school; and the extent and variety of its *curriculum* make it a representative institution. It is more professional in character than ordinary art schools, because of the high standard of instruction to be obtained in its classes; but there is essentially practical and industrial work done in it. The plan of securing one-third of the students' works for the use of the school; copying the best works by photography; the taking of contracts for art workmanship, to be wrought by the students; teaching of casting for the purposes of reproduction, and the making of working drawings for actual use, — are all excellent features, suggestive to us here, as soon as we can get men capable of managing such practical and valuable agencies. It is a feature characteristic of the German system in its best schools, and partially practised at South Kensington in wood-engraving and making of terra-cotta, which is worthy of serious consideration in any state school that may be established in this country. The consciousness in a student, that his work, if good enough, will be made use of in a book or a building, stimulates him to a successful effort; and the test of practical usefulness is an excellent standard by which to judge his productions. Thus an advanced class-room is a middle step between the school and the workshop, and is a means of directing the first exercises in design upon sound principles, the work being subjected in its progress to just criticism. This feature seems to me to be a combination of the good parts of the academy and atelier methods. Students wholly educated in the ateliers of professional artists lose the healthy competition of the class-room; and those who take no part in the production of works which are to be sold, frequently have to mourn their ignorance of the practical requirements in their professions.

The thoroughness which is characteristic of German education generally is displayed also in their methods of art study. The theoretical work is illustrated by the best specimens of its application; and a student who is engaged in working out a project of his own is constantly referred to the successful efforts of others, who have done similar things before, — not in vague statements, but by examination and analysis of the objects themselves. The museum and picture-gallery, however modest in proportion, are adjuncts of the class-room; and book-work is by no means overlooked. It will be seen, by reference to the Nuremberg programme, that a class of students called *listeners* is provided for, who have to pay three times as much for the privilege of looking on as the ordinary students have for their working course. That meets a want in most countries; for there are those everywhere who would like to go through the form of art study if it were not for the labor entailed.

Each of these three systems — the French, English, and German — has specially good points in it; and a catholic regard for the excellent will recognize the good in all, without feeling it necessary to undervalue any one. A man's mind must be very narrow in its area, if there is room in it only for the appreciation of one good thing; and those who cannot admire the good features in very opposite methods, rather than condemning wholesale all schemes of instruction which may have deficiencies, have certainly got much yet to learn. Any system, to be righteous and practical, ought to be elastic enough to embrace every new process that experience may perfect, let it come from whence it may; and if it is otherwise, basing its own methods on the theory that they are already perfect, and that other methods wherein they differ are imperfect, then such a system may succeed in putting strait-jackets on the bodies and souls of its students, but will never make original workers of them. In the adaptation of any scheme of instruction for the development of skill in individual cases, it ought to be possible, and may sometimes be necessary, to turn the whole scheme upside down, beginning at the end, or ending at the beginning, if needs be, any laws or formulæ to the contrary notwithstanding; and if a system won't stand such a strain as that, it is worse than useless, — a dead-weight of red-tape and pedagogism. It seems to me that view is perfectly consistent with belief in the mind of any one man, that a certain process is the best, on the whole, for average powers, and that he is justified in working upon his conviction generally; but every educationist knows how various are the requirements and talents of human beings, and how that, if all be treated exactly alike, without making allowances for difference of character, people may be destroyed as well as saved, "according to law," — or by any law, which, like that of the Medes and Persians, "altereth not."

I should like to see a school of art big enough and catholic enough to have class-rooms in it conducted upon each of these three distinct plans, and administered by the best masters that could be found from France, England, and Germany, or by Americans, whose experience in the several methods would enable them to work the schemes successfully, and that it should be a perfectly voluntary matter into which of the preparatory schools students would enter. Then if it be true, as some believe, that a tree may be known by its fruits, we might come to fair conclusions, and select our fruits according to our ideal of excellence. My own belief is, that they would be found to be like the three porches or gates of a temple, giving admission by different approaches to the same tabernacle, and that the disciples would be finally worshipping at one altar, — that of artistic perfection. If the world has learned any thing by experience, it has come to the conclusion that bigotry and immobility are fatal to its happiness, and that, like the Humpty-Dumpty of our childhood, people who proclaim the doctrine of their own infallibility may immediately afterwards have a very great fall indeed. From such a fall, wise men will guard themselves by not

WORCESTER COUNTY FREE INSTITUTE.

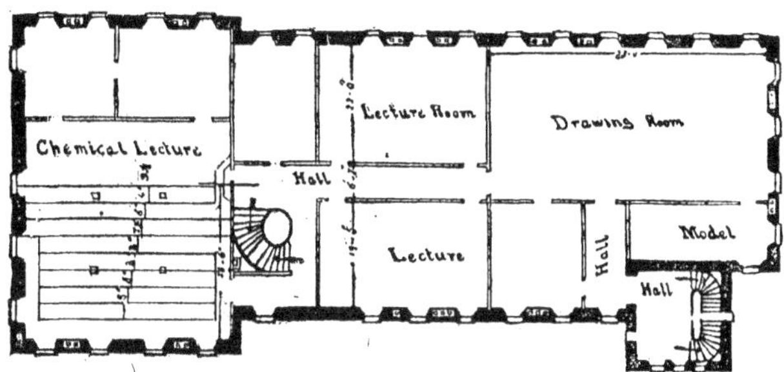

PLAN OF SECOND STORY

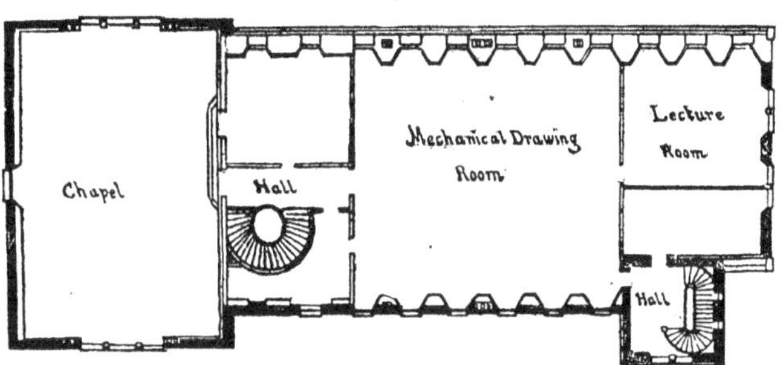

PLAN OF THIRD STORY

climbing to the giddy heights of infallibility; and then they will not need the futile help of "all the king's horses, and all the king's men" to set them, humiliated and self-defiled, "on the wall again."

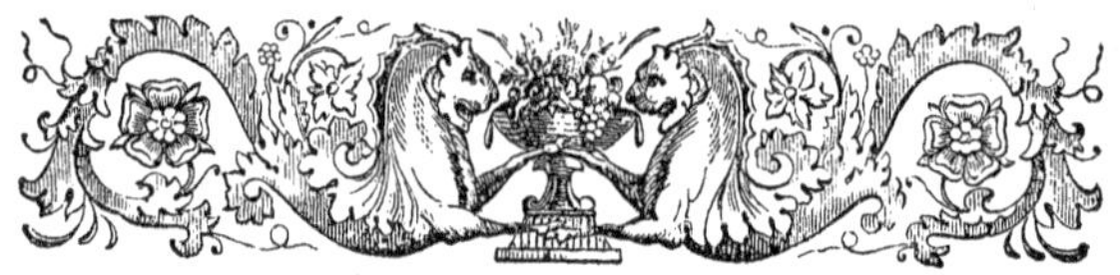

CHAPTER V.

CONDUCT AND MANAGEMENT OF SCHOOLS OF ART.

IN a country like America, where there is so excellent a system of common-school education, it will not be long before a technical development of it in any direction will be organized and administered with the skill already displayed in the general subject. After a few years of experience, there will be little to learn from other countries concerning their systems of art education; for it is but reasonable to suppose, that, in the progress of events, the practical genius for educational organization which distinguishes the people of America will be equally discernible in the adaptation of art and science to the educational wants of this country. I do not, therefore, propose to do more than suggest what appears to me a practical beginning in the conduct and management of schools of art, conscious that probably, to suit the circumstances of a new country, original features of organization will be necessary, and anticipate a success in the conduct of such schools that will place them beyond the needs of either advice or criticism.

I have, however, been made very thoroughly aware of the necessity for some suggestions at the commencement of the introduction of art study generally in this country, by observing the inadequate provision for it in cities, where, apparently to the promoters, they had done all that was necessary to found a school of art; where an empty room, with seats and a blackboard in it, and a draughtsman from the nearest foundry or factory to teach his specialty, seemed to be all that was required to establish industrial art education. This way of looking at the subject is essentially unpractical; and I have seen splendid classes, such as a great teacher would be delighted to instruct, wasting their time in studying technical subjects of drawing which would never be of use to them, because there was no opportunity given them of studying their own individual subjects, or because the teacher was only skilled in one branch of drawing, which he taught of necessity indiscriminately to all. If the students in a class or school represent twenty different kinds of industries, requiring special developments of art skill, and a teacher be employed who is only acquainted with one of these, and has to assist him neither subordinate teachers nor examples of various art subjects competent to teach on or bearing upon the other nineteen subjects, he will only be able to give industrial education to one of the twenty classes of industries requiring art instruction; and the rest will possibly get knowledge of little use to them: to them it will be purely an amusement or an accomplishment, if they do not retire altogether from the classes as being of no practical value to them. The first necessity, then, is, that a school shall be properly fitted and furnished with the required implements of art study, and that the teachers shall be thoroughly well able to teach the subjects in which the school professes to give instruction, and the curriculum be limited to those. Then there can be no disappointment arising from a student, who wants to learn one subject, being forced to learn another: if his subject be down on the programme, it will be taught; and, if not, he must seek instruction somewhere else.

The points to consider in the conduct of a school of art are: 1. The Subjects of Instruction. 2. Regulations concerning Teachers. 3. Regulations concerning Students.

I. — THE SUBJECTS OF INSTRUCTION.

These may be grouped under the two distinct headings, 1 general, 2 technical: of which the first comprises the common subjects required to be taught as the basis of all art instruction, and also the study of general principles of art common to every specialty, such as drawing, composition, light and shade, and principles of design; the second, or technical subjects, will include all those advanced studies in which the knowledge gained in the general course is applied to special subjects, such as modelling, carving in wood and stone, drawing on wood and stone, and wood-engraving, model-making, ship-draughting, etching, designing for manufactures, painting, architectural and machine drawing. Thus we might substitute the words elementary for general, and advanced for technical subjects, without changing the grouping or order of the instruction. It is quite likely that many schools will only at first undertake to give instruction in the general subjects, from a conviction that it would be the most useful course, avoiding thereby the difficulty of obtaining teachers of the advanced subjects. It would be the wisest to secure this elementary instruction at once, rather than to wait for the means of obtaining a school which should be complete in both general and technical studies; for the latter may grow out of success in the former, as a result of wedding art to industry. Provision might, however, very usefully be made in a new school for opportunities in the shape of rooms and materials for some of the technical subjects, so that skilled workmen might be able to practise the artistic rendering of their work, even if they received no special instruction in it, under the general criticism of the principal of the school. Rooms of this character are provided in the design by Messrs. Sturgis & Brigham, the basement giving ample accommodation for studios for every technical study.

In the arrangement of study for the general or elementary subjects, the course should be as varied as possible, so that every student may have the opportunity of discovering in what his strength lies, and of strengthening his weak points. Short lessons, frequently repeated, each containing a clear illustration of some principle of art or mode of working, are much better than a long, monotonous study of one subject only. Some students can be reached through their understanding, and some through their taste; and it will be found generally, that one of these characteristics will be developed out of all proportion to the other, especially if the student has worked much by himself. Varying the subjects of instruction, so as to include the more artistic as well as the scientific phases of study, will tend to equalize these two faculties of taste and understanding, besides broadening the area of the student's knowledge. Two exercises should be practised from the first, — namely, drawing from memory, and time-drawing; and no week ought to be allowed to pass without a definite proportion of time being given to each, the teacher adapting both time and subject to the attainments and opportunities of the student. The object of this is to secure, that drawing be regarded as a language, to be used when called for, and with sufficient rapidity to make it both useful and intelligible, like a true story told in a few words. Infusion of variety in subjects might also be supplemented by varying the vehicle used in drawing; thus lead-pencil, crayon-point, stump and leather with charcoal, pen and ink, sepia or Indian ink, red and white chalk, selected with some reference to the nature of the exercise being performed, will be found to make the student independent of material, and check any disposition to one-sidedness, either in subject or vehicle. This should be done just as children are taught in school many more subjects than they will be required to pursue in after life, in order to cultivate and educate them. It is probable that many subjects or vehicles may be dropped afterwards; but then those will have been discovered and practised which eventually will absorb all the faculties of each individual, and which might never have been even touched upon in a more limited field. The first year of study may be usefully devoted to work in the lecture-room, to acquire knowledge of principles, not necessarily by means of theoretical lectures, but by practice of the alphabet of drawing, such as free-hand ornamental drawing, geometrical drawing, parallel and radial projection, principles of light and shade, — all taught from the blackboard, or whiteboard, by a teacher who will be required to be thoroughly master both of his subjects and of his tongue, or he will never be master of his pupils. The various subjects should be divided into courses of lectures, a given number of lectures to each, and an examination be held at the end of the year's work, to test the student's progress and the master's efficiency. The advancement of students from the general to the technical department should depend upon their success at these annual examinations, in the majority of cases, though there may be exceptional instances of great ability in some one specialty among the pupils, to whom rules ought not to apply. The German method of bringing students face to face with the exigencies and requirements of trade and manufacture, by letting them take commissions to be worked out in the schools, appears to me to be an excellent training; for it seasons theories with practice, and gives opportunities for the development of a determined taste in any practical direction.

Though the education given both to children and adults in the industrial art schools is free (the greatest example which America sets to the civilized world), and students may, therefore, be expected to dispense with any further encouragements to study, yet I think it is a justifiable course to offer prizes for success in the examinations, if they are of a nature to assist the student towards the further prosecution of art study. The action of the English science and art department in this direction is worthy of consideration. The prizes awarded for excellence in the work done at examinations are in the shape of helps to future study. Thus a student succeeding in free-hand outline drawing of ornament or models can choose a box of crayons or a color-box, or works on geometry and perspective, as his prize ; and the same principle holds good in all the examinations. The cost of these marks of approval and encouragements to the students is a very trifling matter to the State ; but the influence of this expenditure can be definitely traced in the popularity and general prosecution of art study. The mere possession of the implements of study will often act as an incentive to take it up ; and, considering how much the interests of society are involved in making of its youth students and producers, I regard all such public investments for the study of art as seed sown in a fruitful soil, which will bear fruit a hundred or a thousand fold.

The grading of drawing, though a matter of detail, is not without its influence upon systematic study. The three distinctions which can be made in it, are 1st, the drawing of children in day schools; 2d, the drawing of adult students in schools of art or industrial drawing-classes; 3d, professional work either of art masters or artists. The grades pursued in schools of art will, therefore, be the second and third grades; for every school should be broad enough both to instruct the artisan and educate the artist and art master. The one feature which ought to be added to the plan of art education as pursued in most European countries is that of technical study, to bring it into immediate contact with industry. The absence of this has been the weakness of systems where it has been ignored; and any new scheme should include it as of vital importance.

In some American cities, the school-boards provide the students of industrial drawing-classes with the more costly implements of study, as well as free instruction; and that seems to me to be a wise and generous action. The cost of such, at that particular time in a young man's or woman's life when they would be most useful and required, might prevent the student from engaging on the study of drawing, which is surely to be avoided if practicable. Thus the city of Boston provides drawing-boards, T and set squares, mathematical instruments, slabs for ink and color, ink and brushes, all free for the student's use; and the same with proper care and custody will last for many years. In addition to these, it would be well that the school-committees provide canvas covers for drawing-boards, modelling-clay, plaster of Paris, and tools for casting; box-wood blocks for drawing and engraving on wood; wood and stone for carving; copper plates for etching; lithographic stones for drawing upon; and the actual materials used for any

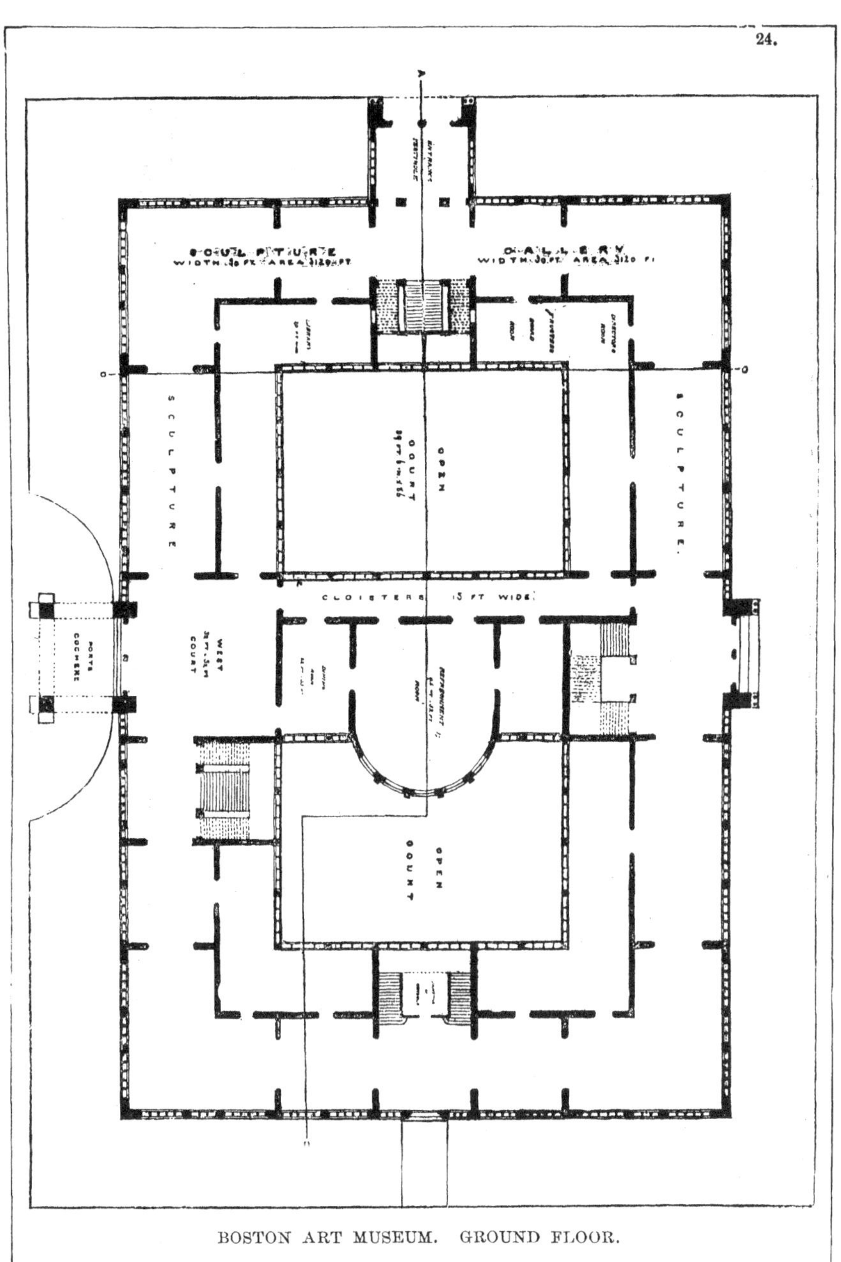

BOSTON ART MUSEUM. GROUND FLOOR.

technical process carried on in the school. The students might be expected to furnish themselves with all the tools or implements used, which are not included in the above list. Thus pencils, crayons, paper, drawing-pins, modelling-tools, gravers, carving-tools, colors, brushes, and etching-tools should all be purchased by the pupils, though it might be of convenience if those for which there was a continual demand were kept in stock by the janitor at his office in the school, and be sold to the students at cost price, — a great advantage to them. If a city could afford to be thoroughly generous, it might, without any serious addition to the whole cost of maintaining a school of art, supply the students with every thing required by them, as freely as it gives them education; but if for economical reasons, or from a conviction that the students themselves should make some sacrifice in order to encourage them to value the education they receive, the burden is shared, the division between what is found for them gratuitously and what they provide for themselves may be taken as indicated above.

II. — REGULATIONS CONCERNING TEACHERS.

The position of the principal of a school of art should be equivalent to that of the master of a school district, where he is held responsible for the working, not only of his grammar-school, but also of the primary schools in the district; the difference being, that the principal of the art school should be the city inspector or superintendent of drawing in the public schools, taught by either special or regular teachers.

[Whilst upon the subject of teachers, I would like to state that the employment of special teachers to teach elementary drawing in the public schools is in my opinion an unmitigated evil. The effect upon the children is to make them regard drawing as so difficult that even their own teachers cannot learn it; and yet they see with wonder that they are expected to learn what their own teachers are excused from. This destroys the influence, and puts entirely in a false position the whole subject of drawing. When a special teacher of drawing be employed, it should be in the capacity of superintendent, and to give instruction to the regular teachers until they become qualified, and not as a direct teacher of children in the public schools.]

In every city, there will in due time be a demand for a school of art; and it ought to be regarded as a centre from which the art education of the district should emanate. The same law of Massachusetts which requires drawing to be taught in the common schools demands also that it shall be taught in free evening classes; and that suggests the practical unity of the want which is thus provided for. If a teacher of ability and reputation be secured for the management of the art school, no one can be better fitted to manage the drawing in the common schools; and the double duty will enable school committees to offer such an inducement as salary that the best men in the profession of art may be commanded. His duty in the art school will be to give instruction generally to all the advanced students, and occasional lectures upon general art topics; to see that the teachers of the various classes are giving instruction upon the principles and plan adopted throughout the school, and be responsible to the committee for the conduct and management of the whole school. To give him authority to carry out the scheme, he should be consulted upon the appointment of all subordinate teachers, and be held responsible for examining their professional qualifications, and reporting on them, for the guidance of the committee in making appointments. In the day schools, his work would be that of superintendent and examiner, directing the teachers, and holding periodical examinations of the pupils. The direct inspection of the classes in each school may be safely intrusted to his assistants in the art schools, who would inspect and report to him; but for their work, as well as his own, he should be responsible to the committee.

The subordinate teachers required in an art school would be, (1), a second master, or, as he is sometimes called, a deputy head-master, or sub-principal, whose duties in the school are to represent the head-master in his absence, and manage the elementary part of the class-work, such as the lecture-room and lower classes, give class-lectures, and be custodian of the school generally; (2), teachers for each distinct subject, as, for instance, free-hand drawing from copies and casts, mechanical and architectural drawing, modelling, and casting; teachers for technical subjects, as ship-draughting, wood-engraving, porcelain-painting, carving, &c. In addition to this, there should be a monitor appointed for each class-room from among the students who are preparing to become teachers, whose duties would be to occasionally assist the teacher, keep the attendance of the classes, and help the students in any way that may be desirable. In the French schools, the students themselves elect their monitors; and I am not sure that it is not a good arrangement. They are not paid for their work, but receive as compensation a professional education from the principal and teachers whom they assist. In large cities, consisting of wide-spread districts, it is well to have elementary drawing-classes, taught by means of class-lectures from the blackboard, in all the distinct localities which are at a distance from the central art school, held in the high-schools or grammar schools of each district; and the teachers of these might be appointed from among the monitors, spending half their evenings at the art schools and half in teaching district classes. Payment for the latter work would enable young men to pursue their studies, who might be otherwise without the means of doing so; and thus the public would be well served, whilst the art education of promising young men would be assisted. That is an arrangement adopted in London, and has resulted admirably. Even to those students who do not propose to become teachers, teaching is an excellent discipline; and I have known many accomplished artists state, that they never saw deeply into the bearings of some art subjects until they were brought by teaching into contact with the difficulties others felt about them, and had to invent explanations which would simplify those difficulties. This had illumined the whole field to them, more than their own studies had done.

There seems an objection in some places to allowing the teachers of the day schools to teach evening classes, supposing that all their energy is required for their work in the daytime. As a rule, this may be true; and with regard to subjects of general education, when the evening work is a mere monotonous repetition of that carried on in the day, I believe it is a wise course to object to the day-school teachers working at night. But when the subjects of study are quite different, such as is the case with art or scientific instruction, the objection does not altogether hold good. It is a relief to the teacher to take up quite a new subject; and, if he is a lover of it and skilled in its practice, then he is probably the best teacher of those subjects that can be found. I have serious misgivings, whether in such subjects it is wisdom to cut off good teachers from public employment at night, and rely only upon such aid as can be got from those who are not teachers by profession. It will be many years in this country before the rare combination of the artist and the teacher is to be found in sufficient individuals to supply the demand for art education. But with the help of the artistic among our general school-teachers, there is a fair chance of supplying the need for elementary instruction in evening classes at once. The teaching of many hundreds of night drawing-classes as well as science-classes in England is carried on entirely by the day-school masters; and the Government highly approves of their employment. The experience of other countries may be of some use to us here in considering how provision is to be made for the future in art and scientific education.

Not that the demand for teachers of the highest order will be met by the employment of day-school teachers: the only course capable of touching that want will be the establishment of professional training-schools, such as that described in Chap. I., — a remedy already successfully adopted both in England and France. A normal art school carried on under State control, with a staff of professors who are accomplished educators each in some special field, and managed by the official representative professionally of the State board of education, will meet the difficulty in every State.

III. — REGULATIONS CONCERNING STUDENTS.

When drawing has been in full operation in the public schools for many years, it will be advantageous to raise the standard of admission to schools of art very considerably. At present, students will have to be accepted who have received no instruction in drawing; and therefore it is somewhat difficult to describe any test to be applied at their admission, except that of age. Those who attend day schools ought to be ineligible, and no one be admitted under fifteen years of age. In a central art school, after a while, students applying for admission should be subjected to an examination of competency in elementary drawing, such as is taught in the day schools, and, failing in that, be refused admission. But for some time to come, in this country, any student who engages to attend regularly should be admitted to the elementary courses carried on in the lecture-room, to be passed on to the higher classes upon examination and success in the subjects taught in that department. Irregularity or unpunctuality of attendance, except in case of sickness or removal from the neighborhood, should be sufficient grounds for suspension or expulsion of the irregular student. It will be better that the time of the teachers be spent upon those who are in earnest to study, and display it by regularity and punctuality, than to waste time over those who value instruction only by fits and starts.

The time usually spent in study per week differs very much in different countries, according to the character of the instruction given. In the night drawing-classes, not held in schools of art, in England, one night per week, of two hours, is the time allotted; in the art schools, three nights per week; and day classes vary from two to five lessons per week. In France, the municipal schools are open at least five nights per week for all students; and some of the classes meet oftener than that. The majority of the classes already established in Massachusetts meet two nights per week for a lesson of two hours; and, until the work in them becomes more advanced, perhaps that is often enough. Home work should be encouraged; and, if the student desires more practice than he can get in two lessons per week, he should work at home, bringing his drawings occasionally for criticism and for direction to his teacher.

Students should be informed, on their first admission to a school of art, that all injuries to the school's property will have to be paid for by those causing such injury, whether it be by accident or wilfulness. This is rendered the more necessary, because, to be available for study, valuable casts and works of art are constantly at the mercy of students, who may by carelessness or frivolty inflict great injury upon those works. It is not without value in the moral training of students, to teach them to respect and even reverence the beautiful works of art of past ages; and the responsibility felt for their destruction ought to be at least equal to that very simple commercial law which makes us "stand by our accidents." Art study, besides having a tangible value in its relation to manufactures, is designed to promote improvement in taste; and the principal of an art school, whilst he may be very merciful towards artistic imperfections, cannot be too severe in his standard of good taste, nor can he apply it too stringently to the students under his charge. In the presence of the Elgin marbles and the antique statues, unless a student feels called upon to be well-behaved, as much so as if he were in a cathedral or at a fashionable assembly, he has more of the savage in him than is desirable, and will have to be reduced to a condition of decency by rough expedients of the street or the market-place before any hope of art work can be entertained concerning him. Nor should a student ever be allowed to seach for copies or handle casts. He is not in a school of art to choose, but to be led; and what direction or placing of examples may be required will be best left in the hands of those who understand such matters. In the art school, as in the common school, the first condition of success is obedience to orders and good behavior; and, until that has been complied with, it is as ridiculous to expect a refined perception of art in students as it would be to seek capacity to lead in a mutinous soldier, or require an Ojibbeway Indian to wear court dress.

All education is a process of reducing things to law and order; and even that most delicate operation of disciplining the hand and eye, training the understanding, and developing the powers of the imagination, must be conducted with due regard to subordination of the immature to the mature mind, or art study will become lawless and experimental. Not that the master of an art school should be a martinet, but that, if he has been appointed to lead, he should do so, and expect, and command, obedience to his instructions. I have seen valuable lives wasted from laxity on the part of teachers, who allowed conceit or youthful frivolity to rule their pupils, rather than exercise their own wills to control the students who were placed under them. A sympathetic feeling should always exist between master and student, and may do so without sacrificing the authority of the one or the interests of the other. But it must not be a reciprocity of feeling which is all on one side. If a master displays interest in his pupil's progress, and goes out of his way to think over and digest what should be done to advance that pupil's studies, the least that the said pupil can do in return is faithfully to comply with his master's directions, whether it be concerning his conduct or his studies. This is the more important; because in the minds of those who believe they have the gift of art power, there is frequently a disposition to regard rules as superfluities, and trust to intermittent efforts of their own initiation, rather than buckle down to the hard collar work of systematic training. That is occasioned by the inexperience and impetuosity of youth, which leads its victims, if uncontrolled, into ill-regulated and non-sequential habits of study, often ending in a narrow mannerism or some contracted groove of subject, incapable of development. The evil of very large art

BOSTON ART MUSEUM. SECOND FLOOR.

schools is, that the master can hardly know and take individual interest in each of his students; and thus many who would become strong men by training are left to wander about in search of the best courses to pursue, coming at last to regard their own crude notions as their only guide. Nothing in after life can ever compensate for this absence of early training under a wise master; and for one student whose powers may be cramped by the strict regulations of a school, perhaps fifty are ruined by the want of sufficient discipline. It is quite true that the capacities of students are so varied that even the same course of study will produce entirely different results in individuals; and it is for the master to discover by his observation and close scrutiny the direction towards which the mental capacity of each is tending, and in which may be found the prospects of a useful and successful life. Perhaps in no other occupation has so much misery been caused as by the mistaken choice of art as a profession by those who had not the capacity nor sustained strength to succeed in it. We seldom hear of architects, lawyers, engineers, or ministers dying in a garret of starvation, when possessing acknowledged powers in their professions; but it has been by no means rare in art. There is a lamentable disposition towards pride and light-headedness in art students, as though they alone monopolized the genius of the world, but were irresponsible for its exercise. Now and then, when this fails them, they wage an unequal war with society, which ends but in one way; but, if it does not so end, men with originally excellent capacities are left to pursue imbittered and disappointed lives, railing against society, and charging it with the responsibility of their own useless careers. That arises from want of discipline to begin with, and the impractical nature of art study generally in the past; by which men have been limited in their studies, and tacitly allowed to regard industrial art as a prosy, inferior vocation, only to be resorted to as a last chance, whilst high art and poetical inspirations were the main business of life. How radically wrong this view is, may be seen by the biographies of many great artists of modern times, — men who as sign-painters, wood-draughtsmen, pattern designers for factories, or stone-carvers, passed through the useful vocation of industrial art to the highest attainments of fine art. Sir Francis Chantrey was a carver before he became the distinguished sculptor, Sir Noel Paton was a pattern-drawer, and Sir John Gilbert a wood-draughtsman, before arriving at surpassing excellence in the highest walks of painting, and wealth and honor from their Queen and countrymen, as a substantial reward. That should be a lesson to light-headed art students, who frothily despise industry, and pine in garrets over some impossible ideal, — the germ of proud idleness, — from which the only thing to deliver them is practical contact with the industrial art necessities of their fellow human beings.

Society has a claim upon every human creature whom it supports and protects for some useful work as a return; and when the facts so strongly point to the highest success in art, resulting from the practice of useful occupations as preparation, it seems to me to be wise and beneficial to require the pursuit of some branch of industrial art from every student, before he is permitted to think about historical or ideal art. I have seen students kept wearily studying for years from the antique and life, with the hope some day of turning them out as historical painters, during which time no one stroke of serviceable work was ever done by them to help forward the business of the world. Out of fifty so employed, not more than two or three have become even decent painters; several have died from actual privation; and the majority have sunk into third or fifth rate positions as artistic hacks, or taken to more useful lives as book-hawkers or storekeepers. They were demoralized by years of useless labor, during which pride was fostered, and idleness generated; and now it is hard work to keep the wolf from the door by employment which was previously despised and for which they have had no preparation. That may seem a very lamentable description; yet how true it has been in past years in almost every country, the lives of art students will show: and it is not easily obliterated from the memories of others who have watched and worked in the same field. The remedy for that cankerworm which has destroyed so many lives is systematic study towards some practical occupation, and a merciful but searching test of the student's powers as his education progresses; whilst the advice of the master concerning what is best for the student's future vocation must be, if necessary, like the knife of the surgeon, — cruel, that it may be kind. The example of Albert Durer, of Cellini, of Flaxman, and other grand old art workmen, ought to be enough to consecrate industrial art even to the most aspiring of art students; and the instances of great and successful artists now living, who are proud of their useful lives as industrial workmen whilst studying for the higher subjects, are so numerous as to be convincing of the value of such experience.

In different parts of this book, I have expressed opinions which show that I believe in art study as equally adapted to the occupations of women as of men, but in this chapter have referred to an art student as of the masculine gender only. That has been merely accidental, just as I suppose it is accidental that angels in the Holy Scriptures are invariably masculine, whether faithful or fallen ; not as suggestive of incapacity on the part of women to become either artists or angels, but simply as representative of a human identity, in the first case, perhaps as a spiritual unit in the second. Any one who has been in the habit of visiting the public galleries of Europe, where students of both sexes are admitted to copy the great works, without any separation of the sexes, will remember how infinitely higher in quality the productions of the lady students are than they seem to be in the female schools of art. This may partly arise from the fact that the best students only are permitted to copy without instruction ; but it is in a great measure to be explained by their artistic contact with their male fellow-students, which gives them the opportunity of seeing various styles of work and methods of painting and handling. Some of the freedom and boldness of treatment which is supposed to be characteristic of the masculine artist become familiar to and are acquired by the ladies, who on their part communicate to their fellow-students many nameless graces and refinements. Good results on both sides from this ; and those who have had much experience in education will bear testimony to many advantages arising from the co-education of the two sexes. Mixed schools for adults are the only ones which should be permitted anywhere, both for the sake of education and morals.

The opening up of the subject of art education in this country seems to me to give a great opportunity to test the natural capacities of women, and will, I hope, be the means of furnishing them with an additional source of employment. At present, men have not here had a very long start before women in the subject of art ; and so we may possibly see whether, if both engage upon it on equal terms, either displays greater faculties than the other. For both economical and artistic reasons, therefore, I would plead for schools of art being mixed schools, and that the education given to both sexes should contemplate their having to live by the artistic labor of their own hands.

ART AS AN OCCUPATION FOR WOMEN.

In speaking about the suitability of art study as a training for women, and its practical value as fitting them for the serious duties of life, by which in any event they make themselves independent members of society, I am conscious that I touch on a subject upon which there is much difference of opinion at least, and latterly much controversy. In view of this, and only recognizing the difference of muscular strength in the sexes, existing for obvious reasons, and which according to every natural law must be compensated for by some special endowment not possessed by the muscularly strong, (or Nature has been less just to her last creation than to all others), I judge from my own experience that the whole subject is one of great interest, and that the compensation referred to takes the form physically of a more delicate organization, and mentally of a greater sensitiveness to outward influences. Theories seem to me to be fairly deducible from practice, by those who may have no claim to be philosophers, or who do not possess the original faculty of inductive reasoning; always supposing that those who practise have sufficiently long and extensive practice, and seek rather to discover a principle for their own guidance than to establish a theory preconceived or borrowed from others. My own fear has been, and now is, that hitherto women have been treated as pets and playthings, to be indulged and delighted in, but not to be held responsible for any thing; have been educated with the view that all should become merely the ornaments of society and not its essentials, and the important half of its structure; that, finally, men have come to regard women with a patronizing feeling, in which there is an infinite amount of good nature in some cases, but no justice in any case. And the terrible thing is, that, when the good nature ceases, or the indulgence necessary to a plaything comes to an end, all the penalties fall on one side only: the whole of the sauce is used up for the goose, whilst the gander stalks away to new fields that are ever verdant and fresh, and indulges his gandorial magnificence.

Christianity and May meetings ought to have had long enough opportunities in nearly nineteen hundred years to test the fairness and justice of this view of human nature; but they seem to me to have failed to discover, that, whatever difference our beneficent Creator meant to exist in his design of human beings, he usually places there with his own Almighty hand, and requires no further journeyman's work on man's part to emphasize or stamp this difference. Yet, in spite of this, we educate women superficially, and then smugly say they have no minds; we withhold all reasoning processes from them, and then say they cannot argue, but jump at conclusions; we train and grind up our boys in athletic sports, in Euclid and conic sections, and the differential calculus, and our girls in Berlin-wool work, in waltz-playing, and the Paris fashions, and then proclaim that men can reason, women only perceive, men can create, women only appreciate; and as Milton the Puritan poet expresses it, —

> "For contemplation he, and valor formed; *
> For softness she, and sweet attractive grace," —

as though contemplation were not equally characteristic of both sexes, the combination of leisure, a stored

* Not trained.

mind, and subject to contemplate; valor, the result of self-confidence in training, and difficulties already overcome, and faith in surmounting future difficulties; softness and sweet attractive grace, the natural appreciation of each sex by the other, as much belonging to men as to women, common to the two sexes, which are alternately the attracted and the attractive.

My own belief is, that we have no grounds for and no right in making any difference whatsoever in human beings on account of sex, either in their education or occupations, more than Nature has done; and that half of the troubles we find in the world arise from, and are a just judgment upon, our presumption in making any distinction between them, in fostering the self-conceit of the one, and sacrificing the independence of the other. Let the same education from the first to the last, physical and mental, be furnished for both sexes; let it be accepted, that, as they require the same physical sustenance, so they will need the same intellectual food; that the two who will in time become one flesh shall be in unison and harmony with each other, in attainments and desires, in their minds as well as their bodies, and then we shall have the perfect harmony in difference, which we see in all God's works, leaving it humbly to him that all His plans shall develop themselves with as much certainty as that He creates each after its kind, without any impertinent help from us. The compensation which it appears to me Nature makes to women for the comparative withholding of muscular strength, is endowing them with greater powers of endurance in the first place, and a gift of natural aptitude and quickness, which, when it exists in men, we call mother-wit. Thus we see that whilst men become irritated and impatient of the repetition of little troubles, and would put a violent end to them, women, like charity, are long-suffering and kind over vexations, which in connection with their children and other cares often last daily for years. The quickness and aptitude they have may be the support which Nature gives them through their instincts, as a balance to men's muscular superiority; and this seems to me to indicate that the sensitive touch and quick perception and delicate hand point out the practice of art as peculiarly adapted for a woman's occupation, being in itself the most refined and delicate of all manual labor, as it is also the most perfect expression of the impressions we receive, through our eyes, of physical phenomena.

It may be, that, should we recognize this view, the fair division of labor, which somehow or other must be made, will be facilitated, and both sexes profit by it. If we remove all masculine protective tariffs, we may find great powers where we have fancied that weakness was inevitable. In literature, we have some of the most powerful works of the imagination written by women; and they fetch the same price in the book market as the novels which men have written. In the picture exhibition, the buyer discusses a work of art in relation to its price, not with reference to the sex of the painter; and those who are familiar with the London exhibitions know that as large a proportion of the works displayed in the exhibition of the Society of Female Artists are sold as in any other exhibition composed principally of the works of men. That, however, is the case with books and pictures only, where women sell their labor at their own time, and choose the purchasers, being proprietors of their own skill. In every other avocation that I know, the same work, performed in the same manner and with equal skill, is paid for at an entirely different rate to the two sexes. This is especially the case in education, whose influence on the

GROUND PLAN OF THE SOUTH KENSINGTON MUSEUM, LONDON.

happiness and safety of the human race cannot be overrated, that, of those who are employed to train up our children in the paths of rectitude and strict morality, nine-tenths of them are paid for their labor at about half the price they would receive if they were men, — an unfortunate example to them of how they should teach rectitude and instil moral principles.

If a woman and a man were by their industry to raise two barrels of potatoes, and each took a barrel to the market, the market price of a barrel of potatoes would be given to both for their goods. If a woman and a man by their industry and training grow the ability to teach, and take their goods to sell in the educational market, both being of the same quality, tried by every test, the man will be paid by the purchaser nearly fifty per cent more than the woman; and the latter is of necessity obliged to take the unrighteous offer. That is to say, when we are buying food for our bodies, or to fatten our hogs, we do fairly to all who have to sell; when we purchase intellectual sustenance, to educate and develop our children, we pay those who have education to sell, if they are women, at fifty per cent less price than we should pay them if we were buying potatoes of them for our swine.

The minds and souls of our children seem to me to be of as much importance as their bodies, and even as the bodies of any other animals; but here, in comparison, by an act of injustice, we undervalue them about fifty per cent. If women supply us with only half as good an article as men, we do an injustice to our children by employing them; if the article supplied by women is as good as that supplied by men, we rob them of every dollar we should pay men for it, but don't pay to women.

So that, in the educational labor market generally, we

act inconsistently, and inflict penalties upon those from whom we require the most exalted service. This cannot be for the public good, but proceeds from the limitation of occupations suitable to women, resulting from their utterly unpractical education, which throws almost all women of the middle class who are without means into the educational market. By this, individual labor is reduced in value, the market being glutted. The purchaser, therefore, goes in and buys up what he wants at half-price, the needy seller sacrificing it, on the principle that half a loaf is better than no bread. This is the explanation of a condition of things, which is, from the public point of view, utterly suicidal economically, and the root of many evils morally. We have drifted helplessly, but, I trust, not yet hopelessly, into social circumstances, by which the intellectual powers of half of the human kind are left dormant, and remain stunted and undeveloped; so much so, that but a very limited number of occupations are possible to women, and of these, from our worship of a fetich called Mrs. Grundy, many are deemed unsuitable. Yet Nature goes on laughing at the little golden calf that we have set up, and bringing into the world more women than men, whose minds and actions we deliberately cramp more than John Chinaman does the foot of his female minister, who is so much his mere chattel as to be drowned by him, or sold to his neighbor, to suit his own convenience, without interference by the law.

I don't regard this as so much a woman's question as a man's question, and not as a sentimental question at all, and decline to be made, by my own consent, a practical sufferer economically by the sentiment which others import into it. I want to feel the sensation of common honesty, — that I pay for a dollar's worth of work with a dollar, and not with fifty cents, whether I buy it of a woman or a man; and I want to see one-half of the human beings that are born do half the work which is to be done, and receive half its recompense. For every portion of that half of the work which men withhold from women, men have to make up by additions to their own half; and for every dollar withheld from them for work done, men have to pay them in some way, directly or indirectly, as a question of sentiment or charity; which destroys self-respect and independence in women, and develops in them slavishness and timidity, distrust in themselves, and absence of self-reliance and self-helpfulness.

I am aware that for this deplorable condition of things no one is directly to blame, and that men are sometimes very hardly judged by women as being wholly responsible for it. We have drifted into it, having set too much store by that Eastern estimate of women we originally received from the Jews, and might as well have adhered to burnt-offerings, peace-offerings, and sacrifices, as to still keep up the senseless distinctions of sex which came to us from the land of harems and fatalism? It is time to wake up from our delusion on this matter, — time for men to reject with the scorn and contempt it deserves the masculine and feminine chirruping of those who accuse women-helpers of a desire to unsex them, as though that were possible. Here we see women of ability and power running off into all kinds of lamentable delusions, and inventing pestilent doctrines concerning their relationship to men, all for the want of sound practical education, good, healthy work, and fair treatment; and yet we fold our hands, and stand idly by, horrified at the phantom our neglect has called up, instead of remedying it by the only possible specific, — work and wages, and plenty of both. We ought to clear away the fanatical cobwebs in women's brains, — engendered by superficial education, by their sense of unjust treatment, and partly by enforced idleness, — with a vigorous blast of wholesome labor in any capacity or occupation they choose themselves, or can do the best at: and let us once for all try and learn the truth, that sin and labor are of no sex, and that any professional or manual occupation a decent woman could not worthily be employed in, a decent man has no right to engage upon; whilst every employment that is necessary and honorable is as much so to one sex as to the other, the fitness of each for any occupation being controlled only by their physical powers. This, I maintain, is not a sentimental view. It is, for aught I know, the view of many besides myself; though having never had time to read either book or pamphlet on the woman's-rights question, I may be advancing very old arguments: but this does not affect the rightness or wrongness of my own judgment, inasmuch as these conclusions have been arrived at independently, by practical observation extending over many years, during which time I have been a daily educator of adult women, and thus know something of their wants and their powers. Experiments for educating women and men together are familiar to me; and so also is the strict separation of the sexes educationally. The former, in every case coming within my observation, has been beneficial to both; and the latter as detrimental. For this reason I would as strongly oppose colleges and universities for women only as for men only, each being but half the story; and the next great act of justice and wisdom which the just and wise should be called upon to perform is opening all the universities and schools and colleges to women, in which they may acquire the educational basis of all the professions. The dangers which sage people with telescopic minds decry in the distance, when "sweet girl graduates" are placed in daily association with their graduating brethren, is a danger which is existing in their own households, at their neighbors' hearthstones, in their own churches, and in all social assemblies every day, without destroying them. If it be true that young men and women cannot meet on the same staircase, listen to the same lectures, and study the same subjects together, without disrespectful treatment of one another, and without influencing each other badly, it is something exactly contrary to my experience for twenty years; but, if it is really the case, the sooner they are taught to do so by actual experience, the better for every one concerned. It is a scandal and disgrace to the nineteenth century, if it be so.

I have dwelt more fully upon this topic than I should have felt warranted in doing, but for the fact that art study especially (in which knowledge of the human form is an essential to success in the highest branches) is one of the subjects which Mrs. Grundy has her opinions about, and darkly hints at the shocking things which sometimes happen, when women take to studying art, anatomy, and other fearful subjects, that ladies of delicate perceptions should never think about. That kind of grundyism must be wiped out; and I know no better way of doing it than by proving or making all such studies so pure and morally harmless that the purest-minded woman can study them without any shock to her most delicate perceptions, and with much profit to her knowledge, and carry on her studies side by side with her masculine fellow-students. If there be any apples on the tree of knowledge which Eve must neither touch nor taste, I think, on the whole, Adam will be better without them; and history, if it sets a precedent at all, records at least one instance where the same fruit was forbidden to both, — not to one only.

It is some comfort to know that many of the preserves of knowledge have been successfully besieged by women, and that colleges of surgeons and physicians, and academies of arts, whether royal or republican, are surrendering unconditionally to the demands of lady students for admission and degrees. In this crusade, men have taken the sorry part of obstructives, helped and encouraged thereto by the cackling of some women who profess in such matters to be anxious only for the happiness of their own sex, but who, if they had ever faced the difficulties of providing for themselves, might very quickly find good grounds for changing their opinions. Remembering, too, the indescribable amount of influence which women have upon their children, I cannot imagine it possible to over-educate them; for every word and thought they utter is unconsciously shaping the minds and lives of their children, whilst yet of tender age; and when we consider how almost invariable it has been, that the great men of all ages have owed their first inspirations and their habits of thought to their mothers, whose superiority to other women has been that of a higher education, it would appear to be established, that, whatever it may be necessary to teach to men in this world, it is a matter of necessity to teach to women, in order that the man's education may begin with his life, and his mind be nurtured with his body, that perfect human education may be accomplished.

CHAPTER VI.

ORNAMENTAL DESIGN IN FORM AND COLOR.

DESIGN may be described as the arrangement, or formation upon a defined plan, of any thing which is for the use or enjoyment of human beings, in which the element of taste is displayed, either in form or color.

Among the many definitions whereby the human animal, *man*, is distinguished from all the other animals, — such as that he cooks his food, or that he is a bargaining animal, or that he is a wearer of clothes, which are half true and wholly amusing, — comes the philosophic definition, that man is a user of tools, and a designing animal.

Perhaps no more interesting subject exists as a study than the consideration of the weapons and implements used by men in all ages, from the flint arrows and hatchets of our nude forefathers, to the revolver, sewing-machine, and steam-plough of this present elaborately clothed race. There is history itself in every one of these; and the student and antiquarian who treasure up and explain these relics of the past, or compare them with their representatives of the present, are themselves an illustration of one of the truest definitions of the human race; for men alone are students and antiquarians.

I believe there exists in the interior of Africa a tribe of human creatures who may be described as a connecting-link between the lowest order of men and the highest order of animals, who are not men. They are arrayed, not in the latest Paris fashions, but in the simple costume of our first parents before their expulsion from paradise: they build no houses nor huts nor tents, but scrape a hole in the earth, or enlarge a crevice already existing, which gives to them shelter, and their name of Earthmen. These men seldom cook their food, but eat it as soon as caught, as the hawk or the lion does, and in a very similar way; and it is believed, that, whenever a bushman or earthman is found to be roasting his meat, it has been the result of his demoralization through contact with civilization. They don't bargain, and they don't design, but they do use tools; i.e., they slay their victims with a wooden brand, or smite their prey with a stone. I have had the honor of a personal introduction to a lady and gentleman of this interesting tribe;* and it was with some difficulty I could bring myself to regard the gentleman as a man and a brother, or the lady as a woman and a sister, especially as they had no names, and for the purpose of conversation, which was rather one-sided, I had to invent one something like Kickaboo, which was acknowledged by a grunt of approbation from the gentleman addressed.

Now, between these creatures and the painter of the Sistine Madonna, or the discoverer and adapter of electricity, there is apparently a great gulf fixed: yet it is only apparently; for, seen closely, the gulf is a ladder, or staircase, of many rounds or steps, Kickaboo being at the

* Their portrait-statues, cast from life, are now in the Crystal Palace, Sydenham.

bottom, and Raphael or Morse at the top. It seems to me, that the first step from the bottom (which is a dead-level, occupied promiscuously by all animals) is the use of tools, and the second step is design. How far the bushman and the gorilla are the same or similar creatures, I am not prepared to say; but they are both on the same round in this ladder at present: they both use brands as implements of attack or defence, and they neither of them design.

Leaving them, we find, that in the condition of most of the savage races, and also of many of the semi-barbarous tribes, though progress may have been arrested at a particular stage, and the stage has in their cases become archaic, yet it is difficult to discover any race of men who have not in some degree practised a species of design. The first step is the making of tools; the second, making them comely and attractive. Whatever man has to make out of a combination which does not exist naturally may be described as an implement. Even a house is an implement of protection against the weather as much as an umbrella is; and so surely as that a race of men begin to make themselves weapons or implements, will they also endeavor to make them beautiful. Here at this low stage of civilization comes in design; and from that up to the highest phases of development, as seen in the Medici tombs or the Elgin marbles, is only a question of degree, not one of kind. The germ of Michael Angelo may be said to have existed in the first savage who cut a rude ornament on his war-club; the first step towards producing a Raphael was taken when colored earth was rubbed over men's bodies to make them attractive to their friends or terrible to their enemies.

All the rest has been a greater or less application of the principle of design, having its roots in the desire to create the beautiful, a desire common to the human race after its first purely animal stages.

Now, as ornamentation does not increase the mere usefulness of any thing, it comes into existence as an expression of some inherent desire; and it is to be noticed, that radically it is an evidence of love, — the objects first ornamented being those prized for their usefulness, and valued and loved by the possessor, who adorns and thus honors them. That is a human thread, or filament, which runs through every human weft, and is as common to civilized men as possession of the physical senses of sight and hearing. We do not wish to ornament things we care nothing about, or put to mean and ignoble purposes; on the other hand, the objects we most love, we love to see beautiful and beautified by all the resources of art. "The king's daughter is all glorious within: her clothing is of wrought gold," — that is merely a description of the desire to lavish on a lovable object the purely human expression of our love, and a statement that it has been done, whatever else it may mean symbolically. When we consider how general this feeling has been in all ages and among all peoples, it can only be explained as a necessity to human happiness; and it is the inevitable sign of progress and civilization: for barbarism, which ignores the past and defies the future, caring only for the present, concerns itself very little with care of antiquities, or thoughtful provision for posterity. Still less does it trouble itself with the ideal, which is the fire burning on the altar of perfection; or the beautiful, which, in its relation to us, is our appreciation of God's laws. Barbarism may be said to be an ignorant or selfish existence from hand to mouth: civilization is a consistent living as tenant in possession of the earth, with reverence and respect for the past and thoughtful provision for the future; whilst it secures all that may be honestly obtained for the present. Thus recklessness and barbarism are suggested by the destruction of accumulated art in the words, "But now they break down all the carved work with axes and hammers:" constructiveness and civilization are equally indicated by the expression, "He hath loved our nation, and built us a synagogue."

It is *prima faciæ* evidence of progress, that a nation will not ignore landmarks, nor despise the wisdom of past ages: it is conclusive proof of advancement when a people estimates past experience at its full value, whilst it claims for itself independent action for the present, and displays consideration for the future. The tendency of art and design is to help forward civilization, by providing a peaceful object on which to expend both love and genius. It is also to be regarded as a thermometer of national development; for so long as the inventive powers are displayed in discoveries of new processes or the improvement of old ones, and art is employed to enrich and ennoble the nation by its triumphs, the meridian of that nation has not yet been reached; but when love of the beautiful decays, and art is on the decline, then, in fact, people are relapsing into barbarism, and neither civilization nor society will long survive their extinction. The influence of good design upon the happiness of people is real, if not direct. A sense of fitness and propriety, of unconscious rest, marks the presence of good design. The opposite sensation is the inevitable accompaniment of bad design.

The perfect adaptation to purpose of every thing which God has made and men have left alone, or which has had strength enough to resist his corruption, has given us a standard by which the arts and works of men may be judged, and by which, consciously or unconsciously, we form an opinion about them. Thus it often happens that a person entirely ignorant of the practice of art, or the canons of taste, may, by intimate acquaintance with natural laws and phenomena, be a keen and impartial judge, by simply criticising a work as though it were nature, not art. That applies only to such phases in it as claim to be like nature, and not to those higher developments of intellectual effort or achievements in processes which are the outcomings of profound knowledge and the ripest technical skill. In considering design adapted to the ornamentation of useful objects, the only sound standard will be that which requires the ornament to increase their beauty, without limiting their usefulness. That is the first and absolutely essential condition ; but it is poor design in which no effort is made to increase the usefulness whilst adding to the beauty of an object, not only in an æsthetic, but a utilitarian point of view. Industrial products capable of displaying taste, and in which it is utterly ignored, may reasonably be supposed to be the work of barbarous originators, as little to be trusted for the choice of good material or practice of sound workmanship as for other indications of skill, which are manifestly deficient: but, on the other hand, simplicity is not barbarism; and infinitely better is the absence of any design than the presence of that which is vulgar or false. Though we may prefer a man with the culture and manners of a gentleman to a man with the ignorance and uncouthness of an agricultural laborer; yet a plain, honest man, however ignorant and uncouth, who affects to be nothing but what he is, is an infinitely better and pleasanter companion than one, who, by vulgar arts, pretends to be better than he is, whose manners, learning, appearance, and character are assumed and worn, like his clothes, to conceal himself, — shams like his jewelry, and base as its metal.

The general principles of design, and their application, seem at once to grow out of a true knowledge of its origin, which I have endeavored to explain.

The ornamentation of an article of use is something which is quite unnecessary to it. It is bad ornament when that use is interfered with, or limited in any way, by the ornament itself. The tendency of ignorant designers is generally in the direction of profusion, — overloading, perhaps, a simple object with excess of ornament, in which the original use of the object is ignored or concealed. This excess of ornament is not enrichment: it is merely ostentatious vulgarity; and, unless there is a large proportion of plain parts in a decorated object, it comes to be like the plum-pudding which was all plums and no flour, — nauseating and of evil influence. In the best periods of art, that was always avoided; and any development in that direction is a certain indication of a low state of public taste. A lavish profusion of ornament or decoration is often resorted to, to cover inferior work in the construction; and you may always regard with suspicion any thing which appears to be more pretentious than its importance warrants. Common sense supplies us with the soundest canons of taste in designs for manufactures. A certain amount of work has to be expended on the production of every object of use: then there is the cost of the material; and out of the sum-total you must subtract the cost of the ornamentation, and you have the utilitarian cost, and possibly value left, of the thing purchased.

It follows, then, that, when too large a proportion of the labor has been expended in ornamentation, too little has been left for good workmanship in the construction, or quality in the material. Take a chair as an illustration. Let it be smothered with carving, and its arms and legs twisted and indented with all kinds of curves and enrichments, and I, for one, avoid it as an object of use, both because some clever bit of sculpture is sure to stick into one at some unsuspected spot, and because, with such flaunting pretension, I suspect the moral character of its workmanship.

Again, that species of design which consists in the mere imitation of a natural object, and making it into an article of use by some talented contrivance, is an abomination: it is an insult to nature, and a confession of utter poverty in design. The application of any object to fulfil a purpose for which the original would have been ill adapted or impracticable, is also an error in design.

I see in the windows crucifixes in green glass, sold as candlesticks. Imagine the bowed head of the Saviour on the cross covered with tallow-grease! The man who designed that, and the man who manufactured it, ought either to be working together in a school of design, or in ——, I am not quite sure which [the reader may supply the omitted alternative workroom according to his own notions of mercy or justice].

We will now glance for a few moments at the influence of color in design, and upon the sensations of sight, through which, indirectly, the mind is affected. Perhaps color may be said to affect the mind more powerfully and directly than form. A man could no more live in a room painted a glaring red color than he could live in a fire, or stare at the noonday sun; and though less positive colors affect the sensations to a slighter degree, every color, as well as every combination of colors, has a sensible influence upon the feelings.

Colors influence the sensations through the eye, the same as sounds affect them through the ear. Arranged systematically, with due regard to proportion and numbers, we describe the arrangement as harmony in painting, or music in sound. There is a close parallelism between painting and music, extending even to details. Each is susceptible of a major and minor key; in painting, the major being light, and the minor shadow.

Disregard of the laws of composition and proportion, in both, results in discord and confusion.

Repose, pleasure, and pain can be suggested by color as by sound. Light decomposed results in color, — red, blue, and yellow, and the tints between them: color, therefore, is decomposed light. The proportion of pure color to produce light is yellow (3), red (5), blue (8); and the fusion of these, seen in a humming-top or disk revolving at great speed, produces a near approximation to white.

The table of colors suggesting the proportion and harmony of the principal is not without use, considering them as elements of ornament. That very generally accepted is as follows: —

Colors are divided into primaries, secondaries, tertiaries, tints, hues, neutrals, shades.

Primaries . .	Original and Simple .	Yellow, Red, Blue.
Secondaries . .	Mixtures and Compound,	Purple, Green, Orange.
Tertiaries . .	" "	Citrine, Russet, Olive.

These harmonize in the following proportions of surface, purity being taken for granted: —

*	*	*	
3. Yellow,	5. Red,	8. Blue,	Harmony of Primaries.
13. Purple,	11. Green,	8. Orange,	" " Secondaries.
19. Citrine,	21. Russet,	24. Olive,	" " Tertiaries.

Where two colors are used, the primary and secondary, with neutrals, black, white, and gold; where three, the primary, secondary, and tertiary, with the neutrals, — will be found to produce harmony. It will be seen that

* Harmony of complementaries.

three of yellow harmonizes with its secondary purple in the proportion resulting from the admixture of the remaining primaries: thus red 5, blue 8, produces purple 13. Three of yellow, therefore, harmonizes with thirteen of purple. The same holds good of the harmonic proportion of the other primaries and secondaries; also, that a secondary, as green, being taken, the tertiary russet, which will be required to balance it, is determined by the fusion of the other two secondaries; viz., green 11, (purple 13, orange 8), russet 21, and so on with the others. A *tint* is the admixture of color with white; a *shade*, its admixture with black; a *hue* is one primary tinged by another; whilst the word "tone" is applied to the general effect produced by all the colors, used in decoration or in a picture, upon the eye simultaneously.

The position of these colors in any scheme of decoration, to be pleasant in appearance, must be very much dependent on their actual position in nature; for though fashion, caprice, or manner may induce people to like what is unnatural, — i.e., contrary to natural laws, — Nature is stronger than fashion, and an outrage of the principles which Nature's works display will become distasteful to, and eventually disgust, even the most artificial taste. Now, if we look around us to see where the primaries, secondaries, and tertiaries exist in the largest proportions and the most generally in nature, it will be found that in the sun, the firmament, and the clouds, tinged by and partially absorbing the sun's rays, there is a predominance of yellow, red, and blue, the primaries, and an absence of the secondaries and tertiaries, white being the prevailing neutral. That suggests primaries and their tints for ceiling decoration, and horizontal planes visible from beneath. Midway between the heavens and the earth, the governing colors are green, purple, and orange, with their tints and shades, as seen in foliage, shadows, fruits, flowers, birds, and insects, relieved by the presence of the primaries in very small proportions: this as clearly indicates the predominance of the medium secondaries for wall decoration and vertical planes. The earth is full of tertiaries, — russet, citrine, and olive, and their hues and shades varied in myriads of combinations, which would seem to point out to us that the duller colors find their place upon the ground we walk upon, and that horizontal planes may be so colored with adherence to natural laws.

Without reference to exact proportion, then, it may be reasonably said that Nature places her most brilliant colors in the heavens above us, her least brilliant and most neutralized tints on the earth beneath us; and the colors which are midway between lightness and darkness are most frequently seen midway between heaven and earth. Without being a theory of color for decorative purposes, that seems to me to suggest a motive-principle, controlled necessarily by special circumstances, of locality, requirements of purpose, means of ornamentation, color of materials used. The amount of neutral color used, as black, white, and gold, may modify any very prominent colors by dividing one from another, — the primary from its complementary tints: but pure primaries or secondaries are seldom satisfactory unalloyed, either by white or black, or modified in the shape of hues; the effect of this reduction in brightness being a blending and harmonizing of color, producing a sense of satisfaction, of seeing without fatigue to the eye. External and internal decoration will necessarily differ in their character, the one great element of light being different in the two cases; for light is color, and color is light, applied judiciously with knowledge and skill. Where light is abundant, as it is externally, then, large masses of bright color are unnecessary and out of place; for

Nature uses brilliant color very sparingly, generally upon the smallest objects, whether in the animal or vegetable kingdoms.

Perhaps the one feature which is most apparent in Greek ornamental design is its fitness, — an entire absence of profusion or excess, with extreme beauty of form; simplicity and severity of subject, yet the highest grace in arrangement. Ornamentation comes in quite as a subordinate feature to a general conception to give fuller expression to the higher features. This is remarkably apparent in the dresses of figures on the Greek vases; the ornament consisting generally of a simple running pattern on the borders and edges of the garment, or a delicate powdering; the ground of it being plain, the figure being principal, the drapery next, and, last of all, the ornament on the garment. The figures themselves, as being applied to a flat surface, are in one tint not shaded into roundness, which would destroy the contour of the vase itself.

There has been a great return to this pure feeling, in Europe, in many branches of modern manufacture, but not as much as could be wished. We have hardly yet got out of the imitative period, so that the longing for purity and grace takes the form of reproduction rather than originality. Still, that is infinitely better than a low type of originality; for it may lead in time, as the Gothic revival and restoration have, to an education of a sound sort, upon which eventually originality may be based. The only fear is, that, among an educated people, imitation is sometimes destructive of originality; and, when it does occur, it is often as a fashion rather than an outward expression of the inward refinement. People who are beating about for a cast-off raiment are not likely to get one which fits them exactly; but beggars cannot be choosers, and any thing will do to wear until another more attractive robe can be assumed to hide the art nakedness of a sterile age. Occasionally, then, a Greek garment may be picked up and worn so long as the fashion remains unchanged; but before we have felicitated ourselves all round that daylight is coming, and Hellenic taste is in the ascendent, some booby will have discovered a piquant barbarism somewhere, which is agonizingly attractive to the feelings of fashionable savages, sometimes restrained into temperance by fashion, but who will bound out of it into ochres and tattooings, as a schoolboy going home for the holidays springs back to the old homestead. That happens as a consequence when art is assumed, not generated. Unless cultivation in art is bred into a people, and either originated by them or assimilated by slow degrees, developing with their increased perceptions, it is like the garment rather than the individual. It is of little use vexing ourselves about and straining after originality of style in architecture and ornamental art, as though it could be invented like a sewing-machine, or drawn up by a committee, like resolutions, preceded by a " whereas : " when people are fit to receive it, the condition of society and of art education will be such that the creators of a new style will have been simultaneously produced. One feature of change in style seems usually to escape the observation of those who most sigh for it; which is, that, in all great changes of which we have data, it has been very gradual, — a process of growth, not an alteration of principle, beginning with details, and finally affecting the whole conception. The student may follow out this operation by closely observing the development of Gothic architecture in the thirteenth, fourteenth, and fifteenth centuries; noticing how the enriched mouldings altered one by one, how piercings for windows became clustered in groups, and finally moulded into tracery as the centuries progressed. The same process is visible in the developments of French Renaissance.

The revival of Gothic, with its multitude of subordinate arts, has undoubtedly introduced one sterling feature into modern design, — a desire for reality and an abhorrence of shams; which, whilst it has already banished much of the pretentious rubbish that afflicted industrial art for so long a time previous to that revival, promises even more beautiful work in the not distant future. Some of the best artists of the Pre-Raphaelite School in England have become designers of furniture; and that manufactured by Morris, Marshall, & Co. is sound, honest work, such as might be expected when painters and poets like Rossetti and Marshall are the foremen of the workshop. The revival of the manufacture of Venetian table-glass by Dr. Salviati, in his factory at Venice, is evidence that we are returning to mediævalism in taste and almost every detail. An illustration borrowed from Mr. Eastlake's admirable book, entitled "Hints on Household Taste," will give the reader an opportunity of comparing Dr. Salviati's modern reproductions with original specimens of Venetian glass which may be found in museums. It is frequently said, that, in the one specialty of glass, modern work of the best kinds is superior to ancient examples. In some features, such as geometric regularity, clearness of metal, and accuracy of cutting, modern glass may compare well with any ancient work; but in other features, such as color, chastity of design, variety of form, and use of many tints, it is not to be for a moment compared to glass which has been produced in many art epochs of past ages.

Design, which is a translation of man's thoughts and aspirations and wants into the language of form or color, must of necessity depend very largely upon impressions

28.

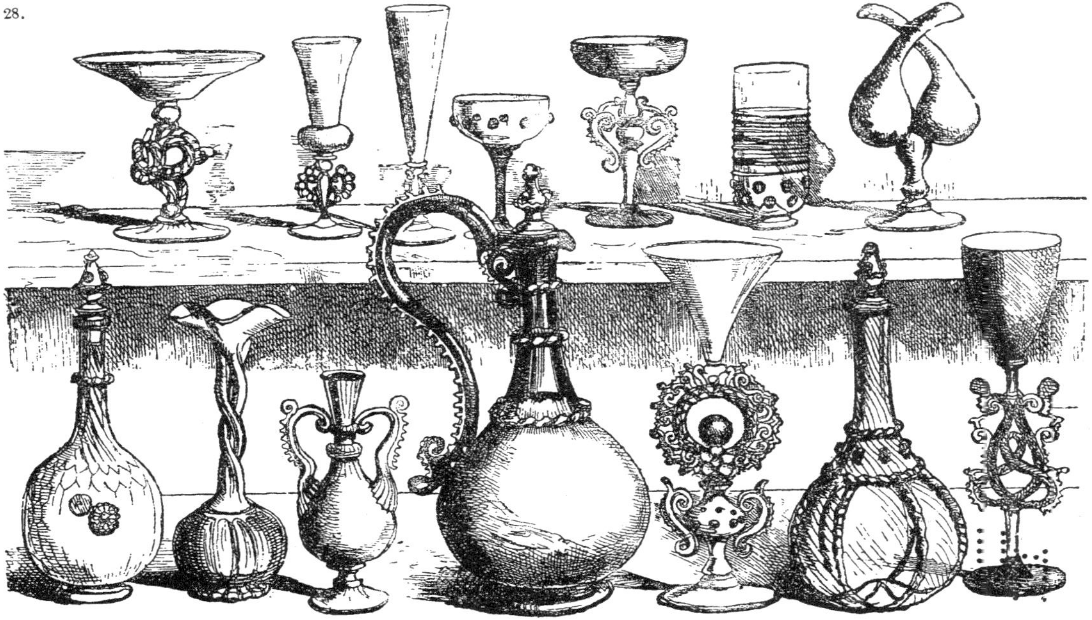

Specimens of Modern Venetian Table-Glass, manufactured by Salviati & Co.

derived from nature, and will be controlled to a certain extent by his powers of expression. The rudeness or conventionality of barbarous art springs probably from undeveloped art powers; and repetition, creating manner, perpetuates imperfections, until, associated in regular sequences, they become accepted as styles. Processes of work, and character of material, will also control the nature of design. A great distinction, however, may be drawn between the conventionality of barbarism and the conventionality of style; the first being the result of immature art power, and the second of mature choice.

The naturalistic in design is the imitation of natural forms, with most of their peculiarities, to create ornamental effects; whilst the conventional treatment adheres to general forms and principles of nature as a motive, omitting unimportant details and individual peculiarities, thus producing a generalization or type-form of ornament based upon first principles.

An imitative natural treatment of design will be found to gratify the tastes of the young and the ignorant, as it does also that of the savage, and the *roué* worn-out taste of a frivolous or luxurious age. Nature, when simply copied as ornament, suggests the incapacity of the designer, as well as his ignorance of historical methods; nature conventionalized is evidence both of knowledge and originality, and in all industrial art will be found adapted to its requirements, and satisfying to the most refined perceptions. In fine art, as distinguished from industrial art, exactly the reverse holds good; conventionality suggesting mannerism and academic stiffness, whilst nature is to be regarded as the direct source and subject of the true artist's work.

The symbolic and æsthetic treatments of ornament are also phases of design which display distinct features; the former being subordinated to or controlled by religion or sentiment, and made to convey its axioms; whilst æsthetic ornament has reference to neither, and attempts to display only its own intrinsic beauty.

Power to design seems to be incommunicable; because in proportion as the motive or inspiration is conveyed from one to another, it results in reproduction rather than originality. The infinite resources of nature in the two directions of form and color, and the laws upon which they are displayed, constitute one portion of the study of design; the application or disregard of those laws in the works of those who have gone before us, so far as we can now ascertain them, is the second part: thus we acquire a knowledge of natural principles and their historical treatment; for the surest foundation of originality is extensive knowledge combined with great executive power and imagination, which, if the necessary creative impulse should seize upon, may result in the conception of original works. The only instruction, therefore, that can be given to the student of design, likely to be of use to him, will be to direct his attention to natural laws and beauties, and to analyze with him the peculiarities of standard examples of good design, — generally accepted specimens which exhibit the qualities of adaptation to purpose, skilfulness of treatment, and a pure imagination.

The existence of much of the bad design we see, when much has been attempted, arises as frequently from the absence of education, as from inherent bad taste. What we want to bring about is a sound and practical art education, which will make, from its comprehension of first principles, intelligent and consistent design possible; and then we may hope that the diffusion of this education generally will cause good design to become a necessity.

The alliance of science and art in the factory and

workshop is of great importance, infusing an intellectual fibre into efforts of the imagination, which they sometimes lack. The harmony of color, a feature of consequence in design for woven or printed fabrics, is, both as regards proportion and hue, as scientific a problem as it is an artistic one; whilst the discovery of new tints, and their chemical effect on each other (both of influence in design), are purely scientific problems, which the designer would be the stronger for comprehending. Some of the loveliest lustres and tints have been discovered in examining microscopically the shells or wings of insects; and quaint colors on manufactured goods, which have startled us sometimes by their originality and novelty, have been copied literally from the glittering armor of a beetle. Scientific knowledge and observation, especially of the animal and vegetable kingdoms, is an excellent preparation for successful designing, to which, if we add skill in drawing and a fertile imagination, we indicate the necessary characteristics of the creative artist. In many places an idea prevails, that, if a man or a woman has not skill or imagination enough to become an artist, it is better to become a designer; in other words, that the weaker vessels of either sex, who cannot pass through the fine-art furnace, should be prepared, as coarser clay at a lower temperature, for the more ignoble occupation of pattern-drawers for the factories. Such a delusion must inevitably result in impoverished and miserable design; and the work so produced contrasts as darkness to light with the conceptions of Durer, Flaxman, or Rossetti. It is from those who fail in art that we get designs originating in the kaleidoscope, and, when that resource fails, imitations of natural leaves or flowers as plucked from the roadside, or arranged to use up a surplus stock of color in the manufacturer's stock-room. Over such designers the enterprising manufacturer rules with a rod of iron; and his monotonous cry is, "Make me something attractive, that will *sell:* never mind about principles;" and thus low taste is perpetuated where once it is in existence.

It is not overstating the case to say that the designer, like the poet or the inventor, needs all the knowledge and all the skill of other men, and a glorious faculty in addition, — creative power; and we know that it is given but to few to possess all the combinations of natural and acquired powers in the proportions which lead up to originality in art, whether it be in poetry, music, painting, sculpture, or architecture. For there are few who can bear the strain of long-continued and constant discipline, which either the love or the ambition of greatness requires from those who are to become creators. Genius has been defined as the union of the desire and the strength to do any amount of work; and it is curious to remember how many men who have achieved the distinction of being considered geniuses seem to have been impelled to labor incessantly, when all ordinary motive for labor as labor had long passed away. We have but to remember, one by one, the master-spirits of every age, and judge them by a common standard, to find that the difference between them and common men is, that they have been "in labors more abundant."

I should not be surprised if some skilful statistician were to prove that the greatest artist had painted the most pictures; the greatest sculptor had modelled the largest number of statues; the greatest poet had written more poems than any other; that the foremost orator had spoken the most frequently; the greatest warrior fought the maximum number of battles; the greatest musical composer had written more pieces than many of his compeers put together; the wealthiest self-made man had worked two hours per diem for the one hour or fifteen minutes occupied in labor of any sort by the majority of human beings: for that would be only supplying a wholesale explanation of phenomena which we see every day happening under our eyes, and in average cases requiring no explanation.

This much we know by experience of the past, — that, to be permanently pleasing, design must be based on principles which are founded upon natural laws, and are therefore unchangeable; that it must generalize its subjects when the work to be performed is simply ornamental and subordinate, rather than as fine art and principal; that it must proceed from a learned and cultivated taste, expressed by matured skill, and cannot result from accidental combinations of vulgar elements imperfectly displayed: moreover, that if, in the final test of judgment, design neither increases the beauty of an object by its construction or its ornament without sacrificing its use, nor adds to the sense of satisfaction either of the cultivated or uncultivated taste, it is immature power wastefully expended upon creating imperfect work, which should have been employed in refining itself from its own grossness, — insuring its own development in some way more profitable to its possessor, and less disagreeable to others, than in permanently recording its own incapacity.

CHAPTER VII.

SURFACE DECORATION.

SURFACE decoration — the covering-up of one material by another to increase the beauty, or entirely to remedy the want of attractiveness in it — is purely a human invention. We have no grounds for supposing that birds and animals are ever influenced by the desire to make their homes beautiful, but rather to construct them well, and make them comfortable. Though acting from natural impulses only, and unconscious of the beautiful nests they build, birds weave sticks and grasses in lovely but strong labyrinths, and line them with soft feathers and hairs, and delicate mosses, that their young may be protected from climatic and other dangers. Strength externally, comfort internally, are the two principles of Nature's architects. Beauty resulting is accident. To create the edifice first, to make it minister to comfort and security secondly, are instincts man shares with many creatures besides his fellow-men; but to add to these instincts another, which does not of necessity spring out of them — viz., that of desiring to secure beauty — is peculiarly human.

I wish it were possible, within the scope of this book, to illustrate, by engravings in color or form, the development of this mental want through the ages and centuries. A subject particularly susceptible of illustration, and not very interesting without, has to be spoken of as a question of abstract principle; and thus I am compelled to call upon your memories, your taste, and your reason, to illustrate the remarks made.

Comparatively a stranger in this country, I am as yet unaware of its resources either in good taste or bad taste; and I should hardly like to engrave a paperhanging or a carpet of villanous design which I had borrowed for the purpose of a man who had it to sell. Imagine my calling upon a highly-respectable firm of dry-goods merchants in Washington Street, and requesting the loan of a few yards of carpets, curtains, furniture covering, and such-like, to illustrate this chapter, and finding, as I don't doubt I should find, a kindly disposition to assist me. Being necessarily interested in the subject of furniture and decoration, one of the heads of the firm is disposed to see what I have to say on the subject, especially as the firm so cheerfully contributed the examples. He reads this chapter, and sees engraved as an illustration the goods he has lent me, and sees, also, I advert to the outrage of good taste in carpets, and refer to an example of execrable design which is illustrated; analyze it, and show how impossible it is for any room to be well furnished which has such a monstrosity in it. All this time my kind friend has been considering the baseness of my conduct in thus betraying his confidence, and wonders also, if I convert the public to my views, what he is going to do with the remaining thousand yards of that pattern, now on sale, at three dollars a yard, in his store on Washington Street. Now, that is the kind of difficulty I should meet with, and cannot very well get over; and so I must appeal to the indulgence of my readers, and tell them, if I sometimes seem abstract and dogmatic in my views, it is for want of the power to convince them by a selection of illustrations, and because I do not want to appear in the character of Judas before those who have treated me with kindness.

A gentleman in London who had never been remarkable for personal beauty — described by his lady-friends as being very plain, and by his male acquaintances as being ugly as sin, and who, as a matter of fact, had been endowed by nature with the physiognomy of a mediæval gargoyle, and had himself contributed to it the expression of a thief — was one day accosted by an artist of eminence, who, though a stranger to him, said that he had been looking out for the gentleman for a long while. "Indeed!" said Mr. Ugly Mug; "and pray for what purpose?" — "I want your head in a picture I am painting," said the artist: "I can't find one to suit me; and some friends of yours have referred me to you, and I now see with what propriety. Your head will just do; and if you will sit to me for a portrait, which I may copy into my picture, the original sketch shall be yours." With the peculiar vanity which, somehow or other, often characterizes plain people as well as others, the gentleman felt flattered, and gave his blushing consent. The sketch was made, copied, and sent home, framed, and hung in the *sanctum sanctorum* of the cockney's house, — his dining-room. And thus the matter would have ended pleasantly for all, if Mrs. Ugly Mug had not one day paid a visit to the Royal-Academy exhibition, where she discovered the faithful portrait of her beloved husband in a large and important picture, playing the part of Judas Iscariot in a subject entitled "The Traitor's Kiss!" Could treachery be better illustrated?

Now, I cannot betray those who would assist me in that way, and therefore I must do without illustrations.

The subject of our consideration is SURFACE DECORATION; and, if I treat it in a superficial manner, you must regard it as consistent with its name.

That innate sense in human beings, to which I have referred, of requiring that not only shall an object be useful, but, as far as it can be made, beautiful also, is perhaps more thoroughly displayed in what may be called surface decoration than in any other form of ornament, because, generally speaking, it is so completely an addition to, and forming no necessary part of, the original purpose of the object ornamented, — a feature added to it to satisfy our craving after the beautiful, just as physically we sometimes yearn for food.

The lowest form of surface ornament is a flat coat of one-colored paint; the highest form, an historical picture. In the same way, the lowest form of sculpture, or relief ornament, is a squared stone; its highest development, an ideal statue.

We may divide the general subject of surface decoration into three classes: —

1st, Material.
2d, Manufacture.
3d, Applied Ornament.

The first comprehends all that vast field of ornament obtained by using only the material as it exists in nature for the purposes of ornament, such as the grain of wood or the color of stone or marble in its dead or polished form. Thus, externally, the contrast of different-colored stones and marble, or encaustic tiles, irrespective of the general design in form, is surface decoration, and in very many respects the most honest and faithful of all the resources of ornament. The beautiful color of several varieties of building-stone as well as marble, to be obtained in America, and its use on some important private buildings, has been productive of a thoroughly-satisfactory effect. Without referring to the question of style in architectural design, I would mention the new hotel at the corner of Boylston and Tremont Streets, and the new house of Mr. Brimmer in Beacon Street, both in Boston, as illustrations of the use of several colors in external construction, and to express a hope that the experiment may be persevered with; for it is one way of solving the problem of how to get color externally which shall be permanent.

On the other hand, the practice of veneering, with marble fronts, houses which are built of brick or wood, is a detestable sham, which all honest men should avoid, as they would a forged check or a spurious greenback.

There is no sound constructiveness in such work, and oftentimes it makes good construction difficult, if not impossible; so that it is both a sham and a peculiarly-dishonest sham.

Veneering of any sort is a make-believe, shuffling sort of transaction, — a thick-skinned layer of respectability covering the carcass of a rogue, — and is about as appropriate as the wig and gown of a lord chief-justice would be on the body of a London pickpocket.

Now, we find on examination that the works of God are not so built up. They are good throughout, from the skin to the marrow; not surface and sham, but solid, like that grand American expression, the most hopeful sign in the language, "right through," which expresses a valuable form of mind and an honest determination of purpose.

Any one who has seen the inside of a church, not rough built and then plastered, but built as carefully internally as externally, with the natural color of the stone showing as well as the joints, especially if the stone be sandstone or red granite, will remember how beautiful the effect is, — how incomparably superior to paint and plaster, — and what a feeling of reality and comely truthfulness is engendered in the mind of the spectator. I believe that in public buildings the age of whitewash and plaster is passing away, and that the material, whether brick, stone, or marble, will be left to form the background of any added sculpture or painted decoration.

I have found that in one specialty there is more good taste shown in America than in any country I have yet visited; and it comes under the head of the use of material in surface decoration. I refer to the preservation of woodwork from paint or stain, displaying the natural grain of the wood in its native color. That is a thoroughly satisfactory way of using a constructive as a decorative agent, true in principle, and more ornamental than any method of disguising it by paint or dye for decorative purposes.

The extreme beauty in the grain, variety in color and appearance, of American woods, points to an unlimited field of ornamental treatment, — combinations in which harmony shall be obtained by judicious associations of different-colored woods, and variety displayed in the contrast of their grain growth.

Whatever scientific process may be necessary for the preservation of wood may be resorted to without destroying its beauty, such as saturating it with gelatine, or varnishing it; but to conceal its lovely grain or destroy its natural color by a coarse veneering of metallic paint, is a desecration.

These sources of ornament only apply to materials which are either valuable or beautiful; and one feature does not seem to me to be sufficiently appreciated, viz., the effect produced by the contrast of dead and polished surfaces in the same material. This is noticeable especially in granite and marble, but may be also used with effect in woodwork. I am gratified to see that wainscoting in oak and walnut is used so much as it is, and becoming popular, both because it makes an excellent background for pictures and other art works, and is a handsome, durable method of covering a wall. Parquetting, or inlaying of wood in ornamental patterns for flooring, is another adaptation of wood, not apparently so general as wainscoting, but essentially legitimate and effective as a means of decoration. It should accompany wainscoting to make a room complete in one feature.

2. Manufacture. — The next kind of surface decoration is that made by the process of manufacture, in which the features of make are displayed; as in weaving in one color, lace-making, mat and basket making, and embroidery.

In this class, design becomes most apparent; for here is no addition of ornament, — the distinction being that *design* includes the whole art character of the object constructed as part of the idea; whilst *ornament* only is something applied to it after construction, to increase its beauty.

The amount of ornamental arrangement of which such processes as mat and basket making are susceptible is very slight; but their constructional features are capable of very great variety. The aim is not high; for, in order of development, this class of work comes next in progress to the display of the natural characteristics of the material, in which neither design nor ornament enters at all, except by selection and juxtaposition of different colors and forms. Nevertheless, so coarse a material as wooden chips or twigs, or grass, may be made, and is made, the vehicle of much refined taste; and, where too much is not attempted, there will be found beautiful effects produced. As a branch of industry of an essentially useful kind, which has not yet had the benefit of much art influence, I regard it as capable of great development, and believe, if some education in art were given to those engaged upon the process, new combinations, especially pleasing, would be originated. Among the many treacherous shams to which the progress of inventiveness has introduced us, this unimportant little industry has retained its honesty and its noble simplicity.

Very similar in their essential character are the two more important subjects of muslin and lace making, each deriving its peculiar ornamentation from the mode of manufacture; but from their more general use, and the far higher purposes to which they are applied, they have absorbed at all times some of the highest skill in design. It may also be said that lace and muslin manufactures have been made the vehicle of much of the very worst and most atrocious taste in design.

I dare not trust myself to enter into the subject of hand-made lace: it is too attractive to me, and capable of such a lengthy and interesting treatment, that I must avoid it, — confining myself to machine-made lace in the form of curtains and garments.

Lace is said to have originated by withdrawing certain threads in regular order from a piece of linen, and then stitching the remaining threads together. All lace, at first, was made by hand, and worked with the needle; and the different points — as point d'Alençon, Venetian, Honiton, and Irish point — have been preserved to this day in the localities which originally produced them; but their peculiarities have been so successfully caught and expressed by machinery, that, at the present time, one of the most beautiful branches of art manufacture is lace-making. If the origination of the process be borne in mind, and that an opaque linen surface was perforated by the withdrawal of part of the fabric, leaving also a part remaining, it will be seen that the first element of lace is semi-transparency; at first, of regular-shaped omissions of material, and secondly, in the conversion of the remaining material into definite forms in one color; so that, while the only art treatment of which it is capable is the contrast of open spaces with masses of closed stitches, the process of manufacture under skilful designers has been made to express very lovely combinations of forms. Curves can only be indicated by little square notches, each the size of a stitch; but that does not limit the direction, nor mar the proportion, of the curves expressed.

The most *general* use to which lace is put is that of curtains, and in this the best and worst taste is displayed. A material which hangs in folds, and part of whose ornamentation must therefore necessarily be hidden, ought to be so designed that no important portion of its ornamental treatment shall be thus concealed. That seems obvious: yet many designs for lace curtains are composed of huge and barbarous scrolls, squandered irregularly over the surface as if by accident, half hidden by the drapery in which the curtain hangs; immense and vulgar bouquets of flowers, in which not only the unsymmetrical natural flower is closely copied, but attempts at shading are made by relying on the curtain having a dark background, and making the parts requiring shadow to be more open than the rest. All such work is a gross outrage upon the material, and a labored effort after something which is meretricious and unattainable. It is manifest that a geometrically-constructed fabric should have, as a basis of ornamentation, forms which can be expressed geometrically without much injury to their distinctness. Also, that when clearness or semi-transparency is required as a quality in the character of the manufactured article, designs which very much cover the surface, and destroy the transparency, are not adapted. The best designs for curtains are those which consist largely of an enriched border, founded on some light and graceful natural foliage forms, in which the outline is characteristic; the body of the curtain being slightly powdered over with some detail of the plant used, such as a conventional treatment of the flower or bud of the subject which forms the border. I need hardly say, that in this branch of surface decoration, and indeed of all ornamentation, nature should be adapted to the purposes and requirements of art, not copied literally; for attempts at copying nature by the clumsiness of any manufacturing process must inevitably end in failure, whilst the decorative character of the work is thereby limited and destroyed: a chaste conventionality, which displays all the prime characteristics of the form chosen, is more satisfying to the refined perception, and results in a purer ornamental effect. One of the most beautiful features of hand-made lace, the snow-point, — imitated from the lovely form of snow-crystals, — has seldom been attempted in machine-made lace; yet considering the whiteness of lace, its suggestiveness of coolness, the geometrical forms of snow-crystals would be excellently adapted for imitation, on account of their great intrinsic beauty, boundless variety, and suitability both in shape to the manufacture and similarity in color to the material used. If we could look from our heated summer apartments, through the gauzy fleeciness of white snow-crystals, to the blazing outside atmosphere, it would be suggestive of arctic luxuries at a time when melting moments most afflict us.

Thus a recognition of the nature of the material in which lace is wrought, and the adaptation of the treatment to suit it, would achieve more satisfactory results than any effort to ignore or supersede the exigencies of manufacture. I have spoken more fully of lace as an element of refinement than I should have done, because its extreme beauty seems to me to be overlooked. It is one of the few subjects susceptible of the highest decorative treatment, without losing its utilitarian character, and, whether in furniture or garments, is a sign of refinement and elegance. In the most sacred offices of the Church and the most exalted secular ceremonials of past ages, lace and embroidery have been prominent as elements of enrichment; and for my part I should be glad to see the revival of the demand for hand-made lace, which cannot be produced by machinery, and for machine-made lace of the highest class which can be so produced; for the two kinds are quite distinct in their character, and appeal to a different range of sympathies. There is the same sort of feeling about a piece of hand-made lace as there is in the manuscript of an author; whilst about machine-made work we have that sort of affection that we feel for a good edition of his works. I have seen an altar draped in lace, which was made by titled English ladies during years of leisure more than a hundred years ago, and regarded it as the converse of the proposition, "the evil that men do lives after them, the good is oft interred with their bones;" for there the pious labor that women had engaged in lived after them; whilst the evil they had been guilty of has long since smouldered with their bones.

In this age of rapid life, almost insect life, which is gay and thoughtless, in which men seldom care to pay onwards to posterity the good they have received from their ancestry, any transmission of refinement, whether in thoughts or tangible things, is a virtue. We ought to encourage the use of leisure, which is a bequest from our forefathers, or a present from our friends, in useful, permanent work, which shall transmit our best qualities to posterity, and save for them our arts.

Among the several kinds of surface decoration must be classed the art of embroidery, by needlework, — such as the tapestry of old, and the working of altar-cloths and of rich garments, whether sacred or secular. That was work for women of leisure, and had all the true characteristics of good art workmanship: it was skilful, intellectual, and permanent. Which means that it required training and education, employed the mind as well as the hand, and was an honest thing, made to last when it was done; and was handsome, useful, and beautiful into the bargain, — mental and physical labor judiciously expended and invested.

I am not able to state from my own experience whether there are any people of leisure now; because, though I am constantly told by all those with whom I come in contact, that they "have just twice as much to do as they can possibly get through," I never have yet found the happy individual who was languishing for an occupation, unless his bread depended upon it and it couldn't be found. Nevertheless, I notice in this country, as in the old one, periodical attacks of social inflammation of a benevolent sort, which breaks out into eruptions, called "Fairs." That is the outward and visible sign of there being leisure somewhere in the past; and, as fairs are hereditary affections, it points in the direction of there being leisure now, and likely to come in the future. The great argument in support of fairs is, that they furnish a benevolent occupation for those who cannot give money to good objects, but can give time; and, therefore, working for a stall is a practical solution of how to make the best of both worlds. Assuming, then, from external evidence, that the piles of objects on the stalls of a fair represent so much leisure time, occupied for good purposes, — the product of busy and delicate fingers actuated by kind and generous hearts, —

I would ask whether the kind of way in which the labor is expended, and the sort of objects which most commonly are produced, fairly represent what should be the skill, taste, and knowledge of the educated feminine leisure of the nineteenth century, and is to be the final expression of its powers.

I know that I am treading on very delicate ground, and do not wish to reach forth my unhallowed hand to touch this ark of the covenant unadvisedly, or rashly to interfere with this sacred privilege of female solitude and leisure; and were it not that the ground is somewhat familiar to me, and that I have modestly touched this ark before, and yet live, I would not dare to venture on either asking a question about it or making a suggestion thereon.

But I will ask whether it might not be possible for some leisure to be spent on work which will outlive its authors, and be utterly noble exercise for all the faculties which have been conferred on a human being.

Would it not be equally interesting as an amusement, and valuable as an investment, if such subjects as water-color painting, and good wholesome embroidery, be undertaken by ladies in their leisure, both in their ways noble surface decoration, instead of what is usually done for fairs? I would say that the Bayeux tapestry is a more creditable and valuable production than the ephemeral work of modern days. The Berlin-wool patterns, the knitting, netting, tatting, and crocheting of this age, are not worthy of the serious attention of accomplished women, and I believe they are less practised here than elsewhere; but I want to see them replaced entirely by work of a character higher artistically and more durable, and in the best sense useful. Art work, intended for useful purposes, and embarked upon a material which will be easily destroyed or rapidly wear out, is waste of life. Two kinds of needlework appear to me to be equally noble, — plain work for a righteous purpose, such as making clothing for the poor or afflicted; and the most elaborate embroidery or lace work, made with the object of draping the walls of a sanctuary or a hall of justice, to tell the story of great deeds, and to encourage, by enshrining, the qualities of morality and patriotism. Both of these are like the box of precious ointment, not wasted but consecrated, by the use to which they are applied.

The terrible tendency in these latter days is, that we are becoming like the machines we have invented, — fast, thoughtless, and monotonous. Year by year our labor becomes less original in its individual character, and hand-work is being supplanted by machine-work. Successful imitation is a current coin: original production is as scarce as spade-guineas or twenty-dollar pieces, which we hang on our watchguards or frame as a picture to show our children what those ancient gentlemen, our forefathers, did in the way of money.

Any kind of original hand-work, not made in dozens or supplied by the gross, is a comfort now; and even the children of past ages may teach us a lesson in this respect in the matter of needlework.

There used to be, and I hope will be again, an old-fashioned method of embroidery practised in the agricultural districts of England, as both an education and recreation of small female fingers, and which, sooner or later, every germinating lady of twelve years or thereabouts had to go through. It was called "*making a sampler.*" Now, a sampler was a compound production; getting its name, I suspect, from its containing samples, or ensamples, of many things. In size it varied from nine inches square to twenty-four inches square. It was worked by the needle with different-colored cottons, or threads, on a groundwork of linen or cotton or canvas. The subjects worked varied, but always included the alphabet and the numerals, often in capital and small letters; and the explanation of their *raison d'etre*, given to me by an aged dame in a wayside village-school, whose spectacled eyes were dim, and whose fingers were horny, was, that such practice was necessary "for every female to enable her to mark clothes and table-linen." But that was not the whole scope of the sampler. The occasion was seized to achieve great triumphs in embroidery: for the alphabet and nine figures only took up a small portion of the surface; and the rest was adorned by illustrated stories, or imitations of many created things, — sometimes, I am bound to say, without serious outrage of that commandment which says, "Thou shalt not make unto thee any likeness of any thing that is in heaven above, or that is in the earth beneath, or that is in the water under the earth."

Yet the work was good, honest, and especially permanent work; for in an English national exhibition I have seen samplers with dates on, showing them to have been done two hundred years ago. There was generally a handsome border made up of zigzag lines, — Greek frets, and scrolls and leaves, — often of extreme beauty, and always of excellent workmanship; but the greatest triumph of all was in the story which the figures represented. There would be the taking of the animals into the ark by Noah, which was a great effort. Side by side and two by two, they walked in procession from the wilderness at the bottom of the sampler — represented by three triangular trees — to the ark at the top, — indicated by a box about as large as one of the elephants who were going into it, at the side of which stood Noah, as master of the ceremonies, bowing in a couple of lions. And the delicious grotesqueness of those spotted leopards, having about nine spots between them; the Egyptian simplicity of those apocalyptic sheep, with rectangular bodies, and passionate-looking, independent tails; and the general delight and profusion which appeared everywhere, — made a beautiful exhibition of rural simplicity and attainments.

Perhaps in another would be put an apotheosis of Adam and Eve in paradise, before the fatal apple was eaten, and the serpent was still on his best behavior, — our first parents sitting side by side on a bank of primroses, hand in hand, looking, as well as black-stitched eyes would allow them, at their prosperous row of beehives in front, or their stores of double Gloster cheeses behind, or the donkey and cart with groceries from the nearest market-town, which the farm-servant had just brought home! That was the ideal of rural felicity; and great was the occasion upon which Mary Ann or Keziah brought home her year's work in a complete form upon the sampler, — to be preserved, and form part of the furniture of her future home. I have seen, hanging side by side together, the needlework samplers of four generations of women, related as mother and child; and, though such features as I have mentioned were very ludicrous and amusing, the workmanship was excellent, and a charming record of childish experience and history. I am not ashamed to confess that I love samplers, because all of them represent the best work of individuals at an age when they were simply delightful people; because there is, as a rule, only one of a sort in the world, and therefore they never are vulgarized by repetition; but, most of all, because samplers were educational: they taught the child to use the needle skilfully for the purpose of enabling each wife to stamp in a permanent manner her household treasures, and gave her, whilst yet of tender age, some knowledge of the elements of art and skilled workmanship; and they expressed the feeling of the ages in which they were executed.

Yet, whilst I advocate the use of the needle as a noble means of surface decoration, I do not wish to over-estimate it. Cases have come to my knowledge of such work monopolizing time which should have been given to the necessities of general education; and one, which is particularly ludicrous, I will relate, occurring in that ancient little Island of Great Britain, which I may be excused for loving. A friend of mine, who, from his distinction at the University of Oxford, was appointed an inspector of schools by the government of the day, had to examine each pupil in his district in those elevating subjects of a comprehensive education, — the three R's, as a member of the school committee described it: Reading, Riting, and Rithmetic. He was inspecting a rural school on the moors of Yorkshire, which are the prairies in miniature of a kingdom which would be lost in one of our prairies; and, taking the head class, had got nearly to the bottom of it, when the next candidate was a big, healthy-looking, strapping, rustic lass, who stood a whole head and shoulders above the rest of the class. My friend asked her to read a passage in the text-book; but she smilingly informed him "she didn't read."

"Will you then kindly write a sentence from my dictation?" asked the inspector.

"Oh, no, sir!" was the reply: "I can't write."

"Not write!" exclaimed her Majesty's representative: "then you can possibly work me a sum in simple addition; for your talents must be mathematical, — you must be absorbed in figures."

"Oh, no, sir! I know nothing about figures."

That was a poser; but, coming up fresh and smiling to the intellectual combat, my friend suggested, —

"As I do not seem to have mentioned your peculiarly-strong points, perhaps you will now kindly inform me what you *can* do."

"Oh, yes, sir!" was the reply; and, dropping a courtesy, she said, "Please, sir, *I can crochet Moses!*"

"Crochet Moses! What on earth does that mean?" asked the inspector.

Whereupon a Berlin-wool picture of Moses striking the rock was produced, in which was a flood of lamb's-wool water rushing out to comfort the thirsty Israelite multitude, which the rustic lass had executed by years of toil; and which having accomplished, her education was complete in her own eyes.

Now, I don't want people to crochet Moses, or to crochet at all; but I do want to see the accomplished ladies who happily possess leisure invest some of it in the most beautiful and most permanent of all feminine accomplishments, — lace-making by hand, and embroidery.

Properly, I should here speak of damasks and carpets, as being woven, but will omit them in their natural order to class them in the group of applied ornament; previous to which I will enumerate some of the general principles of ornamentation applied to flat surfaces.

The first and most important is that which requires modesty and subordination in all ornament covering an even or level surface. It may possibly detract from the luxurious profusion of a saloon to banish from it all the elaborate bouquets of flowers on the carpets, or the birds of paradise which are disporting themselves on the walls or the furniture; but their presence is inconsistent with the first approach to good taste.

I have seen with satisfaction how frequently apartments are painted in one color here, rather than papered; for it is safer to trust to one color than many; but the almost universal custom of dividing the room into panels gives the decorator the opportunity of spoiling the whole effect by efforts at relief and roundness, and the addition of shaded ornament, which kills all the furniture, and, by bringing the walls forward, decreases, apparently, the size of the room. The same effect of decreasing the size of a room is frequently produced by a carpet having a large pattern, which dwarfs the furniture and destroys the sense of repose. The color of a carpet is also of the greatest importance; for if, as I see is almost general in richly-furnished houses, the carpet is very light in color, harmonious combination of general effect is an impossibility.

In furnishing a room, as much skill may be displayed as in the composition of a picture: indeed, they are precisely the same things. The first task is to produce an agreeable combination of colors, to keep all the details in their proper proportion as to size, and to make them consistent in their style. The figures in the pictures are the human beings who inhabit the rooms. And there is the same opportunity given of producing an effect in any special direction, and making definite impressions on the mind. Thus the library or study may, by its sobriety of tint and quietness in arrangement, suggest and induce repose of sensation; whilst it encourages activity of the mental faculties; and the reception-rooms, by their brightness and cheerfulness, may display the qualities of welcome and geniality.

The position of a surface is suggestive of the treatment of its ornamentation. Thus a floor or a ceiling is a horizontal plane, and the ornamentation should neither proceed from right to left nor cross-wise in any direction, but be what is termed an "all over" pattern, covering the surface without leading the eye away from any point. A wall, on the contrary, is a vertical plane, and there the decoration may be vertical; that is, tending upwards, on the principle of the growth of plants.

In all subordinate ornamentation, symmetry and conventionality are essential; and great variety is by no means necessary for producing a pleasing effect. In the best periods of ornament, the actual variety of forms has been slight. Thus, in Greek art, the acanthus, echinus, anthemion, the fret and guilloche, were the only important rudimentary ornaments; and these were repeated and perfected until they became types of beauty.

It is the secret of using colors of a negative character which makes Turkey carpets the most satisfactory to the refined taste; and, again, it is the conventionality of ornament in Indian goods that makes them deservedly popular, — without the reason for this liking always being recognized. On the other hand, Chinese ornament, which endeavors, as nearly as possible, to imitate nature, has never been accepted by ornamentists as any thing but rude and barbarous, except where local tradition has preserved a style of decoration that has been either excellent in its simplicity, or associated with some valuable scientific process of manufacture.

3. Applied Ornament. — I now come to the third class of surface decoration, and will endeavor to define the true position of the carpet and paper-hanging under this head.

Of Carpets. — A carpet should be always chosen as a background, upon which the other articles of furniture are to be placed, and should, from its sober colors and unattractive features, have a tendency rather to improve by comparison objects placed upon it, than command for itself the notice of the spectator. It should vie with nothing, but rather give value to all objects coming in contact with it. Composed of sombre shades and tones, and treated essentially as a *flat* surface, it exerts a most valuable, though subordinate influence upon all the other decorations of the room. Upon it the eye rests whilst surveying the more important furniture; and its presence, properly treated, supplies the necessary material for a satisfactory contrast with other portions of the decoration, which comparison in no wise detracts from its own peculiar degree of merit, but proves, from this circumstance, how valuable it is as contributing to the pleasing effect of the whole apartment.

Of paper and other hangings, Mr. Redgrave has so clearly expressed the uses, that I quote his remarks: —

"If the use of such materials is borne in mind, the proper decoration for them will at once be evident, since this ought to bear the same relation to the objects in the room that a background does to a picture. In art, a background, if well designed, has its own distinctive features; yet these are to be so far suppressed and subdued as not to invite especial attention; while, as a whole, it ought to be entirely subservient to supporting and enchancing the principal figures, — the subject of the picture. The decoration of a wall, if designed on good principles, has a like office: it is a background to the furniture, the objects of art, and the occupants of the apartment. It may enrich the general effect, and add to magnificence, or be made to lighten or deepen the character of the chamber; it may appear to temper the heat of summer, or to give a sense of warmth and comfort to the winter; it may have the effect of increasing the size of a saloon, or of closing in the walls of a library or study, — all which, by a due adaptation of color, can be easily accomplished. But like the background to which it has been compared, although its ornament may have a distinctive character for any of these purposes, it must be subdued, and uncontrasted in light and shade: strictly speaking, it should be flat and conventionalized, and lines or forms harsh or cutting on the ground as far as possible avoided, except where necessary to give expression to the ornamentation." "Well-considered design, thoroughly adapted for the process of printing by machinery, would enable the manufacturer to unite good taste with extreme cheapness; whereas the only present result is, by increased labor, to detract from the beauty of the ornamentation."

All designs which have a tendency to divide the flat surface of a wall-paper into distinct compartments, or have colors so distributed that they attract the eye at intervals; all designs which cut sharply from the ground, and exhibit the ornamentation in strong contrast to that which it is upon, or by a combination of several tints of the same color appear to relieve the ornament from its background, — are false in principle, and deficient in the simplicity which should characterize this branch of decoration. An evenness of effect must be the *sine qua non* of a material which is to cover a surface, that, if it were otherwise than flat, would not be tolerated.

As a rule, all imitations, in whatever material, of a totally different surface from that which characterizes the material itself, are false. It seems a wonderful instance of misdirected talent, that, whilst the art of the engraver has attained the perfection it has, so many young ladies should perseveringly waste their time in attempting to delineate a minute face, full of expression, on a surface which is totally unfit for the reception of a design having any pretension to graceful curves or delicate light or shade.

Vice versa, this peculiarity of Berlin wool is transferred with the greatest nicety to block-printing for paper-hangings, the smoother surface of which renders it capable of receiving the most elegant curves, and the most delicate tints. The very fact of a manufacture attempting to pass muster as something different to what it really is, should condemn it. The fact of an object being a great deal too good for its use should condemn it. Every object in a room may be good in its degree, but it should not attempt to be of more importance than its degree warrants. Supposing the occupants of an apartment to be of primary consideration, as every thing else is for their gratification, then works of high art take the precedency.

Nothing should be more attractive than that which precedes it in importance; and, for this reason, life-size figures, either in painting or sculpture, are out of place in a constantly-occupied apartment: the next degree is taken by the movable furniture; and last of all comes the background on the wall or floor.

It is an axiom in art, that the higher forms should be added to the lower, and neither can be regarded as a substitute for the other, and that the higher forms are out of place unless preceded by the more elementary. It is so in civilization. The hunter's life precedes the agricultural life, the manufacturing epoch succeeds to the agricultural; just as the earth cavern develops into the tent, the hut or tent into the house, the house into the village, the village into the city. But, for human happiness, each should be sterling and consistent, — the honest expression of men's wants, and not aping the characteristics of the other. Progressive development is a delightful study, and is as true in art as in all other honest things. The influence of consistency in decoration and ornament on the sensations, and their mental effect, is not to be ignored or treated as a thing of no consequence.

If it is true that a man may be known by the company he keeps, it is equally true that he may be judged by the books he reads, and the objects which, of his own free-will, and having the means to do as he likes, he surrounds himself by. Of the effect on men's minds of good or bad pictures, there can be no doubt; and the same principle holds good of refined or vulgar ornamentation. The limit which controls the application of this principle is that of means. Taste often outruns a man's means; perhaps as often as that with some people the reverse is true, and that money is the substitute for taste. Still the rough material of even the humble cottage may be made influential for refinement and comfort. There may be as much taste displayed in the appointments of the poor room as in those of a wealthy mansion, each being suitable to the requirements of the possessors; for quantity is unimportant as an element in taste. The evil tendency is, when people can't afford pictures or engravings of works of art, they try to combine their want for something of the kind with the necessity of having their rooms papered; and that spoils both. Art cannot be manufactured; and, if a man cannot afford good pictures, let him be content with a background for them. Machinery and block-printing are incapable of producing good works of art; and any one with even a decent perception of the beautiful will soon tire of bad ones, though their pernicious effect will have depraved his taste and corrupted his power of judgment.

If a man is unable to provide himself with pictures and engravings of the noblest subjects, or portraits of eminent men, distinguished for virtue or patriotism, to be a delight and comfort to him, — if that be impossible, he needn't hang up the likenesses of murderers to lower the tone of his mind or suggest bad thoughts. And so, if richness of decoration be beyond a man's means, simplicity and absence of any meretricious efforts may protect him from outrage to his taste.

A poor man of great taste and eminence was once visited in a house whose bare walls seemed to attract the attention of his visitor. "How is it," he was asked, "that you don't make your rooms more attractive by hanging up a few pictures, or, at any rate, have the walls papered with some lively pattern having nice colored representations on it?" The answer was quick and exhaustive: "I can't afford good works of art, and there's no act of parliament to compel me to have bad ones. As for papers with pictures on them, sixpence a yard for art doesn't fit my taste; and I have done nothing to deserve them as a punishment."

I was once informed of the utter misery inflicted unintentionally upon a man whose life was as valuable to society as to himself, by the presence in a sick-room of a wall-paper which had certain prominent red spots upon it, appearing at intervals in the pattern. He was just past the climax of a typhoid fever, and had arrived at that stage when the mind, not yet in full possession of the exhausted body, conjures up delusions, — an almost inseparable stage in recovery from such a malady, and so critical a time, that any relapse, through excitement or other causes, is almost certain to end fatally. Before the mind was capable of consecutive thought, like that of the child just strong enough to receive impressions only, the patient opened his eyes to perceive on all sides a fiery red eye gazing on him from the walls of the room. That took the form of a delusion, and his semi-delirious efforts to hide these dreadful eyes from his sight almost brought on the fatal relapse. Curtains were hung closely round him, though neither the doctor nor nurses were suspicious of the cause of his delusion. His convalescence was then rapid; but, before he became sufficiently conscious to speak collectedly, the curtains were removed, and then the red balls tortured him in another form. Do what he would, he could not help counting them from floor to ceiling, from one wall to another, casting up the figures mentally, adding and subtracting, without power to control himself, until he was almost in a worse fever than ever; until at last he was sensible enough to beg that he might be taken to a room where there was no paper at all, and then found repose and comfort. The tortures he felt during that time, he said, were indescribable; and his grief was, that he had not strength enough nor clearness of head enough to explain what it was that afflicted him.

Now, that is a true story of the effects of bad art on a sensitive, irritated condition of the body, brought on by exhaustion and prostration; yet it shows what effect a villanous, bad design is capable of producing upon a sensitive mind. I have suffered from the very same cause, and known many others who have also been thus distressed, and have no doubt that, either consciously or unconsciously, it affects every one.

Good ornamental art, fitness, and consistency in that which surrounds us, is like a pleasant melody if simple, and like a chorus of delightful harmony if elaborate: bad art — the ignorant jumbling together of inconsistent elements, or the heaping up of vulgar ostentation — is like a sonorous rhapsody which has neither time nor tune; or like the jangle of sounds produced when all the notes of a piano are struck by one violent blow. It has been said, that "a thing of beauty is a joy forever." And one of the very greatest blessings that can happen to a human being is to have the eyes opened to a perception of beauty. The man who looks at the forest, and sees only lumber, is a poorer man and a less joyous man than he who sees in all things the marvellous beauties of nature, and in a tree the manifestation of almighty power. We may, and often do, degrade things to an earthy level, and live and die without having felt a communion with spiritual laws by our understanding of the beautiful.

I claim for art the position of an element in all education for the increase of human happiness. We know what was said by the poet of mankind concerning music: "The man that hath no music in himself, nor is not moved with concord of sweet sounds, is fit for treasons, stratagems, and spoils: let no such man be trusted."

Rather hard on the unmusical; though, as an old chorister, I can say, that there are very few human beings who answer to the description of not having music in their souls. And if any one doubts it, and wishes to form an opinion, I would ask him to go to any of the primary schools in the city of Boston, and ask the teachers to allow the little scholars to sing some simple melody they have been taught. Let him, if his ear be trained, listen if there be any harsh or discordant sounds, not in the tune, evolved from the little throats, and then see if any lips be closed. If he finds what I have found, he will notice that all sing, and hear no discord, and see no dumb lips. Training has developed the "music in the soul," and education done its faithful duty.

Now, what education has accomplished for music, let us hope to see done for form and color. There are those who love and understand both subjects, who believe that the "music in the soul" produced by art knowledge is a source of as much delight as the melody and harmony of sound.

And we cannot insure the appreciation of art until we make all of its developments pure and chaste. It will be of little avail to build galleries and establish academies, unless they are made to affect the character of popular art in every phase of its use. Pure art never existed side by side with corrupt and vulgar ornament, any more than pure religion consists of very much faith and very indifferent works. Life, if it exists at all, permeates the whole body, brain, blood, bones, marrow; it cannot carry about a dead limb, but shakes it off: so art which exists for the polite and well-dressed, and does not reach to the humble folks clad in fustian, is an art afflicted by paralysis, — a diseased and unnatural condition, to be pitied perhaps, but not imitated nor prolonged. Let us hope, that in the fair field there is before us, which has so early recognized the value and blessings of education, no human faculties will be ignored, no possible human attainments will be neglected, no sources of human happiness will be closed; but that the chief corner-stone of our liberties, inscribed with the words, "All men are born free and equal," shall mean for us, not only freedom from oppression, but freedom from ignorance; not only equality with ourselves, but equality with the best people of the best periods of the world's history; and that, if the corner-stone in the foundation does not express this, the keystone of American progress shall attain unto it.

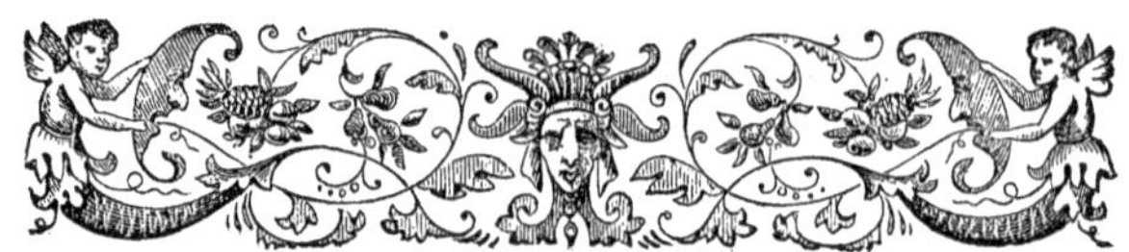

CHAPTER VIII.

RELIEF ORNAMENT, — MODELLING AND CARVING. POTTERY, GLASS, AND TERRA-COTTA.

RELIEF ornament — modelling and carving, working in solid material in imitation of form only, just as surface decoration attempts, by reproduction of outline and color upon a flat surface, to convey the ornamental character of a subject in outline and color, without relying on its roundness — is one of the most important branches of industrial art.

Relief ornament — i.e., ornamental forms relieved or raised from the surface they are upon — is the application of sculpture to industrial purposes, in the same way that surface or flat ornament is the industrial application of the fine art, painting.

In many respects, industrial sculpture is of greater influence and of more importance than ornamental painting; for it is less possible to reproduce it by mechanical means. Many and persevering have been the efforts to invent a carving-machine, which should do for wood and stone what block-printing and chromo-lithography have done for surface decoration. But the man has not yet been born who has succeeded in doing that; and we shall have to wait a little longer before he comes: if by some oversight he should never come at all, it will be a great blessing to mankind.

Attempts have been made to carve by machinery, and certain rough effects have been produced: thus the outline and actual relief of a scroll of wood-work can be obtained in duplicate, after the first model has been made, by a machine now in use in London, and which I have seen in operation, worked somewhat in this manner: —

A panel of ornament is placed flat on its back, and, in a corresponding position near it is placed a solid wood block, in exactly the same plane as to its upper surface as the highest point in the ornament. Two pointed steel pencils — one fixed, and the other gouge-shaped, and revolving by steam-power — are placed parallel to each other. The fixed pencil is held by the operator, who begins by pressing it down to the surface of part of the carving; and the revolving pencil, which acts in perfect sympathy with that which is handled by the operator, descends or ascends, or moves to the right and left, according to the movements of the operator. This revolving pencil is placed over the wood block to be carved, and is, in fact, a very fine cutter; so that, as it traverses the wood block, it removes the material, and leaves what is left on the original carving, over which its twin point in the hands of the operator has been travelling.

Mouldings and unimportant details might thus be reproduced; but the work would always have to be finished by hand.

Another mode of obtaining the effect of carved wood-work was, by making a metal mould red-hot, and impressing it on oak, or other hard wood, charring the material, so that it left the impress of the mould on the panel. That was at one time used to produce book-covers, and resulted in somewhat handsome effects. But practical difficulties prevented its general adoption, and it was a short-lived experiment. It is, in fact, an impossibility to produce the highest forms of sculptured art by mechanical processes; and thus, as a rule, there is more originality in sculpture and carving than in flat ornamentation.

Stone-carving cannot well be accomplished, even in that imperfect way, owing to the more brittle character of the material, which would chip and fracture, where the grain and tenacity of fibre in wood would preserve it from so doing when hard wood was used.

So that there is more originality and handwork in modern relief ornament than in its sister industry, surface ornament; in this respect, more like the same work in the best periods of art, whether Greek, Roman, Gothic, or Renaissance.

Men were sculptors before they were painters. The mud-houses and unbaked clay blocks with which habitations were built in the earliest ages were infant attempts at modelling in clay, much as the cherished dirt-pie of our more innocent days betrayed our love for elementary sculpture.

The stone and the wood used in the construction of huts gave birth to the parent art of architecture when civilization began to dawn upon barbarous races, and men's instincts required something permanent with which to shelter their bodies; when, in fact, there developed a desire for a home, and its centre, the hearthstone: then, when stones were squared, and timber was hewn, Sculpture, or the art of cutting, was added to the human accomplishments.

Afterwards, colored earths or dyes were rubbed over the naked bodies, the walls of the habitations, and the weapons for the chase; and thus Painting came to the help of its elder sisters, Sculpture and Architecture, and the arts were born.

The processes of reproduction of solid forms are, of course, as numerous as for the repetition of flat ornament by the use of plastic material, such as plaster of Paris, cement, clay, metal, and glass; but the difficulties of manufacture very much limit the amount of art work and its special excellence in such productions.

The one process whereby the highest kind of art can be reproduced almost perfectly — viz., by terra-cotta — has never been fully developed in that direction. It is receiving some attention now, both in France and England; and we may expect to see results from the experiments which are being made. Yet we can hardly look upon reproduction in terra-cotta as machine-made sculpture; for, after each piece has been taken from the mould, it has to be fitted to other pieces, and finished by hand by at least as good an artist as the designer of the figure: and thus moulded terra-cotta is only a means whereby the elementary or constructional forms of modelling may be secured; and the finish has to be done entirely by skilled hands.

So that the likelihood is, that, in the future as in the past, there will be a demand for skilled labor in solid materials, because of the difficulty of its reproduction, — and a demand which will increase in proportion to the development of wealth and taste. For this reason I stated, that the act of the Massachusetts Legislature which compelled the cities of the Commonwealth to give instruction in industrial drawing should have also included modelling in the course of studies; for, though drawing is the soul of modelling, it is not soul and body as well.

As I believe there is not a very general understanding of the processes of modelling, moulding, and carving, and some light may be thrown upon the subject of design for relief ornament through a consideration of their peculiarities, I propose to say a few words in describing the processes of each branch of this group of industrial arts.

And firstly as to the difference between modelling and carving.

The great distinction between modelling and carving is that which is to be found in their manipulative processes, and the nature of the materials worked in. Thus, modelling is working in a soft material, as clay or wax, principally with the finger-ends as implements, aided by smooth boxwood tools, made to imitate the end of the thumb or finger. Carving is working in a hard material, whether wood, stone, or marble, with at first heavy tools, and at all times edged tools, having cutting and scraping work to do.

Modelling begins with nothing, and builds up the form: carving begins upon a block of material, and hews the form from it. Thus, in relief ornament, modelling is the art of putting-on or adding-to; carving, the process of taking-off. This distinction is at all times the most important one to impress upon the student; for when clay is used like wood or plaster of Paris, and a lump of material put in a place from which the form is scraped or cut out of the yielding clay, then the peculiar quality of the material is lost: and in this way it is more difficult to succeed in obtaining a good effect than with either stone or plaster, firm to the touch and unyielding.

Statues, busts, and the finest pieces of architectural enrichments, are always first modelled in damp clay mixed with sand; so ground and kneaded with water as to bring it to the consistency of dough or putty, — not wet enough to stick to the fingers, nor stiff enough to be worked with difficulty. With occasional sprinklings whilst the modeller is at work, and by being covered over with a damp cloth when not at work, the model is kept in a workable condition until it is finished: being pliable, the clay easily receives alterations, corrections, and additions, until the designer is satisfied with his work.

Then comes the process of moulding and casting, the object of which is to have the model in a material which will not shrink nor crack. If the work was left in the clay, and not burned, it would soon crumble to pieces, be very fragile, and easily be destroyed.

The methods of obtaining moulds and casts are various; but the most common are, by the use of plaster of Paris for both the mould and the cast, or using wax to obtain a mould, and plaster to make the cast.

Plaster moulds are of two kinds, — the waste-mould and the piece-mould, — the latter being also sometimes called a safe-mould, because out of it many casts may be taken without destroying it; whereas from the waste-mould only one cast can be taken, and the mould is chipped from the cast in removing it, and therefore destroyed. The process of waste-moulding is fully described in the chapter on Casting and Casts.

When the work is in plaster, it can be afterwards produced in stone or marble by means of a pointing-machine, a mechanical contrivance which enables the carver to reproduce a design either in relief or the round with practical accuracy. In the case of a bust or a statue, the artist will make the clay model himself, the moulder produces it in plaster, and the carver reproduces it in marble; the artist putting the finishing touches on the most important portions as the work approaches completion. Small or unimportant details of ornamental sculpture are not considered of sufficient importance to model or point, but are chopped out of the block by a stone carver; a superior workman usually laying or blocking out the work, and one of less skill finishing it But elaborate pieces require to be modelled, cast, pointed, and finished like a bust or a statue.

In the case of a bronze statue or statuette, the same process is repeated, with the exception of the pointing and carving; casting in bronze taking the place of the two latter. Thus a bronze statue is modelled in clay, cast in plaster, and then cast in metal from a mould made on the plaster cast.

The two great distinctions in the working of metals are to be found under the heads of *wrought* and *cast* in the coarser materials, as iron and brass; whilst the precious metals, gold and silver and bronze, are either cast, and afterwards chased, or, when of silver or gold, embossed and chased.

Wrought-iron work — that is, iron which is heated white, and hammered into the required shape upon the anvil — is one of the noblest and truest of the industrial arts. The hammering increases the tensile powers of the material to a great extent; so that it becomes more or less elastic, and will spring back into its shape from a blow which would shiver cast-iron into fragments. There is hardly a limit to the forms which may be obtained in wrought-iron; and its use for some of the highest decorative purposes, in conjunction with brass hammered and worked in the same way, is one of the most successful developments of industrial art in England at the present time. The mediævalists, sickened and disgusted with sham bronze and lacquer, have gone back to wrought-iron and brass as honest work. It has fallen to the lot of Englishmen in this century to have the restoration of all the cathedrals and most of the parish churches; and there are few but what either in the rood-screen, candelabra, or altar-rails, display masterpieces of wrought-iron. Then every considerable town in England has, during this century, built, or is now building, a town hall, exchange, hospitals, or civic buildings of some kind; and with the Gothic revival has come a desire for the best work in all branches of labor, each town vying with its neighbor in the magnificence of its public buildings architecturally. In all there is generally a display of wrought-iron as one of the elements of enrichment; and its practice thus extensively has called into existence a race of art workmen of the highest class.

One feature in its working is unique: whilst the iron is hot, it may be twisted into curves whose beauty cannot be equalled in any other process; but that supposes the workman or artist knows what is beautiful when he sees it, or is striving after an ideal existing in his own mind: the capacity of the material is there, if the laborer is competent to develop it; and accident sometimes helps him considerably.

Cast-iron, which is gradually forming so important an element in our architecture, is incapable of highly-ornamental treatment, limited by one condition of manufacture, — that there must be no undercut, or cutting back beyond the rounded outline of the ornament.

The moulds in which metal is cast have to be made in sand or loam; and it is not possible to get these moulds in many pieces: so that, except for slightly-relieved surface ornament, flat railings, fluted columns, or such-like elementary ornament, cast-iron will be of little avail artistically.

In the Paris Exhibition of 1867, one curious fact was very manifest to all, — that the French seemed to distance the whole world in the artistic character of cast-metal work, as, for instance, bronze and iron; whilst there was not any comparison to be made in wrought metal with that of the English mediævalists: yet the French had no wrought work to speak of, and the English no art castings worth looking at.

Chasing in metal is finishing with a hard steel point and a hammer the surface of a design which the sandy surface of the mould has left granulated or rough, and also removing all flaws and imperfections in the cast. The lines which are often so beautiful on a silver goblet or a medallion are generally the work of the chaser, who probably has not made the design or the model.

It is interesting to see the various stages which a silver candelabrum or a race-cup has to go through before it is fit for delivery to the customer.

In many cases the design is made by the draughtsman; and, when approved, it is handed to the modeller, who copies it in clay the size required. It is then passed on to the plaster-moulder, who cuts it up into as many parts as will enable it to be easily moulded in silver. He then makes a plaster mould of each bit, from which he takes a wax cast, exactly of the thickness which the silver is to be when cast. The whole model, in many little bits, is thus returned to the modeller, who works on the wax until it is more highly finished than in the clay. When completed, it is then sent to the silver-moulder, who makes a sand mould, and casts each half separately in silver, and passes them on to a finisher, who joins them together. He sends them on to the chaser, who, having filled the hollow parts with a hard compound of pitch and resin, so as to make it solid to work upon, chases the surface into brightness, adds all the details which could not be given either in clay or wax, and thus finishes the work. The application of heat takes away all the pitch and resin, and the polisher then puts the burnished surfaces upon it; and it is ready for the warehouse or the customer.

From this, it will be seen that almost any thing may

be done in silver, and also, that, when works of art have to pass through so many hands, each must be skilled, or the work will be spoiled. Sometimes, as in the case of Vechté, a French artist, who was once head of Hunt & Roskell's factory in London, the draughtsman, modeller, and chaser are combined in one man; and that undoubtedly results in the production of the best works of art. Thus it was that Cellini worked; and many of the very best men in modern times have imitated his example.

Perhaps one of the reasons why, in modern times, there is so very little universality of power in individuals is, because we divide and subdivide labor so much, requiring each cobbler to "stick to his last," each man to go blindfolded and grinding round in his own mill. Here I am glad to see this is not so much the case as in Europe, — at any rate, in business matters; though it is a good deal the case in art. Thus an artist is either a painter, sculptor, or architect. If a painter, either a landscape or a figure painter; if an architect, either a Goth or a Greek: and neither painter, sculptor, nor architect deems it safe to step over the margin-line of his own department in his own branch of art into the realms of the next. Compare this with what Michael Angelo did. He was architect, sculptor, painter, engineer, and poet; and some living artists would die happily, if any one of his works in architecture, painting, or sculpture had been done by them.

Then, if we judge Leonardo da Vinci by his own testimony, there was no branch of art he was not acquainted with, or would refuse a commission in; and, if we test him by what he has left behind him, he was a giant among artists, universal in his genius.

Division of labor is economy in the factory: it is paralysis in the studio; and, though life is too short for each man to practise all branches of art, the one he devotes himself to eventually will be more thorough and intelligent by knowledge of the rest, than it can be without that knowledge.

It seems to me that the most valuable men in this country, and in all others, have been made so through having, at an early period of their lives, to rely upon themselves for every thing; and being, in consequence, many-handed and many-minded, ready for every emergency that is new, and preventing many mishaps through foresight which comes of old experience, not by sticking to one last, but by having to be every thing by turns.

We can imagine the force of, say, an old maiden aunt of Michael Angelo's, who could do nothing but knit (antimacassars), sagely advising him to stick to his last, and his mighty scorn of the thoughtless counsel.

It is the handiness and general helpfulness of Americans that Europeans cannot understand; and they express their recognition of it by speaking of an American as the "universal Yankee,"— about the best possible testimony to his education and capacity that could be given.

If we consider the kind of ornament in relief appropriate to wood-work, it will be seen at once the color of the wood has very much to do with that; and the grain of the wood is also an important element. Very bold ornament in very dark wood is apt to look heavy, clumsy, and funereal; and delicate ornament in wood, where the grain is coarse, as in pine or oak, is labor thrown away.

The best work is usually done in boxwood or ebony; mahogany and walnut being unsuitable on account of the variety in color and prominence in the grain.

Perhaps more important even than the consideration of material is the question of where carving is admissible in the design and where inappropriate.

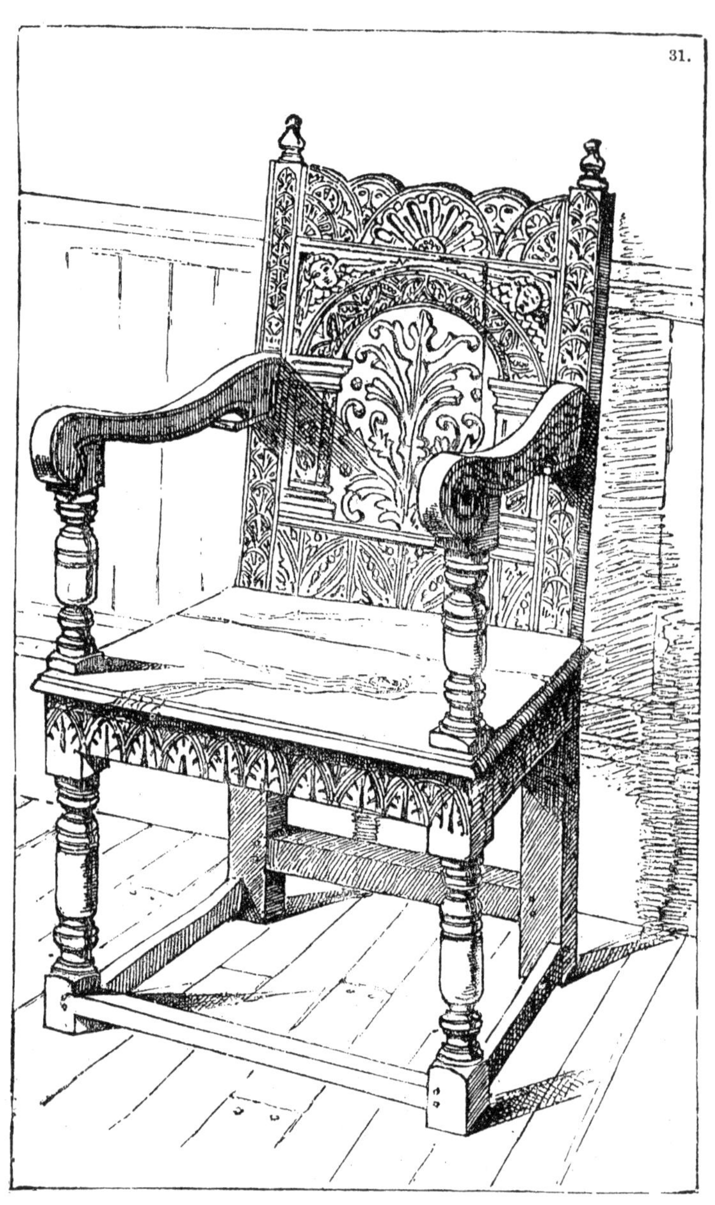

Hall Chair at Cothele, Devon, England; in the possession of the Earl of Mount Edgcumbe.

It should never be used to conceal the constructional features of an object, nor to form any part in any way of construction itself; for that reason, carving should be in recessed or sunken portions of the form, both for its protection when done and for enrichment. It should not be allowed to make the outline of any object, or occur in prominent places; for that will interfere both with its constructional feature and the use of the object itself.

In modern furniture, wood-carving is plastered over the framework as though it were put on with a trowel, or stuck on, as it too often is, with glue; and the result is, that half the furniture that is made is rickety in a month, and its atrocious ornaments come off in your hand as you move it about. Look at the hall chair at Cothele, and compare its honest simplicity and handsome enrichment with the tricky convolutions and over-ornamentation of modern furniture. No man would hesitate to sit on that chair in doubt of its strength, nor could he easily improve its design.

In wood-work, strength means straightness and squareness, with the grain of the wood going from end to end of each piece. The arch is of no account in wood, and curvature of any important constructional feature means weakness and liability to destruction in use.

If, in the use of any piece of furniture made in wood, the carved work must be handled, or it forms part of the object which has to be relied on for strength, it is in bad taste and design.

Again, very high relief, and very round delicate carving, is bad, because wood will split, and parts will chip off, or warp, and crack off.

Some years ago there was a mania in England for carvings of birds, in which every feather and every mark on every feather was exactly imitated; and the string which tied the bird up by the legs, and suspended it to the nail by which it was hanging, was so precisely imitated by the color of the wood — which was pear-tree — and the cutting on its surface, that, if you put real string by the side of the carved string, no one could tell the difference.

That was meretricious art, which has of course disappeared, though people were giving thousands of dollars for one little dead bird in pear-tree wood whilst the fury lasted.

The best test of the best design in an object of use is, that, at the first glance, the ornamentation should not be noticeable at all; coming out only on a second look or further examination. Then we can be sure it is in its right place, not prominent and impertinent, but subordinate and modest. Apply that test to most modern work, and you will see how it fails: the first thing which strikes the eye is some detestable scroll-work or putty-like projection; or, if the object be a chair, the legs and arms will be practising all sorts of gymnastic exercises, — all of which taken together means, bad design, vulgar display, and weak workmanship. The Knole chairs are just what such furniture should be, — simple, strong, handsome, and comfortable; and the settee has the same character.

Apropos of this, I should like to say that ancient carving in wood-work, which is liable to destruction by being worm-eaten, can be restored to almost its first strength by a very simple process. Some five and twenty years ago, an English nobleman who was about to rebuild his castle found that a piece of very elaborate wood-carving, which was, ornamentally, the chief feature of his banqueting-hall, and was perhaps the best work of the best English wood-carver, — Grinling Gibbons, — that this piece was so completely a network of fibres only, the

32.

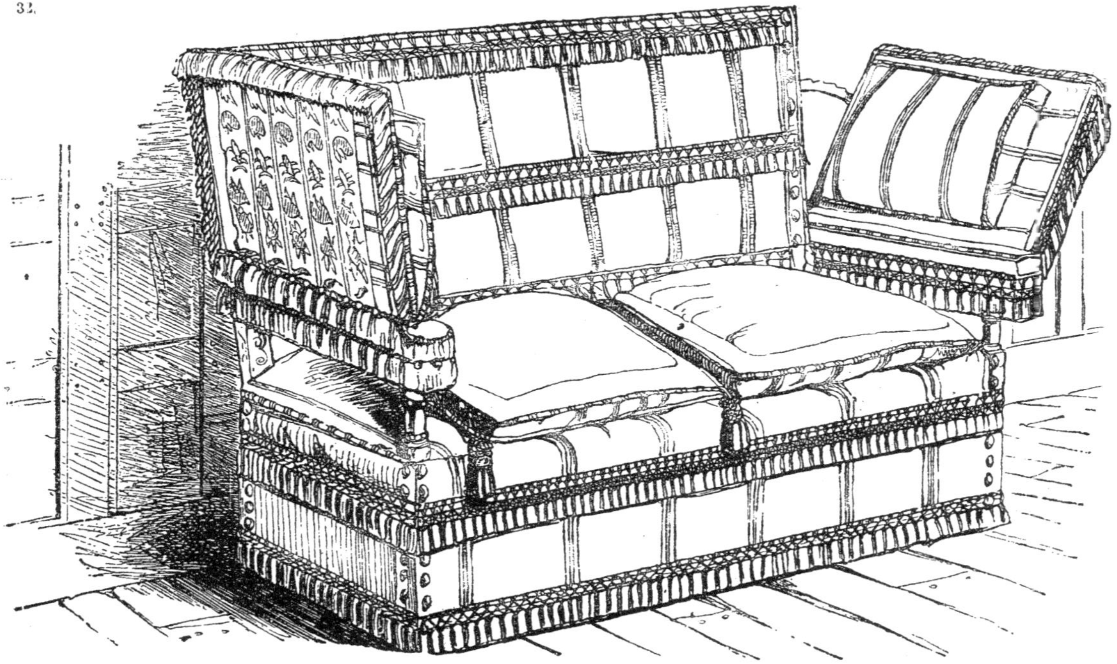

Ancient Sofa in the Long Gallery, Knole, England.

33.

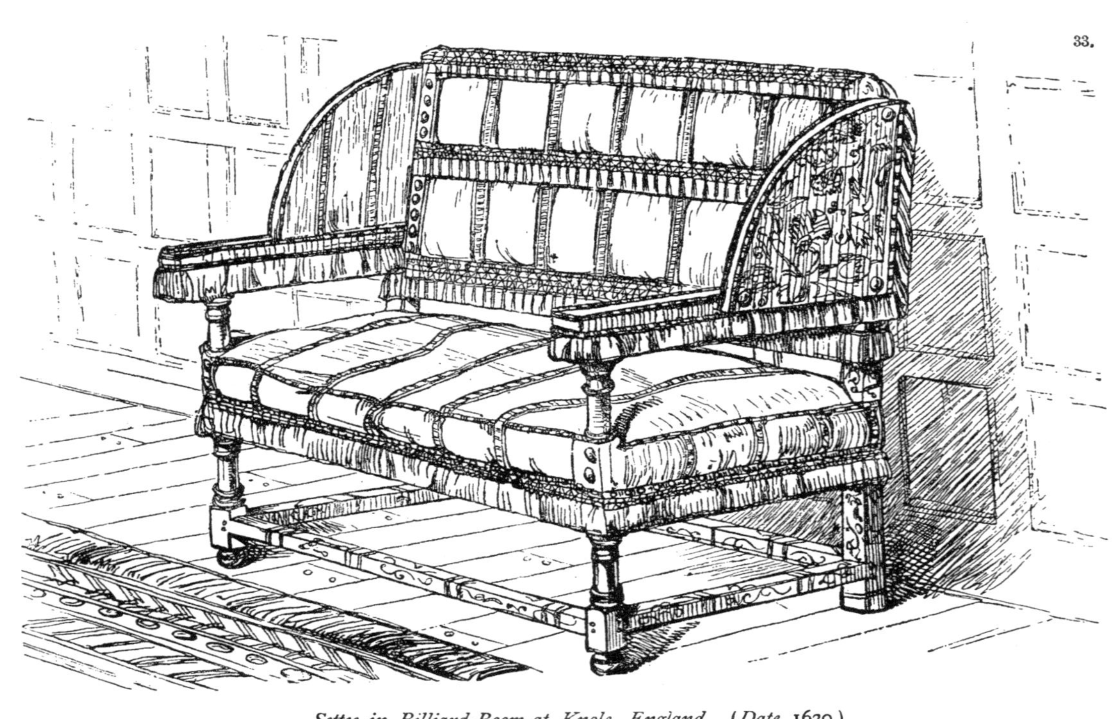

Settee in Billiard-Room at Knole, England. (*Date* 1620.)

34.

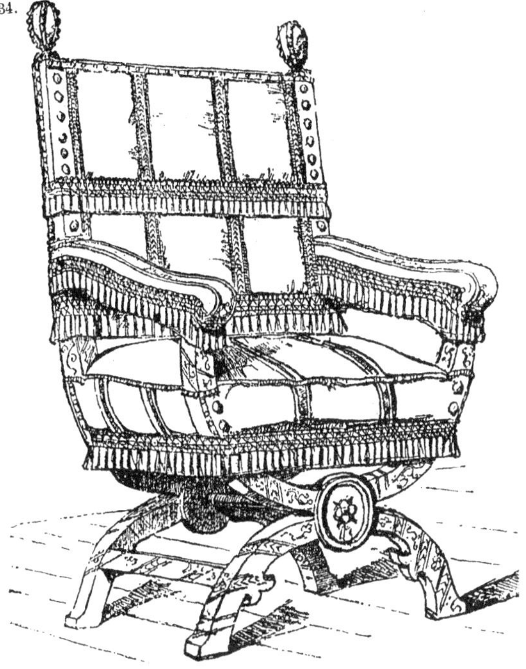

Arm-Chair at Knole, England.

worm having destroyed all the soft parts of the wood, that removal would be destruction; for it crumbled in the hand like a dead leaf. In this dilemma Mr. Rogers, the queen's carver, was consulted; and he, after careful examination, and several experiments on other samples of decayed wood, completely restored it to almost its original strength. His method was this: he steeped the whole piece in a composition of plaster of Paris or fine cement mixed with glue or gelatine, to a consistency as thick as cream, and let the wood absorb this fluid in a hot state, until every worm-hole and every crevice was completely stopped up, making the carving as solid as when it was first done. When the composition was cold, it got as hard as a stone, and, permeating every part of the carving, held it together as if in a vice. A little arsenic with this mixture will make it afterwards an unpalatable dish to future worms.

The experiment was a complete success; and in case any one should be possessed of a valuable piece of wood-carving which is rapidly going to destruction, and may desire to restore it to safety and permanence, I would suggest this remedial process.

There might be some difficulty in thus soaking a book-case or a sideboard; but any small gem of sculpture may be effectually cured by the process.

Stone-carving, which occupies, next to architectural design, the most important place in external decoration of buildings, is one of the weakest, perhaps the very weakest branch of industrial art now practised. For this, several reasons may be assigned: the first is, that carvers have little or no opportunity of studying the art of modelling in clay, which would give them a knowledge of the contrasts of light and shade, and of the effects of certain methods of obtaining relief distinctly: and another is, that the appreciation of old forms is passing away, as unfitting to express our present feeling; and as yet there is no power of design to create new forms. The copying or imitation of natural leaves may be very pretty, but it is not ornament; and the grace and lightness of foliage cannot be imitated in a coarse material like stone.

Then, architectural sculpture, to be honest, must be safe and substantial, well backed up by solid material, and not so cut under, and made thin at the edges, that it becomes fragile and like paper or leather work. In the best styles of architecture, the ornamental carving was strictly conventionalized, and symmetrical in all important parts, — Nature supplying the motive and source of subject, the sculptor applying them to architectural needs.

That must be the course now, as soon as we can get skilled workmen to study nature and design. The splendid foliage of this country will furnish us with new combinations of forms, varied in choicest outlines, and wealthy by contrasts of light and shade on their rich surfaces; and the bright, clear atmosphere will preserve for us the art work we display externally on our public and private buildings.

But that very purity of atmosphere is one argument against a very popular form of stone-carving enrichment, which is almost general now: I mean the incised ornament on flat stone surfaces. If these incisions were filled with colored cement, or if the smoke and dirt of a manufacturing town could be relied upon to fill the sunken device, then incisions, used very sparingly, would be highly ornamental: but in many cities, such as Boston, mill-chimneys are happily scarce; and, so long as it is so, incised ornament will have very little effect.

Carving without power of drawing is an impossibility;

for not only must the complete form be marked on the stone, but the final effect be seen from the first, so that the chisel is only cutting from the solid mass what the pencil has already expressed on paper or the eye sees mentally. If this be not so, then the workman is making experiments where mistakes cannot be remedied; and every stroke may only accidentally help the unseen result, or certainly destroy it. The excellent effect of the sculptured ornament on many of the buildings in Paris results greatly from their being carved in position, not in the workshop. There must be an absolute difference of treatment in the same subject for two positions, — the near and the distant; and a frieze or capital which may look well in the atelier will probably be tame and insipid in its final position, seen from a distance of many yards. Yet that which is effective and refined in appearance at a distance is not disagreeable when seen near at hand, having a certain breadth and noble simplicity which are always attractive and satisfying to the eye and mind of the refined observer.

The resources of art in the form of pottery have at all times, especially in great art epochs, been seized upon to express the art appreciation of different races. The Etruscan vases have made permanent the chaste feeling of their authors, and transmitted to us the refinement of other ages. The Egyptian pottery was exceedingly beautiful in form and outline, though somewhat rude in material; and the vessels which have been used by different peoples, and have been preserved to us, are the clearest manifestation of the condition of domestic industrial art among them.

Perhaps in this branch of industry the progress made during the last twenty years has been greater than in any other; and it has been in the direction of a return to simplicity and ancient forms. The Russian pottery in the Paris Exhibition of 1867 astonished every critic by its beauty of outline and fitness, existing side by side with very curious art displays in other branches. The Russian love of art is princely rather than popular; and the country has yet to produce its first painter or sculptor of European eminence.

Last year, 1871, the International Exhibition at Kensington took for special illustration the subject of porcelain; and it was unquestionably the finest display of specimens ever seen together in one building.

Since the time when Flaxman and Wedgewood, the sculptor and princely manufacturer, combined to bring out the famous Wedgewood ware, the attention of the best designers and potters has been much drawn towards porcelain and pottery; and the existence of the once imperial factory at Sévres, and the now imperial workshop at Berlin, has acted as an impetus to the production of beautiful works. Then, also, the popularity of Palissy ware, and majolica, with its many tints, has led manufacturers to imitate these wonderful masterpieces, with their crafty glazes and subtle lustres.

Some notion of the increase in value of pottery during the last few years may be obtained by an instance quoted by Mr. Robinson, art referee to the South Kensington Museum. Writing in 1857, he says, "Four or five years ago the most beautiful specimens of Italian majolica ware might have been purchased at dealers' shops and London auctions at from a few shillings to at most a few pounds, say five or ten pounds, at the highest; whilst in Italy a few scudi, or dollars, would purchase the finest piece. Now, these same pieces will sell for twenty, fifty, a hundred, two hundred pounds; nay, I dare scarcely place a limit to the finest specimens. As an instance, the most seemingly extravagant price ever heard of until then was given in Italy, not four years ago, for a fine majolica plate. After being refused by dealers and amateurs without number, on account of its supposed exorbitant price, — twelve pounds English ($60), — this long-coveted specimen was purchased by a French dealer. This year the same piece was publicly sold by auction in Paris for the sum of £450 ($2,250), and brought in triumph to this country by its purchaser, a well-known English amateur." He also adds, "The Bernal collection, offered intact to the British Government, and declined, for £40,000, only two years ago, was sold by auction for £60,000, and is to-day worth £100,000."

That shows the rate at which appreciation of pottery and other antiquities is progressing; and what was true in 1857 is doubly and trebly true now.

My own hope is, that, before every specimen of ancient industrial art in Europe is bought up for national collections, the Boston Fine Art Museum will be built, and patriotic Americans will be in the field to furnish it with works of fine and industrial art.

To what extent combinations of different materials in furniture are advisable or in good taste, seems difficult to decide. The French cabinet-makers, who profess to be at the head of the world in this specialty, believe most thoroughly in the use of metal with wood, and recently introduce glass and pottery to an unlimited extent. Bronze and silvered bronze, with either light wood, as sandal-wood, or dark wood, like oak or ebony, have a good effect when the relief of the bronze is not too high. Electrotypes from low-relief friezes or medallions, let in as panels, are quite unexceptionable, because of their flatness. Some of the very best furniture displayed in the Paris Exposition of 1867 introduced enamels in many colors, as medallions and filigrees of porcelain and pottery. Thus the sandal-wood book-case of Wright & Mansfield, which took one of the highest prizes, had some of Flaxman's best medallions, of a chaste sage-green ground, white figures upon it, as its principal ornament. Many of the French specimens used painted porcelain liberally, consisting of groups of flowers, portraits, ideal heads, and such-like: and that was not in good taste; for the brilliant colors destroyed the chaste design, and gave the whole productions a nondescript character, — half fine art, half industrial art, neither prominent enough to decide which was intended as principal.

In many otherwise well-designed and beautifully-executed cabinets, the effort to display the resources of the manufacturer ended in really grotesque confusion as well as profusion. Thus, in one instance, I saw an ebony cabinet, having brass filigree edges, bronze sunk ornaments, enamel inlays, ivory inlays, and points of bright color, obtained by precious stones highly polished, — all squandered over a surface three feet by four. That was like the pudding, — all plums and no flour.

I doubt whether more than two or three distinct materials should ever be used upon an industrial object, even when it comes within the scope of what Mrs. Partington calls "an object of bigotry and virtue."

It is taking a thing out of the realms of industry to elaborate it so much that it should be kept in a glass case for fear of injury; and the price of some of these industrial masterpieces, as they are called, is such, that, together with the risk of destroying them, they are as costly as white elephants. Thus, a small cabinet for coins by Diehl, a French cabinet-maker, was labelled in the 1867 Exhibition at eleven thousand dollars, and was a small one into the bargain. It certainly would not have held a tenth part of the coins required for its purchase.

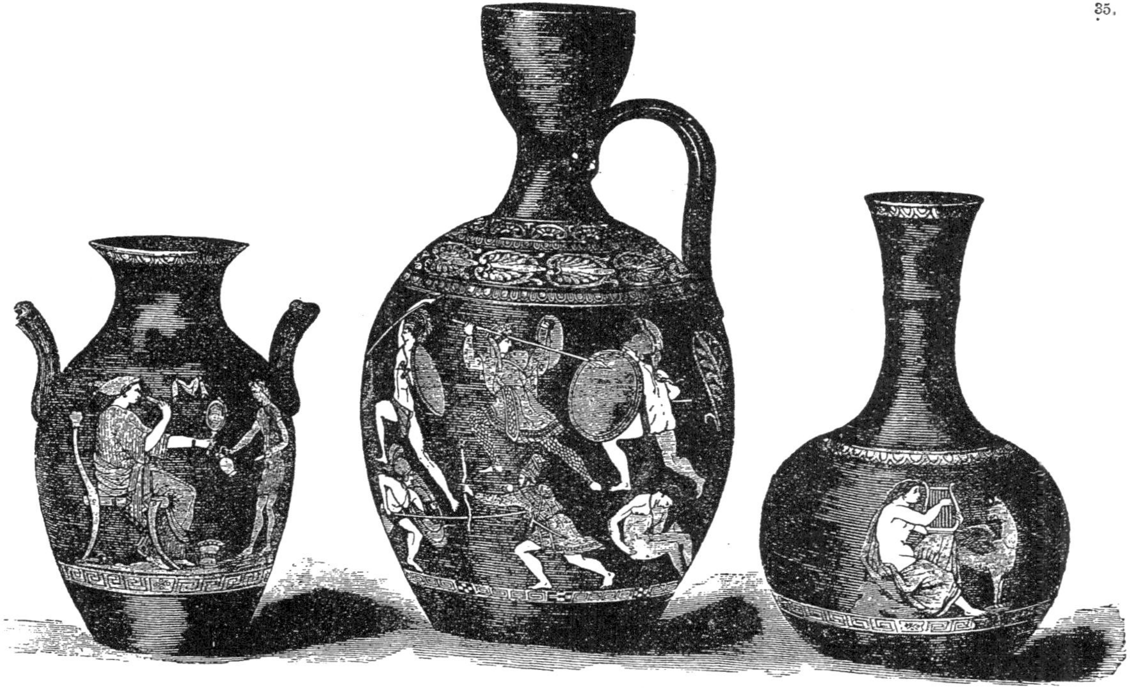

Greek Toilet Ware, manufactured by Messrs. Copeland.

The mischief of all this is, that there can be no gradation of furniture when one thing is so rich and elaborate. It kills the works of art in an apartment; and it makes the man who owns it look like a shabby biped, and the coins it is supposed to protect are not worth so much as the case containing them. What is the inference when the frame is worth more than the picture, the casket more precious than the gems it holds?

Notwithstanding this objection to over-enrichment, I am confident that there is a solid pleasure derived from every sight of an object which is thoroughly adapted to its use, and beautiful as well. The mind dwells on it with satisfaction; and there is the same enjoyment arising from its contemplation as there is, in a fine day, a sense of joyous health or "the concord of sweet sounds."

Of terra-cotta, or burnt earth, which the artist and art connoisseur love, as they do all good things, little practical use has yet been made; and that is the more wonderful, inasmuch as it is practically indestructible, retains the touch of the artist perfectly, and is therefore like a permanent investment of art power.

Most of the old terra-cottas have been modelled in clay solidly, and then burnt. That is not the best way: for clay shrinks in burning, and in proportion to its thickness, so that a thin part does not shrink so much as a thick part; thus distortion takes place.

I have seen a terra-cotta which had been burned for two days, and had only shrunk one-sixteenth of an inch in two feet of height; and that is practically nothing. To attain to that perfection, two things had to be done: first, the statuette had to be hollow, and all parts of the same thickness, which was done by first modelling the figure, taking a mould of it, and then pressing or squeezing the fresh clay into the plaster mould, after being rolled to an even thickness of a quarter of an inch; second, the greater portion of the clay was composed of ground and pulverized burnt clay, in the shape of common clay tobacco-pipes already burnt, and which had therefore been already shrunk, so that when burnt again it did not shrink at all; the actual shrinking being, in the unburnt clay, necessary to bind the particles together. The result was imperishable work, clear and brilliant, every touch of the master's hand sharp and perfect; and, with such care, terra-cotta is a beautiful material.

It is usually regarded as a material for small things only, — sketches and details; but I have seen a life-sized figure made as I have described, and burned without a crack or a flaw: and, if opportunities be ever given here for the highest class of professional study, it is one of the desires I feel, to resuscitate the noble art of terra-cotta upon American soil.

The most notable example of the use of terra-cotta in modern days is in the construction of the permanent portion of the South Kensington Museum in London. Every fraction of the façade, in a sort of Venetian-Renaissance style, is built of burnt earth, — the main body of red brick, the enriched portions of cream-colored terra-cotta. The columns, which are richly covered with figures emblematic of the seven ages and of the arts and sciences, in relief, are in blocks several feet in length and diameter, and the string-courses and mouldings, and wherever the main color of red brick is relieved by the lighter-colored terra-cotta, there are immense blocks of the material as straight and square as worked stone; whilst the surface is as hard as cast-iron, non-absorbent, dead in surface, and almost of uniform color: where the color is varied, the variety is not so great as in the veins of white marble.

Altogether it is a brilliant success; and it has these

advantages: the miserable climate and dense atmosphere of London cannot defile it; for the surface is hard and smooth, and every storm of rain and every gale of wind remove impurities as they would from a white plate; and fog and rain are not altogether unknown in the largest city in the world. I examined these terra-cotta enrichments in September, 1871, after they had been exposed for several years, and they were as fresh as on the day of their erection; whilst stone-work that had been up as long was as black as the inside of a chimney. The entrance hall of the Museum is illustrated on the opposite page, and will give you some idea of the capabilities of terra-cotta, architecturally.

The clear atmosphere of this country, and the absence of a plethora of mill-chimneys, do not so loudly call for permanent and cleanly decorations of buildings as London and Manchester do in the old country; yet, here as there, they would be an honest and pleasing ornament, — art work and hand work, fresh and eternal.

We express our unqualified admiration of a man who is perfect at all points, by saying, in Cockney vernacular, "He's a regular brick." Might we not describe the superlative of this, by stating, that "he's terra-cotta throughout?"

There seems to be a prevailing notion that terra-cotta must be red: yet there are at least three other colors of which it may be composed to my knowledge, for I have seen them; viz., cream-color, white, and gray: and I have no doubt, that, by admixture of oxides of several metals with the clay, almost any color, or tint of color, might be obtained.

Encaustic tiles, which are another form of terra-cotta, display every color known in art, except gold and silver; and their colors no possible condition of the atmosphere can destroy. Even when the earth is consumed with a fervent heat, these tiles and the Greek vases will be left behind us as a permanent record of past civilizations. You may reduce all the pictures in the world to tinder; melt all the bronze statues until they run in the gutters; calcine the marble statues into plaster of Paris; burn all the buildings into lime, and all animal creatures and vegetation into ashes; and all this while terra-cotta will glow red-hot, and remain uninjured, and cool down again into the shape we fashioned it. It is the noblest of all vehicles for the expression of art. It may be difficult to decide what else it is we do which would be even comparatively permanent in any great universal shock or a relapse into barbarism.

Suppose, for instance, an eclipse of European and American civilization as complete as that of ancient Greece, or a cessation of the arts as thorough as in the case of ancient Egypt.

What would be left behind us to tell the future peoples, budding into new forms of civilization, what the pale-faced ancient races did in their confused way of living? After a lapse of two thousand years, our pictures and photographs would be tinder or ashes; our metals, most of them, corroded and destroyed, — an odd bronze coin here and there might tell what our circulation was like; every building now in existence would be a heap of stones or a ruin of bricks, or be scattered in fragments over the earth, — except, perhaps, the Egyptian pyramids. And, though we try to believe that in many respects our civilization is greater than any other yet developed, it seems to me that in the arts, at any rate, it is vastly inferior in the one characteristic of permanence.

But if a straw thrown into the air shows which way the wind blows, and a strong tendency in one direction is an indication of character, then never did wind blow so bravely, nor public sentiment point so decidedly, as now it does towards honest, permanent work.

There is in art a reflex of social life: if refined and noble and original, it points to the maturity of a race; if barbarous, weak, or borrowed, to the infancy or decay of a race.

Let us hope, that, in the youth of this nation, our art progress may be, if slow, permanent; and, if youthful, the youth of a glorious manhood.

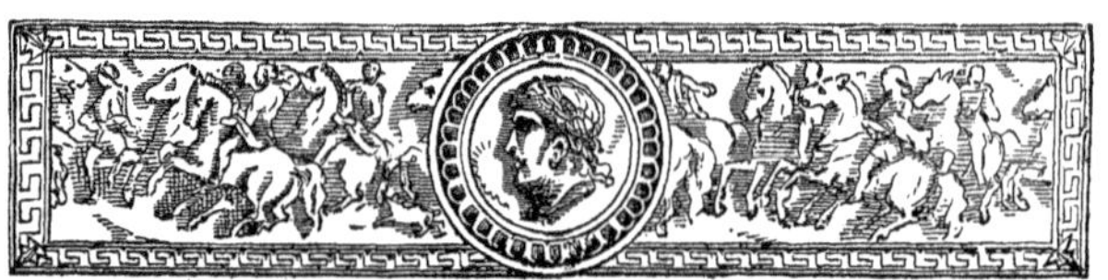

CHAPTER IX.

CASTING AND CASTS.

AS the majority of persons who admire the beautiful sculptured works of antiquity can only have the opportunity of studying and enjoying them through the medium of plaster casts, I purpose giving such information concerning the process of casting as will show what a good cast is, and that, being identical with the original, it may afford the same satisfaction to the cultivated eye.

THE PROCESS OF CASTING.

Casting is an effort to reproduce the exact form of an object by mechanical means, in the same way that modelling attempts to copy the character and form by artistic means. Thus, modelling the original work — a bust or a statue — is the work of an artist; casting it, and (supposing it to be in marble) even carving it, is a mechanical process, done by a mechanic. This statement must be qualified by saying, that to carve a marble bust, even by mechanical assistance (the use of the pointing-machine), though not of the same artistic quality of work as producing the original, yet requires the skill of a practised modeller also; for, without such experience, no carver would be allowed by a sculptor to touch his marble.

In bronze and metal casting, the statue or statuette is finished by the chaser, who must be a good art workman; but the process of casting the work from the plaster into the bronze is carried out by laborers, under the direction of a skilled founder.

WASTE-MOULDS.

Casting from the clay into plaster of Paris is called waste-moulding, because the mould is wasted or destroyed in the process of taking it from the cast; and it is distinguished from the after process of reproducing casts in any numbers from the mould, by the fact that only one cast can be obtained from a waste-mould taken from the clay model: whereas a mould for the purpose of reproducing casts, taken itself from a plaster cast, and called a *piece* mould, or *safe* mould, is so called because a large number of casts may be taken from it safely without destroying the mould.

A waste-mould, then, is a mould in plaster of Paris, or in wax, taken either from a model in clay or from some natural form, such as fruit, foliage, or a human hand or face. We will suppose that a clay model in *basso-relievo* has been made, and it is required to reproduce it in plaster: the following is the method by which it will be done, using a plaster waste-mould. The clay model will be sparely sprinkled with water about ten minutes before the mould is to be put on, to make its surface slightly damp; for plaster will follow water into the angles and small crevices of the model, which it would not otherwise reach. The plaster is then gaged, or mixed with water; and thus, it being settled how much water will be required to make a covering of half an inch thickness over the whole surface of the model, and this water being placed in a white glazed earthenware basin, the moulder takes the plaster by handfuls and shakes it over the side of his hands into the water, letting it fall to the bottom. This is repeated until the plaster begins to appear at the top of the water; and the superfluous water at the top of the plaster should then be poured away. With an iron or wooden spoon, larger than a table-spoon, the plaster is then beaten up, precisely as an egg would be beaten, for perhaps a third of a minute; and it ought then to be rather thicker than good cream. The plaster is then carefully poured over the model, care being taken to make it thoroughly and completely cover the surface, the first coat being spread evenly over, half an inch in thickness. It must be left for twenty minutes or half an hour to allow it to set, — new or quick plaster setting five minutes sooner than old or slow plaster. Having set as hard as a lump of chalk, this first case is oiled or brushed over with a mixture of clay and water, called Italian grease; and then a second coat of about the same or greater thickness of plaster is added to the first. The object of putting the mould on in two thicknesses is, that, when it has to be chipped away, the outer case comes off quite easily, without any danger to the cast, and the thin coat can then be removed with much less difficulty than if the whole mould had to be chipped away in one thickness.

When the outer case is hard, the mould and model together are turned over, exposing the back of the bass-relief, and the clay is picked out of the mould. The mould is washed carefully, and every particle of clay taken from it. The inner surface of the mould is then either oiled or brushed with soap and water to give the surface a slightly greasy character, so that it will leave the cast easily. Very skilful moulders sometimes omit this part of the process, relying upon great experience in chipping off; but it is safer, and necessary for the inexperienced, to grease the mould.

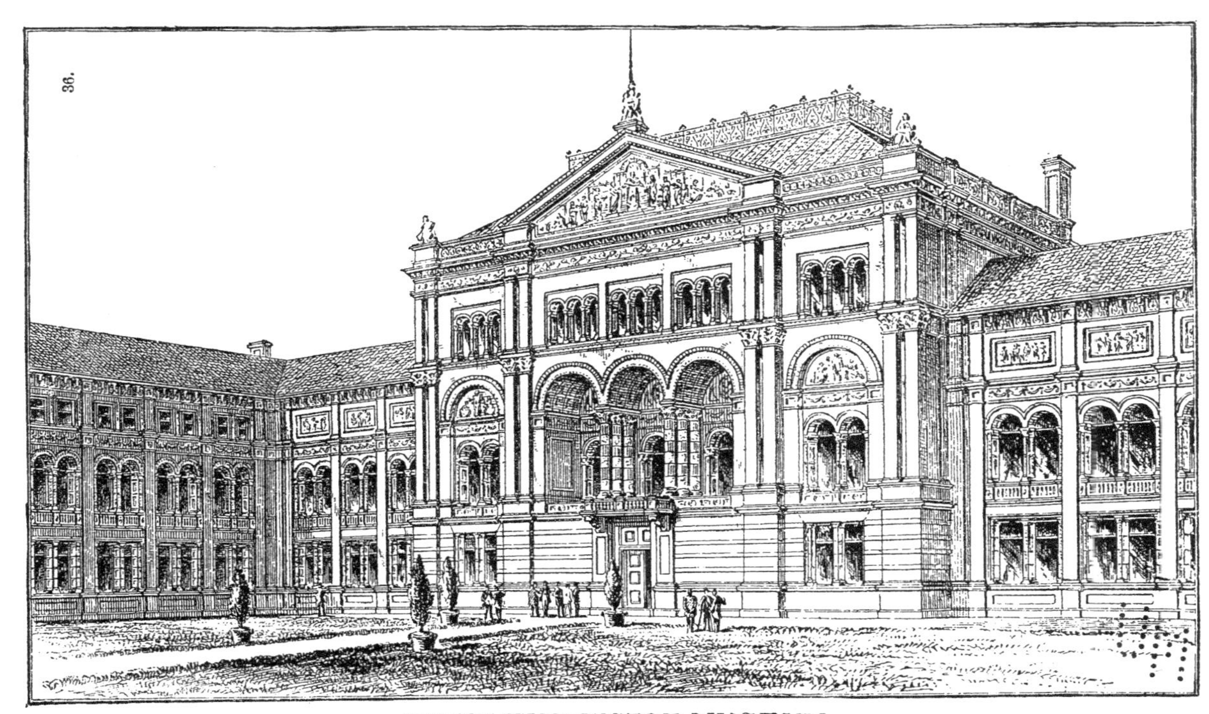

SOUTH KENSINGTON MUSEUM.
CENTRAL HALL.

The mould being thus prepared, the casting may be made. The plaster is gaged in the same manner as for the mould, and poured into the latter. It is well at first to pour into the mould about one fourth enough to fill it, and then to shake it soundly, so as to insure the plaster running into every nook and corner of the mould. Then the remaining plaster is poured in, and the background of the relief made as thick as required, and perfectly smooth at the back. When it is set hard, the chipping away of the mould may be begun. The tools used will be a mallet of wood, about three or four pounds in weight, and blunted chisels of varying sizes, — say about one-fourth, one-third, three-fourths, of an inch, and one broad chisel of about an inch and a half. The outer case of the mould is removed by cracking it off with gentle taps of the mallet upon a chisel, cutting in all cases at right-angles to the surface of the cast. The case will come off in three or four pieces, being prized or levered off; and then comes the particular part of the process of casting which requires skill and the greatest care. The mould which remains will be about half an inch thick everywhere; but in a few places, in angles of the model, it will be sometimes thicker. It is best to *find* a piece of the cast by chipping off a bit of the mould on the outside, and then to follow the cast by chipping off small bits, not more than an inch square, or even less, until a part of the model be reached. Then it is comparatively an easy matter to remove in the same way all the remainder of the mould, by chipping it off gradually, holding the chisel firmly in the left hand; for, if it be allowed to slip, very ugly gashes may be made in the cast. When this has been accomplished, the moulder has to gage some plaster very thinly, and mend up his mistakes; for the best moulders will either chip off or cut into some parts of the cast.

Casting from foliage, or a hand or bird from nature, is done in the same manner: but that, if a leaf be the subject, it has to be delicately propped up behind, so that its form be not distorted; and the plaster should be put on very gradually at first, so that its weight may not force the leaf out of shape, or flatten its projections of surface. In casting a hand or foot or face from the life, the moulder must be an expert, or he will torture his subject, and produce very poor work. Provision must be made, when putting on the mould, for its being taken off without removing fingers or toes; and the best way of securing this is to put a piece of thin, tough string on the surface of the hand or foot, so that, just before the plaster sets, the string may be pulled off, and cut the mould into about two equal parts, dividing it so that all parts of the flesh will be relieved. In casting, the mould will have to be tied tightly together, and, the plaster being run into it, be well shaken and poured out; then poured in again and filled up, if a solid cast is to be made.

All other parts of the process of moulding and casting from the life or nature are the same as from the clay.

PIECE-MOULDING.

The way in which the majority of casts are reproduced is by means of a piece-mould, — a mould made in many pieces, — which can be removed safely from each cast taken, and be ready for the next cast. The process of making this kind of mould is as follows: a plaster cast of great excellence of workmanship is selected or prepared for reproduction, and is, when its art workmanship is perfect, thus treated by the moulder. The cast is carefully dried, and oiled with boiled linseed oil, applied sparingly with a hog's-hair brush. It may, if the plaster be very absorbent, require to be thus oiled two or even three times. Then it becomes perfectly smooth and non-absorbent. Moulders call this cast "*the original.*" In this state, it is ready for the piece-moulding process. We will suppose, to make this description simple, that it be required to make a piece-mould of a cast of a spray of apples and foliage, the apples being highly relieved, but not quite in the round. It is required, that, when the cast has been made, the mould shall be in so many pieces, that each will come away by a slight tap of the hand, and be uninjured. The moulder commences then by placing round some prominent part, such as the top and eye of the apple, a small wall of clay an inch deep, leaving the piece of the cast exposed which is to be moulded. He mixes his plaster, and fills up the cavity. When it is set, he takes it off from the original, and cuts its edges straight and square, with a cunning angle known as the contra-cut, and which any Italian moulder will show the curious inquirer. The next piece is added by letting the first piece make part of the wall, and some clay the other part; which new piece, therefore, perfectly fits the first piece, but has to be taken off when set, and cut square, cut and contra cut, where it has touched the clay. In this way the whole surface of the original is covered with little independent bits of mould, each bit *drawing*, i.e., coming away from the original, without breaking any part of it, or bruising its own surface; to insure which, there must be no *under-cut* in any one piece, or surface cut back from the general surface of the piece. Thus, in an apple, two pieces would not relieve round the apple, but three would; though, if an apple were to be piece-moulded by itself, it would require five pieces, — one for the top, one for the bottom, and three round its sides; and out of such a mould twenty casts could be taken of good quality without much injury to the mould.

When these wedge-shaped little pieces cover the original, a flat, conical hole is drilled into the back of each one: the united surfaces of the backs are then oiled, and covered by a thick case, or matrix, of plaster, which holds them all together firmly in their places over the *original.* When the matrix is taken off, each piece of the piece-mould removed from the original will be found to fit into its place in the matrix, and a perfect mould be thus obtained. Before taking casts from such a mould, it is thoroughly dried, and every part oiled with boiled linseed oil several times, which hardens them, and makes the whole mould safe. When a cast has to be taken out of the piece-mould, the surface has to be first oiled with fine Lucca oil, used very sparingly with a stiff hog's-hair brush. When the cast is set, the matrix is removed, and each piece of the mould tapped with the butt-end of a chisel very slightly, or even with the knuckles; and it comes off easily, and is replaced in the matrix, after being wiped with a linen rag (the inner surface having steam from the new cast on it), ready for the next cast. In the cast taken from a piece-mould, there will be little lines, showing the junction of the several bits of the mould; and these are sometimes erroneously supposed to show where the cast has been joined together. These lines are, in fact, the means whereby a cast may be judged, — a process to be explained farther on.

WAX-MOULDING.

When a subject is very highly relieved from its background, *alto-relievo*, a waste-mould is sometimes made with wax, which has advantages in some ways over plaster. Very delicate work, highly relieved, like the stems of flowers, can hardly be safely trusted to a plaster waste-mould, but may be excellently reproduced by means of a wax-mould. Though called *wax-mould*, the mould is really a composition of wax and resin, to which may be added with advantage a little honey, in about the proportion of wax, one-third; resin, two-thirds; and a table-spoonful of honey for every ten pounds of the two other materials. These are heated over a stove slowly, and well mixed, but never allowed to boil. To make good moulding material out of these ingredients, they should be melted and mixed, and poured out on a wet slate slab, and allowed to cool and shrink two or three times. When cool, the material should be like toffee,—only not greasy, but slightly elastic. Some moulders put a little Canada balsam into the compound, instead of honey.

When the model to be cast is ready, and the wax warmed about to the consistency of molasses, a wall of clay as high as the average height in relief of the model is put round its edges, and the wax poured on the model from one corner, and allowed to flow from it over the whole surface, the higher parts being covered with spoonfuls of the wax, dashed over them. When this coat of wax is cold, it is oiled or greased, and a plaster case is put over it. The clay should be taken out of the mould with great care, as the material is brittle and tender; and water should be freely used to wash out the clay, and harden the surface of the mould. The cast is made as in plaster waste-moulding; and, when set, the outer plaster case is removed with mallet and chisel, leaving the wax-mould to be dealt with. This mould should be placed in front of a moderate fire for half an hour, or until it is warmed through, and will bend easily; and sometimes hot water should be allowed to stand on the wax surface until the wax is thoroughly warmed. Then, taking one end of the mould, by a regular pressure, and very slowly, it may be pulled off, leaving the cast without a mark or a chip. The danger is, in taking off the wax, that hasty removal or irregular pressure may snap off little projections or very round parts; but that can only result from inexperience or careless work. There may be thin, threadlike seams in places where the wax has flowed from two sides and met: for, as the wax flows, the cold surface of the model cools it; and, where two streams meet, they will not join perfectly on the clay surface. For this reason, the wax should, as much as is possible, be run on from one place only. The seams, however, are so thin that an ivory modelling-tool will remove them easily.

The more the wax is used, the better it becomes; and, if it becomes too elastic, resin is added; if too brittle, wax is added: and the same wax may be used any number of times without deterioration.

GELATINE MOULDING.

Gelatine is sometimes used for safe-moulding for bass-reliefs, instead of plaster, though it is not as accurate. The gelatine mould leaves no seams or mould-marks, and thus has one advantage over the plaster-mould; for when such marks are removed by unskilful hands, as is generally the case, much of the beauty of the cast is destroyed.

The material is common glue, or a superior kind called gelatine. This is soaked in cold water until it is elastic, without snapping, and thus put into a tin sauce-pan, and warmed until it is of the consistency of molasses: it is then ready for use.

The cast is thus prepared: An even thickness of modelling-clay is rolled out, and placed all over the cast. Over this a plaster case is put; and a second case is put over the bottom of the cast, which will hold it exactly in the same position in the upper case, when the clay is removed, as it does before the clay is taken away. When the clay is removed, and the plaster cases put together, the cast being left in its place, there will be a vacuum between the case and cast of the thickness of the removed clay. A hole is cut through the upper case; and, the two being firmly tied together, the gelatine, prepared as described, is poured through the hole in the case, and fills up the vacuum left by the clay. The gelatine is left for a space of twenty-four hours to cool; for if removed before that time, or before it is quite cold, it will shrink, and spoil the mould; but, when it is cold and firm, the cast can be taken out: and then, the surface of the mould being oiled, a new cast may be taken, with this care, that, as plaster heats when setting, the mould must be taken off from the cast before the heat melts its surface, or that will destroy the mould. The mould is elastic, like a piece of india-rubber, and, when removed, will spring back into its place, ready for another cast. Not more than twenty casts should be taken from one mould, and then the old mould be melted up again, and recast. As in the case of wax, the material may be used as often as necessary.

Greater skill is used in taking casts by this process than by any other; and the odd distortions sometimes seen in cheap casts result from the overworking and abuse of elastic moulds.

SULPHUR-MOULDING.

This process is used only for casting very small and delicate work, in which there is no relief, such as gems, medals, coins; and a very famous reduction of the Elgin frieze in the British Museum has been so produced. Where there is undercutting, it cannot be used; for the mould must be in one piece, and *draw* easily, or the casts will be spoiled. The plaster must also be superfine, of the highest quality, to get very good casts out of sulphur-moulds.

The process is a simple one. Brimstone is melted in a slow caldron with care, until it becomes as thin as milk or cream. The medal or coin being prepared, by a wall of clay or pasteboard having been placed round it, as high as the mould should be, from one to two inches, the melted brimstone is poured over it. As it is cooling, iron filings should be filed into it, or shaken in from a fine sieve, which will much strengthen the mould. The casts are taken in the ordinary way, the very finest oil procurable being used for the surface of the mould each time a cast is taken.

In using the sulphur for a second mould, it should, when heated, be poured off into another caldron, leaving the iron filings at the bottom of the first; for, if these get on to the surface of the second mould, it will be spoiled. An earthenware pipkin is the best vessel in which to melt the brimstone; which, when melting, should not be allowed to boil, or even, as housewives would express it, simmer.

GOOD AND BAD CASTS.

It may be of some use to the lovers of sculpture to know, by outward signs of workmanship, a good cast from a bad one; and therefore I propose to explain them. Casts on sale will either have been produced by plaster piece-moulds, wax piece-moulds (which are similar but inferior to those in plaster, and therefore need not be referred to), or gelatine moulds, in the case of all subjects larger than gems. Nine-tenths of the casts sold are made by plaster piece-moulds. Upon these casts, the seams, or mould-marks, will either be left, or they will have been removed. The connoisseur should never purchase a cast when the seams have been removed, unless he can trust the moulder who does it, but either take them off himself, or employ a skilful modeller to do it for him. If, however, the moulder be accredited by either a government department or any acknowledged society of *dilettanti*, their credentials will be sufficient evidence of trustworthiness. In any case, it will be safe to stipulate, that, in removing the mould-marks, no sand-paper nor emery-paper shall be used, — nothing but a wooden tool (if the cast be new; or steel if it be old), and Dutch rush for the finer work, — Dutch rush being a ribbed grass, used for fine abrasion.

A cast can only be well judged before the mould-marks, or seams, are removed; and therefore it has been recommended that they be so purchased. If the seams be very thin, and no piece of the cast either project more, or be sunk lower than the next piece to it, it is probably a good cast. The seams ought not to be thicker than thread. If they be as thick as fine string, or if angular projections are found at the junction of two pieces of the mould, the cast has been taken from an old and worthless mould, and should be rejected.

When casts have been taken from gelatine safe-moulds, it requires more skill to detect whether they are good or bad. The most reliable test is by passing the fourth finger of the left hand, *the ring finger* (usually the most sensitive part of either hand), carefully over any rounded, projecting part; and, if it be perfectly smooth, the cast must have been taken from a new mould. But that is not all the test required. Any practised modeller or sculptor will be able to tell by the general appearance whether the mould was a good one, made of well-shrunk gelatine; but a connoisseur, in the absence of technical knowledge, should compare the cast from gelatine with one which has been taken from plaster, especially in the most sunk portions of the cast; and if the angles and crevices be sharp, and generally like the plaster-moulded cast, he may trust to its general accuracy. If, on the other hand, there be blurred parts or little projections on the surface, where they are not to be found in the original, the cast will be bad, — taken from an old mould, or one which has been used hastily before it was well seasoned.

Any one buying a cast from which the seams have been already removed must trust to his knowledge of the original, or art knowledge. But he will be comparatively safe, if he unconditionally rejects every cast upon which sand-paper or emery-paper has been used. The images sold by venders in the streets have usually had all character taken out of them by this method of *finish.* The common plasterman, in his desire to make his images look smooth and finished, always makes smoothness his first object, and with coarse paper, often upon a rough cast to begin with, grinds away all imperfections of used-up moulds, and every atom of character into the bargain. A good mould is a costly implement, and will never be found in the hands of any but first-rate workmen; and it is impossible to get a good cast from a bad mould. Those who have seen wretched engravings from worn-out plates may form some idea of what a cast is which must be sand-papered before it is salable.

Thus, though a good cast is to the artist and art-lover just as attractive and beautiful as the original work, though it may not be associated with the same sentiment, a bad cast is abhorred of all who love the good, as a distorted libel upon the original.

The painting of casts preserves them from discoloration, and is recommended, if it can be well done. But ordinary house-painters and decorators will destroy the finest casts if allowed to treat them as they like. A cast which is to be painted should have its seams removed, because these seams clog the paint, and destroy the sharpness of the cast. The paint should be as thin as milk; and a cast may have six coats of such paint without injury: but it must also have two coats of oil before the first coat of paint. When the casts have become dirty, they should be washed with a soft linen rag with a solution of water and soda, — an ounce of soda to a gallon of water, — which will bring them as clean and fresh as when first painted. In schools of art, casts require to be painted when used for light and shade; but, for connoisseurs, the most satisfactory way of preserving casts, and securing them originally, is to purchase them with the seams on, not to have the seams removed, and, instead of having them painted, give them two coats of boiled oil, at an interval of three days between each coat, and have it applied in the summer to insure absorption. The casts must be thoroughly dry, or the oil will never dry. Casts so prepared become gradually the color of old ivory or marble which has stood the weather: they become seasoned, and beautiful in tint, and harder than those prepared in any other way; and an artist loves his casts thus prepared better than by other means. Whiteness in painted casts should be avoided: a slight tint of yellow ochre or Indian red and black, just sufficient to take the rawness off the white paint, is an improvement. Casts in use in schools of art and drawing-classes should be protected, if hanging upon a wall, by a projecting shelf, — as shown in the fitting-up of the elementary-room, — which will prevent their being touched. A regulation of every school should be, that, under no circumstances, are casts to be touched by the students; that being done, when necessary, by the teachers. The casts should be dusted daily with a feather brush, never by any thing harder. Very delicate casts from nature, either of hands or foliage, may be protected by glass, and will in this manner keep fresh and clean for years; the light and shade showing as clearly through the glass as it does without it.

CHAPTER X.

ARCHITECTURAL ENRICHMENTS.

THE study of architecture, whether to the antiquarian or the lover of art, may be truly described as one of the most interesting and absorbing of subjects. To it all the dependent constructional and decorative arts are allied, as the leaves and flowers are to the tree, — the final developments of its life and beauty, or expressions of its decay and death. We are not now about to consider the tree, but one of its many blossoms, — architectural enrichments.

Architecture, the great and venerated parent of the arts, though considered only through its subordinate details of ornamentation, might well have taken precedence of other less important branches of design; but it seems safe to me that we should approach the greater theme through the less, and, by arriving at main principles in less important subjects, be enabled to form a sound judgment upon the highest.

For this reason I have preferred that we should seek after truth in the byways, and that lastly our inquiries shall turn in the direction of the great highway of architecture. Man is not the only architect, though he is the principal; for to many creatures besides ourselves has been communicated the desire to create a material home.

Yet as if to suggest higher thoughts, and to reveal the essential difference between man, whose mission is to conquer the earth and subdue it, and the fowls of the air and beasts of the field, which only exist and possess the earth, the architecture of man, the builder, is various and ever-changing, as though seeking after the perfect; whilst that of the inferior creatures is forever the same, stereotyped in all its features and unchangeable. The spider spins the same web, the silkworm the same cocoon, as its ancestors; the bird builds the same nest, and uses the same materials, as its parents; the hare rests in the same form, and the lion reclines in a similar den, as hares and lions have always inhabited. Now, as in the ages that are past, and in the times lost in the remotest antiquities, so also at the present time "the high hills are a refuge for the wild goats, and so are the stony rocks for the conies;" but, in contrast to this, each succeeding civilization, every distinct creed, has had among men its own form of expression and its own kind of development architecturally.

I know of no better illustration of the difference between instinct and reason than that; between the beasts that perish and the man created in God's own image than that, whilst they simply reproduce, man recreates; whilst they repeat only, man reforms; and this indicates the great spiritual and organic variety, — the difference between repetition and re-formation, the distinction between the merely animal and the man, — the beasts who are said to perish, and the man who is immortal. Not only do different generations of the same race entirely vary in the character of the buildings they erect, but different individuals in the same generation require an entirely original design for the homes they make. There is nothing more distressing to a cultivated taste than sameness in the highest forms of art, and nothing more destructive of originality than the repetition of important forms. We unfortunately, many of us, have to live in rows of houses, all alike, just as some of the weakest of us, driven by poverty, or compelled by misfortune, or enslaved by our own vices, have to wear liveries, or uniforms, or clothing supplied to us out of the rates; but we don't keep that up when once our backs are turned on the kindly institutions which have given us the workhouse costume or the regulation Sing-Sing uniform.

That system of blocks or rows of similar houses is one of the evils resulting from an unequal division of money and education, and a lax state of the law, whereby any man who has a bit of money to spare forthwith triumphs over his neighbors, by erecting strings of tumble-down contractors' houses *to sell*, and assumes the right of compelling others to wear his shabby livery for the rest of his days. No other races of creatures are so tyrannized over as men are in that respect. I live in a row of houses myself, which are all so identical, that, to find my own at night, I have to count doors from one end, or take bearings from objects on the other side of the square; the numbers on the doors being invisible in the darkness. That is living in a uniform, just as putting on the Sing-Sing dress is wearing a uniform; and neither of them indicates a right state of things. Wherever men degenerate into uniforms, it is an indication of either weakness or wickedness; and when it is necessary, as in the cases of the patriotic soldier, or the friendly policeman, that is a confession of turbulence and lawlessness among our neighbors or ourselves, which requires liveried, disciplined, human machinery to control or put down.

I know of no parallel authenticated cases of this habit of body in the lower creatures, unless the conventionalism of Fable may be taken as an authority; and then it seems to me that I once read of a certain donkey who clothed himself with a lion's skin, and a certain jackdaw who decorated himself with a peacock's feathers; and, if I remember rightly, neither of these experiments ended happily.

The peculiar charm of individualism in architecture may best be seen in the streets of old Flemish and German cities, where each house is harmoniously associated with its neighbors on either side, but entirely different from them; the gables and gablets and flèches and quaint dormers, the carving and metal work and oriel-windows, varied in each, yet together forming a general effect rich in character, and delightful to the eye. A stroll at Frankfort or Malines or Antwerp is as interesting as being in a good picture-gallery; and no man of taste can see these beautiful old houses without comparing the originality of other days with the monotony and sameness of these.

And yet the people who have left behind them these art relics and sources of delight to posterity were not richer than we are; i.e., they had no more money than we have: but I suspect they were a good deal wealthier than we are, — used their means for weal rather than woe; for riches are not necessarily wealth, but merely unnatural accumulations of money, and wealth is its possession for the highest and best purposes; none being higher and better than ministering to the intellectual and spiritual wants of mankind; few channels being more permanent than the perennial delight afforded by good art, none more generous than that which provides an external sculpture gallery, made by noble architecture, open to the sight of all created beings.

There is something to be learned from that distinction between riches and wealth, not often well considered, and which may be of use to us architecturally, as well as socially.

The merely rich man, who possesses his riches only for himself, may be compared to a stagnant pool of water: the wealthy man is like a river that fertilizes the valley in which it flows, and illustrates that grand old proverb, "There is that scattereth, and yet increaseth."

Now, I fear that in modern days we are in the habit — to put it in the vernacular of to-day — of investing our art love rather in personal property than in real estate, — in movable, destructible things, which may make us personally rich, but which do not contribute to the common weal, or common wealth, of our race; and just in proportion as we do so we are rich, but not wealthy.

Those quiet old Germans and Flemish citizens, who left behind them that which sends us thousands of miles to see, were wealthier than we are on all counts; and their works testify to it to this day. In the times they lived, the house was the home of a family; upon it was lavished affection as well as money, and the outside was as beautiful as the inside was domestic and comfortable; neither outside nor inside monopolizing the art of the fabric.

I wish that those who have the means to do so would follow their example, and make it as great a delight to walk in the streets of a modern city as it is to wander through an ancient town; instead of erecting temporary, flippant, or monotonous furnished lodgings, build homes for their families, so permanent, solid, and beautiful that they will communicate stability and refinement to the races of which they are the cradle, — sanctuaries, where the sacred relationships of parents and children shall be consecrated by the hallowing influence of beautiful art; and which shall be, within and without, at the hearthstone and in the gabled windows, truth, strength, and beauty. For let it not be supposed that this outward manifestation of our character is uninfluential. The character and attainments of a people may be fairly estimated by the houses in which they live, taken on a broad average ; and men grow into the likeness of their surrounding influences, or, when these are less strong than men's wills, they are changed into the expression of those wills. There is a marked difference between the general character of the dwellers in an ancient cathedral city and the inhabitants of a modern manufacturing town ; and the difference is not always in favor of the latter.

There is a better tone amongst the people who live in the best parts of a town than among those who inhabit the worst, not to be wholly explained by social circumstances nor variety of occupations. The same family which dwells in the trim and picturesque cottage, peaceable, industrious, and constructive members of society, if removed from it, and made to burrow among the wretched shanties in the slums of a big city, will degenerate into idleness, turbulence, and destructiveness.

I have seen the character, not only of a whole city, but of a community, changed by the influence of architecture ; in which, up to a certain date, there was no civil building deserving to be called architectural, and where there was an almost total lack of institutions for the amelioration of social defects, except those compelled by law, — the workhouse and the jail. The art influence was brought to bear upon it, and some noble buildings were erected, out of all character with every thing that surrounded them. It was stanchly maintained that the beautiful was as economical in the long run as the plain or the ugly, and had a better effect on the character of the people and reputation of the town. People pondered over that, and were converted. In new fabrics, architects were employed as well as builders ; and each succeeding building made a stride upon the last. Old streets were pulled down, and new ones erected in their places, employing all the resources of art; and people were forced to see that the best citizens thought that making money could be combined with decency and order, and that commerce need not be enshrouded in dismal garments, but come to them clad in the pleasing raiments of beauty, as delightful to the eye as its pursuit was profitable and gratifying to the pocket.

I watched this change, and noted, that precisely in the proportion that mere money-grabbing ceased wholly to absorb people's faculties, and this new element of a love of the beautiful was introduced into their thoughts; so an awakening to the performance of other social and moral duties followed,—a gradual elevation of the moral sentiment, initiated by art. The wretched workhouse, where the poor or the unfortunate were thrust as sheep into a slaughter-house or wild beasts into a den, gave place to a handsome building, where poverty was not treated as a crime, nor misfortune made more bitter by cruel hardships. The foul courts and alleys, where rapacious landlords ravished the poor because they were in their nets, now attracted the attention of persons who did not want their city to be like a whited sepulchre,—fair without and foul within; and, both municipally and by private enterprise, pleasant and healthy homes were provided in place of these wretched habitations, whilst men who would invest their money in running up houses for the poor were taught, that, unless they could afford to build them decently and well, they would not be allowed to build them at all, and would have to seek other investments for their superfluous capital.

The waste places, where of old the children defiled themselves in the companionship of ancient refuse and departed cats, were cleansed, and made into gymnasiums and playgrounds; some questionable places of amusements were swept away; and the most beautiful and romantic old park in the locality, which had been ripening into beauty since the time of the Commonwealth, was purchased, and made into a place of public recreation and resort.

That took twenty years to develop; and if you ask me what was the prime, unconscious cause of it all, I should say, the love of the beautiful, initiated by good architecture. This is no ideal sketch of a theoretical possibility, but a real outline of an accomplished fact.

I have noticed that tangible and material good comes frequently as a result of the cultivation of faculties in us which are not directly useful in a material point of view.

You may inquire of me, why I dwell upon these points before I come to the practical part of my subject; and my answer will be, because it is at the foundation of what I have to say. If art in any shape were only the occupation of idle fingers, and useful only as the means for gratification of curiosity, then it would be unworthy of your attention or my examination. I take it that the reason why you and I find ourselves writing or reading this, is because we regard art work as of some importance to that delicate structure called the human mind; and we can only grasp the subject by comprehending the first principles on which art is founded.

A great deal of the distinction between building and architecture, between use and beauty, consists in understanding the true position of each in relation to man's necessities and his aspirations. And this understanding is based on knowledge of many things besides the actual subject under consideration. We want to know why mankind wants art at all, and then what it is wanted for, before we come to the question of what kind of art will meet the demand, and have the effect and influence sought. And then we can supply this need; and, in the natural order, the minister becomes the leader, — that which has been the delight and solace of the unearthly part of our existence supports and leads us, and holds up the standard of our best days to help us through our worst. The most matured embodiment in art of the most highly-cultured minds strikes the key-note; and we join in the chorus.

Yet it is not by looking at any phase of art in detail that we either know the whole field or become closely acquainted even with the details we study. It is rather by comprehending the origin, object, and fulfilment in one glance, that all the features can be seen in perfect relationship.

What is it, then, which makes the difference between a piece of architecture and a building? To put it in few words, architecture comprehends building as its instrument, employs the structure erected for the necessities of the body to provide simultaneously the beautiful, which is the mind's necessity. Architecture and building stand towards each other as the soul to the body, — united being life; and building by itself is the body without the soul, dead and earthly.

I never see a flat, vertical wall, pierced through with rectangular slits for doors and windows, without thinking it the soulless carcass of architectural life; representing the merely animal part of our being, and ignoring all its mental and spiritual faculties.

On the other hand, when, in the effort to meet the living appreciation of the beautiful, necessities are ignored, and the artistic is presented as the be-all and end-all of a building, it becomes equally objectionable, as carrying too much soul for its miserable body.

The useful and the beautiful may be combined by a due consideration of requirements in most objects; but there are many in which no effort whatever should be attempted to make them other than simply useful things; for in them art is an impertinence or criminal waste. Humble obscurity is an element of great value in art; and we sometimes want mere nothingness as a background for some principal figure, — just as silence is necessary for the appreciation of sound.

I have met with no better illustration of the marring of two purposes by their union in one object than the crucifix candlestick, — a green glass candlestick made by a socket placed on the top of a veritable figure of Christ on the cross; for there a beautiful incident was degraded by its application to an ignoble use, and an otherwise useful object was made inconvenient by the bad adaptation of the design to the purpose the object had to fulfil. It was at once shocking and inconvenient.

Architecture gives us the opportunity of uniting these two elements of use and beauty, and in a manner peculiarly attractive to us all.

It is also a case in which we are put into the witness-box, and must testify in the open light of day; for, though a man may hide his face and conceal his thoughts, he cannot put his house under a bushel, nor explain away its meaning by a garbled statement.

Assuming, then, that the function of architecture is to blend the useful and the beautiful into an expression of perfect human requirements, let us look at how this has been and may be attained.

First of all, the circumstances of the climate, and habits of the people, ought to decide the general character of the building. The office to which the structure is to be applied will also control its main feature, and settle the amount of enrichment it is right to adopt in the design. And then comes the golden rule in art, — that no second means of enrichment should be resorted to until the first is exhausted; no third to take precedence of the second.

If there be no means of obtaining the higher resources of ornamentation, we should be the more economical with the lower. If sculpture and color are beyond our reach, let us see that the proportion of masses be well arranged, the light and shade effective, and the lines of construction cunning and harmonious. When a man can only afford to pile up a heap of stones or brick for his house, he ought to employ the very best architect of the day to do it for him; for to do that well requires the ripest skill in art. And the skill of the best architectural designer the country or the world affords is to be obtained at a cost of five per cent on the outlay, which makes the whole account stand at ninety-five per cent for bricks, and five per cent for brains; not an extravagant proportion for brains.

Heaps of bricks and stones, without any ornamentation or enrichment, may be piled up in a very effective manner, delightful to even the most refined and cultivated taste, only it takes consummate power to do it; and the less a building is to cost, the greater ought to be the architect employed. That is a rule which does not prove true in the converse: I should not like it to be understood, that, the more a building costs, the smaller the architect to be intrusted with its design. Great buildings will generally be intrusted to the right people; but lesser ones are usually in the hands of the wrong.

And then, above all things, let not the simple necessity which confines us to mere construction be garbled and confused by sham enrichments. If the material be good, and the lines and masses of composition show skilful design, the first condition of good art has been complied with: it will be consistent and pleasing left in that state, but destroyed at once if shams be introduced to relieve its plainness.

Indeed, the consideration of cost does, as it should, affect not only the accommodation to be given in a building, but every line of the designer's pencil, from the first to the last touch. I know of two instances where an alteration of the sum to be appropriated in the erection of a structure entirely destroyed its character; and, curiously, they are in opposite directions, — the first instance decreasing the cost, and the second increasing it. The first was an illustration of those who begin to build, and do not count the cost until reminded of it in the progress of construction. It was an edifice in the design for which appeared a handsome tower and lofty spire. The spire was half-way up when the funds gave out, and there was nothing for it but to curtail. So the committee took the matter out of the architect's hands; and, instead of completing the spire by the continuation of its first lines, they cut off twenty feet from its height, and finished it by a sort of conical stone nightcap, giving the effect of an humiliated aspiration, — a spire which didn't know its own mind, or exactly where it was going to, or when it intended to arrive at that doubtful point.

The second case was where the founder of an edifice commissioned an architect to design a building to cost fifty thousand dollars. When it was six feet out of the ground, he altered his mind, and determined to spend five hundred thousand dollars upon it. The plan would not carry the increase of expenditure; and it hardly requires an educated eye to detect an overloading of enrichment and disproportion of ornamentation to the general conception in the design.

But, to explain what I have referred to as gradation

in the means of enrichment, I must take a case where a sufficient amount of funds is available to command the best skill in design, and all necessary degrees of ornamentation suitable to the size and character of the fabric contemplated and required.

With regard to material, there seems good ground for supposing that the natural products of a locality are best suited to it; and it certainly comes within the range of art to use native materials to the best advantage: where these are manifold, the scope given by using several kinds in one building is valuable to the skilled eye, and the result is pleasing contrast of color. This association of color in material is not the first step in ornamentation, but the second. The first is the formation of lines in the construction, either in the shape of mouldings or masses of material. That is the primary resource in design, — a sort of architectural study in monochrome, or one color; the color being shadow, a darker tint of the material used in construction. In stone of a dark color, such as the beautiful reddish-brown sandstone used in America, very handsome effects may be thus obtained, and, I am glad to say, have been obtained already, though there is a want of well-pronounced horizontal lines in most of the designs; and the mouldings, which might be made more strictly ornamental by depth and greater contrast of light and shade, are, as a rule, too weak and thin in section.

Then, secondly, comes the use of various material, as stone and marble, or stone, brick, and marble, without carving. Some of the most pleasing and attractive architectural effects are arrived at by employing strong materials, like granite, for shafts and columns, a different stone to make string-courses or bands of horizontal lines, and a third to form the plain wall and mass of coloring. This, however, requires very great skill in design: for it is as easy to place light and dark color in the wrong places in a building as it is in a picture; and, as a rule, it has always appeared the most pleasing in effect when the lightest material forms the main part of the fabric, and the darker is used for variety and constructional ornamentation. There is considerable danger in overdoing this use of colored materials, or of letting each be equally important. A building at Oxford, built of alternate courses of red sandstone and white Caen stone, is always referred to by the undergraduates as "the streaky bacon." And where, in another instance, many different materials of bright color have been employed, they describe it as "the frisky harlequin." There is sound criticism at the bottom of those names; for these terrible children of nineteen and twenty generally get uncomfortably near the truth when they take to calling names.

As a phase in this use of several colors, is the contrast obtained by polished and dead surfaces in the nobler materials, — marble and granite, — or of glazed brick and tiles in brickwork. I know that many of the very best authorities are averse to the employment of any material which shines, or of polishing any dead surface. That, however, can only apply to sculptured work, or work in which direct reflection of rays of light hides the ornament, or destroys the effect of masses of light and shade. In a cylindrical column, the polishing of the surface is an actual advantage; for it increases the sense of strength by expressing the roundness and size of the shaft: the light is reflected in the right place, and suggests the shadow.

Next to these resources comes the use of carving, though I am aware how, in some of the best periods of art, architectural sculpture has preceded the use of color in materials. Thus in the cathedrals of the Middle Ages the most elaborate carving of every phase of subject was resorted to, whether in enriched mouldings, foliage, or the human and animal figures; so that the exteriors were magnificent studies in one color, or monochrome, displaying all the resources of sculptural art, from the simple symmetrical moulding to the figures of saints and kings in their canopied niches.

Yet it must be admitted that these sculptured enrichments are far in advance of simple contrast of color in mechanically-formed blocks of stone, and in any system of gradation ought to be ranged in comparison far higher than granite-polished shafts or sandstone string-courses. When we consider, also, that the æsthetic Greek and symbolic Gothic styles are the only great successful instances of sculptured ornament in architecture, it will be seen that the use of color should precede the higher developments of form.

The gradation in sculptured ornament suitable to enrichment of effect, after the employment of mouldings and colored materials, is in the order of vegetable forms, as foliage and flowers being first; secondly, animal forms; and thirdly, if at all, the human figure. The carving of human heads on keystones of arches, over doors and windows, often of enormous size, is simply an atrocious barbarism. The human figure ought to be considered too important a subject to be used for ornament until all other resources have been exhausted; but to cut it up into fragments, and use the head alone, like John the Baptist's head on a charger, with no regard for proportion to other parts of the building, and often as a substitute for all other ornament, is a sign of nothing but savage ignorance. It is of a piece with that miserable subterfuge of caryatides — human figures bowed down by bearing enormous weights on their heads — in place of columns for the support of pediments, crushed as it were by loaded masses of stone above them. The Gothic artists never fell into that monstrosity. They put a shaft or column to bear the weight; and, if they wanted a human figure there, put it on a pedestal in front, and protected it by a canopy above. Where they did use a figure to bear weight, it was an evil spirit or grotesque creature caught and bound, and pressed into the service of the Church, and showing unmistakable evidence of pain in his enforced employment; one of the fallen angels, who, getting the worst of it in that primeval war, was seized by the monkish artists, and applied to a more useful purpose in stone than he ever fulfilled in the spirit. Such also are the gurgoyles and monsters who are carved as waterspouts to carry off the rain from the roofs of churches, and supplying, by their grotesqueness, the only element of the terrible to be found in Gothic art.

There are resources enough in foliage to satisfy a considerable love of sculpture and carving architecturally, and greater developments may employ the combination with it of animal forms. Last of all should come the human figure, only when all other expression fails, and for the highest purposes of art. To conventionalize the image of God, or to put it to ignoble purposes, is sacrilege. All art processes are feeble conventionalities compared with nature, and all the lower types are more capable of generalization in art than is the human figure. The Greeks understood this, and barbarous races have always misunderstood it; and I take it to be an evidence of good art where the human figure is used sparingly or with reverence, and of savage art where it is employed indiscriminately for many purposes, or repeated as an ornament.

Recurring to the use of polished and dead surfaces, it

may not be without interest to remember, that Edmund Burke, in his essays on the sublime and beautiful, laid it down as a general proposition, that in nature smooth things are beautiful, and rough things are ugly. He says,—

"Smoothness is a quality so essential to beauty, that I do not now recollect any thing beautiful that is not smooth. In trees and flowers, smooth leaves are beautiful; smooth slopes of earth in gardens; smooth streams in the landscape; smooth coats of birds or beasts in animal beauties; in fine women, smooth skins; and in several sorts of ornamental furniture, smooth and polished surfaces. A very considerable part of the effect of beauty is owing to this quality; indeed, the most considerable: for take any beautiful object, and give it a broken or rugged surface, and, however well formed it may be in other respects, it pleases no longer. Whereas, let it want ever so much of the other constituents, if it wants not this, it becomes more pleasing than almost all the others without it. This seems to me so evident, that I am a good deal surprised that none who have handled this subject have made any mention of the quality of smoothness in the enumeration of those that go to the forming of beauty; for, indeed, any rugged, any sudden projection, any sharp angle, is in the highest degree contrary to the idea."

And in his recapitulation he says,—

"On the whole, the qualities of beauty, as they are merely sensible qualities, are the following:—

"*First*, To be comparatively small.

"*Secondly*, To be smooth.

"*Thirdly*, To have a variety in the direction of the parts.

"*Fourthly*, To have those parts not angular, but melted as it were into each other.

"*Fifthly*, To be of a delicate frame, without any remarkable appearance of strength.

"*Sixthly*, To have its colors clear and bright, but not very strong and glaring.

"*Seventhly*, If it should have any glaring color, to have it diversified with others.

"These are, I believe, the properties on which beauty depends, — properties that operate by nature, and are less liable to be altered by caprice, or confounded by a diversity of tastes, than any other."

Now, that testimony is plain enough, and is evidence from one who by his study of the cause of beauty had a right to form and express an opinion.

But, in applying this to art instead of nature, it seems to me not to be wholly true; for smooth surfaces are sometimes, by art processes, roughened to increase their beauty. In nature it may be, and I think is true, that smoothness is a considerable element in beauty; but in art it would have been truer to have said that flat, rough things were ugly, and smooth, round things were beautiful, — flatness being almost incompatible with beauty of the highest order, just as it is a necessity of subordination. And in this our ideas are very much based on the natural forms displayed in the development of the human body. The straight line is less beautiful than the circle, the circle less beautiful than the ellipse, or oval. How the forms of children tend to the round or circular, and suggest health! Whether it be the rounded cheek or the concave dimple, the prevailing shape is spherical. In the most perfectly-developed beauty, as seen in the faces and forms of women, the elliptical form prevails, the face being oval; and the highest types of natural beauty are to be found in the faces and other forms of well-developed women. Decay and old age reduce the elliptical curve to the straight line, or something like it: the roundness of the child has merged into the ovoid face of the woman; and then decay takes the beautiful curves away, and flattens the check and straightens the jaw, and, in fact, destroys the beauty. In this case it is not smoothness only which causes beauty, but roundness.

That same element is to be noted in Egyptian, Greek, and Roman mouldings, progressing on exactly the reverse plan. In Egyptian mouldings, the prevailing line is straight, — chastity; in Greek, the ellipse, — subtlety; in Roman, the circle, — boldness; and here, as in the human form, the subtlest beauty is seen in the Greek or ovoid forms.

There are three elements of enrichment I hope to see extensively used in American architecture, in addition to those I have already referred to; namely, encaustic tiles, having a dead surface, and bas-reliefs, terracotta mouldings, moulded brick, wrought iron, and lead work.

I have already stated that one necessary characteristic of all true, intelligent, and noble art is permanence; and this should control even the material in which a structure is erected. Where peculiar natural or artificial conditions of the atmosphere destroy the softer stones, it is folly to employ them. The British Houses of Parliament, perhaps the most costly building erected in this century, is crumbling away; and you may cut the stone externally with a knife, as you would an apple. On the east coast of Yorkshire there is a building not twenty years old, which externally is more ruinous than an old abbey near it, which is centuries old. That has been caused by the action of the sea-air, charged with salt, on a soft stone; and the old monks who built the abbey either knew of this scientific truth, or they blundered on a stone with which to build their abbey that was proof against all climatic influences.

What is true of the fabric is true of details. To invest labor and skill in art upon delicate, sculptured ornament, which will either be destroyed by decay, or its effect be nullified by discoloration, is not wise. For this reason, terracotta is preferable; and it introduces, also, the element of color. If sculpture be applied to very hard stone, the work must necessarily be rough; and, when the grain of the stone is coarse, the work will be heavy and ponderous.

If a building were erected here in America containing brick as a basis, moulded brick for mouldings, terracotta for its sculptured enrichments, and encaustic tiles to give bands of color, we should see a structure entirely composed externally of burnt earth, indestructible and unchangeable either by climate or other influences, except fire, which would pulverize the mortar in which the burnt earth was set. I hope the time is not far distant when an enlightened public sentiment will create a desire for pictures in public buildings; for until that is the case we shall have no very great artists.

The Puritan feeling of the Anglo-Saxon race, wherever found, has been averse to associating the highest forms of art with religion, as a thing savoring of popery and the Scarlet Lady. But that is rapidly becoming a thing of the past; and, if I mistake not, I have seen beautiful pictures in the windows of a Unitarian church in this city of Boston, which, had our great-grandfathers beheld, they would have exclaimed with the Jews of old, "If we permit this thing, the Romans will come and take away our place and nation."

The revival of Gothic art, which has occurred during the last fifty years, has let considerable daylight into our notions concerning these things. It has been found possible to employ beautiful art to hallow the sanctuary, without reviving dead-and-gone superstitions.

We find that nature, as a rule, is very artistic without being at all sectarian, and true art is a reflex of nature. There will come a time when the Protestantism which has survived the introduction of pictures in windows will not be shocked or destroyed by a fresco or mosaic on the walls of our churches; and then may come again to us the light which shone upon Italy in the Middle Ages, the more brilliant in our day, in that it has been purified from the mists of superstition.

I was once travelling in a stage-coach with an ancient dame, who had not been out of her native village, away up among the Yorkshire hills, for forty years, as she told me. She was a devout Wesleyan, belonging to what she described as "t'owd body" — the first original Wesleyan Methodists, founded by Wesley himself.

As we approached a town, the first she had seen for forty years, we passed by a very elaborate religious edifice in the highest development of Gothic, its windows dull with stained glass leading, and its gable-ends bristling with elaborate crosses. Asking what building that might be, I informed her that it was a Methodist chapel. "Some of them new-fangled bodies," she remarked, "that stick to the old name, whilst they have lost the old spirit." — "On the contrary," I replied, "that is the new chapel of the old body." — "What!" she roared out, "with all them popish symbols on the roof, — their crosses and jinglings and priestcraft!" Wringing her hands, she muttered, "That ever I should have lived to see this day, I rue it, I rue it!" and the old lady wept tears of real Protestant sorrow at the sight of the cross, the symbol of her redemption!

I might have been disposed to commiserate these wasted tears, and attribute them to the forty years spent on that hillside upon the wolds, only that another individual, who could not give that excuse, a very reverend dean of the principal church in London, had just been wringing his hands from a similar cause, and, in reply to the proposition that St. Paul's should be decorated with frescos, had declared, that, so long as he lived, popery should not creep into the cathedral, in whatever guise it came. Alas! for this reverend Mrs. Partington, trying, as Sydney Smith said, to mop up the Atlantic: the good dean has gone to his Protestant bourn, the pictures are to be placed in St. Paul's, and popery is nowhere.

Perhaps the most beautiful form of picture for either external or internal decoration is the mosaic, such as the Roman or Venetian mosaic, composed of minute squares of colored glass or earth: it is also the only form of picture which will stand our northern climate externally. There is a great revival of the practice of working in mosaic going on now in London; and all the portraits of distinguished artists and men of science which decorate the panels, and fill the sunken niches, of the South-Kensington Museum are worked in mosaic. The building in which they are is absolutely fire-proof; so that the objection sometimes urged against frescos and mosaics — their liability to be destroyed by fire — does not apply to them.

The existence of symbolism in architectural enrichments is an element of interest always, whether the building be religious or secular, though it is not so frequent in the latter as in the former: yet in the coats-of-arms, in the mottoes, or seals, on civil buildings, it still lingers amongst us; and latterly it has taken a new form in ornamental carving. Thus in an English northern hospital, a modern Gothic building, the capitals of the columns are carved into the likenesses of all the plants and herbs used in medicine; and, as these capitals are somewhat numerous, it points out to the patients the unlimited field the doctors have for killing or curing them.

The advantage of the symbol is in its conciseness, and where, as in religious art, it conveys at a glance some principle or dogma of creed, or cherished incident in the lives of revered persons, there is consistency and beauty in the use of symbolic emblems.

Yet as this is scarcely to be called an age of faith, the value of the symbol is decreasing; and both people and artists seek in the enjoyment of physical beauty what they have lost in faith. That has led us into æstheticism, — the choice of forms and their expression on account of their attractiveness to us only.

But I do not regard this as a permanent feature of the art of this country. In our veins here to-day runs the same blood as once gave life to the men who built the cathedrals; and that history repeats itself, is true now as heretofore. The Anglo-Saxon race is pre-eminently a believing race, and a Gothic race too; and it has only been at the most barren and miserable portions of its history that it has relapsed into classicalism in art, and rationalism in religion. The French Renaissance taste, which is so popular in America to-day, will not last. It has not a thought or form in harmony with the blood of the people, but is really a passing sentiment; and, with increasing art education, it will cease to express their feeling. The architects who go from America to Europe, and study there as part of their training, come back and build Gothic buildings, which means something for those who have eyes to see. The repetition of history, which gave impulse to Pre-Raphaelism, and infused most of what is vital in English art; the Gothic revival, which has made every branch of art it has embraced honest and living again as it did in the fourteenth and fifteenth centuries, — that art revivalism is already here amongst us to-day, in the persons of the most intelligent American artists, and the most educated of American architects. Climate, a new form of government, and two hundred years of independent education, have not bred out of us what it took six centuries to breed into us; and, when the breath of art life shall call into existence a national school of American art, it will not be rationalistic nor classical: the instincts of our old Gothic forefathers will be revived here as elsewhere; and the art which has to express our whole sentiment will not be found to ignore our Christian faith, nor the art language of our ancestors.

Those miserable nightmare reigns of the four Georges, of which every Englishman is now justly ashamed, may have made the Anglo-Saxon race into two nations; but they could not, even by crime and blundering, transform them into more than one people. And though the waters of the broad Atlantic flow between these two nations, and separate them geographically, the common blood in their veins — blood which is thicker than water — will, let us fervently hope, keep them forever an undivided people.

Their agreement means "peace, and good-will toward men," — the message of heaven to earth: their division and dissension mean fratricide and wickedness. Let us each and all strive to unite this race by mutual charity and forbearance, in which the younger and stronger nation can afford to be generous and just. We ought to honor our national as well as our physical parents; and the reward is, "that our days shall be long in the land which the Lord our God giveth us."

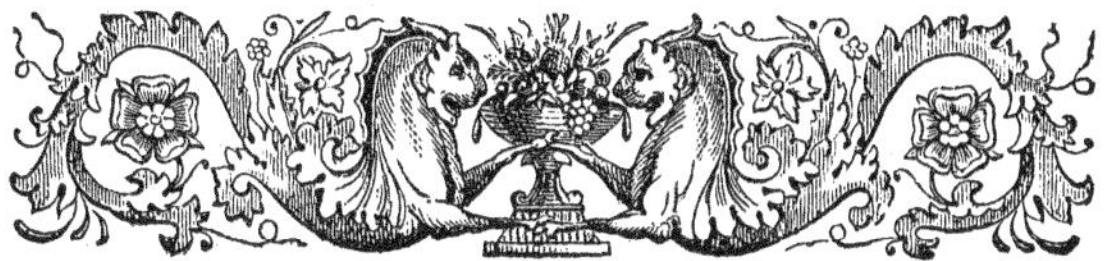

CHAPTER XI.

SYMBOLISM IN ART AND ARCHITECTURE.

THE æsthetic and symbolic are not inaptly illustrated by the legend of that beautiful little blue flower with its golden eye, which grows on the banks of every purling stream or flowing river that meanders through the meadow-lands of old England, — the "forget-me-not." The ancient story, handed down traditionally from generation to generation of young men and maidens, old men and children, is, that a young knight and his true-love were wandering on the margin of a rivulet, talking, no doubt, on the subject which was invented by Adam and Eve in paradise, and maintains its interest to this day, though none has ever been so generally discussed, or resulted so universally in such unanimity of opinion, — a subject called now, from its great antiquity, the "old, old story," ever new and fresh and delightful to those who tell it, as to those who hear it; for "time cannot stale nor custom wither its infinite variety." In an interval of the wooing, the "fayre ladaye" caught sight of a cluster of blue coronets — rivalling the beauty of her own eyes or the tint of the heaven above — growing in rich wantonness on the shady bank opposite to the lovers. An expression of admiration, and of a wish to possess them, on the lady's part, sent the knight of that chivalrous age plunging into the stream; and, battling against its turbulent motion, he grasped the longed-for treasure. Recrossing the rivulet, whilst preserving his chaplet of flowers uninjured, his powers were ill-matched against the violence of the water, but enabled him to approach his lady-love sufficiently near to be able to throw the bouquet at her feet, and exclaim, as he was swept away, "Forget me not." Since which time the flower has been consecrated to lovers as an emblem and symbol of faithfulness and true love.

Before, it was only an æsthetic love of the beautiful which made that "fayre ladaye" admire it; but afterwards it would doubtless be a consecrated emblem, whose beauty, great as that is, was eclipsed by its symbolic meaning. And a symbol it has remained to this day.

Symbolism is the suggestion through form and color in art, through words in language, sound in music, and signs in motion, of something which is beyond and in addition to the mere outward meaning of the thing seen, spoken, heard, or done. It is characteristic alike of the infancy and the maturity of the arts and of social history; but its use marks the existence of a distinct type of mind. What the allegory and parable are in literature; what figurative speaking is in language; what the war-cry is in the death-struggle of contending armies, or the trumpet-note in face of the foe, — what these things were and are in their several ways, the same is symbolism in art and architecture.

Beginning with architecture. Both the ancient and modern styles are divided easily into the æsthetic and the symbolic: the former being the embodiment of the beautiful alone and for itself; the latter striving, through the choice of beautiful forms, to convey a second meaning, either of religion or sentiment. The ancient styles of architecture are the Egyptian, Greek, and Roman; of which the Egyptian is a symbolic style, whilst the Greek and Roman are æsthetic styles.

The distinction may be seen by examining the treatment of a human figure as displayed by the two styles. In the Greek, or æsthetic, nothing but the absolute imitation of the most perfect forms seems to have been considered, — the Venus displaying only the choicest example of female form, the Apollo of male form.

The Gladiator and Discobolus were only athletes in perfect human development of strength and training, without reference to a second thought, save delight in mere excellence, and reproduction of the beautiful or the perfect. The Jupiter exhibited the majesty, Juno the dignity, Hercules the strength, and Bacchus the mirth, of the immortal gods, — not by signs or symbols, but by creation of the divinities themselves. In the Egyptian or symbolic style, a figure was used to embody some idea connected with the theology or history of the nation; and the actual form of its human parts was of little consequence compared to the truth or sentiment it illustrated. The amount of imitative power, as applied to the representation of the human figure, in Egyptian art was slight; yet it conveyed what was meant, because what was meant was something beyond the figure of the person represented: it was symbolic of what the artist thought or believed.

In the modern styles of architecture, Gothic is a symbolic, and Renaissance or Italian or classic is an æsthetic style. I think, from the analogy, symbolism in art is an indication of the association of religious views with the daily life of the people; or that art, being in the hands of the priests, has been used as an exponent of the national creed. We find, for instance, that, where the religious element is the most powerful, there art became the most generally symbolic, as in the case of the Egyptians, and the people living in the Middle Ages who built our cathedrals.

In architecture we see the most permanently preserved forms of symbolism: and I purpose pointing these out to you; because, when the idea of incorporating ideas or creeds with imitative art becomes the leading principle, then we shall see every form as an article of faith, and nothing left out from being affected by the prevailing influence. The same principle which settled that Christian churches should be built east and west, and decreed that Christian men and women should be buried with their feet to the east, — so that, in the first case, the altar should be towards the country whence came Christianity, and, in the second, that the Christian should rise at the last trumpet-call, and face his Saviour, — guided also, with a different application, the laying out of Egyptian temples, which all have their axes to one point of the compass, and also permeated every detail in the ornamentation of those temples. Thus the prosperity of Egypt was associated with the overflowing of the Nile, which brought fruitfulness to the soil, and food for the people: as a recognition of this, we find the prevailing form in ornamentation is the lotus, or water-lily, of the Nile, — symbol of plenty and prosperity. Again, the zigzag, or ornament composed of straight lines, signified the Nile smooth and at rest: the wave scroll, a spiral-curved form used in enrichment, was the emblem of the Nile water in motion.

The winged globe was carved over the doorway of every Egyptian temple; and this symbol was a kind of mixture of the Christian symbol of the cross and national arms, — the two rolled into one. This winged globe was composed of a ball, or sphere, which meant the earth; on each side were spread the eagle's wings, meaning dominion; and between the two were two serpents, or asps; the whole signifying, that, with the wisdom of the serpent, Egypt had dominion over the whole globe, or earth.

There was also a religious interpretation of this symbol, which regarded it as an agatho-demon, or good spirit, — a species of trinity composed of three parts, the globe signifying creation, the sun being the material source of every thing, the wings providence, and the asp order or wisdom. The crook and flail joined together, and occurring constantly on the decorated parts of buildings and garments, denoted the high respect paid to an agricultural and pastoral life in Egypt.

The favorite lotus-flower, used as an emblem of plenty, was further symbolized by the manner in which it was represented. Thus, if the flower was turned upwards, it was a symbol of Upper Egypt; if downward, of Lower Egypt.

In Chinese art, nature is imitated by the designer, either closely or conventionally, without any other idea than copying beautiful forms. It is purely an æsthetic style, meaning nothing but simple ornament, unconnected with religion. At the commencement of the Christian era, the effect of religious influence upon art is very strongly marked, from the entire devotion which the Christian artists showed towards their work. Thus both art and religion became promoted, — the former through the influence of the latter, and religion through the expression of art. The proof of this union is the constant repetition of symbolic forms in all art work.

This lasted for a few centuries; but the influence of religious fervor became less and less. And thus we find that emblems gradually died out: art became more æsthetic, and consequently less symbolic. Much of this change was due to the advancement of art and the increased power of artists. The first Christians were, as a body, uncultured and persecuted, meeting in dens and caves of the earth. To them a cross was sign and symbol of redemption and faith, — a symbol for which they were ready to suffer death if need be; a mark engraved on their hearts and in their secret places of worship, borne aloft in their processions with chants of victory or litanies of prayer, until from the village of Nazareth had proceeded the mysterious conquerors of the Roman Empire: the Gaul and German, Celt and Saxon, were enrolled as soldiers of the cross. In the first rude time the two cross-lines were sufficient to symbolize this suffering and victory; but when Christianity became the dominant religion, and art had developed into maturity, gorgeous pictures of the crucifixion took the place of the simple cross.

In the same way the fish was an emblem of baptism, — the rudest and simplest manner in which so important a part of the creed could be symbolized. Three crosses together were emblematic of the crucifixion before art was able to paint the figures upon them. But as art and architecture progressed, so long as it intimately associated with religion, the symbolic principle prevailed over every plan and every detail.

The churches and cathedrals were built in the form of a cross in plan. The numbers 3, 5, 7, became sacred, — 3 meaning the Trinity, 5 the five wounds, 7 the seven sacraments. The numbers were to be seen in the plan of a church, — a nave and two aisles; in the number of lights in the windows, in the foils of the tracery, in the number of points or leaflets in the sculptural foliage; and even the art of painting so far embraced the principle as to give a special color for the garment of every saint, and a special emblem to denote the sufferings of each martyr. Thus St. Andrew, executed by crucifixion upon a cross in the form of the letter X, stands majestically behind the symbol of his martyrdom.

Another apostle, sawn in two by his persecutors, appears forever in the glorious canopied sculpture of the Middle Ages with the implement of his barbarous execution in his faithful hand, — a never-dying protest against the bigotry of old creeds, and a warning to all future peoples not to persecute the believers in new doctrines.

The architecture of a people, supposing it to be a native and not a borrowed style, will display in its details the governing influence of the period in which it is practised. Wherever it expresses an embodiment of creed, as in ancient Egyptian or mediæval Gothic, there we may be sure religion has been the prime mover in the State. Where, on the other hand, it displays kingly or military symbols, we may draw the inference that the religious element was less powerful.

In Roman art the chief characteristic was the predominance of military trophies, such as triumphal arches and columns, to commemorate victories. In Greek as well as Roman history, we are told it was customary to decorate baths, triumphal arches, and other buildings, with the spoils of vanquished enemies. Thus trophies became a permanent feature of the styles, and indicated the influence of the military power.

Every people that has had a history will be found to be possessed of symbolism; for that is but the expression of history. It is compressing into a small compass the watchwords and principles which have been tried and not found wanting. Nor must it be forgotten, that there is a secular as well as a religious symbolism. The coats-of-arms of ancient families are symbolic of either their characteristics or achievements. The Prince Consort's motto, he who was called by England's greatest modern poet Albert the Good, was "True and Fast." An English nobleman's title, arising from his crest, is "Say and Seal." There is no end to the history contained in the crests and arms of the principal families in every European State ; but it is all expressed symbolically. I once asked the meaning of the words, or motto, on the crest of a family named Cross : it was "Crede Cruce" ("Believe in the Cross"). The answer was simply, that no Cross of that family was ever known to tell a lie! Young or old, in joke or in earnest, a Cross told the truth, be the consequence what it might. That was symbolism of the noblest sort, a whole system of morality in itself. A symbol may be expressed in a word or words, such as "Dieu et mon droit" ("God and my right"); and it is sometimes used to express a local characteristic.

I said that symbolism was the mark of a distinct type of mind; and that type is the *imaginative*, with a tendency to the *religious*. It is the discovery of similitudes between the seen and the unseen ; the co-ordinating of human hearts with spiritual standards; the linking together of the good deeds of all past ages with the present by keeping them forever in remembrance ; the physical outward significance of a principle made sacred or an act deemed noble, spoken in a language without words, appealing to the sentiment and the soul. It will be seen, therefore, how such a characteristic as symbolism would be the product of a religious age, and the more so when an age is both religious and ignorant. For the symbol is more condensed than the cipher, and plainer to understand by the lowest capacity.

Before books were printed and pictures were painted, when knowledge was in the hands of the few, when being learned was to be called a clerk, and being called a clerk meant being in holy orders, or, if not that, a Jesuit, then the symbol was books, pictures, knowledge, all in one, to the masses of the ignorant or superstitious. Having thus gained a foothold in the mind, it retains its place from its own intrinsic beauty ; but before the spread of knowledge, freedom of thought, and a tendency to dissociate the religious principle from art, symbolism must be cherished and kept alive by those who love it, or rationalism and the æsthetic spirit will destroy it altogether. The æsthetic styles of architecture banish symbolism entirely. The rationalistic mind will never tolerate a symbol when it scoffs at the reality. A man who laughs at the sacrifice will not be found to swear by the altar. And thus it will be found that a perpetual struggle goes on between the æsthetic and the symbolic in art and architecture.

In this age we have seen a contest between symbols and æsthetics in the struggle between classic and Gothic architecture for predominance.

This contest is not yet over, nor will it ever be; though the balance of success is very largely in favor of Gothic and symbolism just at present. Nor do I think the advantage will be easily wrested from it; because the basis upon which its appreciation now rests has been widened and strengthened to embrace much of the very little that is good in the spirit of this age, and eliminating from it features which belong to different conditions of society in the ages which invented Gothic, and are inappropriate now. Thus the grotesque and the terrible are very much ignored in modern Gothic, because people like the natural more than the grotesque, and the terrible hardly exists in this age. The time has passed when people could be terrified by pictures of hell, or frightened out of their lives by sculptured devils armed with the implements of torture. In this age a man is good because he loves virtue, not because he is afraid of fire. So that the gurgoyles whose savage forms awed the people of the Middle Ages, and the purgatories which by anticipation frizzled out of them tithes and bequests, made fat monks, and built big monasteries, are powerless now, either to instil fear or enforce contributions.

The chaw-bacon of the thirteenth, fourteenth, and fifteenth centuries could not read, write, or cipher; but he could be kicked and frightened, and skulk off into the mire of servitude, crossing himself the while, and praying to be preserved from hell's torments.

The chaw-bacon of this age reads and writes in daily newspapers, disputes theological points in the Sunday school of the bethel he patronizes with the person appointed to instruct him and lead him to heaven. So that, were the artists of this day capable of reproducing in art and architecture the terrible or the grotesque, — which they are not, — the people are too knowing to be impressed by them; and Gothic architects from their own feelings, and Gothic sculptors from their own tastes, leave out this species of mediæval symbolism altogether, and are developing something healthier and nobler. Thus, in adapting Gothic architecture to the times, the grossness and puerility of ancient symbolism is becoming eliminated, and the stronghold of æsthetic architecture appropriated, its birthright taken away, and the sceptre passing out of its hands.

That which has so conspicuously occurred in architecture has happened not the less surely in painting. The *nimbus* of the saint, which with its golden rays symbolized the holiness of the subject, has disappeared utterly, or is revived occasionally, like miracle-plays, — as great a curiosity as a piece of cloth that is all wool. The one great effort of modern days to return to the symbolic in painting — the establishment of Pre-Raphaelism, — an effort that began with the painting of angular saints and emaciated sinners — ended by producing the most essentially nineteenth-century artists we have amongst us. An importation from the fourteenth century could not live in this age,—pre-eminently a fast age,—but developed in a single decade of years into æstheticism, which previously it took two centuries to produce. Perhaps nothing in the realms of painting has done so much to link the past with the present, or create in our times a revival of the symbolic, as the re-introduction of stained or painted glass. There is in it so much of the spirit of the Middle Ages, whilst its religious subjects and bright colors accord so well with the allegorical or the symbolic, that we seem almost to be in the Middle Ages in presence of a good stained-glass window. Among nations, the most important symbol is the flag, representing the sovereignty of a country. This is the most comprehensive symbol possible: beyond its significance there can be no greater. The colors of a regiment, again, form the symbol of its courage; and the field must be bloody or the demoralization great before they are resigned to the foe. Other symbols are the crown and the signet; and, amongst savage tribes, smoking the calumet of peace (which some civilized people think not a bad practice), in token that war has ceased, and burying the hatchet for the same reason, show the love of symbolism even at the lowest stages of civilization. King Arthur's Round Table was a symbol of equality, having no head, or principal seat. The red and white roses were symbols which cost our mother country many a desolated hearth, and filled the land with widows and orphans.

We can tell the tomb of a Crusader, or Knight of the Holy Sepulchre, because the recumbent effigy has its legs crossed: that of a bishop is distinguished by a shepherd's crook or pastoral staff; whilst the keys of St. Peter betoken the last resting-place of an officer of the sovereign pontiff as he was, the bishop of Rome as he is.

The rose of England, the thistle of Scotland, and the

shamrock of Ireland, are symbols of the three countries, — the shortest and simplest and most universally-understood method of delineating in art the nationalities which form the United Kingdom; and leaving the old country, to come home for an instance, perhaps no more perfect symbolism exists in the world than that which has placed a star for each State in the Union upon the flag which waves gloriously over the United States of America.

In Egypt, the Jews fell into the prevailing symbolism which surrounded them, and, on a memorable occasion, marked the lintels with blood: later on, the concubine of a Levite, cut into twelve pieces, — each piece being sent to one of the twelve tribes of Israel, — knit the people together as one man; and, in revenge for her murder, there was slain of the tribe of Benjamin every living creature, save six hundred warriors who escaped. A terrible symbol that! but its power was irresistible. In thinking over and examining into the bearings of the subject, one must be strongly impressed with the almost universal tendency of the human mind to speak figuratively, and the love which is felt for allegory and symbol at the two extremes of civilization; arising, as I believe, from the value and universality of it in the rudest state, and the sentiment and religious attachment to it in the more advanced degrees of civilization. Where it does not exist, as in Greek and Roman art, there is generally a high development of æsthetic art, unaccompanied by the religious sentiment.

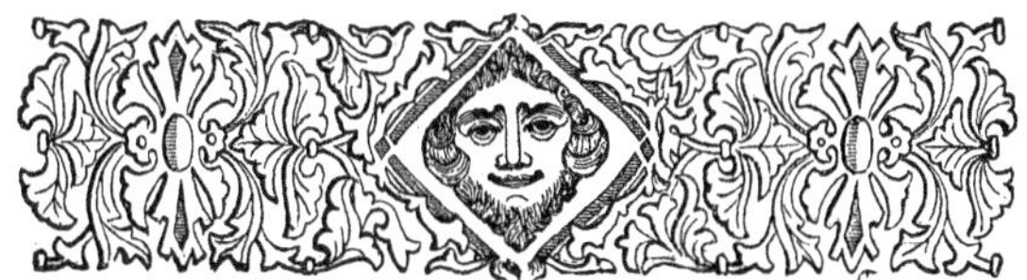

CHAPTER XII.

PROSPECT AND RETROSPECT.

I PURPOSE now to take a bird's-eye view of the subject of art education, and am going to ask you to accompany me, not into the clouds to seek after the ideal, but sufficiently away from the details of earth so that we may see this matter in one general view, — a comprehensive survey, in which all the parts of our view will fall into their relative positions, and none be distorted or ignored.

It is usual to think of the past as something seen through a glass, darkly, and of the future as a vision belonging to that style of architecture which concerns itself principally with building castles in the air; but the present we regard as clear and real, and easily to be understood.

The past we had, the future we may have, the present we have now; and our memory and travail in the days that were and are not, and our hopes and faith for the days that are not, but yet may be, form together a foundation and superstructure in which we enjoy or understand the present, which now is.

Yet it is given to very few rightly to comprehend the present, and understand its closely-veiled meanings. An artist knows what it is to be so near an object that he cannot see it; and the soldier who is fighting in the thick of a hot engagement is the last person to know how the battle went. We are the artists near our subject, and the soldiers fighting in the battle of to-day.

You may know narrow, microscopic persons, by the undue prominence given by them to whatever detail they see and magnify into the whole subject. There are people in every walk of life, and in every vocation, who can never be made to see more than the little bit of any subject which is within an inch of their eyes; and, as a rule, they are those who most loudly assert their own rightness and other people's error. They mention in confiding moments that they know more than they like to tell, and prove it most frequently by telling more than they ever knew. They are, by their own accounts, the really practical people, who are not going to be led away by any nonsensical theories, but will hold fast by the faith as it is in St. Ego.

Then there are the telescopic persons, whose eyes, shrouded from the daylight around them, gaze wistfully back into the ages that are afar off, or forward into the realms of the future. Very harmless folks in comparison with the microscopists, and not only harmless but helpful; for out of them come the generals on the eminence, directing the battle of life, telescope in hand, and who, by virtue of their broader survey, command the movements and direct the power of other men.

Yet all are not generals who see through telescopes; and some telescopic people who are peering disconsolately into the golden days of the good old times, or contemplating with rapture the vista stretching out into the millennial future, have a habit of treading on other people's feet, or bruising their own shins against material obstacles, in the uncomfortable present.

These two little instruments for seeing smaller and greater things than can be grasped by common eyesight, the microscope and the telescope, are typical of two phases of mind, neither of which alone comprehends the whole truth.

Then, again, there is the clear glance of healthy vision, not shrouded to confine its range, nor staring directly at the noonday sun, whose images are limited by natural laws possibly, but by laws which display as much of the past as we need, as much of the future as is good for us, and all there is of the present, — vision which is not hysterical over the millions of dragons which inhabit a drop of water, nor hushed with terror at the approach from afar of armies of fallen angels who are coming to disturb our peace. That is rational and natural vision, healthy and responsible. It is only by knowledge of the past, and consideration of the future, that the best use can be made of the present; for our work, unless it be controlled by law and directed by method, — experience crystallized into wisdom, — will be of no great value to us now or hereafter.

In my recapitulation I shall endeavor, so far as one fallible man may, to avoid falling into that telescopic error; and in my prospective enunciations will try to keep clear of unduly enlarging my microscopic atom.

The reason why I selected this comparatively dry subject for my first appearance as an American writer is, because it has enabled me to say something upon themes which are not yet exhausted in this country, but which, on the contrary, are now becoming interesting to many. It would have been more agreeable to me, and might have been more merciful to my readers, had I chosen some topic already familiar to the public mind, and thereby enlisted interest and sympathy in its discussion.

I am not unconscious of the proportion of people who want to be amused to those who want to be informed; but I would rather aspire to inform a few than amuse many.

At the foundation of all consideration of the question of industrial art lies the one great subject of education, necessary alike both for creation and appreciation; and that is why we first dwelt upon it. It is also the first step taken here to bring into existence a system of art culture. And perhaps it would not be out of place to look for a while at some of the needs that have existed in other places and times for art work, and see how they have been met; comparing our present wants with past necessities, and measuring the remedies found effective in other cases with the result looked for here.

The association of art with religion gave it for ages the character of an exponent of pious feelings and religious thought; and some of the greatest triumphs in art have been either inspired by or made the vehicle of such thought. There are not wanting those who advocate, that, until these two exalted expressions of human desires are again united, the highest forms of art will be impossible to us, and that, with the decay of faith, commenced the decline of art, only to rise again, if ever, with the revival of faith. It is perhaps needless to say, that I have no sympathy with that view, because it assumes what appears to me untenable, — that faith and religion are of one kind only; and what is referred to is the Christian religion. Now, we may alter the form of a thing without changing its area or its substance, or destroying its nature; and we do know that Greek art was as highly developed and as perfect a realization, as any subsequent revival, before Christianity was in existence, or had been manifested to us as a creed. On the other hand, the fading away of heathen creeds and the decline of Greek art did not prevent the glorious art revival of the fourteenth and fifteenth centuries in Europe; nor will many be made to believe that the faith of the people in those centuries was less, or less pure, than that of the believers in the deities of Mount Olympus.

Though the religion had changed, the art element remained the same, moulded only by the difference in race and creed into national or theological expression.

The same change is undoubtedly occurring now both in art and creed. The cherished idols of former epochs are broken and gone; and the last leaps of the accumulating avalanche will be more rapid and destructive than its first sliding motion. Yet we should be both forgetful of history and wilfully blind to that which surrounds us if we believed that transformation meant destruction, and guilty of grievous folly if we mourned uselessly over the irrevocable change.

The Panathenaic frieze will not be received again from mortal hands, and holy families will never again be painted; but if either or both, in some new development of society or religion, be demanded of the human family, then Phidias or Raphael will come again in the flesh to provide them in some new form.

I do not think that another distinctly-religious picture will ever be again produced in the limited sense attached to that name; for even the best modern artists, with perhaps one great exception, successful in all else, have made utter failures of those subjects: and moreover, as we are now circumstanced, I do not think that this is a matter of very deep regret. The religious picture was a sort of triangular mixture of the Apostle's Creed, the Thirty-nine Articles, and a daily newspaper; and, as we are beginning now to keep all these excellent things apart from one another, there will be no need of further mixture from that prescription.

But, seriously, the picture of the fifteenth century was the creed, sermon, and book of the people; and so it is now where society is much in the same condition as it was then, — which, if any one doubts, let him betake himself to a village in Belgium, or the Forest of the Ardennes, where the kirtled maidens still wear homespun raiment, and where Gascony love-songs are lightly warbled by the merry spinsters, sitting outside the cottage-doors at eventide, whilst the shovel-hatted priest smiles approvingly at them. Let him go to the ancient church, and watch the devotional exercises of the people, — not at mass-time, for that is mere ceremonial, but when people steal into the sacred building, which is always open day and night, to say their prayers or murmur their praise. He will see what I have seen hundreds of times: that perhaps a shoeless peasant-woman will go and sit or kneel for even hours, steadfastly gazing at a picture of Christ's passion, or the crucifixion, or a group of the Holy Family, until it seems to magnetize her. She is addressed by it through her sense of sight, appealed to on her human nature by all the influences that affect a sensitive creature. The language is unmistakable: it is neither threatening nor fawning, clouded by dogma nor mystified by hard words. She understands it, because she is a human being, not because she is a Catholic; for probably she never learned to read, and does not know the meaning of that word. And it speaks to her eloquently; and thus in contemplation, often in deep study, it is to her creed, sermon, book.

Now, I am far from saying that the time for such an exercise as that is passed away altogether; for, to those who have the priceless blessing of honest leisure, it might not be injurious if they sat as often in contemplation before a good picture as they do before a bad play or a trashy book. But if we look around us, and think how far the Ardennes village resembles modern American cities, we shall see how much our habits and thoughts are likely to be influenced by the same sort of agencies. We print our books, we say our creeds, and we listen to our sermons; and with that change of circumstances the vocation of the religious picture is gone.

Nevertheless, there is as much purity of feeling, as much of motive for good purposes, in many modern paintings, as in the fifteenth-century holy families; only the best artists of modern days, not being willing or able to paint such works, tell their stories in their own way, usually from secular subjects, — social or historical commentaries upon sentiments they delight to honor or wish to condemn. Here I am speaking only of the best work in all countries: the worst is about the same at all times and in all countries, — neither good, bad, nor indifferent, only misapplied labor.

The art of the future will be different from that which has preceded it, just as the thought of the present day is in channels which are as yet untravelled if they are not new. But I do not believe it will be a degraded or an incompetent development. The education of to-day is better than it ever has been; better because broader and fairer, and not monopolized by the few. Technical skill in art is as great as in the fifteenth century, — Millais paints as well as Giorgione; and, when modern thought finds its expressive formula, we shall have as great work done then as before, only it will be of a totally different sentiment. There may be as wide a departure from present types as ours is already from mediæval; but I have faith enough to believe that it will, in many features, show progress and not decay. One great peculiarity of modern art is its popularization by reproductions; and it may, to some extent, explain the archaic change that has occurred in our sentiment with regard to the whole subject. The artist now appeals to the people, not only by his original work, but by engravings, photographs, and a multitude of other channels. Where the men of old painted for a congregation or a city, men of the present paint for a country or a continent; so that, instead of appealing to a few and their special forms of delight, the modern artist appeals to the many. That peculiarity, of course, gives a sort of trivial or temporary character to modern art, which contrasts unfavorably with the quiet, sterling character of older art.

But it is a change that has taken place in almost every thing else as well. In proportion as we increase the power of many men politically, we decrease the power of some. The tendency now is towards diffusion of every thing, — power, land, money, government, art; and new phases will be assumed in all, not of necessity either better or worse than what is displaced, but having original features.

Where men once built a grand cathedral, we build twenty churches; and that is a sign and a type of many other changes. Where the stake once stood with its holocaust of martyrs, asserting uniformity of creed and worship, we erect a monument in commemoration of religious liberty. The pictures which once only hung in solemn grandeur in churches and halls now are to be found, as engravings, enlivening the house and the cottage.

This alteration in sentiment has been brought about, like all other great changes, gradually, and without any special effort, — spontaneously. It is perhaps more directly traceable to education than to any other cause; and, in the elevation and development of that blessing, we may expect many other great transformations besides.

In the matter of art education, we have not much to learn from the remote past. Almost all that has been done in it, except for professional or trade education, has been initiated in this century. The trade schools of the French Bronzists, the Free Industrial School at Toulouse, the drawing and painting school of the Sevres porcelain manufactory, and a few others, are, before the beginning of the present century, the most important, if not the only efforts to give technical art education, even in France, which lays claim to be the most highly-educated art producer of modern times. Professional schools have existed longer than that in most countries. Thus the British Royal Academy is just one hundred years old; and the École des Beaux Arts is, I believe, older. Schools and classes for art study used not to be the accepted form of art education; but the young artist was sent into the studio of a great artist to clean his brushes and palette and pick up his style. That accounts, also, for the prevalence of similar modes and thoughts which produced schools. Style was inherited by a pupil from his master; and, though often varied by individual pupils of a great master, the prevailing influence of an acknowledged leader is felt in contemporary and subsequent works.

But the public and the art workman have been ignored in the dispensation of art education in the centuries gone by, so far as means of instruction went. This must be qualified by the admission that the public has had, in countries where professional art has been long practised, the insensible education obtainable by public collections and monuments. And that is not a slight advantage, either in the formation of general taste or the development of skill and power in the individual. The influence of good buildings and galleries of art open free to the public is a rapid fertilizer of the artistic spirit in all, and creates it in many.

People whose eyes are constantly, or even occasionally, seeing beautiful forms, are receiving an education, whether they know it or not; and thus, in countries such as Italy, France, and Germany, public taste is higher than it is in other places where art is not ever-present in street, church, and gallery. This fact, the reproductive quality of art, was rather curiously illustrated by a circumstance happening some years ago, which demonstrated two things: the first, that originality depends upon knowledge of the works of other men, and the constant presence of artistic influences from without; and the second, that the withdrawal of such an influence is destructive of art power.

A manufacturer of fabrics, on the design for which much of their value in the market depended, a resident in a manufacturing district in the north of England, had been paying a large sum annually to foreign artists for designs (and that points to a time gone by, so that I shall hurt no one's feelings by mentioning the incident): conceiving that he would be better served, and obtain a more even quality of excellence in his productions, if he employed one good designer entirely in his factory, he found out the best designer in Paris, from whom he had long purchased his best work, and invited him to become his master-workman, offering a salary almost as great as that of a cabinet minister to tempt him to comply. The artist gave up his beautiful Paris, and located himself in a luxurious home on the bleak hill-side of a Yorkshire moor, and within sight of the tall mill-chimney and town where his designs were manufactured. For a short time the experiment succeeded; but he rapidly found, that, among the smoke and dirt and hideous ugliness of a manufacturing town, virtue was going out of him. His work became first tame and then ugly, and within a year he threw up his appointment; confessing, that, in such a place, he could not design, and what power he had originally possessed he was losing day by day.

That is a complete confirmation of what John Ruskin says in his "Two Paths," in a lecture delivered in a Yorkshire manufacturing town. It is as follows: —

"Beautiful art can only be produced by people who have beautiful things about them, and leisure to look at them; and, unless you provide some elements of beauty for your workmen to be surrounded by, you will find that no element of beauty can be invented by them."

That is a principle recognized by the founders of fine-arts museums, and will, I hope, to some extent, meet the difficulty here. In a beautiful contrast of two scenes, Ruskin further illustrates his meaning in a short passage I must quote, because it is too original to describe: —

"I was struck forcibly by the bearing of this great fact upon our modern efforts at ornamentation in an afternoon walk, last week, in the suburbs of one of our large manufacturing towns. I was thinking of the difference in the effect upon the designer's mind between the scene which I then came upon and the scene which would have presented itself to the eyes of any designer of the Middle Ages when he left his workshop. Just outside the town I came upon an old English cottage or mansion, — I hardly know which to call it, — set close under the hill, and beside the river, perhaps built somewhere in the Charleses' times, with mullioned windows, and a low, arched porch, round which, in the little triangular garden, one can imagine the family as they used to sit in old summer times, — the ripple of the river heard faintly through the sweetbrier hedge, and the sheep on the far-off wolds shining in the evening sunlight. There, uninhabited for many and many a year, it has been left in unregarded havoc of ruin, — the garden-gate still swung loose to its latch; the garden, blighted utterly in a field of ashes, not even a weed taking root there;

the roof torn into shapeless rents, the shutters hanging about the windows in rags of rotten wood; before its gate, the stream which had gladdened it now soaking slowly by, black as ebony, and thick with curdling scum; the bank above it trodden into unctuous, sooty slime; far in front of it, between it and the old hills, the furnaces of the city foaming forth perpetual plague of sulphurous darkness; the volumes of their storm-clouds coiling low over a waste of grassless fields, fenced from each other, not by hedges, but by slabs of square stone, like gravestones, riveted together with iron. That was your scene for the designer's contemplation in his afternoon walk at Rochdale. Now fancy what was the scene which presented itself, in his afternoon walk, to a designer of the Gothic school of Pisa, — Nino Pisano or any of his men.

"On each side of a bright river, he saw rise a line of brighter palaces, arched and pillared, and inlaid with deep-red porphyry and with serpentine; along the quays before their gates were riding troops of knights, noble in face and form, dazzling in crest and shield, — horse and man one labyrinth of quaint color and gleaming light, the purple, the silver, and scarlet fringes flowing over the strong limbs and clashing mail like sea-waves over rocks at sunset; opening on each side from the river were gardens, courts, and cloisters; long successions of white pillars among wreaths of vine; leaping of fountains through buds of pomegranate and orange; and still along the garden-paths, and under and through the crimson of the pomegranate shadows, moving slowly, groups of the fairest women that Italy ever saw, — fairest, because purest and thoughtfullest, trained in all high knowledge as in all courteous art, — in dance, in song, in sweet wit, in lofty learning, in loftier courage, in loftiest love, — able alike to cheer, to enchant, or save, the souls of men. Above all this scenery of perfect human life rose dome and bell-tower, burning with white alabaster and gold; beyond dome and bell-tower the slopes of mighty hills, hoary with olive; far in the north, above a purple sea of peaks of solemn Apennine, the clear, sharp-cloven Carrara mountains sent up their steadfast flames of marble summit into amber sky; the great sea itself, scorching with expanse of light, stretching from their feet to the Gorgonian Isles; and over all these, ever present, near or far, seen through the leaves of vines, or imaged with all its march of clouds in the Arno's stream, or set with its depth of blue close against the golden hair and burning cheek of lady and knight, that untroubled and sacred sky, which was to all men, in those days of innocent faith, indeed the unquestioned abode of spirits, as the earth was of men; and which opened straight through its gates of cloud, and veils of dew, into the awfulness of the eternal world, — a heaven in which every cloud that passed was literally the chariot of an angel, and every ray of its evening and morning streamed from the throne of God.

"What think you of that for a school of design? I do not bring this contrast before you as a ground of hopelessness in our task: neither do I look for any possible renovation of the Republic of Pisa at Bradford in the nineteenth century; but I put it before you in order that you may be aware precisely of the kind of difficulty you have to meet, and may then consider with yourselves how far you can meet it. To men surrounded by the depressing and monotonous circumstances of English manufacturing life, depend upon it, design is simply impossible. This is the most distinct of all the experiences I have had in dealing with the modern workman. He is intelligent and ingenious in the highest degree, subtle in touch, and keen in sight; but he is, generally speaking, wholly destitute of designing power.

"And if you want to give him the power, you must give him the materials, and put him in the circumstances for it. Design is not the offspring of idle fancy: it is the studied result of accumulative observation and delightful habit. Without observation and experience, no design; without peace and pleasurableness in occupation, no design; and all the lecturings and teachings and prizes and principles of art in the world are of no use, so long as you don't surround your men with happy influences and beautiful things. It is impossible for them to have right ideas about color, unless you see the lovely colors of nature unspoiled; impossible for them to supply beautiful incident and action in their ornament, unless they see beautiful incident and action in the world about them. Inform their minds, refine their habits, and you form and refine their designs; but keep them illiterate, uncomfortable, and in the midst of unbeautiful things, and whatever they do will still be spurious, vulgar, and valueless."

Yet even where works of art are not available for public exhibition, and where the surrounding circumstances have not been provocative of taste, it has been found possible to create much artistic feeling by education. The class-room, supplied with beautiful details of ancient art and intelligent instruction to explain them, has not been wholly uninfluential, even in the very locality where the lecture of Mr. Ruskin was delivered, or to which his comparison refers.

And, though I most thoroughly believe that it is infinitely easier for people to become tasteful in their habits and skilful in their works where there is an art atmosphere which they breathe from their infancy to their old age, there must be, of necessity, times when taste and skill have preceded these influences, or the buildings originally would never have been built nor the pictures painted: so that here, as elsewhere, the inner education must precede and create the outer; and then there will be a re-action from without, and all will go on merrily.

The one grand advance made upon the action of the past is the recognition of the principle, that art education must be general to be efficient; that human beings are fairly treated by Nature in this matter, as in some others, by her impartially dealing out to all the elementary faculties of sight and understanding to receive, and voice and touch to express. When drawing was by law introduced into the common schools of the State of Massachusetts, there was done by a stroke what it took European nations a good many centuries to accomplish, and some of whom have not yet succeeded in realizing. Yet where any solid advancement has been made, either in the fine arts or the industrial arts, it is to a great degree owing to the intelligence displayed by this recognition of general natural powers.

For the general culture obtained through the study of art, even in its lowest elements, cuts both ways: it provides not only the opportunity for development of exceptional taste and skill, but furnishes also the ability to appreciate good art in those who do not possess unusual attainments. It creates the demand as well as the supply, tills the field, and sows the seed which is to fructify into the harvest of the future, makes the audience and the orator, the discerning public and the designing craftsman.

And that is the only consistent basis upon which education can be faithfully carried on, — the principle of treating all alike, and leaving to individual circumstances the use to which its developments may be applied.

We have the advantage of beginning with that principle acknowledged: the net is large enough to catch all fish; and we shall find in time that no possibly great artist will be "born to blush unseen;" but we shall find him early in the rough, and catch him, and hew out of him the shape his nature wants to assume. The compulsory teaching of drawing in the common schools is such a step, that all which may be required afterwards will follow as a natural consequence. In the State of Massachusetts the history of the American school of painters is begun: before two years ago individual artists may have existed at long intervals and with very varying success. But, when history speaks of the future eminence of New England in art matters, it will start with a statement of the brilliant light of Stuart and some others illuminating the surrounding darkness, and pass on directly to the legislative acts of 1870, which say, that, in future, drawing is to be taught to all children in the common schools; and then art history commenced.

What is now being done in European countries to advance the interests of industry, by elevating the taste and skill of workmen, must necessarily be a matter of much interest to us just now, when we are trying to bring our workmen up to the same level. In many parts of Germany instruction in industrial art in night classes is gratuitous, as it is here; and almost every important village even has classes. In France the municipal schools are not all of them free, though a few are; and the immediate money value of art power keeps the schools always crowded with students.

Perhaps the most important retrospect with regard to French art education is that which reviews the effects upon them of the English International Exhibition of 1862. The enormous strides which art education had made in England since the previous great exhibition in 1851, and which was reflected in every object of industrial art displayed in the exhibition of 1862, set the sensitive French manufacturers at work inquiring the cause, fearful that their own industrial art supremacy was endangered. A commission which visited England, and examined into the subject with characteristic sagacity, soon discovered the cause of improvement, and paid special attention to the administration of the South Kensington Museum and its training-school for art masters. The city of Paris, always ready to advance art, appointed a commission in 1863 to examine and draw up a scheme for re-organizing the municipal art schools, and suggest some plan by which the whole system of instruction could be improved. The recommendations of this commission embraced the following suggestions: —

1. The holding of annual examinations for granting diplomas to male and female professors of drawing, and to whom alone the city schools should be intrusted.

2. Division of the teaching into artistic and geometrical education, in order that special masters might be employed in each of these departments.

3. The selection and production of superior models and examples.

4. Improvement of the class-rooms, and separation of the various classes.

5. Annual competitions amongst all classes, in order to stimulate the zeal of the pupils.

6. Better remuneration of teachers, combining a fixed sum in conjunction with fees dependent on the number of pupils attending the schools, the number admitted to the competitions, and the number of rewards there obtained. [These regulations were borrowed entirely from South Kensington.]

7. Drawing to be made obligatory in all the public schools, whether for boys or girls.

8. Nomination of two inspectors to watch the progress of the schools, and report on it, and upon the improvements which seemed called for.

Those recommendations having been adopted with some few modifications, and accepted by the minister of public instruction, the plan was immediately carried into operation by an examination of candidates for teacherships in the city. The value of this step may be seen by its results. The first examination was conducted in 1865; and, of persons who believed themselves eligible for such appointments, there were a hundred and seventy-one who presented themselves. Of this number, only twenty-seven passed in the artistic, and only thirteen in the geometrical subjects, — a practical commentary upon taking people at their own estimate; for, without such a test, there would have been a hundred and seventy-one persons ready for positions as art teachers, of whose qualification no evidence of a satisfactory kind could be given, and who, when tested, shrunk away to forty in number, the rest presumably going back again to their studies to create or increase their qualifications. But in 1866, ninety females becoming candidates for diplomas, eleven only received them; and in 1867, of ninety-two male candidates, nineteen only were not found wanting. This is conclusive evidence of the need for such a professional examination for teachers' diplomas as that suggested in Chap. I., page 30; and I feel convinced, that, until it is established in America, there can be no great results secured for art education here.

The establishment of the normal school at Cluny, for the training of art and science teachers, by M. Duruy, after the law of 1865 was passed, was a powerful step in the right direction. That law laid down the axiom, that education in art and science should not be considered subordinate to classical education, but of the same rank; and M. Duruy, proceeding on this view in the law which owed its origin to him, carried it out by organizing at Cluny a noble institution for the advancement of industrial education in art and science. The old abbey of the Benedictines, then unoccupied, was transformed into a normal art school, with its courses of study arranged for two years, but permission in special cases for talented pupils to remain an additional year; admission being given only to those between eighteen and twenty-five years of age. The whole cost to each pupil is about two hundred and twenty dollars a year (gold) for instruction, board, lodging, and even washing and repairs of clothing.

Both in France and Germany a greater prominence is given to what are called schools of industrial sciences than to schools of art, in which art study forms a section of the general plan of industrial education.

It seems to me, that, now the question of industrial schools is being so much discussed here, very valuable information concerning such schemes might be obtained from an examination of these foreign schools by some intelligent educationists sent for that purpose by the Government of this country.

In England the experience is the reverse of this, and scientific or industrial classes form a part of the schools of art. But the demand for and extreme popularity of scientific study, as compared with that of art, may be estimated by one fact gleaned from the annual blue-book, or report of the government department of science and art for the year 1870. Though the organization and examination of science schools and classes are not yet ten years old, and five years ago there were hardly any established, yet, at the end of the year 1870, there were 943 schools of industrial science in the United Kingdom, having 2,684 classes, and 34,435 students in them; whilst, at the end of twenty years' experience in establishing schools of art, there were at the end of 1870 only 117 schools and 20,290 students.

In addition to these schools and students, it is, however, only right to add, that of night classes for industrial drawing, similar to what have been established in the State of Massachusetts and taught by certificated art teachers, there were 352 schools and 12,119 students; and the public schools which were instructed by certificated art teachers numbered 1,359 schools and 147,243 pupils: all these returns being for the same year, 1870, and all the schools and classes and individual pupils having been examined by the government inspectors during the year.

It is rather interesting to note the rapid progress made in this subject in four years in the United Kingdom in the matter of art: —

In 1866,	night schools instructed,	32;	in 1870,	352
"	public schools "	560;	"	1,359
"	schools of art established,	99;	"	119

In industrial science, though I cannot compare the progress made in four years, I can say, from my own knowledge of the subject, that, in the year 1866, science classes were rare, and at the end of 1870 the report shows 2,684 classes examined; and, in addition to that, I have incidentally heard from science teachers, that, in 1871, the number of classes before existing was almost doubled, and the students increasing in the same ratio.

To show the practical nature of the sciences studied in these classes, I will here enumerate a list of the subjects of instruction: —

1. Practical plane and solid geometry.
2. Machine construction and drawing.
3. Building construction and naval architecture.

4, 5. Pure mathematics.

6. Theoretical mathematics.
7. Applied mechanics.
8. Acoustics, light, and heat.
9. Magnetism and electricity.
10. Inorganic chemistry.
11. Organic chemistry.
12. Geology.
13. Mineralogy.
14. Animal physiology.
15. Zoölogy.
16. Vegetable anatomy and physiology.
17. Systematic and economic botany.
18. Mining.
19. Metallurgy.
20. Navigation.
21. Nautical astronomy.
22. Steam.
23. Physical geography.

The stages of art instruction also number twenty-three, with above sixty subdivisions, and are as practical in their bearing on industrial art as the above subjects are upon industrial science.

There may be cases in other countries showing a parallel development of art-and-science instruction; but I am not aware of them, if they exist. It is sufficient for us to know, that in a country peopled by the same race as America, speaking the same language, and a manufacturing nation as we are, this wonderful progress has actually occurred in the space of four years; that the classes in all subjects are nearly doubling year by year: and any practical educationist will see at a glance what must be the effect of such advancement.

If it be asked, how has this been brought about, I

shall say, by a little practical wisdom on the part of the Government, learned by its art experience. The first care was to offer great inducements to teachers to study the several subjects, and become certificated by passing examinations, and thus qualified to teach others. They, in their turns, were employed to instruct teachers' classes in many centres; and, as a consequence, thousands of teachers, competent in some one or more subjects, were planted broadcast over the land. These are not special teachers, whose profession it is to teach a particular branch of science, but the regular day-school teachers, whose evenings, being unoccupied, are most profitably employed in imparting secondary or technical instruction to artisans and others.

I look for a similar development in this country when the same steps are taken to insure it, and not before. What we are doing is right as far as it goes; but how far it does go, in comparison with what is being done in Europe, any person knowing the above facts, and capable of thinking, is able to decide.

What England is doing in this matter of industrial education is probably greater than in most countries; but they are all doing much: and in proportion to what they do is their commercial success in manufacturing industry.

Nevertheless, I believe, that, so soon as this country awakens to the sense of her deficiencies in this subject, there will be as great a rush to do great things as there has been tardiness in commencing them; for the ground will be fully prepared, and the demand for its cultivation general.

With regard to the best methods or systems of study in art or science, that will right itself; for the only ones which will succeed here will be American. Those whose experience is worth any thing, or who have watched or read of the initiation and development of great movements, know that you cannot fit any branch of civilization upon a people who have not originated it.

The genius of a country impresses itself upon those who are not too old to learn; and, when they are too old to learn, they are unfitted to teach: and this spirit will fit the work to the men or the men to the work. The only sort of system which will be found to work is that which we make as we go on; and, if the right sort of workmen are employed, they will not be in any difficulty about plans or schemes, which will develop as the need comes. For a plan of education is not like the erection of a building, which has to be settled from foundation to roof before a stone is laid. It is rather like the cultivation of a new farm, whose soil has to be tested to see what it will best grow, — corn or roots or wheat; and it will be many seasons before that will display itself.

It may have occurred to some that my notions and illustrations have been drawn almost entirely from experience in another half of the world, which is different from this half, comparatively unknown to Americans, and having another history and dissimilar wants.

To those I would say, that I am conscious of this, and can plead in extenuation of such an offence, that I have regarded my task as a responsible one, however unimportant it may be considered socially, and that, in endeavoring to display certain principles and to find some light to guide us in our common path, my position has been that of a witness in the witness-box, — not to detail hearsay evidence, but his own experiences; not to be discursive on the merits of the case, but to state his own share in the transaction: and, in doing so, how could I, who have spent but a few months in this country, do other than "speak of that which I know, and testify of that which I have seen," to use language which most aptly expresses my own individual case. The time may come when, by my own experience and the progress of art education here, the most pertinent facts I refer to and the most illustrative images I portray may be American in every detail; until that time arrives, and considering my infancy as an American citizen, I feel sure my readers will gently excuse Old-World illustrations, and believe that practical evidence is worth as much as any other evidence I could give.

I shall conclude this very imperfect treatment of my subject by again quoting from the thoughtful language of the greatest art master this century has produced. I would wish for no better indication that the tendency of American manufacture was in the right direction, than that both masters and students could approve of the lofty ideal set forth in the following words. Mr. Ruskin was addressing an audience in the town of Bradford, an important Yorkshire manufacturing centre. Speaking of the education of the workmen, and the character of the manufactures, he said, —

"I repeat, that I do not ask you, nor wish you, to build a new Pisa for them. We don't want either the life or the decorations of the thirteenth century back again; and the circumstances with which you must surround your workmen are those simply of happy modern English life, because the designs you have now to ask for from your workmen are such as will make modern English life beautiful. All that gorgeousness of the Middle Ages, beautiful as it sounds in description, noble as in many respects it was in reality, had nevertheless, for foundation and for end, nothing but the pride of life, — the pride of the so-called superior classes; a pride which supported itself by violence and robbery, and led, in the end, to the destruction both of the arts themselves and the states in which they flourished.

The great lesson of history is, that all the fine arts hitherto having been supported by the selfish power of the *noblesse*, and never having extended their range to the comfort or the relief of the mass of the people, — the arts, I say, thus practised and thus matured, have only accelerated the ruin of the states they adorned; and at the moment when, in any kingdom, you point to the triumphs of its greatest artists, you point also to the determined hour of the kingdom's decline. The names of great painters are like passing bells: in the name of Velasquez you hear sounded the fall of Spain; in the name of Titian, that of Venice; in the name of Leonardo, that of Milan; in the name of Raphael, that of Rome.

"And there is profound justice in this: for in proportion to the nobleness of the power is the guilt of its use for purposes vain or vile; and hitherto the greater the art, the more surely has it been used, and used solely, for the decoration of pride,* or the provoking of sensuality. Another course lies open to us. We may abandon the hope — or, if you like the words better, we may disdain the temptation — of the pomp and grace of Italy in her youth. For us there can be no more the throne of marble, for us no more the vault of gold; but for us there is the loftier and lovelier privilege of bringing the power and charm of art within the reach of the humble and the poor: and, as the magnificence of past ages failed by its narrowness and its pride, ours may prevail and continue by its universality and its lowliness.

"And thus, between the picture of too laborious England, which we imagined as future, and the picture of too luxurious Italy, which we remember in the past, there may exist — there will exist if we do our duty — an intermediate condition, neither oppressed by labor

* Whether religious or profane pride, — chapel or banqueting-room, — is no matter.

nor wasted in vanity, — the condition of a peaceful and thoughtful temperance in aims and acts and arts. We are about to enter upon a period of our world's history in which domestic life, aided by the arts of peace, will slowly, but at last entirely, supersede public life and the arts of war. For our own England, she will not, I believe, be blasted throughout with furnaces, nor will she be encumbered with palaces. I trust she will keep her green fields, her cottages, and her homes of middle life; but these ought to be, and I trust will be, enriched with a useful, truthful, substantial form of art. We want now no more feasts of the gods, nor martyrdoms of saints: we have no need of sensuality, no place for superstition or for costly insolence. Let us have learned and faithful historical paintings, touching and thoughtful representations of human nature in dramatic painting, poetical and familiar renderings of natural objects and of landscape, and rational, deeply-felt realizations of the events which are the subjects of our religious faith. And let these things we want, as far as possible, be scattered abroad, and made accessible to all men. So, also, in manufacture: we require work substantial rather than rich in make, and refined rather than splendid in design. Your stuffs need not be such as would catch the eye of a duchess; but they should be such as may at once serve the need and refine the taste of a cottager. The prevailing error in English dress, especially among the lower orders, is a tendency to flimsiness and gaudiness, arising mainly from the awkward imitation of their superiors. It should be one of the first objects of all manufacturers to produce stuffs, not only beautiful and quaint in design, but also adapted for every-day service, and decorous in humble and secluded life. And you must remember always, that your business, as manufacturers, is to form the market as much as to supply it. If, in short-sighted and reckless eagerness for wealth, you catch at every humor of the populace as it shapes itself into momentary demand; if in jealous rivalry with neighboring States, or with other producers, you try to attract attention by singularities, novelties, and gaudinesses, to make every design an advertisement, and pilfer every idea of a successful neighbor's, that you may insidiously imitate it or pompously eclipse, no good design will ever be possible to you. You may by accident snatch the market, or by energy command it; you may obtain the confidence of the public, and cause the ruin of opponent houses; or you may, with equal justice of fortune, be ruined by them. But, whatever happens to you, this at least is certain, that the whole of your life will have been spent in corrupting public taste and encouraging public extravagance. Every preference you have won by gaudiness must have been based on the purchaser's vanity; every demand you have created by novelty has fostered in the consumer a habit of discontent; and, when you retire into inactive life, you may, as a subject of consolation for your declining years, reflect, that, precisely according to the extent of your past operations, your life has been successful in retarding the arts, tarnishing the virtues, and confusing the manners, of your country.

"But, on the other hand, if you resolve from the first, that, so far as you can ascertain or discern what is best, you will produce what is best, on an intelligent consideration of the probable tendencies and possible tastes of the people whom you supply, you may literally become more influential for all kinds of good than many lecturers on art or many treatise-writers on morality. Considering the materials dealt with, and the crude state of art knowledge at the time, I do not know that any more wide or effective influence in public taste was ever exercised than that of the Staffordshire manufacture of pottery under William Wedgewood; and it only rests with the manufacturer in every other business to determine whether he will, in like manner, make his wares educational instruments or mere drugs of the market.

"You all should be, in a certain sense, authors: you must, indeed, first catch the public eye, as an author must the public ear; but once gain your audience or observance, and as it is in the writer's power thenceforward to publish what will educate as it amuses, so it is in yours to publish what will educate as it adorns. Nor is this surely a subject of poor ambition. I hear it said continually that men are too ambitious: alas! to me it seems they are never enough ambitious. How many are content to be merely the thriving merchants of a state, when they might be its guides, counsellors, and rulers; wielding powers of subtle but gigantic beneficence in restraining its follies, while they supplied its wants. Let such duty, such ambition, be once accepted in their fulness, and the best glory of European art and of European manufacture may yet be to come. The paintings of Raphael and of Buonarotti gave force to the falsehoods of superstition, and majesty to the imaginations of sin; but the arts of England may have for their task to inform the soul with truth, and touch the heart with compassion. The steel of Toledo and the silk of Genoa did but give strength to oppression, and lustre to pride: let it be for the furnace and for the loom of England, as they have already richly earned, still more abundantly to bestow comfort on the indigent, civilization on the rude, and to dispense, through the peaceful homes of nations, the grace and the preciousness of simple adornment and useful possession."

I have made these long extracts from "The Two Paths" because the counsel given is as applicable here to-day in America as it was in England ten years ago, and is now; because it expresses precisely my own feeling with regard to the quickest way of arriving at a consistent development of art industry, fitted to the circumstances of this age and this country. Knowing from a long course of observation how important an influence the author has had upon the art of England by such utterly noble thoughts and language as that I have quoted, I reproduce them as likely to be not without similar results here.

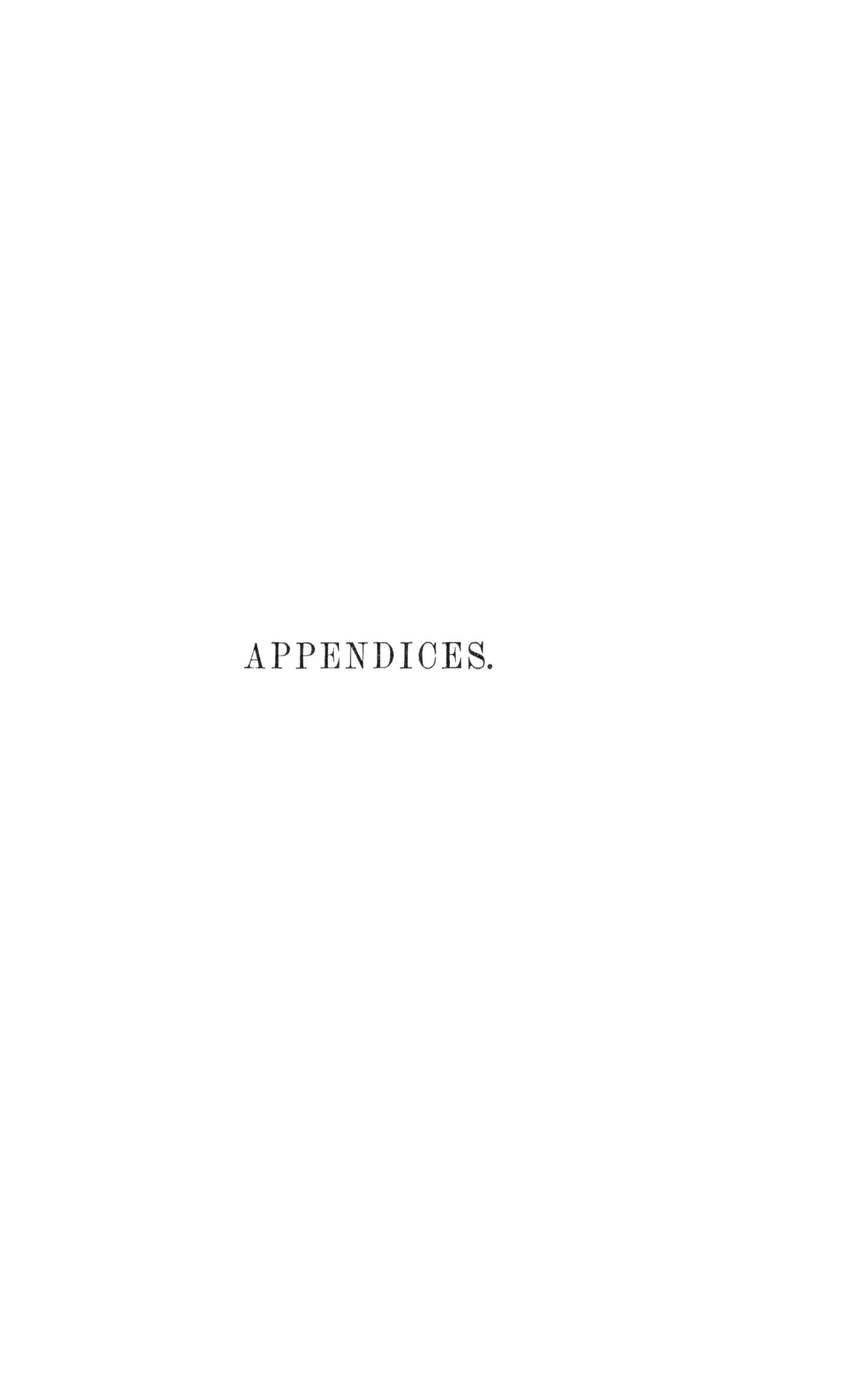

APPENDICES.

APPENDIX I.

FLAT EXAMPLES, MODELS, AND BOOKS.

THE want of examples and casts for art study which have been examined and approved of by competent authorities in art has long been felt in America. Possibly, until such works are designed or reproduced here, we may have to depend upon our supplies from abroad. The following lists may therefore be of service to such as have to provide examples for classes. To the prices given, fifty per cent must be added for package, freightage, and dues; but works of art for the purposes of public instruction enter the United States free of duty. My experience is, that carriage by steamer is preferable to by sailing vessel for works of art, and that all cases used for packing such works must be lined with tin or zinc. If only flat copies are required, without models or vases, thirty per cent will cover the extra cost of package, etc.

Agent in London, Sig. D. Brucciani, 40 Russell Street, Covent Garden, London, England.

List of Examples, &c., approved by the Science and Art Department, and supplied to National and other Public Schools, Institutions, &c.

Rotation number.

18–20 Letters A. O. S., 3*s*.
33–45 Simpson's 12 plates of Outlines for Blackboard, on canvas, 7*s*.
Ditto on sheets, 3*s*.
375–377 Richson's Elementary Free-hand Copies, five parts, 2*s*. 6*d*.
1710 Delarue's Free-hand Outlines of Common Things, 48 subjects, 5*s*.
95–98 Familiar Objects, 9*d*.

COPIES FOR OUTLINE DRAWING.

2120 Delarue's Outlines of Animals, 1*s*.
148–222 Dyce's Elementary Outlines of Ornament, 50 selected plates, unmounted, 5*s*.
223–234 Weitbreicht's Outlines of Ornament, reproduced by Herman, 12 plates, one set, unmounted, 2*s*.
235–254 Morghen's Outlines of the Human Figure, reproduced by Herman, one set, 20 plates, unmounted, 3*s*. 4*d*.
255–258 One set of 4 plates. Outlines of Tarsia, from Gruner, unmounted (size, 17½ in. x 22 in.), 7*d*.
259–262 Albertolli's Foliage, one set of 4 plates, unmounted (size 20 in. x 8 in.), 5*d*.
1272 Wallis's Drawing-Book, unmounted, 3*s*. 6*d*.
1701–1708 Outline Drawings of Flowers, 8 sheets, unmounted, 8*d*.
1271 Outline of Trajan Frieze, mounted, 1*s*.
Elementary Drawing-Books. For the use of children from four years old and upwards, in schools and families, 4 to 7 books, at 8*d*. each, London, Chapman & Hall, 1864. The set, 4*s*. 6*d*.

COPIES FOR SHADED DRAWING.

Selections from the Course of Design, by Ch. Bargue (French), 20 sheets, each 2*s*.
2160 Renaissance Rosette, unmounted, 3*d*.
2226 Shaded Ornament, unmounted, 4*d*.
2110 Ornament from a Greek Frieze, unmounted, 3*d*.
Four plates of Flowers, shaded:—
2106 Virginian Creeper, unmounted, 9*d*.
2107 White Grapes, unmounted, 9*d*.
2108 Burdock, unmounted, 4*d*.
2109 Poppy, unmounted, 4*d*.
2235 Column from the Vatican, unmounted, 1*s*.
2241 Early English Capital, unmounted, 4*d*.
2247 Gothic Patera, unmounted, 4*d*.
2246 Renaissance Scroll, Tomb in S. M. Dei Frari, Venice, unmounted, 1*s*. 4*d*.
2248 Moulding of Sculptured Foliage, decorated, 7*d*.

ARCHITECTURAL AND MACHINE DRAWING.

Selected Examples of Machines, of Iron and Wood Work (French), by Stanislas Petit, 60 sheets, at 13*s*. per dozen, £3. 5*s*.
Bradley's Practical Geometry, Perspective and Projection, 2 vols. each, 16*s*.
Architectural Studies, by I. B. Tripon, 20 plates, £1. 13*s*. 4*d*.
Glenny's Examples of Building Construction, 12 large plates, £1. 1*s*.
969-1030 Engineer and Machinist's Drawing-Book, 71 plates, published, sewed in numbers, unmounted, at 2*s*. per number, £1. 12*s*.
Laxton's Examples of Building Construction in Divisions (1st division, containing 16 imp. plates), 10*s*.
Ditto (2d division, containing 16 imp. plates), 10*s*.

COLORED EXAMPLES.

285 A Small Diagram of Color, unmounted, 9*d*.
287 Redgrave's Manual and Catechism on Color (3d edition), 36 pages, 9*d*.
618-618*a* Two Plates of Elementary Design, 1*s*.
301 Petunia, unmounted, 2*s*. 9*d*.
300 Pelargonium, unmounted, 2*s*. 9*d*.
1649 Group of Camellias, 12*s*.
302 Nasturtium, unmounted, 2*s*. 9*d*.
305 Althæa Frutex, unmounted, 2*s*. 9*d*.
Pyne's Landscapes in Chromo-Lithography (six), each mounted, 7*s*. 6*d*.
Cotman's Pencil Landscapes (nine), set, mounted, 15*s*.
Cotman's Sepia Landscapes (five), set, mounted, £1.

SOLID MODELS, ETC.

The models, or part of them, should be included in the outfit of a night class for elementary drawing.
3 Rigg's large Compasses, with Chalk-holder, 4*s*. 3*d*.
6-7-8 Slip, two set squares and T square, 5*s*.
16 Elliott's Case of Instruments, containing 6-inch compasses, with pen and pencil leg, 6*s*. 9*d*.
1694 Elliott's Prize Instrumental Case, with 6-inch compasses, pen and pencil leg, two small Compasses, pen and scale, 18*s*.
1676 Elliott's 6-inch Compasses, with shifting pen and point, 4*s*.
317 A Box of Models for Parochial Schools, £1. 4*s*.
318 A Stand with a Universal Joint, to show the solid models, &c., £1. 10*s*.
319-328 One Wire Quadrangle, with a circle and cross within it, and one straight wire, one solid cube, one skeleton wire cube, one sphere, one cone, one cylinder, one hexagonal prism, £2. 2*s*.
1612 Skeleton Cube in Wood, 3*s*. 6*d*.
2000-2006 Mr. Binn's Models for Illustrating the Elementary Principles of Orthographic Projection as applied to Mechanical Drawing, in box, £1. 10*s*.
Three Objects of Form in Pottery (Minton's):—
332 Indian Jar, 5*s*.
333 Celadon Jar, 3*s*. 9*d*.
334 Bottle, 5*s*.
336-338
& 1541 Five Selected Vases in Majolica Ware (Minton's), each 8*s*. 6*d*.,—£1. 2*s*. 6*d*.
341-343 Three Selected Vases in Earthenware (Wedgewood's), 4*s*. 9*d*., 4*s*. 9*d*., and 6*s*.
Imperial Deal Frames, glazed, without sunk rings, 10*s*.

BOOKS, ETC.

359 Robinson's Manual for teaching Elementary Drawing, 7d.
99 Burchett's Practical Geometry, 5s.
100 Burchett's Perspective, 7s.
360 Burchett's Definitions of Geometry, 5d.
362 Art and Science Directories, each 6d.
2023 Davidson's Elementary Drawing, 8vo cloth, 3s.
365 Redgrave on the Necessity of Principles in Teaching Design, 6d.
287 Redgrave's Manual and Catechism on Color, 9d.
366 Principles of Decorative Art, 1s.
367–371 Five Placards of the Principles of Decorative Art, 10d.
Anatomical Method of Drawing the Figure, by Ad. Yvon, 18s.
316 Text to Dyce's Drawing-Book, 6d.
1270 Wornum's Catalogue of Casts, stitched, 1s.
1270a " " " bound in cloth, 1s. 6d.
2234 Dicksee's Perspective, 5s.
378 Lineal Drawing Copies for the Earliest Instruction, comprising upwards of 200 subjects, on 24 sheets, mounted on thick pasteboard, in a portfolio, 5s. 6d.
379 Easy Drawing Copies for Beginners, 6s. 6d.
380 Drawing for Young Children, 3s. 6d.
Examples for First Practice in Free-hand Outline Drawing, by Walter Smith, 2s.
Smith's Elements of Geometry, First Grade, 1s.
Smith's Elements of Practical Geometry, Second Grade, 1s. 6d.
First Grade Practical Geometry, by John Kennedy, New Edition, 6d.
First Grade Free-hand Drawing Book, by John Kennedy, 1s. 6d.
Gregory's First Grade Free-hand Outline Drawing, enlarged for the blackboard, 2s. 6d.
Sciography, or Radial Projection of Shadows, by R. C. Puckett, Ph. D., 5s.
Drawing-Book for Beginners, by P. H. Delamotte, F.S.A., 2s. 6d.

The following is a list of French examples, flat copies, chosen for the City of Boston Normal Art School, with prices marked. The copies were unmounted. All of them came from Paris, but may be ordered in England from Sig. D. Brucciani, 40 Russell Street, Covent Garden, London, who will procure them, and forward them to America: —

3 books Free-hand Outline Drawing (at 1s. 4d.), 4s.
2 sets, 81 plates, small Ornaments (2s. 6d. doz.), £1. 13s. 9d.
1 set, 100 " petits Matériaux (2s. 6d.), £1. 10d.
1 " 100 " small Architectural, 8s. 4d.
1 " 100 " " Mechanical, 8s. 4d.
1 " 36 " " Blery's Flowers (2½d.), 7s. 6d.
1 " 100 " " Bucollet's Models (2½d.), £1. 10d.
4 lessons in Sepia (9d.), 3s.
2 doz. small Sepia Copies (9d.), 18s.
1 set, 40 plates, Habitations, Cosmo (12d.), £2.
1 " 50 " Tripon's Mechanical (9d.), £1. 17s. 6d.
1 " 50 " " Architectural (9d.), £1. 17s. 6d.
1 " 67 " Petits Mechanical (9d.), £2. 10s. 3d.
1 " 9 " Tripon's New Architectural (9d.), 6s. 9d.
1 First Year Tripon's Geometrical, 15s.
1 Second " " " £1.
1 set, 40 plates, Numa's Ornaments (4½d.), 15s.
1 " 72 " large, Mechanical Outline (2d.), 12s.
1 " 50 " large, Architectural (2d.), 8s. 4d.
1 " 9 " Animals' Heads (4½d.), 3s. 4½d.
1 " 95 " large, Lalaisse Animals (4s. 6d.), £1. 15s. 7½d.
1 " 24 " " Blery's Plants (4½d.), 9s.
1 " 38 " Models from Nature (4½d.), 14s. 3d.
1 " 84 " Julien's Preparatory Course (9d.), £3. 3s.
2 " 24 " " Ornaments (7½d.), £1. 10s.
1 " 48 " Rosa Bonheur's Small Studies (7½d.), £1. 10s.
50 Calamo's large Landscapes (9d.), £1. 17s. 6d.
30 Plantar's Ornaments (9d.), £1. 2s. 6d.
17 Rosa Bonheur's Large Studies (2s.), £1. 14s.
8 Photographs from the Antique (4s.), £1. 12s.
Lined Packing Case, 12s.

APPENDIX II.

CASTS OF FIGURE, ORNAMENT, AND FROM NATURE.

The lists here given may be trusted to contain only such works as are of a high character, according to their several subjects. Those on Sig. Brucciani's list, as approved by the art referees of the Science and Art Department, England, are in use in the schools of art and drawing-classes there. Casts should be ordered painted, if from accredited agents of artistic societies, or the government of the country from which they are obtained; the cost in England being fifteen per cent additional. In calculating expenditure on casts, fifty per cent must be added for package, freight, and incidental expenses. Casts for public instruction are admitted into America duty free.

I.

List of Casts, with Prices, approved by the Department of Science and Art of the English Government, for the Use of the National Schools of Art. Sig. D. Brucciani, 40 Russell Street, Covent Garden, London, England, Agent.

CASTS OF HISTORICAL ORNAMENT.

GREEK.

English official numbers.

347 Section of Frieze, from the Erectheium, Athens, 6*s.*
495 Stele Top, from the British Museum, 4*s.*
492A Enriched Moulding (Echinus, from the Erectheium), 5*s.*
1634 Lysicrates Scroll (Athens), 4*s.*
495A Stele top, from British Museum, 4*s.*

ROMAN.

348 Small Acanthus Scroll, 6*s.* 6*d.*
344 Rosette, from the Capitol, Rome, 4*s.*
345 Another " " " 4*s.*
346 Rosette, from the Cloisters of Sta. Maria del Popolo, 3*s.*
474 Florentine Panel, with Swan, £1. 5*s.*
1631 Nest of Scroll of Pilaster, from Villa Medici, 15*s.*
471 Large Scroll, from Trajan Forum, £4.
490 Small Acanthus Leaf, Temple of Jupiter Stator, 6*s.*
494A Small Rosette, from the Tomb of the Scipios, 1*s.* 6*d.*
494B Another " " " " 1*s.* 6*d.*
472 Large Frieze, Trajan Forum, £4.
1630 Nest of the Florentine Scroll, with the Swan, 10*s.* 6*d.*
473 Pilaster, from the Villa Medici, Rome, £3. 10*s.*
1540 Centre Rosette, from Trojan Scroll, 7*s.* 6*d.*
491 A Griffin. 5*s.*
492C Leaf Moulding, Temple of Mars Ultor, 5*s.*
492D Enriched Moulding, from the Upper Cornice of Pedestal of Trajan's Pillar, 5*s.*
493 A Rosette, from the Capitol, 4*s.*
494 A Rosette, from the Antique, 4*s.*

RENAISSANCE.

English official numbers.

349 Pomegranate Portion of the Frieze of the Ghiberti Gates, Florence, 1424-52, 6*s*. 6*d*.
1542E Pilaster, from Tomb of Louis XII., 5*s*.
1543E Another " " " " 5*s*.
476A Another " " " " 5*s*.
476B Another " " " " 5*s*.
483 Egg-Plant and Pomegranate, Ghiberti Gates, 15*s*.
475 Pilaster, from Florence (cinquecento), formerly called from "Sta. Maria del Popolo," £1. 1*s*.
489 Acanthus Leaf, from St. Eustache, Paris, 4*s*.
481 A portion of the Architrave of the Ghiberti Gates, with Eagle, 15*s*.
482 Another, with Squirrel, 15*s*.
476C Pilaster, from Louis XII.'s Tomb, 5*s*.
476D Another, " " " " 5*s*.
496 Diamond Rosette, Brescia, 3*s*.
1645 Panel, from the Martinengo Tomb, Brescia, with cinquecento Arabesque and Figures, £1. 10*s*.
1646 Panel, from Chateau D'Anet, with Cartouche, 4*s*.
1647 Pilaster, from Notre Dame, Louis XV., 10*s*.
484A Piece of Architrave of Ghiberti Gates (the Pomegranate portion), 5*s*.
484B Piece of Architrave of Ghiberti Gates (the Egg-Plant portion), 5*s*.
484C Piece of Architrave of Ghiberti Gates (the Bird portion), 5*s*.
475A Lower portion of Florentine Pilaster, 7*s*.
475B Middle " " " 7*s*.
475C Upper " " " 7*s*.
1625 Panel, with cinquecento Arabesque, from the Martinengo Tomb at Brescia, £1. 10*s*.
477 Pilaster, from the Madeleine Gates, 12*s*.

MODERN RENAISSANCE.

478 Pilaster, from the Madeleine, Paris (from the Bronze of Triquetti, c. 1840), 12*s*.
478A A section of the above, 8*s*.
478A Portion of Pilaster, from the Madeleine, 3*s*.
478B Another " " " 3*s*.
478C Another " " " 3*s*.
478D Another " " " 3*s*.

GOTHIC.

487 Finial, from Lincoln, 3*s*. 6*d*.
488 Capital, from Temple Church, 7*s*.
1640 Capital, from Stone Church, Kent, 7*s*. 6*d*.
485 Moulding Boss, from St. Stephen's, Westminster, 4*s*.
1639 Spandrel, from Stone Church, Kent, £1.
1641 Small carved Panel, Tracery, 3*s*.
1642 Another " " " 3*s*. 6*d*.
486 A Moulding Boss, from St. Stephen's, Westminster, 4*s*.

BYZANTINE.

1636 Piece of Architrave, from St. Denis, Paris, 10*s*.
1635 Panel, from Bonn, 4*s*.
1637 Iron Scroll Work, Hinge, Notre Dame, Paris, 12*s*.
1638 Another portion, 7*s*. 6*d*.

SARACENIC.

1643 An Alhambra Panel, 3*s*. 6*d*.
1644 Another " " 3*s*. 6*d*.

CASTS OF FRUIT, ETC., FROM NATURE.

2111 A Group of Blackberries, 15*s*.
2112 " Apples, 7*s*. 6*d*.
2113 " " (different), 7*s*. 6*d*.

English official numbers.

2114 A Group of Pears, 7*s.* 6*d.*
2115 " Plums, 7*s.* 6*d.*
2116 " Vine and Leaf, 7*s.* 6*d.*
2117 " Vine and Leaves (large), **£1. 1*s.***
2118 A Bunch of Grapes, 7*s.* 6*d.*
2121 Cast of Shaddock, from Nature, 1*s.*
2122 " Orange, " 6*d.*
2123 " " " 6*d.*
2124 " Melon, " 1*s.* 6*d.*
2125 " Pomegranate, " 9*d.*
2126 " " " 1*s.*
2127 " " " 9*d.*
2128 " Bottle Gourd, " 1*s.*
2129 " Apple, " 6*d.*
2130 " " " 6*d.*
2131 " " " 6*d.*
2132 " Pear, " 1*s.*
2433 " " " (different), **1*s.***
2134 " Pine, " 1*s.*
2135 " Citron, " 1*s.*
2161 " Giant Gourd, 2*s.*
2162 " A Group of Plums, 7*s.* 6*d.*
2163 " Lemon, from Nature, 6*d.*
2164 " Rock Gourd, 1*s.*
2165 " A Lily, from Nature, 7*s.* 6*d.*
2166 " Funeral Fern of New Zealand, 2*s.*
2167 " Vine Branch, from Nature, 5*s.*
2168 " Dock Leaf, from Nature, 2*s.*
2169 " Dock, from Nature, 2*s.*
2170 " Bean and Leaf, from Nature, 2*s.* 6d.
2171 " Study of a Stalk, from Wood, 1*s.* 6*d.*
2172 " " " " " 1*s.* 6*d.*
2176 " a Hand, from Nature (with compass), 2*s.* 6*d.*
2177 " Hand resting, from Nature, 1*s.* 6*d.*
2178 " Hand, drawing, from Nature, 2*s.*
2179 " Open Hand, from Nature, 1*s.* 6*d.*
2180 " Open Hand (male), from Nature, 2*s.*
2181 " " " " " 2*s.*
2182 " a Group of Female Hands, from Nature, 3*s.*
2183 " " " " " 7*s.* 6*d.*
2184 " Female Hand, on cushion, from Nature, 2*s.*
2185 " " " from Nature, 1*s.* 6*d.*
2186 " " " with bracelet, from Nature, 1*s.* 6*d.*
2187 " Male Hand, from Nature, 1*s.* 6*d.*
2188 " " " 1*s.* 6*d.*
2189 " " throwing, from Nature, 1*s.* 6*d.*
2190 " " on stone, " 1*s.* 6*d.*
2191 " " with stick, " 1*s.* 6*d.*
2192 " a Clenched Male Hand, " 1*s.* 6*d.*
2193 " Hand with Scroll, on stand, from Nature, 3*s.* 6*d.*
2194 " Child's Hand, from Nature, 1*s.*
2195 " " " 1*s.*
2196 " " " 1*s.*
2197 " " with stick, from Nature, 1*s.*
2198 " a Group of Four Hands, " 5*s.*
2199 " a Pair of Feet, from Nature, 3*s.*
2200 " " large Ears, from Nature, 2*s.* 6*d.*
2201 " " small " " 1*s.* 6*d.*
1198 A Group of Arbutus and Foliage, 7*s.* 6*d.*
1199 " the White-Lily, from Nature, 12*s.*
2100 " Apples (bunch), " 7*s.* 6*d.*
2101 " the Water-Lily, " 7*s.* 6*d.*
2102 " Sunflower and Foliage, from Nature, 10*s.* 6*d.*
2103 " Wheat, from Nature, 7*s.* 6*d.*
2104 " Lemon and Foliage, from Nature, 3*s.* 6*d.*
2105 " Orange, from Nature, 3*s.* 6*d.*
2106 " the Passion Flower and Foliage, 3*s.* 6*d.*
2107 " Vine, Foliage, and Lizard, from Marble, 7*s.* 6*d.*
2108 A Thistle Leaf, front view, 5*s.*
2109 " " back " 5*s.*
2110 A Small Group of Apples and Foliage (Nature), 3*s.* 6*d.*

English official numbers.

2241 A Hand bearing Orange, from Nature, 2*s*. 6*d*.
2242 " " Apple, " 2*s*. 6*d*.
2243 A Female Hand, on slab, " 2*s*.
2244 A Pair of Female Clasped Hands, from Nature, 3*s*. 6*d*.
2245 " " Crossed " " 3*s*. 6*d*.
2246 A Female open Hand, from Nature, 2*s*. 6*d*.
2247 A Male Hand holding Painter's Brush, from Nature, 3*s*. 6*d*.

CASTS OF THE FIGURE.

1617 Bust of Diana robing, 10*s*. 6*d*.
458 Bust of the Young Augustus, 6*s*.
452 Anatomical Figure by Houdon, £5. 10*s*.
1554 Discobolus of Naucydes, Naples, £5.
455 Torso of Venus, British Museum, 8*s*.
459 Bronze Hercules, " " 10*s*.
457 Bust of Diomede, " " 10*s*.
463 Bust of Clytie, " " 10*s*.
498 Dancing Girl, with wreath, 14*s*.
497A Portion of Panathenaic Frieze, from the Parthenon, 18*s*.
464C Hand, with scroll (antique), 2*s*.
464D " with stick, 1*s*. 6*d*.
464E " Female, from Nature, 1*s*.
464F " Anatomical, 1*s*.
464G Foot of the Laocoön (right), 1*s*. 6*d*.
464I " of the Venus de Medici (right and left), 2*s*.
464K " from the Antique (male), 1*s*. 6*d*.
464L " Anatomical, 1*s*. 6*d*.
462 Mask, Child of Niobe, 3*s*.
462A Another, 3*s*.
453 Discobolus of Myron, British Museum, £5.
1614 Fighting Gladiator, Louvre, £5.
1613 Venus de Medici, Florence, £4.
1615 Bust of Apollo, 15*s*.
1616 " Venus of Milo, Louvre, 15*s*.
461 Mask of Moses, by Michael Angelo, 5*s*.
464 Foot of Farnese Hercules, 5*s*.
1626 An Anatomical Arm, 3*s*. 6*d*.
1627 " Leg, 3*s*. 6*d*.
1628 Cast of Leg, from Nature, 5*s*.
1629 " an Arm, " 4*s*.
464B Hand of St. Peter, 2*s*. 6*d*.
463 Mask of a Child (Nature), 2*s*. 6*d*.
463A Another " " 2*s*. 6*d*.
454 Statue of Dancing Fawn, from Florence, £3. 10*s*.
460 Statuette of Apollo, British Museum, 12*s*.
2202 Cast of an Anatomical Foot, 2*s*. 6*d*.
2203 Mask of Juno, 3*s*. 6*d*.
2204 Cast of Mask of Madonna (M. Angelo), 3*s*. 6*d*.
2205 " Nose and Mouth of Æsculapius, 1*s*.
2206 " " " Caracalla, 1*s*.
2207 " " " Adonis, 1*s*.
2208 " " " Antinous, 9*d*.
2209 " " " Venus d'Arles, 9*d*.
2210 " " " Lucius Verus, 9*d*.
2211 " " " Hadrian, 1*s*.
2212 " " " Juno, 9*d*.
2213 " Eye and Nose of Laocoön, 9*d*.
2214 " " " " 9*d*.
2215 " " " Bacchante, 9*d*.
2216 " " " " 1*s*.
2217 " " " Jupiter, 1*s*.
2218 " " " " 1*s*.
2219 " " " Hadrian, 1*s*.
2248 Section of Face of David (left eye), M. Angelo, 2*s*. 6*d*.
2249 Another " " (right eye), " 2*s*. 6*d*.
2250 " " " (mouth), " 2*s*. 6*d*.
2251 " " " (nose), " 2*s*. 6*d*.

CASTS.

English official numbers.

470ABC Three Anatomical Figures of Animals, **£1. 1s.**
465 Horse's Leg, from Nature, *4s. 6d.*
465A Another, *4s. 6d.*
467 Head of a Lion, from Nature, *10s.*
468 " Lioness, *7s.*
469 " Goat, *3s. 6d.*
466 Greyhound's Leg, from Nature, *2s. 6d.*
466A Another, *2s. 6d.*
1618 A Horse, *5s.*
1619 A Cow, *5s.*
1620 A Dog, *3s. 6d.*
1621 A Stag, *5s.*
1622 A Lion, *3s. 6d.*
1623 A Goat, *5s.*

II.

REPRODUCTIONS FROM ANCIENT MARBLES, BRONZES, ETC., IN THE BRITISH MUSEUM.

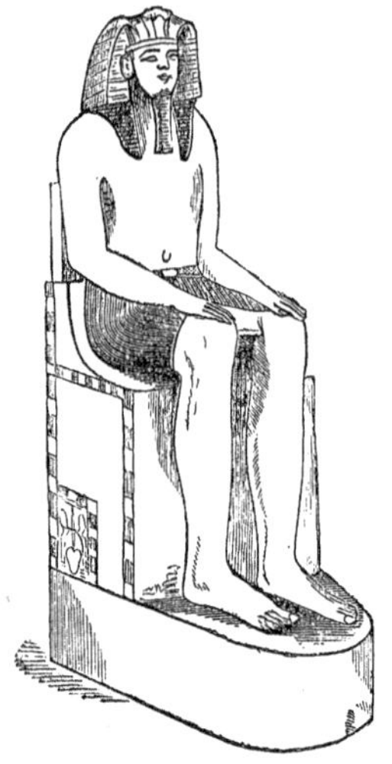

EGYPTIAN SCULPTURES.

STATUES.

No.

14 Amenophis III., called by the Greeks Memnon [XVIII. Dynasty], Thebes, £10.

48 Banofre, a Scribe, dedicated to Osiris [XVIII. Dynasty], Thebes, £1. 12*s.*

98 An Officer (upper part of), 10*s.*

An Egyptian Monarch (upper part of). Presented by Her Majesty, 1854, 12*s.*

462 Amen-em-ha, a Functionary [XII. Dynasty], 10*s.*

70C Betmes, High Functionary, 10*s.*

Upper part of a Statue of an Officer of Rank, inscribed with the name Psammetichus I. [XXVI. Dynasty], 3*s.*

BUSTS.

No.
41 Head of Pasht (part of figure), Goddess of Fire, 5*s*.
16 Amenophis III., £2 2*s*.
26 Seti Menephtah II., 12*s*.
88 Head of Pasht (Bubastis), with the name of Amenophis III. (Memnon) [XVIII. Dynasty], Karnak, 5*s*.
1 Head of a Lion [reign of Amenophis III]. 12*s*.
[97] Head of a Sphinx [Roman period], 15*s*.
17 Head from a Sarcophagus of Sebaksi, Priest of Ptah [uncertain period], £1. 10*s*.

MISCELLANEOUS.

17 Lid of Sarcophagus of Sebaksi, Priest of Ptah [uncertain period], £2. 10*s*.

No.
523 East side of Obelisk (facing entrance), erected by Nekhtherhebi before the Temple of Thoth [XXX. Dynasty], Cairo, £1. 10*s*.
523 One other (south side). £1. 10*s*.
10 Part of Sarcophagus, captured in Egypt by the British. 1801. Presented by King George III., £3.
22 Intercolumnar Slab from a Temple, with inscription and figure of Nectanebo [XXX. Dynasty], Alexandria, 18*s*.
24 Rosetta Stone Inscription in honor of Ptolemy V., in Hieroglyphic, Enchorial, and Greek characters. Rosetta [Ptolemaic period], 6*s*.
6* Basin, 6*s*.
Seti-Menephtah I. (upper part of), 10*s*.
Amen-ra (upper part of), 10*s*.

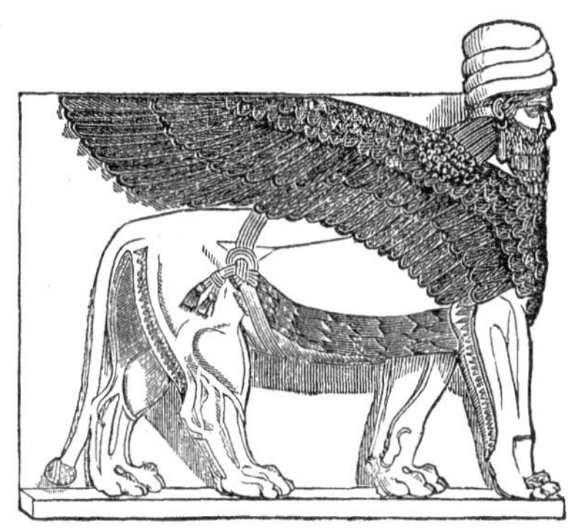

ASSYRIAN SCULPTURES.

No.
1 Four-winged Figure with Mace, £5.
2 King and Winged Figures with Mystic Offerings, beside a Sacred Tree. £9.
3A King hunting the Bull, £2. 3*s*.
3B Return from the Bull Hunt, £2. 3*s*.
4A King hunting the Lion. £2 3*s*.
4B Return from the Lion Hunt. £2. 3*s*.
5A King besieging a City, £2. 3*s*
5B Sardanapalus receiving Prisoners and Spoil £2 3*s*.
6B The same, £2 3*s*.
6A Fugitives swimming to a Fortress, £2. 3*s*.
7A King and his Army in Battle with an Enemy, £2 3*s*.
8A The same, £2. 3*s*.
9A The same, £2 3*s*.
10A The same, £2. 3*s*.
7B Sardanapalus I. and his Army crossing a River, £2. 3*s*.

No.
8B The same, £2. 3*s*.
9B The same, £2. 3*s*.
10B Capitulation of a City, and Reception of Prisoners by Sardanapalus I., £2. 3*s*.
11B The same, £2. 3*s*.
11A Triumphal Return of King from Battle to the Camp. £2. 3*s*.
12A The same, £2 3*s*.
13A The same, £2. 3*s*.
13B Siege of a City by Sardanapalus I., £2. 3*s*.
14B The same, £2 3*s*.
15B The same, £2. 3*s*.
14A King in Battle, before a Besieged City, £2. 3*s*.
15A The same, £2. 3*s*.
16B Horsemen flying before the Assyrians, £2. 3*s*.
17 Winged Figure, with Stag and Branch of Flowers, £4. 10*s*.

No.
18 Winged Figure, with Ibex and Ear of Corn, £4. 10*s*.
19 Foreigners bringing Tribute, £8.
20 Sardanapalus I., £5. 5*s*.
21 Sardanapalus I. enthroned between Attendants and Winged Figures with Mystic Offerings, £7.
22 The same, £7.
23 The same, £7.
24 Sardanapalus I. and Winged Figure with offerings, £7.
25 Winged Figure with Offerings, and Royal Attendant, £7.
26 Sardanapalus I. and Attendant, £7.
32 Priest offering Flowers, £2. 10*s*.
33 Eagle-headed Deity with Offerings, £6.
34 Eagle-headed Deity with Offerings, £2. 15*s*.
35 Four winged Female offering Necklace, £5.
36 Lion Hunt, £1. 6*s*.
37A Winged Figures kneeling beside a Sacred Tree, £2. 3*s*.
39 Sardanapalus I. between Eagle-headed Deities with Mystic Offerings, beside a Sacred Tree, £7.
40 The same, £7.
41 Winged Figure with Offerings, £5. 5*s*.
Human-headed winged Lion, £15.
Small human-headed Bull, £15. 3*s*.
Slab with Flocks, £2. 3*s*.
Ditto, £2. 3*s*.
Horsemen pursuing Enemy, £2. 3*s*.
Female with Camels, £2. 3*s*.
Evacuation of a City (upper half), £1. 14*s*
Triumphal Procession (lower half), £2. 10*s*.
Winged Figure, £1.
Ditto, £1.
Ditto, £1.
Ditto, £1.
Eunuch's Head, 12*s*.

KONYUNIK COLLECTION.—BASS-RELIEFS.

39 Wounded Lioness. From slab of Sardanapalus III. Hunting Lions [Chamber C 20–27], 7*s*. 6*d*.
78 Man-headed Lion From slab of Mythological or Sacerdotal Figures [Chamber T. b. 2], 15*s*.
107 Two Horses and two Lions, one Rider. From slab, Hunting Lions and Disposing of their Carcasses [Chamber S. 14–11], 15*s*.
108 Two Horses and Male and Female. From slab, Hunting Lions and Disposing of their Carcasses [Chamber S. 14–11], 15*s*.
108 Five Horses, three Riders,—one leading. From slab, Hunting Lions and Disposing of their Carcasses [Chamber S. 14–11], £1. 10*s*.

No.
118 Sardanapalus III. at an Altar, pouring a Libation over, 15*s*.
119 Dead Lions, 15*s*.
121 Sardanapalus III. and his Queen Feasting in a Garden, £1. 1*s*.
124A Musicians and Attendants, 7*s*. 6*d*.
124B Attendants, 7*s*. 6*d*.
124C Wild Boar in Reeds, 7*s*. 6*d*.
56 Sardanapalus III. receiving Prisoners and Spoil, £5. 5*s*.
57 A portion of the Pavement [Chamber I. C.], about four feet, £2. 2*s*.

GREAT MOUND.

Obelisk set up by Shalmaneser, King of Assyria [about B.C. 850], £3.

MISCELLANEOUS.

1 Lion Weight, 7*s*.
3 " " 4*s*.
4 " " 4*s*.
9 " " 4*s*.
13 " " 4*s*.
Stone Duck, 5*s*.

SCULPTURES AND INSCRIPTIONS FROM PERSEPOLIS.

84 8*s*.
85 8*s*.
86 7*s*.
88 5*s*.
89 2*s*. 6*d*.
90 7*s*. 6*d*.
91 7*s*. 6*d*.
92 7*s*. 6*d*.

INSCRIPTIONS FROM HADJI ABAD.

Six pieces, £2. 2*s*.
Stone containing Inscription of Addon, King of Assyria. Presented by the Earl of Aberdeen, K.G., 1860, 2*s*.
Stone with Cuneiform Characters, 3*s*.

ARABIC MONUMENTS.

Arabic Inscription on Tombstone, £1. 5*s*.

BABYLONIAN.

Stone, containing the record of the sale of a field, in the reign of Merodach-Adan-Akhi. King of Babylon [about 1120 B.C.], 7*s*. 6*d*.
Stone with the figure of a king in relief, and the record of the sale of a field in the reign of Merodach-Adan-Akhi. King of Babylon [about 1120 B.C.], 7*s*. 6*d*.

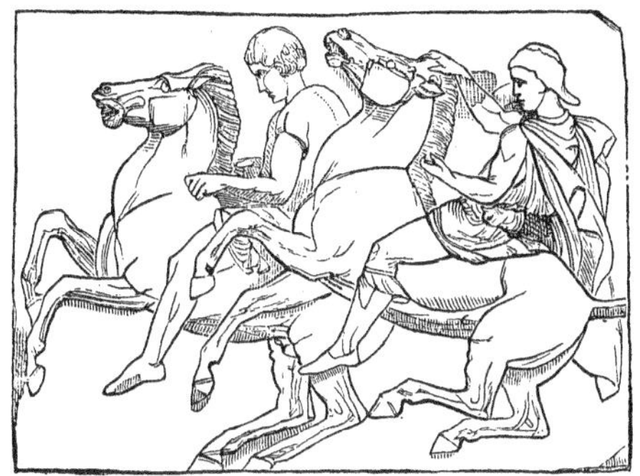

GREEK SCULPTURES.

LYCIAN ROOM.

No.
1 Harpy Tomb (the whole), £9.
1A Youth offering a Cock to Male seated Deity (3 slabs), £2 10s.
1B Demeter, Persephone, Three Horæ and Cow (4 slabs), £2. 10s.
1C Male seated Figure giving a Helmet to a Youthful Warrior, Harpies carrying off the Daughters of Pandaros (3 slabs), £2. 10s.
1D Female Figure bringing Offering to Male seated Deity, Harpies carrying off the Daughters of Pandaros, £2. 10s.

Cast of No. 17 Slab, £1. 1s.
" 18 " 19s.
" 19 " 19s.
" 26 " 13s.
" 27 " 13s.
" 34 " 11s. 6d.
" 35 " £1. 15s. 6d.
" 36 " 11s. 6d.
" 37 " £2. 7s.
" 38 " £1. 18s. 6d.
" 39 " £1. 14s.
" 40 " £1. 11s.
" 41 " £1. 8s. 6d.
" 42 " £2. 7s.
" 43 " £1. 11s.
" 44 " £1. 8s. 6d.
Cast of No. 45 Slab, £1. 14s.
" 46 " £2. 8s. 6d.
" 47 " £1. 11s.
" 48 " £1. 8s. 6d.
" 49 " £1. 13s.
" 50 " £1. 14s.
" 51 " £1. 7s. 6d.
" 52 " 15s. 6d.
" 53 " £1. 13s.
" 54 " £1. 11s.
" 55 " £1. 12s.
" 56 " £1. 7s. 6d.
" 57 " £1. 9s.
" 58 " 16s.
" 59 " £1.
" 60 " £1. 2s. 6d.
" 61 " 14s.
" 62 " £1. 9s. 6d.
" 63 " £1. 9s. 6d.
" 64 " £1. 14s.
" 65 " £1. 6s.
" 66 " 17s.
" 67 " £1. 2s. 6d.
" 69 " 16s.
" 70 " 15s.
" 71 " 12s.
" 142 " £9. 7s.
" 162 " 13s.
" 163 " 10s.
" 172 " 15s.

ELGIN SALOON.

PARTHENON PEDIMENTS.

[The first Nos. are those painted black. The Nos. in brackets are painted red.]

No.
65 Hyperion [91], 16s.
Hyperion, Right Arm of (separate), 4s
66 Horses of Hyperion, Heads of [92], £1 10s.
71 Theseus [93], £4. 10s.
77 Ceres and Proserpine [94], £18.
74 Iris [95], £5.

No.
72 Victory, Torso of [96], £1. 10s.
One of the Fates [97], £7.
The Two other Fates [97], £18.
68 Horse's Head [98], 10s.
70 Ilissus [99], £5.
76 Cecrops, Torso of [100], £1. 10s.
118 Minerva, Fragment of the Head of [101], 3s.
75 Minerva, Fragment of the Body of [102], 12s.
201 Minerva, Fragment of the Feet of, and Laurel Tree [356], 16s.

No.
265 Minerva, Fragment of the [338], 7*s.*
64 Neptune, Torso of [103], £1.
271 Serpent, Fragment of [104], 2*s.* 6*d.*
69 Victory without Wings, Torso of [105], £1.
73 Latona, Fragment of [106], £1 5*s.*
156 Fragment of a Female Figure [178], 15*s.*
104* Head, 8*s.*
105* " 7*s.*
261 Fragment of an Arm [310], 4*s.*
264 " " [311], 4*s.*
267 " a Leg [312], 4*s.*
274 " an Arm [313], 4*s.*
271* " " [315], 10*s.*
269 " a Figure [339], 5*s.*
244 " " [340], 5*s.*
256 " " [341], 4*s.*
268 " " [342], 5*s.*
144 " " [343], 7*s.* 6*d.*
272 Fragment [314], 4*s.*
207 Capital of a Column, one quarter [112], 18*s.*

METOPES OF THE PARTHENON.

11 Metope [1], £1. 15*s.*
2 " [1], £2.
8 " [3], £2.
12 " [4], £1. 12*s.*
15 " [5], £1. 15*s.*
6 " [6], £1. 17*s.* 6*d.*
4 " [7], £1. 15*s.*
5 " [8], £1. 15*s.*
13 " [10], £1. 17*s.* 6*d.*
7 " [11], £2.
1 " [12], £2.
3 " [13], £1. 15*s.*
9 " [14], £2.
14 " [15], £2.
10 " [16], £1. 15*s.*
A 56 " 16*s.*
A 57 " £1. 4*s.*
A 64 " £2.
A 65 " £2.
143 Fragment, Torso of Youth [319], 3*s.*
79 Fragment, Torso of Female [321], 3*s.*
294 Fragment, Torso of Youth [323], 3*s.*
Lion's Head, Spout. Cast from plaster [392], 9*s.*
Antefixal or Tile Ornament [391], 10*s.*

FRIEZE OF THE PARTHENON.

16 Three slabs [17], £3.
17 " " [18], £3.
18 " " [19], £3.
18* Slab of Youth. Cast from plaster [20], 8*s.*
Slab (cast presented by Sir F. Chantrey) Old Man leaning on Staff, 12*s.*
19 Single slab [21], £1.
19* Cast from plaster [21], 10*s.*
20 Single slab [22], £1.
A 100 Cast from plaster [23], £1. 18*s.*
21 Single slab [24], £1.
22 " [24], 7*s.* 6*d.*
A 25 Cast from plaster [25], £1.

No.
23 Single slab [26], £1.
35* " [26], 10*s.*
24 " [27], £1.
34 " [28], £1.
98 " [29], 3*s.*
177* " [29], 4*s.*
35 " [30], £1.
35** " [31], £1.
37 " [32], £1.
A 5 Cast from plaster [33], £1.
36 Single slab [34], £1.
178* Fragment, 3*s.* 6*d.*
A 6 Cast from plaster [35], £1.
38 Single slab [36], £1.
25 " [37], £1.
26 " [38], £1.
27 " [39], £1.
28 " [40], £1.
29 " [41], £1.
30 " [42], £1.
31 " [43], £1.
38* " [44], £1.
32 " [45], £1.
33 " [46], £1.
33 Return [46], 7*s.*
39 Single slab [47], £1.
A 75 Cast from plaster [48], £1.
A 76 " " [49], £1.
A 77 " " [50], £1.
A 78 " " [51], £1.
A 79 " " [52], £1.
A 80 " " [53], £1.
A 81 " " [54], £1.
A 82 " " [55], £1.
A 83 " " [56], £1.
A 84 " " [57], £1.
A 85 " " [58], £1.
A 86 " " [59], £1.
A 86* " " 3*s.* 6*d.*
A 87 " " [60], £1.
A 88 " " [61], 10*s.*
A 13 " " [61*], £1.
40* Single slab [62], 13*s.*
A 14 Cast from plaster [62*], £1.
41 Single slab [63], £1.
44* Fragment [64], 1*s.* 6*d.*
38** " [65], £1.
46 " [66], £1.
50 " [67], £1.
47 " [68], £1.
52 " [69], £1.
40 " [70], £1.
42 " [71], £1.
49 " [72], £1.
45 " [73], £1.
48 " [74], £1.
43 " [75], £1.
44 " [76], £1.
51 " [77], £1.
38*** " [78], 13*s.*
53 " [79], £1.
54 " [80], £1.
56 " [81], £1.
55 " [82], £1.
15* " [83], 16*s.*
57 " [84], £1.
59 " [85], £1.
61 " [86], £1.
60 " [87], £1.
58 " [88], £1.
96 " [89], 3*s.*
62 " [90], £1.

No.
62 Return [90], 9*s*.
145 4*s*.
A 1 [Cast from plaster], £1.
A 2 " " £1.
A 3 " " £1.
A 4 " " £1.
A 7 " " 16*s*.
A 8 " " 16*s*.
A 9 " " 12*s*.
A 10 " " 12*s*.
A 11 " " 12*s*.
A 12 " " 12*s*.

ERECTHEUM.

A 47 Ionic Capital, one-half [125], £1. 16*s*.
Ionic Capital, one-quarter, 9*s*.
Pilaster of Capital, £1. 18*s*.
I 27 Part of Coffer [117], 2*s*. 6*d*.
299 Part of Ceiling [108], 8*s*.
Part of Jamb of Door [115], 3*s*. 6*d*.
A 42 Caryatis, from Temple of Pandrosos, £6.

TEMPLE OF NIKE APTEROS.

258 Frieze, single slab [158], 14*s*. 6*d*.
257 " " " [159], 14*s*. 6*d*.
259 " " " [160], 17*s*.
260 " " " [161], 17*s*.
Volute of Capital [404], 5*s*.
Bass-relief with two figures. Cast from plaster [159*], £1. 16*s*.
Bass-relief with single figure. Cast from plaster [160*], £1. 2*s*.
Ditto [161], 11*s*.
Bass-relief of Victory, 17*s*.
Fragment of Victory, 6*s*.

TEMPLE OF ARTEMIS, AT DAPHNE.

295 Capital of Column, one-half [264], 15*s*.
I 23 Ditto Face [388], 8*s*.
297 Quarter of Shaft [265], 15*s*.
A 45 Part of Shaft [134], £1. 6*s*.
A 46 Base of Column [135], 16*s*.

TEMPLE OF CERES, AT ELEUSIS.

173 Fleuron [169], 18*s*.

ARCHITECTURAL FRAGMENTS FROM ATHENS.

102 Fragment of Capital of Corinthian Column [268], 6*s*.
I 34 Volute, N. Front of Acropolis [410], 2*s*. 6*d*.
I 35 Moulding [407], 2*s*. 6*d*.
I 41 Antefixal, or Tile Ornament [412], 2*s*. 6*d*.
Ditto [413], 2*s*. 6*d*.
I 42 " [414], 2*s*. 6*d*.
I 33 " [417], 2*s*. 6*d*.
" 2*s*.

STATUES.

306 Icarus (Apollo) [113], £2. 12*s*.
Head, cast from plaster [106*], 7*s*.

No.

SEPULCHRAL URNS.

148 [199], 12*s*.
104 [275], 6*s*.

BASS-RELIEFS.

107 [176], 12*s*.
I 183 [177*], 8*s*. 6*d*.
284 [189], 3*s*.
235 [193], £1.
236 [197], 12*s*.
109 [198], 5*s*.
247 [209], 1*s*. 6*d*.
251 [214], 1*s*. 6*d*.
163 [263], 10*s*.
238 [278], 7*s*.
94 [279], 3*s*.
292* [283], 2*s*. 6*d*.
103* [300], 3*s*. 6*d*.
99 [324], 15*s*.
112 [330], 4*s*.
126 [335], 2*s*.
236* [336], 1*s*.
175 [351], 2*s*. 6*d*.
84 [361], 1*s*. 6*d*.
89 [371], 1*s*. 6*d*.
82 [375], 2*s*. 6*d*.
227 [376], 5*s*.
101 [380], 4*s*.
108 [383], 3*s*. 6*d*.
213 [384], 6*s*.
Fleuron [418], 8*s*.
" [429*], 3*s*. 6*d*.
" [435], 4*s*. 6*d*.
" [436], 18*s*.
Cast from plaster [437], 10*s*.
" " [438], 12*s*.
" " [439], 16*s*.
" " [442], 5*s*.
" " [444], 10*s*.
Ornament of Stele, No. 7, 18*s*.

TOMB OF AGAMEMNON, AT MYCENÆ.

220 Part of Frieze [177], 6*s*. 6*d*.
221 " " [180], 6*s*.

GREEK INSCRIPTIONS.

XII. 53 Inscription [E 167*], 9*s*.
92 " [E 173], 7*s*.
214 " [E 266], 5*s*.
177 " [E 377], 8*s*.
302 " [E 378], 8*s*.
200 " [E 379], 7*s*.
XI. 13 I. " 5*s*.
XI. 51 4. " 6*s*.
III. 36 Alcamenes, Shield of, 11*s*.
Damasicreon, Inscription in honor of, 5*s*.

PHIGALEIAN SALOON.

Temple of Apollo.

25 Fragment of Metope, 8*s*.
28 " " 7*s*.
29 " " 7*s*.
30 " " 7*s*.
25 Part of Capital, 8*s*.
26 Part of Cornice, 5*s*.
27 " " 5*s*.

No.
39 Tile, 6*s*.
40 " 5*s*.
The whole frieze, in twenty-three pieces, £30.
Single slabs in proportion.

MAUSOLEUM AT HALICARNASSUS.

Statue.

Mausolos, found under the steps of the Pyramid, outside the Northern Peribolis wall of the Mausoleum [C. T. N. 1857], £15.

Busts.

Mausolus, ditto, 15*s*.
A Bearded Head, ditto, 5*s*.
Head of Apollo, 5*s*.

Frieze.

The whole set, including four slabs recently moulded, £36.
No. 1, 15*s*.
Nos. 2, 3, and 4, £1. 15*s*. each.

No.
Nos. 5, 6, 7, and 8, £2. 5*s*. each.
No. 9, 18*s*.
Nos. 10 to 18, inclusive, £2. 5*s*. each.
Part of a Cornice from the Mausoleum of Halicarnassus, 5*s*.
A Lion, from Castle of St. Peter, Budrum, £5.

OLD TEMPLE OF SELINUS.

Heads of Perseus, Athene, and Gorgon, 15*s*.

BASSI-RELIEVI.

XI. 6 3 Offering of Philombrotus, 4*s*.
XI. 6 4 Lustration of a Horse, by Hecate, 5*s*.
III. 5 Consulting the Delphic Deities, 14*s*.
III. 7 Hercules and Mænalian Stag, 4*s*.
III. 13 Offering to Apollo, 8*s*.
III. 41 Sepulchral Monument, 15*s*.
III. 63 Stele of Exacestes, 10*s*.
XI. 6 1 Tablet of Abeita, 1*s*. 6*d*.
Sepulchral Stele, 10*s*.

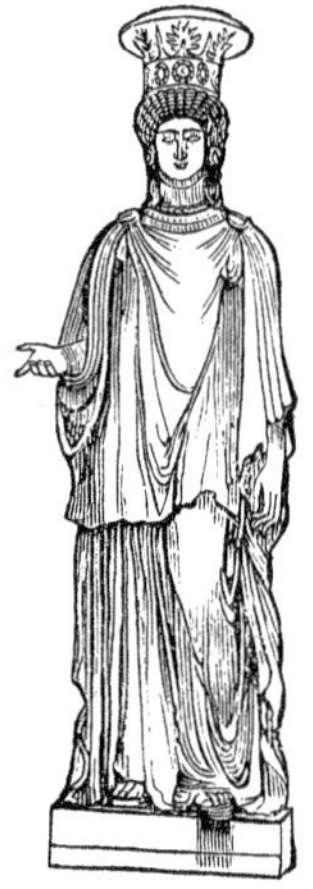

GRÆCO-ROMAN SCULPTURES.

STATUES.

T 15 Venus (Aphrodite), Ostia, £5.
T 43 Discobolus (Disk thrower), ancient copy from a bronze statue by Myron, who flourished B.C. 431, £7. 10*s*.
T 13 Astragalizusa, from the Villa Verospi, Rome, £1. 10*s*.
T 18 Venus Architis 37, 12*s*.
T 17 Venus (Aphrodite) (Torso), stooping to adjust her Sandal, 5*s*.
Venus (Aphrodite) (Torso). Shattered in a fire at Richmond House, 1791, 9*s*.
T 16 Venus (Aphrodite), Ostia, £1.
T 19 Cupid (Eros), Rome, £2. 10*s*.
T 121 Cupid (Eros), found inside a large Amphora, at Castello-di-Guido, near Rome, 15*s*.
T 21 Boy Bacchus. Villa of Antoninus Piuss Lanuvium, £3.
T 1 Bacchus and Ampelus. La Storta, near Rome, £5.

No.

T 22 Ariadne. Roma Vecchia, near Rome, £3. 15*s*.

T 26 Pan (Terminal), 35, found near Civita Lavinia Lanuvium, £1. 10*s*.

Satyr (Rondinini Faun), formerly in Rondinini Palace, Rome, £4.

T 30 Satyr, Maccarani Palace, Rome, £1. 15*s*.

T 29 Satyr (Paniskos), Civita Lavinia (Lanuvium), £1. 5*s*.

T 37 Muse inscribed Eumousia, 12*s*.

No.

T 44 Canephora. £5.

T 38 The Muse Erato, £1. 5*s*.

T 3 Actæon devoured by his Dogs, Villa of Antoninus Pius, £2.

II. 15 Victory. £1. 10*s*.

VI. 31 Victory sacrificing a Bull, £3. 10*s*.

VI. 26 Victory sacrificing a Bull, £3. 10*s*.

VI. 56 Sphinx, £2. 10*s*.

II. 13 Chimera, 12*s*.

II. 40* Hercules (Torso), 5*s*.

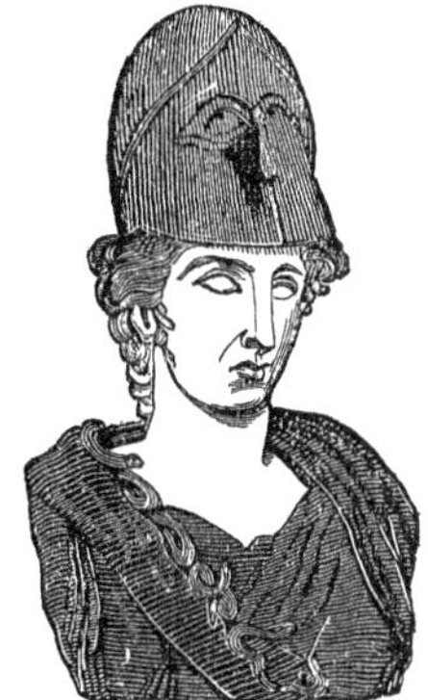

BUSTS.

Caius *Julius* ***Cæsar.*** Born B.C. 101. Assassinated B.C. 44. 6*s*.

C. Jul. Octavianus Cæsar *Augustus*. Born B.C. 63. Died A.D 14, 10*s*.

Luc. Domitius *Nero*. Born A D. 37. Emp. A.D. 54–68. — Athens, 7*s*.

T 93 M. Ulpius Crinitus *Trajanus*. Born A.D. 52. Emp. A D 98–117.—Campagna of Rome, 13*s*.

T 97 *Antinous* in the character of Bacchus. Died about A.D. 132. — Villa Pamfili, Rome, 18*s*.

T 100 *Marcus Aurelius*, (as frater Arvalis). Born A.D. 121. Emp. A.D. 161–180, 15*s*.

T 101 Annia *Faustina* Junior, wife of the Emp. M. Aurelius. Born A.D. 140. Died A.D. 175. — Pozzuolo, 15*s*.

Another of same, different, 6*s*. 6*d*.

T 104 L. Septimius *Severus*. Born A.D. 145. Emp. A.D. 193–211. — Palatine Hill, Rome, 11*s*.

T 102 M. Aurelius Antoninus ***Caracalla.*** Born A.D. 188. Emp. A.D. 211–217. — Esquiline Hill, Rome, 11*s*.

T 167 Octacilia Severa, wife of the Emp. Philippus I., 6*s*. 6*d*.

T 106 Unknown (probably a barbarian chieftain). — Forum of Trajan, Rome, 8*s*.

Unknown (of doubtful antiquity). — Presented by Peter Ducane, Esq., 9*s*.

T 85 Homer. — Baiæ, 12*s*.

T 87 Greek Poet. — Albanó, 10*s*.

T 90 Sophocles, 10*s*.

T 88 Periander. Seventh century B.C., 11*s*.

T 91 Pericles. B.C. 497 - 429. — Tivoli, 7*s*.

Demosthenes. B.C. 384–322, 10*s*.

Diogenes. Bequeathed by R. Payne Knight, 1824. 9*s*.

T 89 Epicurus. B.C. 342 - 271. — Rome, 10*s*.

T 92 Hippocrates. Born B.C. 460. Found near Albano, 12*s*.

Æschines, 11*s*.

T 50 Jupiter (Zeus), part of a statue, 12*s*.

No.	
T 51	Jupiter Serapis, with a modius decorated with olives, the face colored, 8*s*.
T 53	Juno (Hera) wearing a frontal, (Rome), 12*s*.
T 242	Minerva. Found near Rome, 15*s*.
	Minerva (Athens), the helmet and drapery restored, in Bronze. — Rome, 18*s*.
T 57	Minerva (Athens). — Rome, 7*s*. 6*d*.
	Mercurius (Hermes), of early style, 10*s*.
T 70	Mercurius, Small Head of, 10*s*.
T 60	Apollo (Apollon), ancient copy from an early bronze, 10*s*.
T 59	Apollo, 10*s*.
	Apollo, 7*s*. 6*d*.
T 61	Diana (Artemis), 10*s*.
	Diana, 8*s*.
T 12	Diana from statue of Diana (Artemis), hurling a Javelin. — La Storta, near Rome, 8*s*.
T 62	Mercurius (Hermes), 9*s*.
T 63	Bacchus, 14*s*.
T 64	Bacchus [29], 15*s*.
T 65	Bacchus, 10*s*. 6*d*.
	Libera, 9*s*.
	Satyr. Bequeathed by R. Payne Knight, 7*s*. 6*d*.
	Heroic Head. From the collection of the late S. Rogers, 7*s*. 6*d*.
	Hercules. Colossal No. 2. Found in the lava at foot of Mount Vesuvius, £1. 10*s*.
T 77	Hercules. — Barbarini Palace, Rome, 10*s*.
T 72	Atys, 5*s*. 6*d*.
T 76	Hercules (terminal bust of), 10*s*.
T 76	Muse, 5*s*.
T 86	Ajax (Diomede). Found in Villa of Hadrian, 1771, 10*s*. 6*d*.
T 54	Dione, 10*s*.
T 79	Unknown (Clytie). Probably an Empress of the Augustan Period, 10*s*. 6*d*.
	Head XII. 3, 10*s*.
	Head of a seated Demeter, 5*s*.
XII. 2	Female Head, 9*s*.
VI. 42	" " 9*s*.
XII. 13	Bust of Youth, 6*s*.
XI. 2	Female Head, 5*s*. 6*d*.
T 42	Diana, 18*s*.
T 71	Female Head (unknown), 6*s*. 6*d*.
	Venus (Aphrodite). From the collection of Sir William Hamilton, 6*s*.
	Female Head. Perhaps copied from a bronze found near Censano, 6*s*.
	Apollo (Pourtalis Collection), £1.
	Æsculapius. Blacas Collection, £1.
	Hadrian, from bronze, 7*s*. 6*d*.

STATUETTES FROM BRONZE.

T 38	Hercules in the Garden of the Hesperides, 15*s*.

No.	
T 10	Apollo, wearing a Chlamys, 15*s*.
R.P.K. V. 2	Apollo bending his Bow, 8*s*.
	Apollo, K., 4*s*.
	Apollo, 6*s*. 6*d*.
	Jupiter, Serapis, 5*s*.
	Jupiter (one arm), 5*s*. 6*d*.
	Minerva 6*s*.
	Minerva, 6*s*.
	Diana, K., 5*s*.
	Vulcan, K., 4*s*.
	Venus, K. Bequeathed by R. P. Knight, Esq., 6*s*.
	Venus, 5*s*.
	Venus, 5*s*.
	Venus, 4*s*. 6*d*.
	Cupid, K., 2*s*.
	Cupid, K. 4, 2*s*.
	Cupid, K. 13, 2*s*.
	Cupid, K., 2*s*.
R.P.K. LX. 4	Mercury, 4*s*.
	Bacchus, 6*s*.
	Silenus, 5*s*.
	Satyr, 5*s*.
	Faun, 5*s*. 6*d*.
	Hercules, without tree, £1. 1*s*.
	Hercules, 5*s*.
	Hercules, 6*s*.
	Hercules, 5*s*.
	Hercules, with club in right hand, 5*s*.
	Salus, 5*s*.
	Fortune, 7*s*.
R.P.K. XXVIII. 1	Isis, 5*s*.
	Atys, 3*s*. 6*d*.
	Victory, 7*s*.
	Victory, 4*s*.
	Sophocles, 8*s*.
	Alexander, 8*s*.
	Hadrian, 7*s*. 6*d*.
	Roman in Toga, Case 29, No 36, 4*s*. 6*d*.
	Ditto with Mask, on pedestal, 4*s*. 6*d*.
	Horse, 7*s*. 6*d*.
	Bull, 7*s*.

BUSTS FROM BRONZES.

Minerva, K., 3*s*.
Bacchus (youthful), 2*s*. 6*d*.
Satyr, 1*s*.
Amazon, 5*s*.

MISCELLANEOUS, FROM BRONZES.

Lamp, 2*s*. 6*d*.
" Eagle, 4*s*.
" Peacock Handle, 5*s*.
" Leaf Pattern, K., 2*s*.
" Lion's Head, 2*s*.
" A Foot, 2*s*.
" " smaller, 1*s*.

BASSI-RELIEVI.

XI. 11	Minerva, 4*s*.
XI. 22	Apollo at the Altar. From altar sacred to Apollo [22], 3*s*.
XII. 22	Sacrifice to Apollo. From altar sacred to Apollo, 3*s*.
XI4.	Pluto and Fortune, 7*s*.

No.		
III.	12	Bacchanalian Group, £1. 2*s*.
		Satyr and Nymphs, 7*s*. 6*d*.
III.	II	Dioscuri, 6*s*.
		Castor, 10*s*.
VI.	54	Priam and Achilles, 8*s*.
III.	23	Apotheosis of Homer, £2.
VI.	28	T. 131 Bacchante, from a candelabrum, 3*s*. 6*d*.
T.	149	Bacchus and Attendants visiting Icarius, £2. 2*s*.
		Castor and Pollux, 7*s*. 6*d*.
T	121	Castor with a Horse and Dog, 10*s*.
	12	Two Satyrs and Bacchante, Procession of, £1. 10*s*. 6*d*.
T	139	Apollo, Diana, Latona, and Three Suppliants, 10*s*. 6*d*.
		Apollo, Musagetes, and Victory, 10*s*.
T	131	Bacchante, from a candelabrum, 3*s*. 6*d*.
T	137	Hercules and Stag, 3*s*. 6*d*.
		Leda and Swan, 10*s*. 6*d*.

VASES.

No.		
II.	7	Vase, 19*s*.
II.	9	Bacchic Vase, 16*s*.
		Portland, 5*s*.

URNS.

V.	2	Roman Urn, 12*s*.
V.	12	" " 15*s*.
V.	14	" " 15*s*.
V.	36	" " 12*s*.
V.	37	" " 14*s*.
		Cast of Alabaster Urn, with Cover, 5*s*.

TERRA-COTTAS.

Bellerophon and the Chimæra, 1*s*. 6*d*.
Perseus and Medusa, 1*s*. 6*d*.
Alcæsus and Sappho, 1*s*. 6*d*.
Vase. 4*s*.
Ewer, 3*s*.
Basin, 2*s*. 6*d*.
Lamp, A.N. 41, 1*s*. 6*d*.
Lamp, B.E. No. 1, 2*s*.
Lamp, No. 2, 2*s*.

MISCELLANEOUS.

		The Elgin Bronze Tablet, 1*s*. 6*d*.
		The Potidœan Inscription, 6*s*.
		Small monumental slab with skeleton on it. T 211, 6*s*.
		An Etruscan Mirror, with incised figure. 2*s*. 6*d*.
		Wishing Lamp, 5*s*.
		Fragment of a Muse, CNIDUS, 3*s*. 6*d*.
		Torso of Aphrodite, CNIDUS, 3*s*. 6*d*.
		Bust of Ray, the Naturalist, 10*s*. 6*d*.
XII.	13	Hand holding Butterfly (1250), 7*s*.
XII.	13	Hand holding Butterfly, 3*s*.
VI.	30	Colossal Toe, 2*s*. 6*d*.
III.	21*	Foot, 1*s*. 6*d*.
VI.	19	Goat's Head, 7*s*.
II.	VI.	Triangular base of a Candelabrum, Cupids with Armor £1. 15*s*.
		Pig of Lead, inscribed Domitianus, 4*s*.
		Small Eagle. 10*s*.
		Head of a large Eagle, 2*s*.
XI.	II.	Sleeping Child, 4*s*. 6*d*.
III.	23*	Masks, Comic and Tragic, 6*s*.
III.	24*	Comic and Tragic Masks on a revolving Panel, 14*s*.
III.	25*	Mask. 2*s*.
XII.	5	Lion's Head, 12*s*.
II.	14	Pedestal, with Terminal Figures and Birds, 8*s*.
XII.	1	Olive and Vine Branches, 10*s*.
VI.	21	Ornament, 5*s*.
	3	Trapezopheron, large, £1. 10*s*.
		" small, 15*s*.
		" 15*s*.
III.	10	Festoon. 8*s*.
		Keystone of Triumphal Arch, Frascati [15], 10*s*.
III.	14	Branch Ornament, 8*s*.
		Cellini Cup, 7*s*.
VI.	64	Latin Inscription on Cippus of Antoninus, 9*s*.

III.

MUSÉE IMPÉRIAL DU LOUVRE.

Catalogue des Plâtres qui se trouvent au Bureau de Vente du Moulage, Palais du Louvre. — Pavillon Daru.

I.—GROUPES ANTIQUES.

Antinoüs et Adrien, groupe de Saint-Ildefonse (Musée de Madrid). Haut., 1m. 50c.m.; prix, 120f.

Bacchus et Silène de la Villa Borghèse. Musée des Antiques, par Pierre Bouillon III, pl. 8. Haut., 75c.m.; prix, 40f.

Centaure prisonnier de l'Amour, marbre de la Villa Borghèse. Musée des Antiques, I, 64. Haut., 1m. 47c.m.; prix, 120 f.
Diane chasseresse, avec la Biche, groupe de Versailles. Haut., 2m. 13c.m.; prix, 300f.
Enfant à l'Oie. Musée des Antiques, II, 30 Haut.. 92c.m.; prix, 60f
Esculape et Télesphore. Musée des Antiques, III, 11. Haut., 73c.m ; prix. 15f.
Laocoön, marbre du Vatican. trouvé en 1506 sur le mont Esquilin, œuvre d'Agésandre, de Polydore et d'Athénodore de Rhodes. Haut., 2m. 23c.m.; prix, 400f.
Lutteurs de Florence. Galleria di Firenze, III, 121, 122. Haut., 1m.; prix, 120f.
Fils de Niobé avec son Pédagogue, trouvé à Soissons en 1831. Clarac, pl. 589, n. 1281. Haut.. 1m. 76c.m.; prix, 200f
Deux Parques du Parthénon (British Museum). Clarac, pl. 824, n. 2071, F. Haut., 1m. 50c.m.; larg., 2m.; prix, 100f.
Satyre tirant une épine du pied d'un Faune, groupe de la Villa Borghèse. Musée des Antiques, III, 13. Haut.. 65c.m.; prix. 25f.
Silène portant le jeune Bacchus, marbre de la Villa Borghèse, dit Faune à l'Enfant. Musée des Antiques, I, 54. Haut., 2m. 3c.m.; prix, 200f.

II. — GROUPES MODERNES.

Amour et Psyché, par F. Delaistre. Haut., 1m. 61c m.; prix, 100f.
Bacchante portant un Faunisque. par Clodion. Haut., 1m. 60c.m.; prix. 80f.
Les trois Grâces, par Germain Pilon, 1560. Haut., 1m. 50c.m.; prix, 300f.
Léda jouant avec le cygne. par Jean Thierry, 1717. Haut.. 81c m.; prix. 50f.
Mercure et Psyché, bronze par Adrien de Vries Haut., 2m. 15c.m.; prix, 150f.
Milon de Crotone, par Pierre Puget. 1682. Haut , 2m. 80c.m.; prix, 500f.
Milon de Crotone. par Falconnet. 1754. Haut., 70c.m.; prix. 50f.
Nymphe et chèvre Amalthée, par Julien, 1791. Haut., 1 n. 80c.m.; prix, 250f.
Zéphyre et Psyché, par Rutchiel, 1814. Haut., 1m. 55c.m.; prix, 150f.

III. — STATUES ANTIQUES.

A. STATUES ÉGYPTIENNES.

Sévekhotep III, roi de la XIIIe dynastie. Haut., 2m.; prix, 200f.
Ouaphrês, fonctionnaire royal de l'époque saïtique. Haut., 1m.; prix, 60f.

B. STATUES GRECQUES ET ROMAINES.

Achille Borghèse. Musée des Antiques. II, 14. Haut., 2m. 30c.m.; prix, 150f.
Adonis du Vatican. Musée des Antiques, II, 12. Haut., 1m. 91c.m.; prix. 100f.
Adorant, dit Génie suppliant, bronze du musée Berlin. Musée des Antiques, II, 19. Haut., 1m. 44c.m.; prix, 50f.
Amazone Mattei, du musée Capitolin. Musée des Antiques, II, 10. Haut., 2m. 10c.m.; prix, 200f.
Amour jouant au ballon. Musée des Antiques, III, 9. Haut., 1m.; prix, 50f.
Amour en Hercule. Musée des Antiques, III, 9 Haut., 1m.; prix, 30f.
Antinoüs du Capitole. Musée des Antiques, II, 49. Haut., 1m. 93c.m.; prix, 120f.
Antinoüs du Belvédère. Museo Pio-Clementino, I, pl. 7; Musée des Antiques, I, 27. Haut., 2m 75c.m.; prix, 140f.
Apollino de Florence. Haut., 1m. 40c m.; prix, 60f.
Apollon du Belvédère. Haut., 2m. 33c.m.; prix. 150f.
Apollon Sauroctone, de la Villa Borghèse. Musée des Antiques, I, 19. Haut., 1m. 67c.m.; prix. 110f.
Apollon Sauroctone. Haut., 1m. 7c m.; prix. 25f.
Ariadne abandonnée, bronze du Primatice dans le jardin des Tuileries, marbre du Vatican. Musée des Antiques, II, 9. Larg., 2m ; prix, 200f.
Atalante ajustant sa chlamyde, dite Diane de Gabies. Musée des Antiques, I, 21. Haut., 1m. 76c.m.; prix, 150f.
Athlète Cestiaire du Musée de Dresde. Augusteum, pl. 109. Haut., 1m. 68c.m.; prix, 80f.
Athlète versant de l'huile dans sa main, statue de la Villa Borghèse. Musée des Antiques, III, 17. 3. Haut., 1m. 60c.m.; prix, 90f.
Auguste du Palais Giustiniani (Venise). Museo Pio-Clementino, II, 45; Musée des Antiques, II, 33. Haut., 2m. 7c.m ; prix. 120f.
Bacchus Richelieu. Musée des Antiques, I, 31. Haut., 1m. 94c.m.; prix, 150f.
Bacchus tenant une coupe. Clarac, Musée de Sculpture, pl. 273, n. 1575. Haut., 1m. 48c.m ; prix, 80f.
Suivant de Bacchus (restauré en Hercule). Musée des Antiques, III, pl. 16, 4. Haut., 1m. 45c.m.; prix. 80f.
Cérès Mattei, du Vatican. Musée des Antiques, I, 7. Haut., 1m. 8c.m.; prix, 25f.
Cérès du Louvre. Clarac, pl. 278, n. 754. Haut., 1m. 24c.m.; prix, 50f.

Cérès assise du Musée de Berlin. Gerhard, Antike Bildwerke, pl. 21. Haut., 1m. 4c.m.; prix, 72f.
Commode jeune de Gabies. Musée des Antiques, III, pl. 20, 4. Haut., 1m. 76c.m.; prix, 200f.
Discobole du Musée Pie-Clémentin. Musée des Antiques, II, 17. Haut., 1m. 80c.m.; prix, 120f.
Eschine, dit Aristide, du Musée de Naples. Real Museo Borbonico, I, 50. Haut., 2m. 11c.m.; prix, 120f.
Esculape Assis. Haut., 67c.m.; prix, 15f.
Euripide assis de la Villa Albani, trouvé sur le mont Esquilin. Musée des Antiques, III, 18, 1. Haut., 60c.m.; prix, 15f.
Euterpe Borghèse. Musée des Antiques, I, 44. Haut., 1m. 50c.m.; prix, 80f.
Faune dansant du Musée de Turin. Haut., 1m. 52c.m.; prix, 80f.
Faunes flûteurs (deux), de la Villa Borghèse. Musée des Antiques, I, 53; Clarac, pl. 296, n. 1670, 1671. Haut., 1m. 39c.m.; prix, chacun, 60f.
Faune au chevreau de Madrid. Clarac, pl. 726e, n. 1671b. Haut., 1m. 47c.m.; prix, 80f.
Faune en repos du Capitole. Musée des Antiques, I, 55. Haut., 1m. 84c.m.; prix, 120f.
Jeune Fille romaine. Musée des Antiques, II, 65. Haut., 1m. 35 c.m.; prix, 70f.
Jeune Fille romaine, dite Julie, trouvée à Bengazi. Clarac, pl. 311, n. 2482. Haut., 1m. 51c.m; prix, 80f.
Flore Borghèse. Musée des Antiques, I, 52. Haut., 1m. 58c.m.; prix, 120f.
Génie du repos éternel. Musée des Antiques, I, 59. Haut., 1m 91c.m.; prix, 110f.
Guerrier grec, dit Hector, du temple d'Egine (Glyptothèque de Munich). Haut., 1m. 50c.m.; prix, 60f.
Hermaphrodite Borghèse. Haut., 89c.m.; larg., 1m. 48c.m.; prix, 92f.
Hermès (deux), têtes de jeunes Grecs, de la salle de la sculpture grecque primitive du Louvre. Haut., 1m. 30c.m.; prix, chacun, 3f.
Héros combattant, dit le Gladiateur Borghèse, œuvre d'Agasias, fils de Dosithée, Éphésien. Haut., 1m. 63c.m.; prix, 200f.
Hygiée. Clarac. Musée de Sculpture, pl. 3051, n. 1170. Haut., 1m. 50c.m.; prix, 80f.
Joueuse aux osselets du Musée de Berlin. Musée des Antiques, II, 30. Haut., 70c.m.; prix, 50f.
Julie en Cérès. Musée des Antiques, II, 54. Haut., 1m. 70c.m.; prix, 70f.
Julien l'Apostat. Clarac, pl. 978, n. 2528. Haut., 1m. 50c.m.; prix, 80f.
Mars, dit Alexandre de Gabies, œuvre d'Héraclide et d'Harmatios. Musée des Antiques, III, 18, 2. Haut., 80c.m.; prix, 25f.
Melpomène, statue colossale. Musée des Antiques, I, 43. Haut., 3m 92c.m.; prix, 600f.
Melpomène. Musée des Antiques, III, 11, 4. Haut., 90c.m.; prix, 20f.
Mercure assis, bronze de Portici au Musée de Naples. Real Museo Borbonico, III, 41, 42. Haut., 1m. 25c.m.; prix, 120f.
Mercure attachant sa chaussure, dit Jason. Musée des Antiques, II, 6. Haut. 1m. 75c.m.; prix, 160f.
Mercure de Versailles, dit Germanicus, œuvre de Cléomène, fils de Cléomène, Athénien. Haut., 1m. 95c.m.; prix, 140f.
Muse (restaurée en Clio). Musée des Antiques, III, 10, 5. Haut., 90c.m.; prix, 20f.
Niobide agenouillé, de la Glyptothèque de Munich. Haut., 1m. 23c.m.; prix, 100f.
Pallas de Velletri. Haut., 3m. 18c.m.; prix, 400f.
Polymnie Borghèse. Haut., 1m. 86c.m.; prix, 150f.
La Pudicité. Musée des Antiques, II, 64. Haut., 2m.; prix, 100f.
Silène à l'Outre. Musée des Antiques, III, pl. 12, 2. Haut., 1m.; prix, 25f.
Thalie. Musée des Antiques, III, pl. 11, 1. Haut., 1m. 76c.m.; prix, 150f.
Tireur d'épine du Vatican. Haut., 73c.m.; prix, 36f.
Vénus accroupie. Musée des Antiques, I, 14. Haut., 96c.m.; prix, 25f.
Vénus d'Arles. Musée des Antiques, I, 13. Haut., 2m. 10c.m.; prix, 150f.
Vénus à la coquille. Musée des Antiques, I, 15. Haut., 66c.m.; prix, 50f.
Vénus de Versailles, dite Génitrix. Musée des Antiques, I, 12. Haut., 1m. 75c.m.; prix, 150f.
Vénus de Médicis (Musée de Florence), œuvre de Cléomène, fils d'Apollodore, Athénien. Haut., 1m. 64c.m.; prix, 100f.
Vénus de Milo. Haut., 2m. 16c.m.; prix, 120f.

IV.—STATUES MODERNES.

L'Abondance, par Barthélemy Prieur, bronze du Louvre. Haut., 1m. 28c.m.; prix, 60f.
Amour présentant une rose à un papillon, par Chaudet, 1810. Haut., 80c.m.; prix, 60f.
Atalante faisant sa toilette, par James Pradier, 1850. Haut., 1m.; prix, 80f.
Baigneuse, par Falconnet, 1757. Haut., 70c.m.; prix, 40f.

Crépuscule, Aurore, Jour et Nuit, tombeau des Médicis à Florence, par Michel-Ange. Copies réduites des quatre figures couchées. Prix, chacune, 30f.
Cyparisse pleurant son faon, par Chaudet, 1798. Haut., 1m. 50c.m.; larg., 56c.m.; prix, 120f.
Jeanne d'Arc, par la princesse Mathilde d'Orléans. Haut., 2m. 20c.m.; prix, 200f.
Judith, par Ladatte, 1741. Haut., 89c.m.; prix, 50f.
Marie Leczinska, par Guillaume Coustou. Clarac, Musée de Sculpture, pl. 368°, n. 2650b. Haut., 2m.; prix, 200f.
Roberte Legendre, épouse de Louis Poncher, morte en 1522 (figure couchée). Larg., 1m. 85c.m.; prix, 80f.
Louis XIV., statue équestre par Girardon, 1699. Haut., 1m. 2c.m.; prix, 120f.
Mercure attachant ses talonnières, par Pigalle, 1745. Haut., 58c.m.; prix, 40f.
Milon de Crotone, par Edme Dumont, 1768. Haut., 81c.m.; prix, 50f.
Nymphe Salmacis, par François-Joseph Bosio, 1819. Haut., 83c.m.; prix, 80f.
Pâris le Berger, par Gillet, 1757. Haut., 85c.m.; prix, 40f.
Philopœmen, par David d'Angers (Jardin des Tuileries). Haut., 2m. 40c.m.: prix, 200f.
Prisonnier, les bras liés, par Michel-Ange. Clarac, Musée de Sculpture, pl. 357, n. 2596. Haut., 2m. 15c.m.; prix, 100f.
Jeune Prisonnier, le bras replié au-dessus de la tête, par Michel-Ange. Clarac, pl. 357, n. 2597. Haut., 2m. 35c.m.; prix, 120f.
Prométhée enchaîné, par Pradier (Jardin des Tuileries). Haut., 1m. 50c.m.; larg., 2m.; prix, 200f.
Ulysse tendant son arc, par J. Bousseau, 1715. Haut., 86c.m.; prix, 50f.
Vénus au bain, par Allegrain, 1767. Haut., 1m. 60c.m.; prix, 200f.
Voltaire dans son fauteuil (Comédie-Française), par Houdon. Haut., 1m. 65c.m.; prix, 250f.

V.—FRAGMENTS DE STATUES ET TORSES.

Amour grec du Vatican. Musée des Antiques, I, 15. Haut., 73c.m.; prix, 15f.
Ésope de la Villa Albani (Musée du Capitole). Clarac, pl. 1023, n. 2905. Haut., 50c.m.; prix, 20f.
Faune cymballier. Musée des Antiques, III. pl. 13, 3. Haut., 73c.m.; prix, 7f.
Femmes, deux torses du Louvre. Haut., 81c.m.; prix, 6f.
" " " " 48c.m.; " 2f. 50c.
Hercule du Belvédère, œuvre d'Apollonius, fils de Nestor, Athénien. Musée des Antiques, II, 4. Haut., 1m. 48c.m.; prix, 72f.
Hermaphrodite Borghèse. Haut., 60c.m.; prix, 5f.
Hommes, trois torses du Louvre. Haut., 88c.m.; prix, 6f.
" " " " 70c.m., " 6f.
" " " " 51c.m., " 3f. 50c.
Inopus. Clarac, pl. 750 et 1086, n. 1820. Haut., 97c.m.; prix, 18f.
Laocoön, torse avec la tête. Haut, 1m. 12c.m.; prix, 30f.
Marsyas, torse avec la tête. Musée des Antiques, I, 56. Haut., 1m. 22c.m.; prix, 30f.
Poseidon du Parthénon (Musée Britannique). Haut., 1m.; prix, 20f.
Psyche du Musée de Naples. Haut. 94c.m.; prix, 10f.
Vénus de Médicis. Haut., 69c.m.; prix, 6f.
Vénus de Milo. Haut., 1m. 5c.m.; prix, 40f.
Milon de Crotone, par Pierre Puget. Haut., 1m. 45 c.m.; prix, 60f.

VI.—STATUETTES ANTIQUES.

A. STATUETTES ÉGYPTIENNES.

La déesse Pacht. Haut., 60c.m.; prix, 10f.
Le roi Aménophis IV. Clarac, pl. 995, n. 2549°. Haut., 1m.; prix, 10f.

B. MARBRES GRECS.

Pallas d'ancien style. Musée des Antiques, III, pl. 1, 1. Haut., 1m.; prix, 10f.
Pallas du Parthénon, imitation de l'œuvre de Phidias. Gerhard, Denkmäler, 1860, pl. 135, 3, 4. Haut., 40c.m.; prix, 3f.

C. FIGURINES EN BRONZE.

Jeune Acteur. Haut., 15c.m.: prix, 2f. 50c.
Enfant romain. Haut., 10c.m.; prix, 3f. 50c.
Faune. Haut., 31c.m.; larg., 7c.m.; prix, 6f.
Génie sphériste. Haut., 12c.m.; prix, 3f. 50c.
Hercule Philopotis. Haut., 14c.m.; prix, 3f. 50c.
Hercule décoré d'une couronne de peuplier. Haut., 15m.; prix, 3f.
Jupiter. Haut., 15c.m.: prix, 1f. 50c.
Mars. Haut., 25c.m; prix, 5f.

Mercure. Haut., 18c.m.; prix, 1f. 50c.
" " 26c.m., " 5f.
" " 22c.m., " 6f.
Neptune. Haut., 22 c.m.; prix, 1f.
Silène. Haut., 22c.m.; prix, 5f.
Vénus. Haut., 12c m.; prix, 1f. 50c.
" " 14c.m., " 1f. 50.
" " 17c.m., " 1f. 50c.

VII.—STATUETTES MODERNES.

Enfant effrayé, imitation de l'antique. Haut., 10c.m.; prix, 2f. 50c.
Faune accroupi de Florence, style de Michel-Ange. Haut., 22 c.m.; prix, 4f.
Henri IV. Haut., 47c.m.; prix, 15f.
Hercule tenant les pommes des Hespérides, imitation de l'antique. Haut., 19c.m.; prix, 4f.
Enfant Jésus à la crèche. Larg., 40c.m.; prix, 10f.
Marie de Médicis. Haut., 49c.m.; prix, 15f.

VIII.—BUSTES ANTIQUES.

Achille Borghèse. Haut., 90c.m.; prix, 8f.
Agrippa de Gabies. Clarac, Musée de Sculpture, pl. 1070, n. 3252. Haut., 46c.m.; prix, 5f.
Alexandre le Grand de Tivoli. Visconti, Iconographie grecque, 39, 1. Haut. 68c.m.; prix, 12f.
Alexandre Sévère du Palais Braschi. Musée des Antiques, III, Bustes, 9, 2. Haut., 66c.m.; prix, 6f.
Amazone blessée. Musée des Antiques, II, 11. Haut., 60c.m.; prix. 8f.
Amour grec du Vatican. Haut., 61c.m.; prix, 5f.
Antinoüs du Capitole. Haut., 62c.m.; prix, 4f.
Antinoüs, buste colossal de la Villa Mondragone à Frascati Musée des Antiques, II, 83. Haut., 94c m.; prix, 12f.
Antinoüs, du Belvédère. Haut., 75c.m.; prix, 8f.
Apollon du Belvédère. Haut., 85c m.; prix, 12f.
Apollon égyptien, bronze du Louvre. Haut., 50c.m.; prix, 3f.
Apollonius de Tyanes (Buste dit d') bronze du Louvre. Clarac, pl. 1078, n. 2762[a]. Haut., 71c.m.; prix, 5f.
Ariadne du Capitole. Musée des Antiques, I, 70. Haut., 73c m.; prix, 12f.
Atalante, dite Diane de Gabies. Haut., 50c.m; prix, 5f.
Auguste portant la couronne civique du Palais Bevilacqua à Vérone. Musée des Antiques, III, pl. 5, 4. Haut., 70c.m.; prix, 9f.
Bacchus indien au turban, marbre de Versailles. Musée des Antiques, I, 70. Haut., 46c.m.; prix, 10f.
Bacchus indien, marbre rouge antique du Louvre. Clarac pl. 1086, n. 2760[d]. Haut., 50c m.; prix, 10f.
Caracalla, marbre de la Villa Borghèse. Clarac, pl. 1075, n. 3319[b]. Haut., 61c.m.; prix, 5f.
Cérès, buste pris sur une statue de la Villa Borghèse Clarac, pl. 279, n. 753. Haut., 51c m.; prix, 4f.
Jules César, buste pris sur la statue du Louvre. Haut., 60c.m; prix, 10f.
Cicéron. Haut., 60c m.; prix, 5f.
Démosthène de la Villa Albani. Musée des Antiques, III, bustes, pl. 4, 5. Haut., 44c.m.; prix, 6f.
Diane Borghèse, buste colossal. Musée des Antiques, III, bustes, pl. 1, 8. Haut., 83c m.; prix, 8f.
Élius Vérus, de la Villa Borghèse. Clarac, pl. 1081, n. 2440. Haut., 76c.m.; prix, 10f.
Esculape Albani. Musée des Antiques, I, 48. Haut., 70c.m.; prix, 15f.
Euripide de Mantoue. Musée des Antiques, II, 69. Haut., 55c.m.; prix, 7f. 50c.
Faune à la tache de la Villa Albani. Musée des Antiques, II, 72. Haut., 48c.m.; prix, 8f.
Faune Borghèse. Haut., 38c.m.; prix, 2f.
Faunes porteurs (deux), de la Villa Albani. Musée des Antiques, III, 13. Haut., 58c.m.; prix, chacun, 12f.
Faustine la Jeune. Haut., 60c.m.; prix, 12f.
Jeune Fille romaine. Musée des Antiques, II, 65. Haut., 40c m.; prix, 3f.
Gordien Pie de Gabies. Musée des Antiques, II, 90. Haut., 61c.m.; prix, 5f.
Jeune Hercule. Musée des Antiques, II, 67. Haut., 61c m.; prix, 1f.
Héros grec, marbre de la Villa Borghèse. Clarac, pl. 1085, n. 2810[a]. Haut., 1m.; prix, 12f.

Hippocrate de Cos. Musée des Antiques, II, 72. Haut., 42c.m.; prix, 6f.
Homère du Louvre. Haut., 55c m.; prix, 7f. 50c.
Isis grecque. Clarac, pl. 1087, n. 2733[a]. Haut., 41c.m.; prix, 8f.
Jupiter d'Otricoli, du Musée du Vatican. Haut., 58c.m.; prix, 4f.
Laocoön. Haut., 63c.m.; prix, 12f.
Les deux Fils de Laocoön. Haut., 43c.m.; prix, chacun, 3f.
Laocoön de Bruxelles (Musée du duc d'Aremberg). Monumenti dell' Instituto, II, 41[b]. Haut., 64c.m.; prix, 8f.
Marc-Aurèle, buste du Louvre. Haut., 50c.m.; prix, 8f.
Mercure, buste pris sur le groupe de Mercure et Vulcain. Musée des Antiques, I, 22. Haut., 50c m.; prix, 5f.
Miltiade de la Villa Albani. Clarac, pl. 1094, n. 2912. Haut., 57c.m.; prix, 6f.
Néron Borghèse. Clarac, pl. 1095, n. 3272[b]. Haut., 67c m.; prix, 5f.
Omphale Albani. Musée des Antiques, II, 67. Haut., 66c.m.; prix, 6f.
Dieu marin, dit Palémon. Musée des Antiques, I, 72. Haut., 52c.m.; prix, 4f.
Pallas de Vellétri. Haut., 80c m.; prix, 20f.
Pallas couverte du casque aux têtes de bélier. Musée des Antiques, III, pl. 1, 2. Haut., 86c.m.; prix, 8f.
Pâris. Clarac, pl. 1097, n. 2904[e]. Haut., 73c.m.; prix, 6f.
Rome de la Villa Borghèse, buste colossal. Musée des Antiques, I, 74. Haut., 92c.m.; prix, 25f.
Rome en Amazone. Clarac, pl. 1100, n. 2820[e]. Haut., 77c.m.; prix, 8f.
Sapho du Capitole. Haut., 44c.m.; prix, 3f.
Sénèque, marbre du Louvre. Haut., 50c.m.; prix, 3f.
Socrate. Musée des Antiques, II, 73. Haut., 52c.m.; prix, 4f.
Tibère Albani. Clarac, pl. 1103, n. 3255. Haut., 69c.m.; prix, 8f.
Tibère couronné de chêne, marbre de Gabies. Haut., 57c.m.; prix, 8f.
Trajan, buste du Louvre. Haut., 50c.m.: prix, 8f.
Vénus d'Arles. Haut., 67c.m.; prix, 7f. 50c.
Vénus du Capitole. Haut., 56c.m.; prix, 5f.
Vénus de Cnide, marbre de la Villa Borghèse. Musée des Antiques, I, 68. Haut., 1m.; prix, 12f.
Vénus de Versailles, dite Génitrix. Haut., 52c.m.; prix, 4f.
Vénus de Médicis. Haut., 64c.m.; prix, 5f.
Vénus de Milo. Haut., 70c.m.; prix, 8f.
Lucius Vérus, buste colossal de la Villa Borghèse. Musée des Antiques, III, bustes, pl. 6. Haut., 1m. 30c m.; prix, 40f.
Vitellius. Clarac, pl. 1106, n. 72. Haut., 62c.m.; prix, 5f.

IX. — BUSTES MODERNES.

Caryatide, par Jean Goujon. Haut., 70c.m.; prix, 12f.
Milon de Crotone, par Pierre Puget. Haut., 65c.m.; prix, 10f.
Jeune Femme inconnue, marbre du xve siècle (Louvre, n. 79). Haut., 50c.m.; prix, 5f.
Enfant, par Germain Pilon. Clarac, Musée de Sculpture, pl. 1116, n. 3533. Haut., 32c.m.; prix, 2f.
Louis XII, par Laurent de Mugiano. Haut., 61c.m.; prix, 6f.
François Ier, bronze de l'École française du xvie siècle. Haut., 90c.m.; larg., 72c.m.; prix 30f.
Henri II, par Germain Pilon. Haut., 77c.m.; prix, 20f.
Henri II, buste attribué à Jean Goujon. Haut., 80c.m.; prix, 30f.
Charles IX, par Germain Pilon, 1568. Haut., 77c.m.; prix, 25f.
Henri III, par Germain Pilon. Haut., 77c.m.; prix, 25f.
Henri IV. Haut., 60c.m.; prix, 20f.
Henri IV, attribué à Barthélemy Prieur. Clarac, pl. 1119, n. 3545. Haut., 80c.m.; prix, 25f.
Henri IV, buste avec un bras. Haut., 70c m.; prix, 25f.
Louis XIII, par Simon Guillain. Clarac, pl. 1122, n. 3564. Haut., 1m.; prix, 25f.
Louis XIV enfant, par Simon Guillain. Clarac, pl. 364, n. 2611. Haut., 60c.m.; prix, 20f.
Louis XV. Clarac, pl. 1124, n. 3569. Haut., 70c.m.; prix, 20f.
Louis XV. Haut., 1m; prix, 30f.
Marie-Antoinette. Haut., 90c.m.; prix, 20f.
Napoléon Ier, par Houdon. Haut., 75c.m.; prix, 15f.
Béatrix d'Este, marbre du xve siècle, attribué à Desiderio de Settignano. Clarac, pl. 1117, n. 3537. Haut., 62c m.; prix, 8f.
Diane de Poitiers. Clarac, pl. 359, n. 2600. Haut., 80c.m.; prix, 20f.
Diane dite Diane de Poitiers, par Jean Goujon. Haut., 70c.m.; prix, 10f.
Mme du Barry, par Pajou, 1773. Haut., 70c m.; prix, 10f.
Boileau-Despréaux, par Girardon. Clarac, pl. 1122, n. 3567. Haut., 90c.m.; prix, 25f.
Bossuet, par A. Coyzevox. Clarac, pl. 1123, n. 3560[a]. Haut., 75c.m.; prix, 15f.

Buffon, par Pajou, 1773. Clarac, pl. 1123, n. 3568. Haut., 80c.m.; prix, 15f.
L'amiral de Chabot, par Jean Cousin. Clarac, pl. 358, n. 2601. Haut., 80c.m.; prix, 12f.
Jean-Baptiste Colbert, par Michel Anguier. Clarac, pl. 1121, n. 3557. Haut., 85c.m.; prix, 25f.
Édouard Colbert (frère du ministre), par Desjardins. Clarac, pl. 1121, n. 3558. Haut., 1m 5c m.; prix, 30f.
L'amiral de Coligny, par Jean Goujon. Clarac, pl. 1120, n. 3553. Haut., 70c.m.; prix, 25f.
Condé, bronze du xviie siècle. Clarac, pl. 1122, n. 3563. Haut., 90c.m.; prix, 25f.
Pierre Corneille. Haut., 90c.m.; prix, 25f.
Thomas Corneille. Haut., 90c.m.; prix, 25f.
Coyzevox, par lui-même. Clarac, pl. 1123, n. 3560d. Haut., 67c.m.; prix, 15f.
Cuvier. Haut., 85c.m.; prix, 30f.
Jacques-Louis David, par Rude, 1833. Clarac, pl. 1134, n. 3637. Haut., 88c.m., prix, 30f.
Philibert de l'Orme, bronze du xvie siècle. Clarac, pl. 1129, n. 3605. Haut., 80c.m.; prix, 10f.
Descartes. Haut., 88c.m.; prix, 20f.
Christophe de Thou, école française du xvie siècle. Clarac, pl. 1120, n. 3551. Haut., 70c.m ; prix, 20f.
Du Couëdic, capitaine de vaisseau, par Bougron, 1830. Clarac, pl. 1125a, n. 3574. Haut., 90c.m.; prix, 25f.
Fénelon. Clarac, pl. 1122. n. 3560b. Haut., 1m ; prix, 25f.
Comte de Forbin, chef d'escadre, par Petitot, 1822. Haut., 97c.m.; prix, 25f.
Comte de Forbin, directeur des Musées du Louvre, par Ramus. Clarac, pl. 1136, n. 3653. Haut., 1m ; prix, 12f.
Franklin. Haut., 65c.m.; prix, 10f.
Martin Fréminet, peintre. Clarac, pl. 1119, n. 3548. Haut., 49c m.; prix, 20f.
François Gérard, par Pradier. Clarac pl. 1135, n. 3645. Haut., 90c.m.; prix, 30f.
Girodet-Trioson, par Roman. Clarac. pl. 1135, n. 3644. Haut., 79c.m.; prix, 30f.
Gluck, par Francin fils. Clarac, pl. 1123, n 3556a. Haut., 80c.m ; prix, 20f.
Jean Goujon. Clarac, pl. 1120, n. 3552. Haut., 80c.m ; prix, 20f.
Le baron Gros, par Debay père. Clarac, pl. 1135, n 3643. Haut., 84c.m.; prix, 30f.
Jean de Bologne, buste attribué à Pierre Franqueville. Clarac, pl. 1119, n. 3546. Haut., 70c m.; prix, 10f.
Bernard Jussieu. Haut., 80c.m.; prix, 30f.
Antoine-Laurent Jussieu. Haut., 70c.m.; prix, 15f.
Lacépède. Haut., 60c m.; prix, 10f.
La Fontaine. Haut., 85c.m.; prix, 20f.
Lamoignon. Haut., 85c.m.; prix, 25f.
Comte de Lamothe-Piquet, par Brion, 1823. Clarac, pl. 1125a, n. 3574a. Haut., 75c.m.; prix, 20f.
Lapérouse, navigateur, par Rude, 1828. Clarac, pl. 1125a, n. 3574b. Haut., 80c.m.; prix, 30f.
Charles Le Brun, par Coyzevox, 1679. Clarac, pl. 1133, n. 3630. Haut., 85c.m.; prix, 25f.
Le Nôtre, par Gourdel. Clarac, pl. 1136, n. 3647. Haut., 85c.m.; prix, 25f.
Olivier Le Febvre, seigneur d'Ormesson, buste attribué à Ponce. Clarac, pl. 1119, n. 3547. Haut., 48c.m.; prix, 10f.
Eustache Lesueur, par Roland. 1806. Haut., 1m ; prix, 30f.
Linné. Haut., 80c.m.; prix, 20f.
Louvois, par Desjardins. Clarac, pl. 1119, n. 3550. Haut., 80c.m.; prix, 25f.
Lulli. Haut., 90c.m.; prix, 25f.
Mansart, par Lemoyne, 1705. Clarac. pl. 1123, n. 3566. Haut., 1m. 10c m.; prix, 40f.
Maurice, comte de Saxe, maréchal de France, par Pigalle. Haut., 80c m.; prix, 20f.
Mazarin, par Coyzevox. Clarac, pl 1122, n. 3560a. Haut., 80c m.; prix. 20f.
Pierre Mignard, par Coyzevox. Clarac, pl. 1132. n. 3623. Haut., 78c.m ; prix, 20f.
Peiresc, par Francin fils. Clarac, pl. 1120, n. 3556. Haut., 67c.m.; prix, 20f.
Le Primatice, par Foyatier. 1826. Clarac, pl. 1129, n. 3607. Haut., 58c.m.; prix, 10f.
Jean Racine. Haut., 80c.m.; prix, 20f.
Réaumur. Haut., 70c.m.; prix, 10f.
Richelieu, par Coyzevox. Clarac, pl. 1119, n. 3549. Haut., 84c.m.; prix, 25f.
Jean-Jacques Rousseau, par Houdon, 1778. Haut., 45c.m.; prix, 10f.
Pierre Séguier, chancelier de France, bronze attribué à Jacques Sarrazin. Clarac, pl. 1120, n. 3554. Haut., 72 c.m.; prix, 20f.
Soufflot, par Prévot. Clarac, pl. 1125, n. 3566a. Haut., 60c.m.; prix, 20f.

X.—TÊTES.

Antonin le Pieux. Musée des Antiques, II, 85. Haut., 55c.m.; prix, 12f.
Centaures (deux), des métopes du Parthénon (Musée Britannique). Haut., 33c.m.; prix, 3f. Haut., 43c.m.; prix, 5f.

Claude, bronze du Louvre. Musée des Antiques, III, bustes, pl. 5. Haut., 47c.m.; prix, 6f.
Femme voilée (Louvre, salle de la Psyché). Haut., 30c.m.; prix, 3f.
Femme frisée, bronze du Louvre. Haut., 40c.m.; prix, 5f.
Inconnu, marbre du Louvre. Haut., 48c m.; prix, 3f.
Jupiter Trophonius, dit Jupiter Talleyrand. Clarac, pl. 1086, n. 2722e. Haut., 42c.m.; prix, 6f.
Ptolémée, fils de Juba, roi de Maurétanie (Musée d'Afrique). Clarac, pl. 1093, n. 3487f. Haut., 35c.m.; prix, 4f.
Le Rémouleur (Arrotino), du Musée de Florence. Haut., 40c.m.; prix, 5f.
Enfant (École florentine). Haut., 13c.m.; prix, 2f.

XI. — MASQUES.

Apollon du Belvédère. Prix, 3f.
Apollon dit l'Espagne. Musée des Antiques, I, 74. Prix, 50f.
Jupiter. Prix, 1f. 50c.
Jupiter d'Otricoli, au Vatican. Prix, 8f.
Lucilla, masque colossal du Louvre. Haut., 1m.; prix, 80f.
Omphale Albani. Prix, 3f.
Dieu Marin dit Palémon. Prix, 1f. 50c.
Psyché du Musée de Naples. Prix, 1f. 50c.
Sapho du Capitole. Prix, 1f. 50c.
Thucydide. Musée des Antiques, III, bustes, pl. 4. Prix, 1f. 50c.
Vénus d'Arles. Prix, 2f.
Vénus de Versailles dite Génétrix. Prix, 1f. 50c.
Vénus de Médicis. Prix, 1f. 50c.
Vénus de Milo. Prix, 2f.
Prisonnier, par Michel-Ange. Prix, 3f.

XII. — ANIMAUX.

Têtes des chevaux d'Hypérion et de la Nuit sur le fronton du Parthénon (Musée Britannique). Prix, chacune, 12f.
Chien Borghèse. Clarac, pl. 350, n. 216. Haut., 57c.m.; prix, 25f.
Lion assyrien du palais royal de Khorsabad. Larg., 41c.m.; prix, 4f.
Panthère bachique. Haut., 19c.m ; prix, 2f. 50c.
Chien couché, par Giraud. Haut., 50c.m.; prix, 25f.
Lions du jardin des Tuileries, par Barye. Haut., 2m.; prix, 250f. Haut., 1m. 20c.m.; prix, 200f.

XIII. — MEMBRES DÉTACHES.

Achille Borghèse, 2 bras. Prix, chacun, 5f. 50c.
Antinous du Vatican, 2 bras. Prix, chacun, 6f.
L'Enfant Bacchus (du groupe dit Faune à l'Enfant), 2 jambes et 1 bras. Prix, la pièce, 1f.
Combattant grec dit le Gladiateur Borghèse, 2 bras. Prix, chacun, 2f.
Idem. 2 jambes. Prix, chacune, 3f.
Idem. 2 pieds. Prix, chacun, 1f. 50c.
Diane de Versailles, 2 jambes. Prix, chacune, 4f.
Idem. 2 pieds. Prix, chacun, 2f.
Hermaphrodite Borghèse, 2 pieds. Prix, chacun, 50c.
Laocoön, 1 bras. Prix, 6f.
Idem. 1 cuisse, 2 jambes, et 1 genou. Prix, la pièce, 3f.
Idem. 2 pieds. Prix, chacun, 1f. 50c.
Marsyas, 2 pieds. Prix, chacun, 1f. 50c.
Mercure, dit Germanicus, 1 bras. Prix, 5f.
Idem. 2 jambes. Prix, chacune, 3f.
Idem 2 pieds. Prix, chacun, 1f. 50c.
Mercure dit Jason, 1 jambe. Prix, 3f.
Silène dit Faune à l'Enfant. 2 jambes. Prix, chacune, 3f.
Idem. 2 pieds. Prix, chacun, 75c.
Vénus de Médicis, 2 bras. Prix, chacun, 2f.
Idem. 2 jambes. Prix, chacune, 3f.
Milon de Crotone, par Pierre Puget, 2 jambes. Prix, chacune, 5f.
Idem. Patte du lion. Prix, 2f.
Moïse, par Michel-Ange, 1 bras. Prix, 8f.
Prisonnier, par Michel-Ange, bras replié. Prix, 6f.
Jeune Prisonnier, par Michel-Ange, 2 bras. Prix, chacun, 4f.
Idem. 2 jambes. Prix, chacune, 5f.

XIV.—BAS-RELIEFS ANTIQUES.

A. RELIEFS ÉGYPTIENS.

Le Pharaon Snéfrou terrassant un homme de race asiatique (relief provenant du mont Sinaï). Haut., 1m.; larg., 40c.m.; prix, 10f.

B. RELIEFS ASSYRIENS.

I. Du palais royal de Khorsabad.

Taureaux ailés à face humaine (trois). Haut., 4m. 20c.m.; prix, chacun, 500f.
Divinité tenant une corbeille et une pomme de pin. Haut., 83c.m.; prix, 10f.
Divinité à tête d'aigle. Haut., 1m. 2c m.; prix, 10f.
Prêtre portant une tige de pavot. Haut., 95c.m.; prix, 10f.

II. Du palais royal de Ninive.

Sardanapale III. tuant des lions. Haut., 1m.; larg., 5m.; prix, 20f.
Sardanapale V, dans son char. Haut., 1m. 20c.m.; larg., 80c.m.; prix, 10f.
Tributaires conduisant des bœufs. Haut., 1m 50c.m.; larg., 1m. 50c.m.; prix, 20f.
Guerriers dans leurs chars. Haut., 1m. 20c.m.; larg., 80c.m.; prix, 10f.
Siége d'une ville. Haut., 1m.; larg., 8m.; prix, 40f.
Fragment d'un homme tenant deux chevaux. Haut., 50c.m.; prix, 4f.

C. BAS-RELIEFS GRECS ET ROMAINS.

Agamemnon, Épéus. et le héraut Talthybius, relief de Samothrace. Clarac, pl. 116, n. 238. Haut., 46c.m.; larg., 45c.m ; prix, 3f.
Combat d'Amazones, sarcophage de Salonique. Clarac, pl. 117[a], n. 232[a]. Haut., 78c.m.; larg., 2m. 53c m.; prix, 60f
Apollon, Diane, et Latone devant une idole. Musée des Antiques, III, bas-reliefs, pl. 26, 9. Haut., 58c.m ; larg., 58c m ; prix, 4f.
Bas-relief du temple d'Assos en Mysie (scène du Repas), Clarac, pl. 116[a], n. 238[a]. Haut., 80c.m.; larg., 2m.; prix, 40f.
Bacchante. Musée des Antiques, III. pl. 10, 7 Haut., 65c.m.; larg., 44c.m.; prix, 6f.
Bacchante en fureur. Musée des Antiques, I, 75. Haut, 50c.m.; larg., 32c.m.; prix, 3f.
Bacchus et Ariadne, camée du Louvre. Haut., 43c.m.; larg., 54c.m.; prix, 3f.
Tête de Bœuf (prise sur la colonne Trajane). Haut, 30c.m.; larg., 45c.m.; prix, 1f.
Combat de Centaures, frise du temple de Phigalie. Haut., 1m. 30c.m ; larg., 22c.m.; prix, 40f.
Danseuses. Musée des Antiques, II, 97. Haut., 75c.m.; larg., 1m. 87c.m.; prix, 40f.
Diane, médaillon d'un autel Borghèse. Musée des Antiques, III, autels, pl. 4. Haut., 40c m ; prix, 5f.
Invocation à Esculape pour une femme et un enfant malades. Haut., 48c m.; larg., 90c m ; prix, 10f.
Faune chasseur. Musée des Antiques, I, 81. Haut., 1m. 78c.m.; larg, 1m. 17c.m.; prix, 30f.
Faune dansant. Musée des Antiques, III, pl. 10, 6. Haut., 45c.m.; larg., 30c.m ; prix, 3f.
Femme appuyée sur un cippe. Clarac, pl. 180, n. 334. Haut., 67c.m.; larg., 73c.m.; prix, 6f.
Femme appuyée sur un vase, bas-relief sépulcral trouvé à Cherchell. Gerhard, Denkmäler, 1863, pl. 166. Haut., 35c m ; larg., 33c.m.; prix, 3f.
Deux Griffons. Clarac, pl 193, n. 55. Haut., 73c m.; larg., 2m 18c.m.; prix, 40f.
Hercule enlevant le trépied d'Apollon. Musée des Antiques, III, pl. 26, 2. Haut., 52c.m.; larg., 63c.m.; prix, 4f.
Invocation à Jupiter. Bas-relief trouvé à Gortyne en Crète. Clarac, pl. 224[a], n. 36[a]. Haut., 39c.m ; larg., 36c.m.; prix, 3f.
Frise du monument choragique de Lysicrate, dit Lanterne de Démosthène, dix-sept reliefs. Haut., 26c.m ; prix, chacun, 3f.
Tête de Minerve (salle de l'Aruspice au Louvre). Haut., 22c.m.; larg., 17c.m.; prix, 1f. 50c.
Les Muses, sarcophage. Musée des Antiques, I, 78. Haut, 61c.m ; larg., 2m. 7c.m.; prix, 60f.
Deux Musiciennes. Musée des Antiques, III, pl. 24, 6. Haut., 86c.m.; larg., 58c.m.; prix, 18f.

Métopes du temple de Jupiter à Olympié.

a. Pallas assise. Clarac, pl. 195[b], n. 211[b]. Haut., 1m. 59c.m.; larg., 87c.m; prix, 30f.
b. Hercule arrêtant le Taureau de Crète. Clarac, pl. 195[b], n. 211[c]. Haut., 1m. 15c.m.; larg., 1m. 54c.m.; prix, 40f.

Bas-reliefs du Parthénon.

I. Métope du Louvre. Centaure arrêtant une femme (marbre Choiseul). Musée des Antiques, III, 11. Haut., 1m. 41c.m.; larg., 1m. 34c.m.; prix, 60f.
II. Métope du Musée Britannique. Centaure étranglant un jeune Lapithe. Haut., 83c.m ; larg., 90c.m.; prix, 40f.
III. Frise du Louvre. Musée des Antiques, II, 96. Haut., 62c.m.; larg., 2m. 7c.m ; prix, 40f.
IV. Frise du Musée Britannique, vingt pièces. Prix, 400f.
b. Deux cavaliers. Trésor de Glyptique, pl. 1, 4 (deuxième groupe). Haut., 1m. 8c.m.; larg., 1m. 55c.m.; prix, 30f.
c. Éphèbes conduisant leurs chevaux. Trésor. pl. 2, 3. Haut., 1m. 7c.m.; larg. 1m. 56c.m.; prix, 30f
d. Deux cavaliers. Trésor, pl. 1, 3. Haut., 1m. 8c.m.; larg., 1m. 50c.m.; prix, 30f.
e. Deux cavaliers. Trésor. pl. 1, 2. (Groupe du milieu.) Haut., 1m. 7c.m.; larg., 1m. 55c.m.; prix, 30f.
f. Homme frappant un cheval qui se cabre. Trésor, pl. 1, 3. Haut., 1m. 2c.m.; larg., 1m. 39c.m.; prix, 30f.
g. Quatre cavaliers. Trésor, pl. 2, 3. Haut., 1m. 3c.m.; larg., 1m. 24c.m.; prix, 30f.
h. Deux cavaliers. Trésor, pl. 1, 1. Haut., 1m. 8c.m.; larg., 1m. 74c.m.; prix, 30f.
i. Deux cavaliers coiffés du pétase. Trésor, pl. 1, 4. Haut., 1m. 10c.m.; larg., 1m. 48c.m.; prix, 30f.
j. Cavalier casqué. Trésor, pl. 1, 3. Haut., 1m. 8c.m.; larg., 1m. 2c.m.; prix, 20f.
k. Cheval, homme barbu, et éphèbe. Trésor, pl. 1, 2. Haut., 1m.; larg., 1m.; prix, 20f.
l. Le jeune Érechthée et Pandrosos. Haut., 1m. 7c.m.; larg., 88c.m.; prix, 20f.
m. Cheval qui frotte ses naseaux contre sa jambe. Trésor, pl. 2, 1. Haut., 1m. 2c.m.; larg., 88c.m.; prix, 15f.
n. Jeune homme tenant un cheval. Trésor, pl. 1, 2. Haut., 1m. 9c.m.; larg., 90c.m.; prix, 15f.
o. Vieillard s'appuyant sur un bâton. et jeune homme derrière lui. Trésor, pl. 10, 3. Haut., 1m. 3c m.; larg., 87c.m.; prix, 15f.
p. Deux éphèbes appuyés l'un sur l'autre. Trésor, pl. 10, 3. Haut., 1m. 8c.m.; larg., 90c.m.; prix, 15f.
q. Guerrier remettant sa chaussure. Trésor, pl. 1, 3. Haut., 1m. 4c.m.; larg., 47c.m.; prix, 8f.
r. Cheval et jeune homme mettant sa chaussure. Trésor, pl. 2, 3. Haut., 1m. 3c.m.; larg., 52c.m; prix, 8f.
s. Jeune homme. Trésor, pl. 10, 3. (Le sixième.) Haut., 1m. 2c.m.; larg., 47c.m.; prix, 8f
t. Jeune homme. Trésor, pl. 2, 1. (Le premier.) Haut., 1m.; larg., 44c.m.; prix, 8f.
u. Jeune homme tenant un cheval. Trésor, pl. 1, 2. Haut., 1m. 5c.m.; larg., 47c.m.; prix, 8f.
Bas-reliefs des Propylées d'Athènes. Deux pièces à 12 et à 15 francs. Haut., 45c.m.; larg., 45c.m.; prix, 27f.
Quadriges (deux), reliefs trouvés à Herculanum. Haut., 75m.; prix, chacun, 30f.
Sacrifice à Cérès. Musée des Antiques, III, pl. 25. Haut., 55c m.; larg., 60c.m.; prix, 4f.
Trône de Saturne. Clarac, pl. 218, n. 10. Haut., 77c.m.; larg., 2m. 2c.m.; prix, 60f.

Métopes du Temple de Sélinonte.

a. Persée tuant la Gorgone. Haut., 1m. 10c.m.; larg., 1m. 10c.m.; prix, 20f.
b. Hercule portant les Cercopes. Haut., 1m. 10c.m.; larg., 1m. 10c.m.; prix, 20f.
Taureau attaqué par un lion. Clarac, pl. 223, n. 189. Haut., 92c.m.; larg., 1m. 12c.m.; prix, 20f.
Thétis invoquant le secours de Jupiter. Musée des Antiques, I, 75. Haut., 52c.m.; larg., 59c.m.; prix, 4f.
Tibère sur son char de triomphe. Grand camée de Vienne. Clarac, pl. 1053. Haut., 19c.m : larg., 43c.m.; prix, 2f.
Thémistocle vainqueur. Clarac, pl. 223, n. 255. Haut., 43c.m.; larg., 47c.m.; prix, 4f.

Métopes du Temple de Thésée, représentant les exploits d'Hercule et le combat des Centaures et des Lapithes.

a. Haut., 67c.m.; larg., 1m. 8c.m.; prix, 20f.
b. Haut., 84c.m.; larg., 1m. 2c.m.; prix, 20f.
c. Haut., 83c.m.; larg., 1m. 15c.m.; prix, 20f.

d. Haut., 74c.m.; larg., 1m. 5c.m.; prix, 15f.
e. Haut., 78c.m.; larg., 82c.m.; prix, 15f.
f. Haut., 77c.m.; larg., 92c.m.; prix, 15f.
g. Haut., 76c.m.; larg., 77c.m.; prix, 15f.
h. Haut., 75c.m.; larg., 78c.m.; prix, 15f.
i. Haut., 80c.m.; larg., 80c.m.; prix, 15f.
j. Haut., 78c.m.; larg., 78c.m.; prix, 15f.
k. Haut., 76c.m.; larg., 41c.m.; prix, 8f.
l. Haut., 77c.m.; larg., 47c.m.; prix, 8f.

Trajan (tête prise sur la colonne Trajane). Haut., 26c.m.; larg., 20c.m.; prix, 1f.
Ulysse consultant le devin Tirésias. Musée des Antiques, III, pl. 23. Haut., 60c.m.; larg., 62c.m.; prix, 5f.
Vase Albani, six bas-reliefs. Haut., 32c.m.; larg., 28c.m.; prix, chacun, 1f.
Vase Borghèse. Musée des Antiques, I, 76, 77. Haut., 67c.m.
a. Silène ivre soutenu par un faune. Prix, 10f.
b. Bacchante aux Castagnettes. Prix, 5f.
c. Satyre jouant de la double flûte. Prix, 5f.
d. Faune et Bacchante. Prix, 10f.
e. Joueuse de tambourin. Prix, 5f.
f. Bacchus appuyé sur une joueuse de lyre. Prix, 10f.
g. Satyre dansant. Prix, 5f.
Victoire et Apollon. Musée des Antiques, III, pl. 26, 6. Haut., 42c.m.; larg., 45c.m.; prix, 4f.
Victoire, Apollon, et Diane. Musée des Antiques, III, pl. 26, 5. Haut., 49c.m.; larg., 61c.m.; prix, 4f.
Victoire, Bacchus, et Diane. Musée des Antiques, III, pl. 26, 3. Haut., 57c.m.; larg., 63c.m.; prix, 6f.
Trois villes personnifiées. Clarac, pl. 222, n. 301. Haut., 91c.m.; larg., 82c.m.; prix, 18f.
Forges de Vulcain. Musée des Antiques, III, pl. 4, 1. Haut., 65c.m.; larg., 1m. 8c.m.; prix, 10f.

XV.—BAS-RELIEFS MODERNES.

Cheminée du château de Mennecy, par Germain Pilon. Haut., 4m. 62c.m.; larg., 2m. 54c.m.; prix, 600f.
Descente de croix, par Daniel de Volterre. Haut., 79c.m.; larg., 1m. 95c.m.; prix, 40f.
Descente de croix, par Germain Pilon. Haut., 48c.m.; larg., 81c.m.; prix, 30f.
Quatre bas-reliefs du Tombeau du chancelier Duprat (mort en 1535) à la cathédrale de Sens.
1 et 2, haut., 44c.m.; larg., 1m. 75c.m.; prix chacun, 40f.
3 et 4, haut., 44c.m.; larg., 74c.m.; prix, chacun, 20f.
Les quatre Évangélistes de l'autel du château d'Écouen, par Jean Goujon. Haut., 80c.m.; larg., 5m.; prix, 80f.
Sainte Famille (Louvre, n. 15). Haut., 33c.m.; larg., 21c.m.; prix, 3f.
Cinq reliefs de la Fontaine des Innocents, par Jean Goujon. Clarac, pl. 231, 231ª, n. 366, 367, 368ª.
a. Trois nymphes. Haut., 73c.m.; larg., 5m. 85c.m.; prix, 40f.
b. Vénus Anadyomène. Haut., 45c.m.; larg. 26c.m.; prix, 2f.
c. Nymphe de Paris. Haut., 45c.m.; larg., 23c.m.; prix 2f.
d. Nymphe de la Seine. Haut., 45c.m.; larg., 26c.m.; prix, 2f.
e. Nymphe d'un autre fleuve. Haut., 45c.m.; larg., 26c.m.; prix, 2f.
Fuite en Égypte, prise sur une cheminée à Versailles. Haut., 28c.m.; larg., 57c.m.; prix, 3f.
Nymphe de Fontainebleau, par Benvenuto Cellini. Haut., 2m. 5c.m.; larg., 4m. 9c.m.; prix, 600f.
Le Réveil, par Fremyn Roussel. Haut., 43c.m.; larg., 44c.m.; prix, 10f.
Rocquencourt (André Blondel de), contrôleur général des finances, mort en 1558. Figure couchée. Bronze de Ponce. Haut., 73c.m.; larg., 60c.m.; prix, 20f.
Suzanne au bain, de la cheminée de Bruges. Haut., 48c.m.; larg., 75c.m.; prix, 3f.
Vie du médecin Jérôme de la Torre, bronze d'Andréa Riccio (porte de la salle des Caryatides). Clarac, pl. 47 à 50.
a. Jérôme enseignant la médecine. Haut., 49c.m.; larg., 37c.m.; prix, 15f.
b. Maladie de Jérôme. Haut., 49c.m.; larg., 37c.m.; prix, 15f.
c. Sacrifice à Esculape. Haut., 49c.m.; larg., 37c.m.; prix, 15f.
d. Mort de Jérôme. Haut., 49c.m.; larg., 37c.m.; prix, 15f.
e. Funérailles. Haut., 49c.m.; larg., 37c.m.; prix, 15f.
f. L'âme de Jérôme traverse le Styx. Haut., 49c.m.; larg., 37c.m.; prix, 15f.
g. Les Champs Élysées. Haut., 49c.m.; larg., 37c.m.; prix, 15f.
h. Renommée de Jérôme. Haut., 49c.m.; larg., 37c.m.; prix, 15f.

XVI.—INSCRIPTIONS.

Inscriptions cunéiformes (Quatre), au Louvre, n. 602, 606, 612, 613. Prix, chacune, 5f.

XVII.—AUTELS.

Autel Borghèse. Haut., 1m. 30c.m.; prix, 70f.
Autel astronomique des douze Dieux. Haut., 90c.m.; larg., 42c.m.; prix, 30f.

XVIII.—CANDÉLABRES.

Grand candélabre composé par Piranesi. Musée des Antiques, III cand. pl. 1, Clarac, pl. 141, n. 120. Haut., 3m. 58c m.; prix, 600f.
Candélabre de la salle de la Paix. Musée des Antiques, III, pl. 3, 2. Haut. 2m. 20c m.; prix, 100f.
Candélabre aux Atlantes. Clarac, pl. 257, n. 642. Haut., 2m.; prix, 40f.

XIX.—VASES.

Vase Albani. Haut., 77c.m.; prix, 50f.
Vase Borghèse. Musée des Antiques, I, 76, 77. Haut., 1m. 78c.m.; prix, 200f.
Vases de Marathon (deux). Clarac, pl. 152, n. 271, 272, 274. Haut., 45c.m.; prix, chacun, 12f.
Vase aux masques bachiques. Clarac, pl 145, n. 124. Haut., 79c.m.; prix, 30f.
Vase de Sosibius. Musée des Antiques, III, vases, pl. 8. Haut., 75c.m.; prix, 20f.
Coupe, dite de Benvenuto Cellini. Haut., 25c.m.; prix, 12f.
Vase, dit de Benvenuto Cellini Clarac, pl. 51, 2. Haut., 30c.m.; prix, 15f.
Vases modernes du jardin de Versailles (neuf). Haut. 1m.; prix, chacun, 50f.

XX.—OBJETS DIVERS.

Trépied moderne en marbre rouge antique. Clarac, pl. 261, n. 652; Haut., 83c.m.; prix, 50f.
Piédestal décoré d'attributs de chasse (jardin de Versailles). Haut., 1m.; prix, 60f.
Casque d'Henri IV. Prix, 22f.

Casts not included in either of the previous Lists, but which are procurable at the Addresses given.

PARIS.

Ecole des Beaux Arts, Atelier du Moulage. Address M. Desachy.

Bas-Relief from Eleusis, 70f.
4. Bas-Reliefs from the Temple of Victory at Athens (*en staffe*), 95f.

ROME.

Casts may be ordered from Leopoldo Malpieri or from Giuseppe Candiotti, whose address can be obtained from Messrs. Hooker, Maquay, & Co., Bankers, Piazza di Spagna.

MALPIERI.

Ludovis Juno (bust), 70f.
Sophocles, 200f.

CANDIOTTI.

Minerva Medica, 200f.
Pudicitia, 188f.
The Athlete, 134f.
Aristides, 161f.
Sophocles, 161f.
Venus of the Capitol, 188f.
Faustina, 290f.
Amazon, 215f.
Dying Gladiator, 400f.
Caryatide, 300f.
Euripides, 250f.

DRESDEN.

Royal Museum of Casts. Address Dr. Hermann Hettner.

The Tripods with Reliefs, 30 thalers; 120f.
The Dresden Pallas, 25 thalers; 110f.

PROCURABLE AT MUNICH.

Information concerning them may be obtained of Professor Mozet, of the Royal Polytechnical School, Munich.

1, 5. Figures from the Eastern Pediment of the Temple at Ægina, 172f.
6, 15. Ten figures from the Western Pediment of the Temple at Ægina, 172f.
Doric Capital from the Temple of Ægina, 43f.
Bas-Relief. The Marriage of Neptune and Amphitrite, 643f.
The Rondanini Medusa (superb), 54f.
Ilioneus, 140f.

Applications for the purchase of Casts should be addressed to Professor Mozet, Directorium der Königl Polytechnichen Schule, München, Bayern.

APPENDIX III.

EXAMINATION PAPERS.

The examples of examination papers given here are illustrations of the graded system of the English Science and Art Department, in the Art Section. The standard for each grade is considerably lower than that at present applied, the papers being all of dates previous to 1870. It is therefore more applicable to this country, where the subject has not been taught so long as in England. The grades adopted — first, second, and third — are convenient and simple. The first grade should apply to all school children up to fifteen years of age; the second to all above that age, to students of night classes, and the teachers of the common schools; the third to professional teachers of art, or professional artists, architects, or engineers. Of the third grade there are six groups or certificates granted in England; the specimens here given being the first or most elementary group.

EXAMINATIONS BY THE ENGLISH SCIENCE AND ART DEPARTMENT.

Specimens of the examination papers for the first certificate of third grade, — the elementary certificate, — which must be held by masters or mistresses of schools of art. In addition to these papers, the examination includes also a chalk-drawing, in two hours, from a cast of foliage, and a drawing of models in a group, in two hours, the subject for 1868 being a chair leaning backwards upon a machine, in which toothed wheels were visible.

PERSPECTIVE THEORY.

FEBRUARY, 1868.

1. What is the difference between orthographic and perspective projection?
2. Upon what laws in optics are the principles of perspective founded?
3. Give reasons for or against any change by curvature or otherwise in long horizontal or vertical lines parallel to the picture.
4. In order to be able to measure right lines in a given plane, what conditions are necessarily predetermined?
5. By how many methods could you determine the geometric lengths of lines in horizontal planes, the necessary conditions being given?
6. What is the relation of a vanishing plane to the eye?
7. Is the perspective representation of a circle upon an oblique plane invariably a perfect ellipse?
8. Is the distance of the spectator from the picture arbitrarily fixed, or would any change of distance necessarily tend to render the drawing inaccurate?
9. Under what circumstances must a horizontal line be represented by a vertical one?
10. Explain the use of proportional measuring points.

Two hours allowed.

PERSPECTIVE.

FEBRUARY, 1868.

These problems are to be worked to a scale of one-half inch to the foot, the distance of the spectator from the picture being in each case thirteen feet, and the ground-plane five feet below the eye.

1. A right cylinder ten feet long and six feet in diameter lies upon its side on the ground-plane. The visible base is in a vertical plane at an angle of 45° with the picture, towards the left hand, and touches the ground-plane three feet within the picture, and two feet on the left of the spectator. Give its perspective representation.
2. A plane making an angle of 30° with the ground-plane intersects it in a line inclined towards the left hand, at an angle of 45° with the picture-plane. This line intersects the picture at a point, A, one foot to the right of the spectator. Find a point, B, upon the intersecting line of the oblique plane with the ground-plane, four feet from point A; and another point, C, ten feet from point A, upon this line. The line BC is one edge of a cube resting upon the inclined plane. Give a perspective representation of the solid.
3. A line upon the ground plane touches the base-line of the picture at a point, A, two feet to the right of the line of direction, and inclines towards the left hand at an angle of 45° with the picture: find a point, B, upon this line, two feet from point A, and another point, C, eight feet from point A. The line BC is one edge of a solid wedge, the base of which rests upon the ground-plane, and is square. Three sides of the solid are vertical, and its upper surface makes an angle of 60° with the ground-plane from the line BC. Complete its perspective representation without the use of plan or elevation, and give the vanishing line of the oblique plane.

Two hours allowed.

ELEMENTARY ARCHITECTURE.

FEBRUARY, 1868.

In all cases add the names of the parts. Scale at pleasure, but always to be sent up with the drawings.

1. Show by drawings the various joints made use of in wood-work.
2. Show by drawings the meaning of the following terms: wall-plate, pole-plate, tie beam, principal rafter, common rafter, purlins, strut, and king-post.
3. Show also the meaning of the following: bridging and binding joists, girder, and ceiling joist.
4. Give a sectional plan, elevation, and vertical section of a four-panelled door, showing details of framework.
5. Give a sectional plan, elevation, and vertical section of a window-frame arranged for sashes.

Four hours allowed.

GEOMETRY.

FEBRUARY, 1868.

1. Find a third and fourth proportional to two right lines of respectively three inches and two inches in length.
2. Construct a regular pentagon of one and one-half inches side, and an equilateral triangle containing the same area.
3. Give a general method of inscribing a regular polygon within a circle, applying it to a nonagon in a circle of one and one-half inches radius.
4. Give a general method of constructing a polygon upon a given line, applying it to a heptagon of one and one-half inches side.
5. Within the last polygon (fig. 4) place another heptagon, having sides of one inch parallel to the sides of the first polygon, and having the same centre.
6. Describe a circle of three inches diameter, and without it a second circle of one inch diameter, the circumference of which will be one-half inch from the first circle at its nearest point. Describe a third circle of three-quarters of an inch radius, which shall be tangential to these two.
7. The transverse diameter of an ellipse is five inches long, its conjugate diameter being equal to four-sixths of the length of the transverse. Draw the curve of the ellipse by means of intersecting arcs of circles.
8. Two similar triangles have bases of two inches, and one and one-half inches length, respectively. Construct a similar triangle of equal area to these two.
9. Draw a cinquefoil of tengential arcs of circles of one-half inch radius.
10. Construct a triangle, the base of which is one inch long, the altitude two inches, and one side of which is three inches long.

Two hours allowed.

ELEMENTARY MECHANICAL.

FEBRUARY, 1868.

1. A pyramid, base hexagonal, of one-inch side, four inches high, is to be represented by a plan and elevation.
   (*a*) When one edge is vertical.
   (*b*) When the axis is inclined 40°.
   (*c*) When one edge is horizontal, the adjacent faces being equally inclined.
2. A cone four inches high, standing on its base, the diameter of which is two inches, is cut completely through its curved surface by a plane inclined 40°. Draw it in plan and elevation, and show the true form of the section. Show also the shape of the paper required to wrap exactly round the part of the cone below the section.
3. A cylinder, nine inches long, diameter of base six inches, rests on the ground; and on it is placed a brick nine inches by four and a half by three inches, with one of the short edges of a face on the ground, the face being inclined 45°. Draw plan and elevation; the elevation being drawn on a plane taken at 30°, with the horizontal edges. Scale one-third.
4. A prism, with square base of two-inch sides, edges five inches and vertical, one face inclined 30° to the vertical plane, is intersected by another prism of the same dimensions, the edges of which are horizontal, and inclined 40° to the vertical plane. One face of the horizontal prism is inclined 30° to the horizontal plane, and its axis is two inches high, and five inches from the axis of the other prism. Draw plan and elevation.

Four hours allowed.

The following specimens of art-examination papers, given at South Kensington, will indicate some features of the standard of knowledge required to pass in the several groups. They are not selected papers, but what I happen to have by me. The standard in every subject has been raised very much within the last few years.

ELEMENTARY ARCHITECTURE.

GROUP 1. — FIRST CERTIFICATE. — FEBRUARY, 1871.

1. Draw a Grecian Doric entablature three feet in depth, and compare it with an Ionic entablature of the same depth, pointing out the chief differences in the mouldings and enrichments.
2. What were the chief changes effected in the Grecian orders of architecture under the Roman influence?
3. Draw the angle of a pediment showing the method in which the mouldings of the corona and bed-mould are returned and mitred.
4. Give a sketch of an early English capital and base with any details you may remember of the characteristic foliage of the thirteenth century.
5. Distinguish between the early and late decorated styles of English Gothic architecture, by a comparison of the tracery of each period.

Four hours allowed for this paper.

GROUP 1. — FIRST CERTIFICATE. — FEBRUARY, 1872.

1. What were the principal mouldings and enrichments used in the Grecian Doric and Grecian Ionic orders.
2. Draw a Roman Doric column with its capital, and the base usually found in ancient examples. Show also an Attic base for a shaft of the same diameter, and name each of the component mouldings.
3. What orders among the ancients and at the time of the Italian Renaissance are considered to be the best authorities upon the proportions of the five orders? Mention any of their works you can remember.
4. Draw in section and elevation a clustered shaft of the Decorated Period, with its characteristic base mouldings.
5. State what were the chief signs of the decadence of English Gothic architecture, and show how your remarks apply to Henry VII.'s. chapel or any similar building of the Perpendicular Period.

INSTRUCTION. — Except when a sketch only is asked for, the drawing should be to scale, — such scale to be clearly indicated against each question.

Four hours allowed for this paper.

ARCHITECTURE.

Group 6. — Sixth Certificate (Paper Work).

1. Give a design in plan and section of a fire-proof floor of Yorkshire stone laid on 1½ brick arches turned between iron girders; the whole depth of the floor not to exceed two feet.
2. Show by plan and sections the construction of a trough gutter between two quarter-pitch roofs, carried on a nine-inch wall, the gutter to be forty feet long, and the proper fall to be indicated on a longitudinal section.
3. It is required to construct a stone stair 4′ 6″ wide in the hall of a house. The height from floor to floor is fifteen feet, and it is necessary to provide head-room of eight feet in the cellar for a door under the hall landing, no windows to be used, the stairs to have eleven inches treads, exclusive of nosing, and six and one-half inches rises. The space available is ten feet wide, with a length of twenty feet, measured from the lowest step to the back wall.
4. Give examples of at least four of the best kinds of roofing tiles, and show by plan and two sections the method of laying each description of tile. State also briefly the advantages and disadvantages of employing each particular kind.

Four hours allowed for this paper.

ADVANCED ARCHITECTURE.

Group 6. — Sixth Certificate (Practice).

Design for a Provincial School of Art.

1. Plans, elevations, and sections are required for a school of art for one hundred students, with small museum attached.
2. Economy must enter into the consideration of the design, as the sum available for the work is only £3,000.
3. All designs must be drawn to the same scale, viz., one-eighth of an inch to the foot, and colors may only be used to distinguished the material.
4. To be strictly in accordance with minute of Council of Education, No. 359.
5. Competitors will see the necessity of gaining an abundance of light, and also of providing in their plans for an efficient and simple mode of heating and ventilating, to be included in the estimates.
6. No building must advance beyond the line marked in ground-plan.
7. From the character of the adjoining buildings a classical style of architecture is not suitable for the site.
8. Materials to be used: brick, red or white, or the stone of the neighborhood, which is bluish gray and easily worked.

Five days allowed for this paper.

PAINTING.

Group 2. — Second Certificate. — July, 1863.

1. Of what substances are the pigments constant white, chrome yellow, Naples yellow, gamboge, vermilion, lake, light red, Indian red, ultramarine, cobalt, and Vandyke brown, composed?
2. Write explanations of the following terms: tint, tone, hue, breadth, local color, chiaroscuro, handling, glazing, scumbling.
3. Give in chronological order the names of the Italian schools of painting, and of the principal masters in each.
4. Give some account of Albert Durer and his works.
5. Give some account of Michael Angelo and of his works.
6. Give some account of Rubens and of his works.
7. Give some account of Reynolds and of his works.
8. Name some of the best works of the French, Spanish, and Dutch schools.
9. Describe the various materials and processes of oil painting.
10. Describe the various materials and processes of water-color painting.

Group 2. — Second Certificate. — February, 1863.

1. Describe the method of painting large subjects on linen, which was peculiar to England in the fourteenth century.
2. Describe the process of fresco-painting, and the distinctive features between "buon fresco" and "fresco secco."
3. Describe the progress of a picture in the hands of an early Flemish painter in oil.
4. What were the principles of the school of the Carraci, and when and where was it established?

5. What occasions the cracking, the wrinkling of the surface, and the discoloration observable in various oil-color pictures?
6. With what medium are Cuyp's pictures painted?
7. What colors were used in the first, second, and third paintings of a head by Reynolds, in his most usual manner?
8. What are most usually considered the greatest works of Leonardo da Vinci, of Michael Angelo, of Raphael, of Rubens, of Dominichino, of Titian, and of Tintoretto, respectively?
9. Who were the principal Spanish painters, and what were the characteristics of their work?

BOTANY.

Group 2. — Second Certificate. — February, 1864.

1. What is the object of the root of a plant?
2. In what way does the root derive fluids from the earth?
3. Give the three typical varieties of the venation of the leaf.
4. The leaves of certain plants fall annually from their parent by a clean fracture. What is the characteristic feature of such leaves?
5. What is the internal structure of those stems from which the leaves annually fall?
6. Name the parts in what may be termed a perfectly developed or typical flower.
7. What is the object of the stamens?
8. What is the object of the pistil?
9. To how many typical organs are the parts of the plant referable?
10. In what way does the plant repeat itself by growth?
11. Name some instances in which the plant appears peculiarly adapted to the circumstances by which it is surrounded, or to the work it has to perform.
12. Give the characters of the four great classes of plants, i.e., Exogens, Endogens, Acrogens, and Thallogens.

One hour and a half allowed for this paper.

HISTORIC ORNAMENT.

Groups 3, 5, and 6.

Each candidate will be required to produce two sets of six studies each from the ornament of ornamental objects in the Museum of the Department, to be accompanied with the dates and a brief explanation of the principal and distinguishing characteristics of the two styles.

One of the subjects named below will be given out to each candidate by the examiner, and three clear days allowed to each candidate for the completion of the twelve studies and explanation. Where the ornament is colored, the color must be indicated in the sketches.

Each set of the works to be contained on a sheet of imperial paper, the explanations having figured references, and being carefully written.

1. Chinese enamels and Limoges enamels, prior to the end of thirteenth century.
2. Persian and Hispano-Moresco.
3. Sixteenth-century metal work, Italian and French.
4. Sixteenth-century metal work, Italian and German.
5. Damascene work, Saracenic and Italian.
6. Sixteenth-century French pottery.
7. Seventeenth-century English and Italian wood-carving.
8. German and Italian marqueterie.
9. Stained glass prior to end of seventeenth century, Italian and Flemish.
10. Stained glass prior to seventeenth century, Italian and German.
11. Borders of illuminated missals prior to seventeenth century, and Persian manuscript borders.
12. Arabesques, Urbino ware, sixteenth century; Frenza ware, same date.
13. Italian diapered silk prior to seventeenth century; Indian silk diapers.

TECHNICAL ORNAMENT.

GROUP 4. — FOURTH CERTIFICATE. — FEBRUARY, 1862.

1. What are the proper modifications of design for wrought-iron?
2. What are the proper modifications of design for casting in iron, bronze, &c.?
3. Should any distinctive character of relief be observed in the subordinate parts of architectural decoration?
4. What are the technical peculiarities in mediæval (fifteenth century) wood-carving, as distinguished from carvings executed in other materials?
5. In architectural decoration, if the relief is intended to be finished by gilding, &c., would there be any special requirement in the treatment of foliage ornament?

Two hours allowed for this paper.

SPECIMEN OF FIRST GRADE

EXAMINATION PAPER FOR FREEHAND OUTLINE.

FORTY MINUTES ALLOWED.

FOR CHILDREN OF TWELVE YEARS AND UNDER.

This example is intended to be copied the same size on paper. An HB or F pencil should be used. Measuring is not to be resorted to.

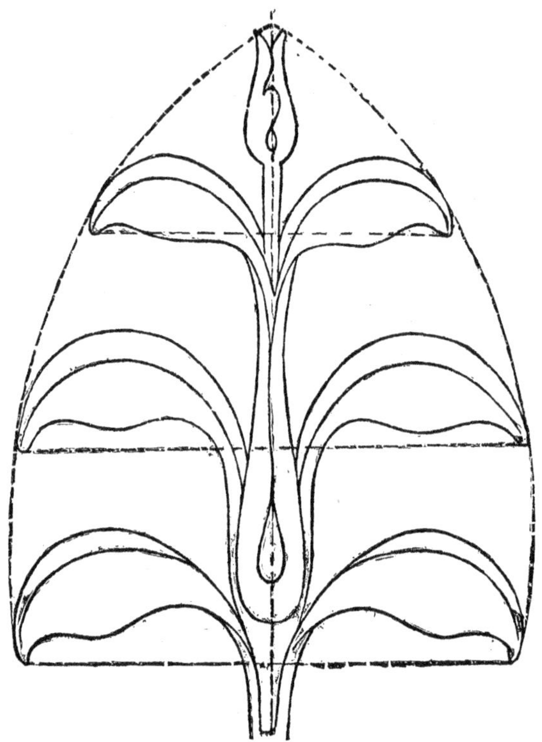

WRITE 1. Your name.
2. Your age.
3. Your school.

SPECIMEN OF

SUBJECT SET UP FOR MODEL-DRAWING.

FIRST GRADE. FORTY MINUTES ALLOWED.

FOR CHILDREN OF TWELVE YEARS AND UNDER.

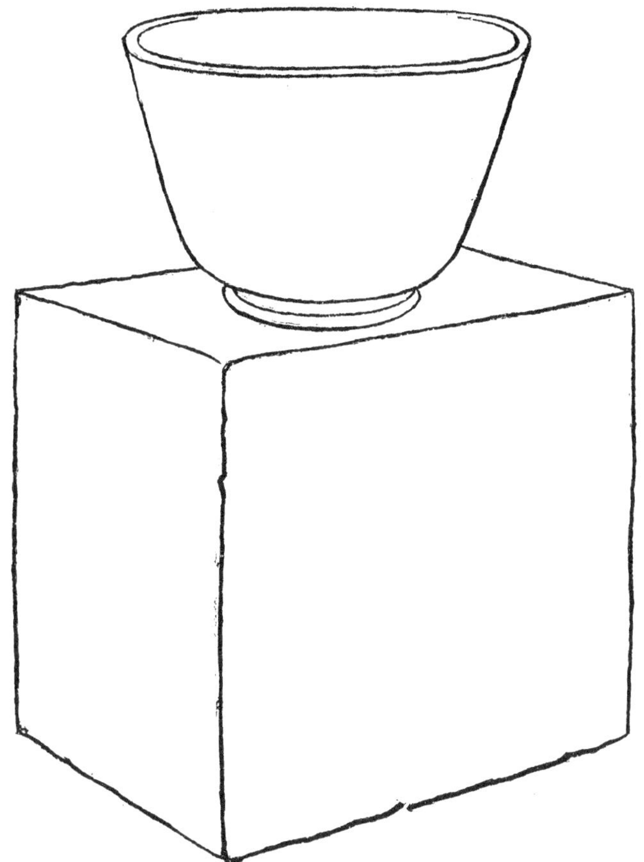

[NOTE.—This paper, and also the geometrical paper, is one-fourth the size of that used.]

WRITE 1. Your name.
2. Your age.
3. Your school.

SPECIMEN OF

EXAMINATION PAPER, GEOMETRICAL DRAWING.

FIRST GRADE. FORTY MINUTES ALLOWED.

FOR CHILDREN OF TWELVE YEARS AND UNDER.

1.

A B

1. Make a right angle at B.
   Divide it into four equal parts.

2.

A B

2. On A B make an equilateral triangle.
   Find its centre.

3.

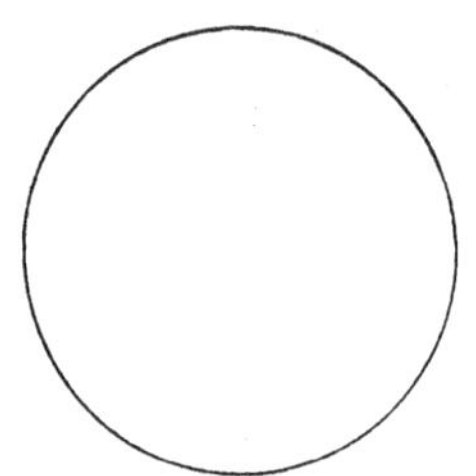

3. Find the centre of this circle.
   Inscribe a square within it.

4.

A B

4. On A B make a regular pentagon.

5.

A——B

5. Divide A B into five equal parts.

6.

B

A

6. A B is the diagonal of a square.
   Construct it.

WRITE 1. Your name.
2. Your age.
3. Your school.

SPECIMEN OF SECOND-GRADE EXAMINATION PAPER, *FREEHAND OUTLINE DRAWING*. TIME ALLOWED, ONE HOUR.

Second Grade is for Teachers of Public Schools and Students of Schools of Art.

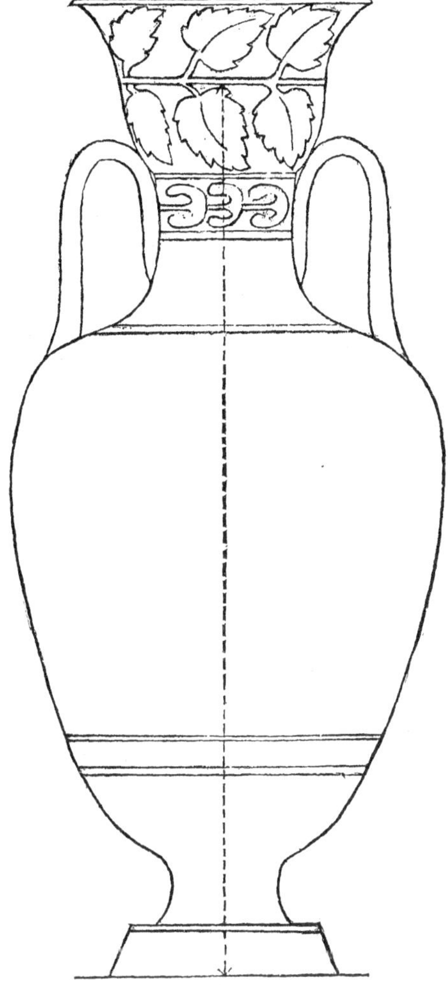

To be drawn on a centre line equal to the dotted line. No measuring allowed.

WRITE 1. Your name at full length.
2. Your age last birthday.
3. The school where you learn drawing.

SPECIMEN OF

GROUP PLACED FOR MODEL-DRAWING.

FOR SECOND-GRADE EXAMINATION.

TIME ALLOWED, ONE HOUR.

To be drawn as large as the paper will allow.

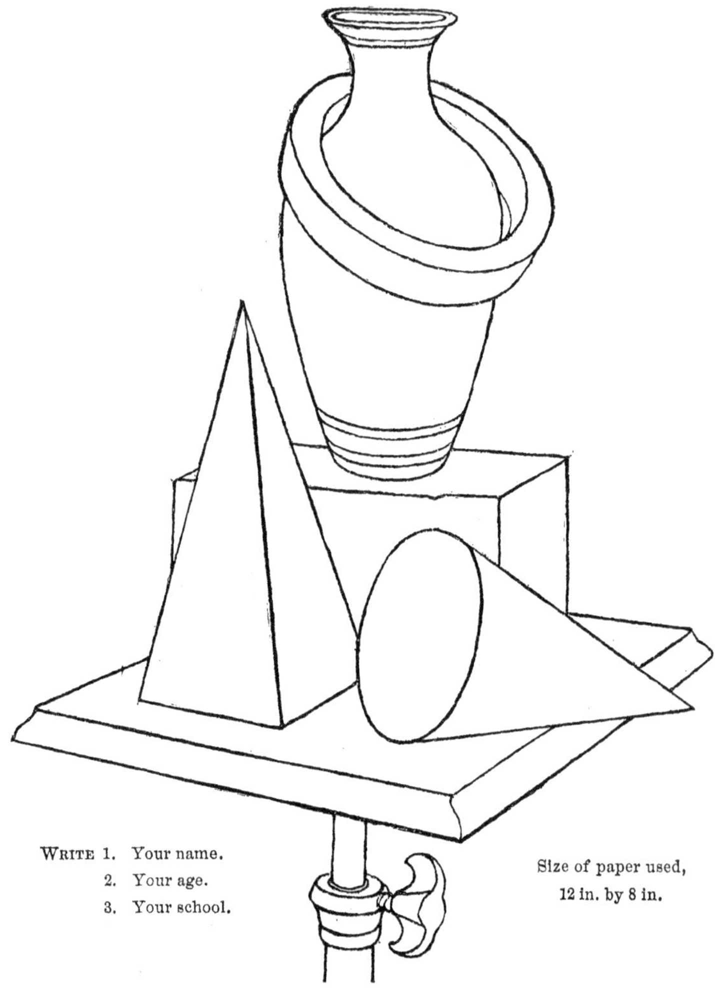

WRITE 1. Your name.
2. Your age.
3. Your school.

Size of paper used,
12 in. by 8 in.

SPECIMEN OF SECOND-GRADE

EXAMINATION PAPER, MEMORY DRAWING

UPON THE BLACKBOARD, AND UPON THE SHEET OF PAPER FURNISHED.

Time allowed, to be settled by the Examiner, according to the difficulty of the subject chosen. [Usual time, fifteen minutes for each.]

DIRECTIONS. — Choose from the subjoined list any two subjects you can draw from memory.

1. A Chair (corner in front).
2. A Chair (side in front).
3. A Tea-kettle.
4. A Branch of Maple.
5. A Pitcher.
6. The Letter M (Roman character).
7. A Round Table.
8. A Barrel.
9. Street Lamp.
10. A Boat.
11. An Animal.
12. A House.

The pencil-drawing to fill the space beneath. The blackboard-drawing to be two feet high.

WRITE 1. Your name at full length.
2. Your age last birthday.
3. The school where you learn drawing.

SPECIMEN OF SECOND-GRADE

EXAMINATION PAPER, GEOMETRICAL DRAWING.

TIME ALLOWED, ONE HOUR.

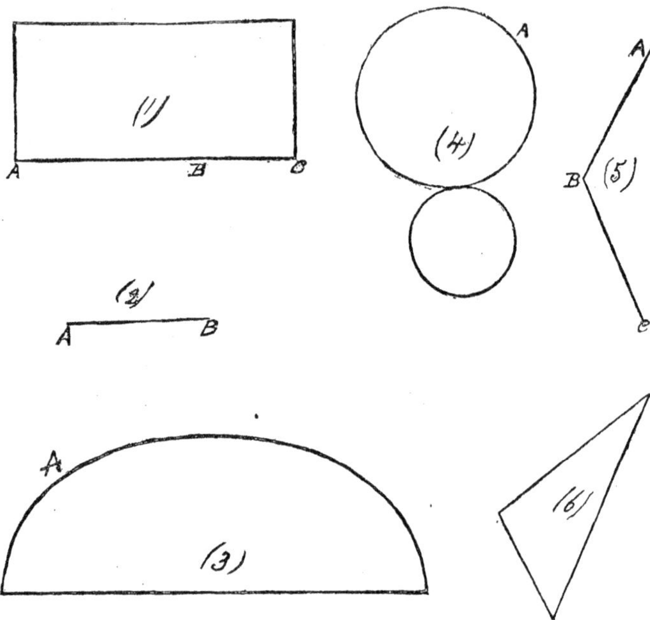

1. On the part A B of the side A C, construct a rectangle similar to the given one.

2. On A B construct a pentagon, then a triangle and a square equal in area to it.

3. Complete the ellipse, of which the transverse diameter and half the curve are given, by means of the foci and intersecting arcs. Then raise a perpendicular at A.

4. Describe a tangential arc to the two given circles which shall touch the largest in point A.

5. Complete the polygon of which A B, B C, are two sides.

6. Construct an equilateral triangle equal in area to the given triangle.

WRITE 1. Your name in full.
2. Your age last birthday.
3. The school where you learn to draw.

SPECIMEN OF SECOND-GRADE EXAMINATION PAPER, *LINEAR PERSPECTIVE*. TIME ALLOWED, ONE HOUR.

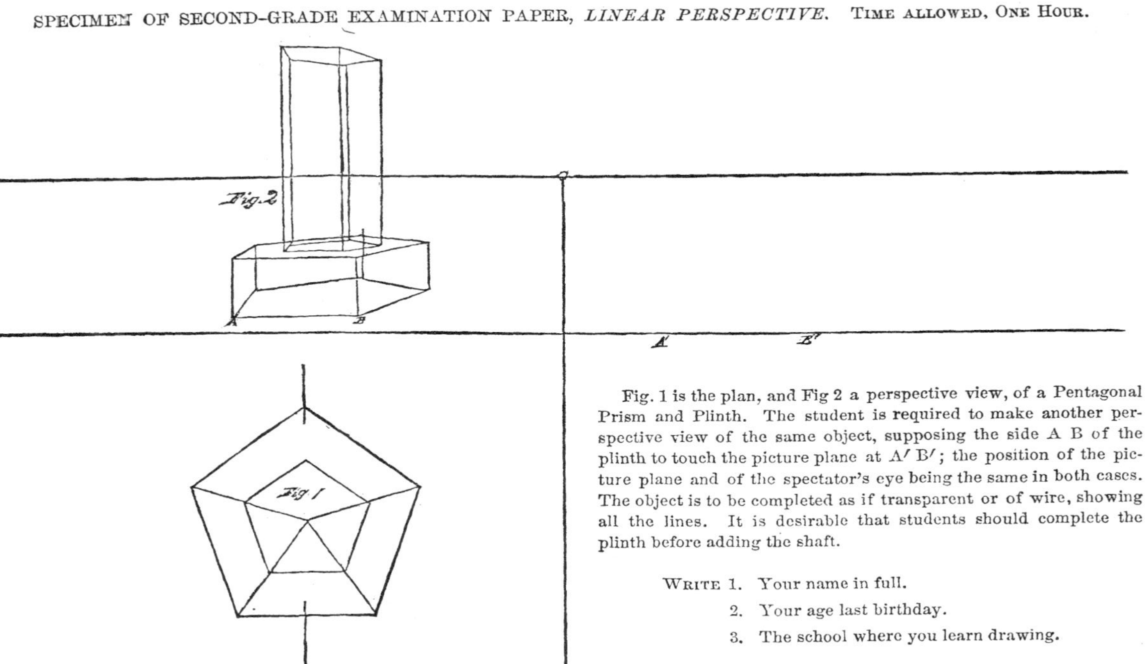

Fig. 1 is the plan, and Fig 2 a perspective view, of a Pentagonal Prism and Plinth. The student is required to make another perspective view of the same object, supposing the side A B of the plinth to touch the picture plane at A′ B′; the position of the picture plane and of the spectator's eye being the same in both cases. The object is to be completed as if transparent or of wire, showing all the lines. It is desirable that students should complete the plinth before adding the shaft.

WRITE 1. Your name in full.

2. Your age last birthday.

3. The school where you learn drawing.

APPENDIX IV.

PROGRAMMES OF SCHOOLS OF ART. 1. AMERICAN; 2. ENGLISH; 3. FRENCH; 4. GERMAN.

I.—AMERICAN SCHOOLS OF DESIGN.

In order that it may be seen what is accomplished already in the way of industrial art education, I give the prospectuses and codes of rules of such American institutions as have come under my observation. Those classes I have seen in this country, or whose premises and collections I have examined, seem to me to suffer from ill-adapted arrangements and a want of good examples,—both so easily removable, that it is a subject of astonishment to me the evils have not been long since remedied. This remark does not apply specially to the following American schools, but is general in its application; and it was with the view of assisting to overcome these difficulties that the principal part of this book has been prepared.

NEW YORK.

NATIONAL ACADEMY OF DESIGN,

CORNER TWENTY-THIRD STREET AND FOURTH AVENUE, NEW YORK.

The schools of the Academy, which have been in operation, *free*, day and evening, male and female, for forty-seven years, embrace, at present, an Antique (or Statuary) School, Life (nude) School, School of Anatomy, and also of Perspective. Schools of Painting and Modelling will be supplied as required. The present Antique Class numbers 175; the Life Class, 55. The lectures upon Anatomy and Perspective, and the general lectures, are attended by all classes of students. An annual exhibition of selected drawings, and rewards of merit, takes place about the close of each school year. The academic system is generally very similar to that of the Royal Academy in London, and of other European institutions of that kind.

NATIONAL ACADEMY OF DESIGN,
NEW YORK, Mar. 1, 1865.

To Artists, Art-Students, and others making inquiry as to the terms of admission into the Academy as Academicians, Associates, Fellows, Honorary Members, or Students.

ACADEMICIANS.

Academicians are chosen only from the body of Associates, or from such *professional* honorary members as reside permanently in the city or vicinity of New York. They are elected only at the annual meetings, on the second Wednesdays of May, and after their names shall have been duly entered by an Academician on the record provided for that purpose, which record is finally closed each year six days before the meeting. They must be exhibiters in the annual exhibition of the year of their nomination. A vote of two-thirds of the members present at an annual meeting is required to elect. To confirm and make legal their election, they must, within one year thereafter, present to the Academy a specimen of their art, to be preserved in the gallery of the institution. The Academicians are the body corporate; and in their election distinguished professional ability and personal character are the only claims entertained.

ASSOCIATES.

Associates of the Academy must be professional artists residing in the city or vicinity of New York. They must be nominated and balloted for at the same time, and in the same manner, as the Academicians, and must also be exhibiters in the exhibition of the year in which they are proposed as Associates. It is also an advantage, though not a necessity, to have been for some years previous to their nomination exhibiters in the galleries of the Academy, since (as in the case of candidates as Academicians) the only claims which they can present for election are those of personal character and of professional merit. Associates elect must (to confirm and make legal their election) present to the Academy, within one year thereafter, their portraits, on canvas twenty-five by thirty inches, painted by themselves or by other artists, at their option.

FELLOWS.

The grade of Fellows was established Jan. 14, 1863, for the double purpose of increasing the financial means of the Academy, and to add to its *moral* force by promoting more general and more intimate association and intercourse between artists and lovers of art; which very desirable objects it promises to advance, to the pleasure and profit of all.

Connoisseurs, amateurs, and all lovers of art, may become Fellows of the Academy for life, and receive their diplomas as such, on the payment of a subscription of one hundred dollars to the Fellowship Fund of the Academy.

The privileges of Fellows will be to receive five season-tickets for each of the annual exhibitions, which they may distribute as they please, in their own names; to be invited to all the receptions of the society, and to have access to the library and reading-rooms; also to nominate two students annually to the schools.

Subscribers of five hundred dollars to the Fellowship Fund are constituted Fellows IN PERPETUITY, with all the privileges of Fellows for Life, and the additional one of transferring or transmitting the same.

HONORARY MEMBERS.

Honorary membership is conferred at the same time and in the same manner as in the election of Associates and of Academicians, upon distinguished artists and lovers of art, at home or abroad.

STUDENTS.

Students should have already mastered the simple elementary difficulties of the art, as the Academy schools are intended for professional students who have already acquired a certain degree of skill in the use of the crayon or pencil, rather than for mere beginners.

On entering the Antique (or Statuary) School, the student must submit to the council such a drawing, in light and shade, of a plaster head, foot, face, or other portion of the human figure, as shall be considered to indicate talent worthy of further cultivation.

Before entering the Life School, an approved drawing of a full-length statue must be submitted to the council, which drawing *may* be best made in the Antique School.

Certificates, which admit the holders also to the annual exhibitions, the lectures of the Academy, and other like privileges, are granted to students on admission. The schools are open from seven to nine o'clock every evening through the autumn and winter months of each year. No fees are required.

Applicants for either of the schools, when nominated by Fellows of the Academy, should send to the council, or bring with them, such nomination, which should be an assurance of their merit, in character, industry, and earnestness.

T. ADDISON RICHARDS, *Cor. Sec. N. A.*

National Academy of Design, Schools, 1870–71.

The Antique School will recommence for the season on Monday, Oct. 3, and will be followed in due course with the re-opening of the Life Class. It is proposed also (as the number and qualification of students may demand, and as the means of the Academy may warrant) to establish classes for the study of painting, both from the nude and the draped figure, in landscape and from still life; classes also in modelling, perspective, and anatomy, lectures on art, and an annual concourse or competition between students, and an exhibition of their works with awards of merit, including the Suydam and Elliott Medals, now in course of preparation.

The schools will be open day and evening free of charge, the students furnishing only their easels and materials.

For admission to the Antique School, the applicant will be required to submit to the council an approved shaded drawing of a hand, foot, or other part of a cast of the human figure. Advancement to other classes will be made according to progress and merit.

By order of the Council,

T. ADDISON RICHARDS, *Cor. Sec. N. A.*

TWENTY-THIRD STREET AND FOURTH AVENUE,
NEW YORK, June 1, 1870.

COOPER UNION FOR THE ADVANCEMENT OF SCIENCE AND ART.

FEMALE ART SCHOOL.

MISS ELLEN E. CHILDE, *Principal.*
MISS FANNIE POWELL, *Teacher of Model and Ornament Drawing from Cast.*
MR. J. F. ENGEL, *Teacher of Figure Drawing from Cast.*
MISS CHARLOTTE B. COGSWELL, *Teacher of Wood Engraving.*
MISS ANNA CURTIS, *Clerk.*

This department of the Cooper Union has been established by the Trustees in accordance with the provisions of the trust deed, for the purpose of affording free instruction in the arts of design to females, who, having the requisite taste and natural capacity, intend to apply the knowledge acquired in the institution to their support, either by teaching or pursuing art as a profession. The following Rules have been adopted for the government of the school; strict compliance with which is necessary in order to secure good order and progress.

RULES AND REGULATIONS.

1. The annual term commences on the 1st of October, and terminates on the thirtieth day of May, in each year Students are not admitted for less than one school year; but if compelled, by illness or any other cause, to leave sooner or be absent for any time, they are required in all cases to communicate with the principal.

2. Pupils are not permitted to pay for any instruction given in the school, but must provide, at their own expense, all the materials required for their instruction, such as paper, pencils, crayons, colors, brushes, and instruments, but not models or easels, which are provided by the trustees

3. The hours of attendance are from 9, A.M., to 1, P M., daily, except Saturdays and Sundays. All pupils are required to enter not later than nine o'clock, and to be in their places *before* a quarter past nine, when the bell rings. An intermission of ten minutes will occur at 11.15, A.M.; and at 1, P M., an interval of half an hour will be allowed for luncheon, at which time *only*, eating will be allowed in school.

Students may remain for practice from 1, P.M., until 4, P M., but *not later*.

4. The art instruction of the school will be conducted by the principal, and the business under the charge of the clerk. The teachers, clerk, and monitors are each required to assist the principal in the good order and discipline of the school; and the students are required to follow their directions

5. No unnecessary conversation will be allowed during the hours of study; and students cannot be permitted to wander from their own classes, or to change the seats assigned to them, without the permission of the principal.

6. Students cannot leave the school during the hours of study without the consent of the principal, nor receive visitors during school-hours, or at all at the school, except on visiting-days; in cases of emergency, the student will be summoned to the office for the purpose of seeing visitors. Letters will be delivered *only* at the close of the hours of study.

7. Visitors will be received only on Fridays from 11, A.M. to 12½, P M; but they must not remain for conversation; and no gentleman unaccompanied by a lady will

be allowed to visit the school without the written permit of one of the trustees or of the advisory council of ladies.

8. Students are in all cases required to follow the direction and course of study prescribed by the principal, and will not be permitted to change seats, classes, or models, without her consent.

9. Every student is required to write her name *legibly, and before she begins*, on the right-hand top corner of the paper used for any drawing executed in the school. The drawings will be the property of the students, with the exception of such as are retained by the principal; every student being required to give one at the expiration of every school term if wanted, but no drawings can be removed from the school until after the annual exhibition at that time. All drawings are to be given in at the office every month, to be kept in a place appointed for their reception. Students who attend the lectures on geometry and perspective are expected at the time to copy the drawings from the blackboard, and afterward to work them out more neatly and carefully and to give them in weekly, at the office (signed with their name), to be examined. All students are required to put their paper and all their other materials away neatly every day.

10. The annual exhibition will take place during the last week in May. when certificates and medals will be awarded to deserving students.

The income of the Prize Fund founded by A. A. Low, Esq., and F. A. Lane, Esq., amounting each to $60 in gold, will be distributed as follows: —

The principal shall select a model, being either the cast of a head or a part of the human figure, from which the students competing for the prize shall make their drawings. To the best drawing $30; to the second-best, $20; and to the third-best $10 will be awarded.

In like manner, the principal shall select a model, either in natural flowers or foliage, or casts of ornament, from which the pupils competing for the prize shall make their drawings. To the best drawing, $30; to the second-best, $20; and to the third-best $10 shall be awarded. The awards shall be made by a committee of three artists, to be selected by the ladies of the advisory council, or the trustees, and the drawings must be ready by the second day of May.

The prize of $30 in gold, founded by the late Robert C. Goodhue, will be awarded to the best drawing on wood made in the school during the term, to be decided by a competent committee in like manner.

Students who have received a money prize will be excluded from the competition for the same grade of prize, in the same department, but will be free to compete for a higher prize.

11. In order that students may become familiar with their duties as teachers, the principal is required to appoint monitresses, who shall supervise the instruction of the beginners. All drawings required for the Cooper Union shall be executed in the school without charge.

12. The school is visited by an advisory council of ladies and artists, whose duty it is to report to the trustees, in a book provided for the purpose, on the condition of the school, and the progress of the pupils. Complaints may be addressed to the ladies of the advisory council, or to the secretary. Pupils, who, from lack of talent or industry, do not give evidence of satisfactory progress, will be dismissed from the school. Any breach of good behavior will be followed by prompt dismissal.

13. A special teacher is provided for engraving on wood, and a special class formed, into which pupils are admitted as soon as they have acquired an adequate knowledge of drawing. Orders are received for engraving, and will be executed by the pupils to whom they may be assigned by the teacher, and the money thus earned is paid to the pupils who may be entitled to it. But it is distinctly announced that the school is not intended to be a workshop, except for instruction; and, when the number of skilled pupils becomes inconveniently large, the more advanced must give place to the learners: but orders will be received at the school, and given out to those who have been pupils, to be executed at home.

14. Pupils must not absent themselves from the school, or come later than nine o'clock in the morning, without the consent of the principal; and three absences, not excused by the principal, will forfeit the place of the pupil so absenting herself. Places will not be retained in the school for students who may desire to defer their attendance, to the exclusion of those who may be prepared to attend at once; but the principal is authorized to grant leave of absence when the circumstances of the case may render it proper.

15. The proper care of the models and other property of the school is confided to the students; and their good sense is appealed to, to preserve the order of the school, and to exercise a reasonable forbearance towards each other and the teachers, whose duties are so difficult and trying.

By order of the trustees,

ABRAM S. HEWITT, *Secretary*.

Commonwealth of Massachusetts.

BOARD OF EDUCATION, STATE HOUSE.

Department of Art Education.

Scheme of Instruction in Drawing suggested for graded Public Schools in Massachusetts, complying with the Act of 1870, concerning Industrial Drawing.

ARRANGED BY WALTER SMITH, STATE DIRECTOR OF ART EDUCATION, MASS.

Schools.	Classes.	Time Given per Week.	Lessons per Week	Length of Lesson.	Drawing on	Taught by
1. Primary Schools.	6, 5, 4.	Two hours.	Four.	30 minutes.	Slates.	Regular Teachers.
2. Primary Schools.	* 3, 2, 1.	Two hours.	Four.	30 minutes.	Paper in blank books	Regular Teachers.
3. Grammar Schools.	* 6, 5, 4.	Two hours.	Three.	40 minutes.	Paper in blank books and text-books.	Regular Teachers.
4. Grammar Schools.	* 3, 2, 1.	Two hours.	Three.	40 minutes.	Paper in blank books and text-books.	Regular Teachers.
5. Latin and High Schools.	* Lower Classes.	Two hours.	Two.	60 minutes.	Paper in blank books and text-books.	Regular Teachers.
6. Latin and High Schools.	* Higher Classes.	Two hours.	Two.	60 minutes.	Paper in blank books and on sheets.	Special Instructors.
7. Normal Schools.	* All the Classes.	Two hours.	Two.	60 minutes.	Paper in blank books	Special Instructors.

SUBJECTS TAUGHT, AND ORDER OF LESSONS FOR EACH WEEK.

The figures 1, 2, 3, 4, signify the first, second, third, and fourth lessons in each week.

Where two alternative subjects are named, one is to be taken one week and another the following week.

Reference to a text-book means, that whatever drawing-book is in use in the schools shall be drawn from as a distinct exercise.

* All the classes marked thus are to draw upon the blackboard when the lesson is suitable to such an exercise; one-third of the class to draw each lesson, so that the whole class will have drawn upon the board every three lessons.

---

1. Freehand outline from cards, charts, and blackboard lessons, the first copies. Memory lessons, drawing previous exercises from memory. Definition of plane geometry, to be learned by heart, and illustrations drawn. Dictation lessons of right line figures and simple curves.

ORDER OF LESSONS.—1. From cards or charts. 2. From blackboard. 3. Memory and dictation, alternately. 4. Geometric definitions.

2. The more advanced copies in cards, charts, and blackboard lessons. Memory and dictation lessons (without illustrations). Object-lessons, illustrated by drawings. Geometric definitions, drawn on a large scale.

ORDER OF LESSONS.—1. From cards or chart. 2. From blackboard. 3. Memory and dictation, alternately. 4. Object-lessons and geometric definitions, alternately.

---

3. Freehand outlines of ornament and objects, from blackboard. Lessons in text-book. Map-drawing. Memory and dictation lessons. Geometrical exercises, plane geometry, up to fifty problems of constructional figures.

ORDER OF LESSONS.—1. Objects from blackboard and drawing from text-book, alternately. 2. Memory-drawing and dictation exercises, alternately. 3. Geometrical and map drawing, alternately.

4. Freehand outline drawing, from solid models. Geometrical drawing, up to the end of the course. Design in geometric forms, from the blackboard. Memory-drawing. Map-drawing. Dictation lessons.

ORDER OF LESSONS.—1. Model-drawing, from object. 2. Geometrical and memory drawing, alternately. 3. Map-drawing and design, alternately.

---

5. Model and object drawing, with exercises in perspective, drawn by the freehand. Object-lessons, illustrating historical art and architecture. Shading from models and copies. Harmony and mixture of colors. Design from natural foliage.

ORDER OF LESSONS.—1. Model-shading and object-lessons, alternately. 2. Lessons in color and exercises in design, alternately.

6. Perspective by instruments. Shading in chalk and color, from models and natural objects and foliage. Design in color and shadow. Projection. Lectures on painting, sculpture, and architecture.

ORDER OF LESSONS.—1. Perspective and projection, alternately. 2. Painting or shading or design, alternately.

---

7. Object-drawing and design. Ornamental design. Historical lessons. Advanced dictation and memory lessons. Lessons in teaching drawing. Perspective, advanced. Designing blackboard examples.

ORDER OF LESSONS.—1. Object-drawing and design, alternately. 2. Perspective and dictation or memory lessons, alternately. 3. Lessons in teaching drawing, occasionally.

BOSTON.

FREE EVENING CLASSES IN BOSTON FOR THE STUDY OF INDUSTRIAL DRAWING,

Held in the Normal Art School, Appleton Street, and in the Institute of Technology, Boylston Street.

Days and hours of study, Monday, Tuesday, Thursday, and Friday, 7, P.M., to 9, P.M.

Students allowed to attend either on Monday and Thursday, or Tuesday and Friday evenings, but not oftener.

STAGES AND SUBJECTS OF STUDY.

ELEMENTARY COURSE, FROM COPIES; ADVANCED COURSE, FROM THE REAL OBJECT OR DESIGN.

STAGE 1. *Instrumental drawing.*
- *a.* Linear geometry.
- *b.* Mechanical and machine drawing.
- *c.* Linear perspective.
- *d.* Details of architectural drawing and building construction.
- *e.* Ship-drafting.

[Stage 1, consisting of instrumental drawing, is at present carried on at the Institute of Technology.]

ELEMENTARY COURSE.

STAGE 2. *Free-hand outline drawing of rigid forms, from flat examples, or copies.*
- *a.* Objects.
- *b.* Ornament.
- *c.* Flowers, foliage, and objects of natural history.
- *d.* The human and animal figure.

Mediums used: 1, pencil; 2, chalk; 4, ink.

STAGE 3. *Free-hand outline drawing, from the "round" or solid forms.*
- *a.* Geometric solids, vases, etc.
- *b.* Ornament from the cast.
- *c.* Flowers and foliage from nature.
- *d.* Details of the human figure, and animal forms from the cast.

Mediums used: 1, pencil; 2, chalk; 4, ink or sepia.

ADVANCED COURSE.

STAGE 4. *Shading, from flat examples or copies.*
- *a.* Models and objects.
- *b.* Ornament.
- *c.* Flowers and foliage.
- *d.* Details of human and animal figures.
- *e.* Landscape details.

Mediums used: 1, pencil; 2, chalk; 3, charcoal; 4, ink or sepia.

STAGE 5. *Shading from the "round" or solid forms.*
- *a.* Geometrical solids and vases.
- *b.* Ornament from the cast.
- *c.* Flowers and foliage from nature.
- *d.* Details of human and animal figures from the cast.

Mediums used: 1, pencil; 2, chalk; 3, charcoal; 4, ink or sepia.

ELEMENTARY AND ADVANCED COURSES.

STAGE 6. *Original design.*
- *a.* Elementary design of geometric forms to fill given spaces.
- *b.* Ornamental arrangements of natural forms, conventionalized in one color, or monochrome, to cover given spaces.
- *c.* Ditto in color, harmonized
- *d.* Applied design for surface decorations.
- *e.* Applied design for the "round," in wood, stone, metal, or clay.

Mediums used: 1, pencil; 2, chalk; 3, charcoal; 4, monochrome; 5, color.

This provisional course is arranged, both as to stages and sections, in progressive order. Students who are not beginners should show the teachers some work already done by them, that they may be placed in their right position in the course. Beginners are to commence at Stage II.; and they will be promoted by the masters according to progress made.

No drawing will be considered finished until stamped by the master of the class in which it is done; and a new drawing must not be commenced until the old one is so stamped. All finished drawings are to be left in the schools; and the drawing committee reserve the right of retaining selected works, — others will be returned to their authors after each annual exhibition.

Voluntary examinations will be held at the end of each term, in April, for those who wish to obtain certificates of proficiency.

WM. T. BRIGHAM, *Chairman.*
WALTER SMITH, *Director of the Classes.*

LOWELL INSTITUTE, BOSTON.

FREE DRAWING-SCHOOL.

FOR YOUNG MEN: two evenings each week, from October to April.

Applications must be made in the handwriting of the applicant; stating name in full, age, residence, occupation, and be accompanied with certificates from parents or employers, and such specimens of drawing as the applicant may wish to offer.

Those applicants will be received who can furnish the best evidence of good moral character, of general intelligence and ability, of industry and skill, together with a taste for design and drawing.

Applicants will assemble at the Institute, Room No. 3, on Thursday evening, Sept. 28, at seven o'clock, for examination and admission.

FOR YOUNG WOMEN: two afternoons each week, from October to April.

Applications to be made as above.

Applicants will assemble at the Institute, Room No. 3, on Thursday, Sept. 28, at two o'clock, P.M.

Former pupils who wish to rejoin the school will simply make written application to that effect, and assemble as above, with other applicants.

Applications must be directed, post-paid, to the Curator of the Institute, Boston, on or before Sept. 23, 1871.

B. E. COTTING, *Curator.*

BOSTON, Sept. 4, 1871.

YALE.

YALE SCHOOL OF THE FINE ARTS, A DEPARTMENT OF YALE COLLEGE.

FACULTY.

NOAH PORTER, D.D., LL.D., *President.*
JOHN F. WEIR, N.A. M.A., *Professor of Painting.*
JOHN H. NIEMEYER, *Professor of Drawing.*
D. CADY EATON, M.A., *Professor of the History of Art.*

The objects of this School are: —

1. The education of practical artists.
2. The furnishing of men desiring a liberal education, an acquaintance with the practice, principles, and history of art, by means of practical work and lectures.

This institution is in a flourishing working condition. It has upwards of ninety students that receive instruction. These students are mostly members of the Sheffield Scientific School, who are qualifying themselves for strictly scientific pursuits. Free-hand drawing has been made an important part of their regular *curriculum.*

The course of study is based upon progressive methods, with the human form, as is the practice in the best schools of art in Europe.

Lectures are given, in regular courses, on the history of art, its practice and aesthetics.

The "Art Building" is a fine massive structure, containing two large picture-galleries, in one of which is an historical collection of the Italian school of painting, dating from the earliest masters to the sixteenth century. These pictures are one hundred and twenty in number, and were collected during a period of twenty years' residence in Europe, by Mr. James Jackson Jarves. The advantage of such a col lection to the art student cannot be over-estimated.

Besides these galleries, this building contains large, well-lighted studios for professors, and ample class-rooms for students.

This School was founded by the free gift of $250,000 by the late Mr. Augustus Russell Street, in 1864. Two hundred thousand dollars was the cost of erecting the Art Building.

Pupils are received for periods varying from one to four years, determined by their proficiency and talent.

PHILADELPHIA.

THE PHILADELPHIA SCHOOL OF DESIGN FOR WOMEN.

RULES FOR GOVERNMENT.

1. The teachers are required to call their classes to order punctually at ten o'clock, A.M., at which hour the school will open. Every pupil shall be at her seat, ready to commence her duties, and to remain diligently occupied till the close of the lesson.
2. No pupil will be permitted to enter after ten o'clock, except by consent of the principal.
3. No pupil can be permitted to leave her place, or enter into any conversation unconnected with her occupation, during school-hours.
4. Punctual and regular attendance is expected from all the pupils. When absence is unavoidable, satisfactory explanations will be required when they return to their studies.
5. Hours of study from *ten* to *three* o'clock, with an intermission of half an hour at half-past twelve.
6. Pupils are requested not to have letters or notes directed to them at the school: should any be received, they will be forwarded by mail to the residence of the students.
7. The pupils are not permitted to receive visitors at the schoolhouse.
8. The pupils will be charged for casts, other examples, or books belonging to the school, which they may have injured or lost; and no pupil can take out of the school any pattern or model belonging to it.
9. Each pupil will furnish her own stationery and a portfolio for her work, which must be deposited in its proper place at the close of her lesson.
10. The drawings of the students must be placed on the walls, and remain there for exhibition, and for the inspection of the directors at their regular stated meetings.
11. A daily record of the presence or absence of each member of the school, and also of any circumstances worthy of note, must be laid before the directors at their monthly meetings.
12. Under no circumstances will students be allowed to present, or the teachers to receive, presents from the students.
13. Every student is required to attend the lectures.

*** It is earnestly hoped by the directors, that all concerned will aid them in maintaining these regulations, which are enacted solely for the benefit of the pupil, and the best interests of the school.

The parents and guardians of students are respectfully urged to visit the institution; also those interested in its objects.

FEES FOR THE SCHOOL YEAR.

Elementary Course. $40.00; Figure and Landscape in Oil, each, $20.00.

Applicants for admission can receive all information at the school, where, also, blank forms of application will be furnished.

The school year will begin Sept. 12, 1870, and close on the second Friday of June, 1871. There will be a vacation of *two* weeks at Christmas.

Students will be received at any time. *The fees are payable in advance.*

Students, before leaving the institution, are expected to communicate, by letter, with the principal.

COURSE OF INSTRUCTION.

"The courses of instruction pursued in the school have for their object the systematic training of young women in the practice of art, and in the knowledge of its scientific principles, with the view of qualifying them to impart to others a careful art education, and to develop its application to the common uses of life, and its relation to the requirements of trade and manufactures."

The stages in the Elementary Course, with the lectures, have been arranged solely in view of developing a knowledge of form, the laws of light and shade, color and perspective, none of which can safely be dispensed with, whether in the practice of the "Fine" or "Applied Arts;" and the desire of the directors is, that all concerned may co-operate in carrying out the "Order of Studies" herein prescribed. The course lasts from two and a half to four and a half years, depending upon the industry of the student.

ORDER OF STUDIES.

Preliminary Stages.

STAGE 1. *a.* Drawing in outline, and shading, from casts of geometrical figures and vases, in different positions.
b. Pencil drawing from flat examples.
c. Practice in the handling of instruments.
d. Ornamental geometry.
e. Primary perspective.

STAGE 2. *a.* Drawing and shading from groups composed of casts of geometrical solids and vases.
b. Pencil drawing from flat examples of ornamental details.
c. Ornamental geometry.
d. Elementary perspective.
e. Coloring diagrams with the *three* primary colors, by which the student sees how the secondary, tertiary, and complementary colors are produced, and the modification which colors undergo by being brought in contact with each other.

NOTE. — All these works must be executed with an intelligent clearness and precision, and the last drawing in the group section must be commenced and finished without instruction; that is, it will be a "test group," determining whether the student will be passed, or retained for further practice in the preliminary stages.

Advanced Stages.

STAGE 1. *a.* Drawing and shading from casts of single leaves, from nature.
b. Drawing and shading, from casts of details of architectural ornament, consisting of a leaf-moulding from the Temple of Mars, the centre rosette from Trajan's Scroll, and a moulding boss from St. Stephen's, Westminster.
c. At this point the student must exhibit well-executed diagrams, illustrating the primary rules of perspective.
d. Landscape, from the flat, in pencil.
e. Ornamental geometry.
f. Drawing and shading, from casts from nature of the Callo Ethiopica, water lily branch of apples, branch of gourd and leaf, branch of grapes, and a branch of blackberries.
g. Drawing and shading, from details of architectural ornament, consisting of casts from the upper cornice of Trajan's Pillar; a Gothic capital from stone church, Kent; a Saracenic panel from the Alhambra; a Byzantine panel from Bonn; and Gothic spandrel, from stone church, Kent.
h. The students at this point must be able to answer questions satisfactorily, relating to the human skeleton.

STAGE 2. *a.* Drawing the upper and lower extremities and head of the human skeleton, in different positions; the names of the details to be written thereon.
b. Drawing and shading, from casts of antique features, consisting of the nose and eye of Hadrian, Bacchante, Laocoön, and a pair of ears, the nose and mouth of Hadrian, Esculapius, Antinous, Venus d'Arles, Juno, Caracalla, and Adonis.
c. Drawing from copies of the antique, from the flat, in pencil.
d. Anatomical drawing from casts of the muscular system, on which must be written the names of the principal bones and superficial muscles, — the origin and insertion of the latter to be carefully expressed.
e. Drawing and shading, from casts from the antique and from life, of hands, feet, arms, and faces.
f. Landscape painting, from the flat, in monochrome (water colors).
g. Drawing and shading, from casts of antique busts, viz., Dione, Venus of Milo, the Young Hercules, Mercury, Juno, Hercules, Antinous, German Prisoner, Ajax, and the Apollo Belvedere.

NOTE.—Students, while passing through the two preceding stages, will, every Monday, be engaged in drawing and painting in water-colors, plant-forms, mostly from nature; and students in these stages, desirous of entering the wood-engraving or designing, or the class of landscape painting in oil, from the flat for introductory study, can do so; but the studies in the regular stages cannot be discontinued.

At the end of the "advanced stages" students may enter any of the technical branches taught in the institution; such are designated as follows:—

PROFESSIONAL CLASSES.

DESIGNING.
Designing patterns for calico and oilcloth printers, &c.
WOOD ENGRAVING.
LITHOGRAPHY.
DRAWING AND PAINTING.
Figure drawing and painting from the antique and from life.
Landscape painting in oil and water colors.
ART TEACHING.

The work to be done in each of the technical classes is designated on another printed sheet.

LECTURES.

In the term commencing Sept. 12, 1870, the following course of lectures was delivered before the students of the school, by Prof. T W. Braidwood.

LECTURE 1, *Oct.* 6.—The present social status of woman, in connection with the objects of schools of design for women.

LECTURE 2, *Nov.* 3.—Science in the decoration of our homes.

LECTURE 3, *Dec.* 1.—The characteristics of historic ornament, or how we can know architectural styles, and distinguish all styles of decoration.

LECTURE 4, *Jan.* 12.—Color practically considered.

Lectures on *Perspective*, on Fridays, by Prof. E. Croasdale.
Lectures on *Artistic Anatomy*, on Wednesdays, by Prof. A. R. Thomas.
Lectures on the *General Principles of Art*, by Prof. A. G. Heaton.

These lectures are free to the public. Tickets of admission may be had by applying at the school.

II.—ENGLISH.

THE ENGLISH NATIONAL ART TRAINING-SCHOOL IN LONDON.

The National Art Training School at South Kensington is established for the purpose of training art masters and mistresses for the United Kingdom, and for the instruction of students in drawing, designing, and modelling, to be applied to the requirements of trade and manufactures.

The Course of Instruction is as follows (it should be understood that it is not progressive in the order in which the stages are named):—

COURSE OF INSTRUCTION.

STAGE 1. *Linear drawing by aid of instruments.*
- *a.* Linear geometry.
- *b.* Mechanical and machine drawing, and details of architecture from copies.
- *c.* Linear perspective.

STAGE 2. *Free-hand outline drawing of rigid forms from examples or copies.*
- *a.* Objects.
- *b.* Ornament.

STAGE 3. *Free-hand outline drawing from the "round."*
- *a.* Models and objects.
- *b.* Ornament.

STAGE 4. *Shading from flat examples or copies.*
- *a.* Models and objects.
- *b.* Ornament.

STAGE 5. *Shading from the round or solid forms.*
- *a.* Models and objects.
- *b.* Ornament.
- *c.* Time sketching, and sketching from memory.

STAGE 6. *Drawing from the human figure, and animal forms from copies.*
- *a.* In outline.
- *b.* Shaded.

STAGE 7. *Drawing flowers, foliage, and objects of natural history, from flat examples or copies.*
- *a.* In outline.
- *b.* Shaded.

STAGE 8. *Drawing the human figure or animal forms from the "round" or nature.*
- *a.* In outline from casts.
- *b* 1. Shaded (details).
- *b* 2. Shaded (whole figures).
- *c.* Studies of the human figure, from nude model.
- *d.* Studies of the human figure draped.
- *e.* Time sketching and sketching from memory.

STAGE 9. *Anatomical studies.*
- *a.* Of the human figure.
- *b.* Of animal forms.
- *c.* Of either modelled.

STAGE 10. *Drawing flowers, foliage, landscape details, and objects of natural history, from nature.*
- *a.* In outline.
- *b.* Shaded.

STAGE 11. *Painting ornament from the "flat" or copies.*
- *a.* In monochrome } either in water colors, tempera, or oil.
- *b.* In colors. }

STAGE 12. *Painting ornament from the cast, &c.*
- *a* In monochrome, either in water-color, oil, or tempera.

STAGE 13. *Painting (general), from flat examples or copies, flowers, still life, &c.*
- *a.* Flowers or natural objects, in water-color, in oil, or in tempera.
- *b.* Landscapes.

STAGE 14. *Painting (general), direct from nature.*
- *a.* Flowers, or still life, in water-color, oil, or tempera, without backgrounds.
- *b.* Landscapes.

STAGE 15. *Painting groups as composition of colors.*
- *a.* In water-color, oil, or tempera.

STAGE 16. *Painting the human figure or animals in monochrome from casts.*
- *a.* In oil, water-color, or tempera.

STAGE 17. *Painting the human figure or animals in color.*
- *a.* From the flat or copies.
- *b.* From nature, nude or draped.
- *c.* Time sketches and compositions.

STAGE 18. *Modelling ornament.*
- *a.* Elementary, from casts.
- *b.* Advanced, from casts.
- *c.* From drawings.
- *d.* Time sketches from examples, and from memory.

STAGE 19. *Modelling the human figure or animals.*
- *a.* Elementary, from casts of hands, feet, masks, &c.
- *b.* Advanced, from casts or solid examples.
- *c.* From drawings.
- *d.* From nature, nude or draped.

STAGE 20. *Modelling fruits, flowers, foliage, and objects of natural history, from nature.*

STAGE 21. *Time sketches in clay of the human figure, or animals, from nature.*

STAGE 22. *Elementary design.*
- *a.* Studies treating natural objects ornamentally.
- *b.* Ornamental arrangements to fill given spaces in monochrome.
- *c.* Ornamental arrangements to fill given spaces in color.
- *d.* Studies of historic styles of ornament, drawn or modelled.

STAGE 23. *Applied designs, technical, or miscellaneous studies.*
- *a.* Machine and mechanical drawing, plan drawing, mapping, and surveys done from actual measurement.
- *b.* Architectural design.
- *c.* Surface design.
- *d.* Plastic design.

ART CERTIFICATES OF THIRD GRADE.

Masters and Mistresses of Schools of Art must hold one or more of the Certificates of Third Grade.

The twenty-three stages of instruction are divided into six groups.

Certificates of competency to teach the subjects included in each group are given to candidates who pass the necessary examinations.

These are called certificates of the third grade.

The following are the groups which form the subjects of certificates:—

GROUP 1. Elementary drawing and coloring.

STAGES 1, 2, 3, 4, 5, 6, 7, 10, AND 13.

GROUP 2. Painting, with examination in styles of art, and in the elementary principles of ornament.

STAGES 11, 12, 14, 15, AND 22.

GROUP 3. The figure drawn and painted, with examination in the historic styles of ornament.

STAGES 8, 9, 16, AND 17.

GROUP 4. Modelling ornament, with examination in styles of art, and in the elementary principles of ornament.

STAGES 18, 20, AND 22.

GROUP 5. Modelling the figure, with examination in the historic styles of ornament.

STAGES 8, 9, 19, AND 21.

GROUP 6. Technical instruction.

EXAMINATIONS.

The examinations of the third grade will take place annually at the offices of the department, South Kensington, in the month of February.

Candidates who are desirous of passing such examinations must forward their names, together with all the requisite works, to the secretary of the department, on the first Saturday in February. They must state the group or groups for which they seek to obtain certificates. These works if accepted, will be retained by the department. Works of unsuccessful candidates, and candidates not proposing to earn payments from the State, will be returned. They will be informed whether their drawings have been accepted, and whether permission can be granted to them to present themselves for examination.

These examinations will take place before the inspector-general for art, assisted by other examiners who may be associated with him. They will be conducted partly by written exercises, and partly by studies made in a given time. Each candidate may be required to teach a class in the presence of the examiner.

FIRST GROUP.

Candidates for certificates for the first group:—

1. If they have attended the training-school of the department, at South Kensington, they must have obtained a recommendation for admission to examination from the head-master. Candidates from the provincial or other schools will be required to execute an extra work in the presence of the examiner.

2. They must be prepared to instruct a class in the presence of the examiners either in free-hand drawing, geometrical drawing, perspective, or model drawing.

3. To sketch, in a given time, a group of models, placed by the examiners for that purpose.

4. To solve, in writing, questions on geometry, perspective, orthographic projection,* and the rudiments of constructive architecture.*

For the first group, the following works are necessary, ten in number:—

STAGE 1*a*. A sheet of geometrical problems.
" 1*b*. A sheet of mechanical drawings.*
" 1*c*. A sheet of perspective diagrams.
" 1*d*. A sheet of architectural details.*
" 3. An outline from the Madeleine pilaster.
" 5*a*. A sheet of drawings from models, shaded in chalk or pencils.
" 5*b*. A sheet of ornament shaded from the cast in chalk.
" 6. An outline of the figure from the flat.
" 10. A sheet of foliage drawn from nature.
" 13. A sheet of flowers painted from the flat.

---

* Female candidates are not examined in mechanical or architectural drawing.

SECOND GROUP.

For the second group each candidate: —

1. Must already have obtained a certificate for the first group.
2. Will be required to sketch in color, in a given time, a group placed by the examiners for that purpose, using any medium or vehicle which the examiners may propose.
3. Will be required to answer, in writing, a paper of technical questions on art, and on the general principles and execution of the several historic schools, and a paper of questions on the nomenclature of structural botany.*

For the second group, the following works are required, six in number: —

STAGE 13 or 14. A landscape in oil from nature, or from some approved example.
" 12. A painting of ornament in monochrome from the cast, in oil or tempera.
" 14. A study of flowers painted from nature, in water-colors.
" 15. A study of a group as a composition of color, in oil.
" 22*c*. A sheet of at least two studies of ornamental arrangements in color.
" 22*a*. A sheet of studies of some plant or plants botanically analyzed with a view to ornamental details.
" 22*d*. A set of studies executed during the period of training, from some one class of objects in the South Kensington Museum, sufficiently extensive to represent the history of the class selected.

THIRD GROUP.

For the third group each candidate —

1. Must already have obtained certificates for the first and second groups.
2. Will be required to answer, in writing, a paper of questions on the anatomy of the human figure.
3. To answer, in writing, a paper on the history of ornament of the various periods and styles; and a paper of questions on the elementary principles of ornament, and on the history and peculiarities of the ornamentation of the class chosen for illustration in the drawings sent up in Stage 22*d*.
4. To draw in a given time the bones or muscles within the outline of an antique figure, from memory.
5. The living model will be posed for a time-study by each candidate.

From candidates who are, or have been, students of the Royal Academy, and have been there admitted to study from the living model, this last exercise will not be required.

For the third group, the following works are necessary, seven in number: —

STAGE 8*b*. An antique figure, shaded from the cast, in chalk.
" 8*c*. A study in chalk from the living model.
" 9. The bones and muscles placed within outlines of an antique figure.
" 16. A painting of the human figure, from a picture in oil.
" 17*a*. A painting of the nude or draped figure from the life, in oil.
" 22*d*.† Varied studies of historic styles of ornament, sufficiently extensive to represent the history of the classes selected, sketched from works in the Museum, the authority in each case being appended. If they are from colored ornament, the sketches are to be colored also.

FOURTH GROUP.

For the fourth group, each candidate —

1. Must already have obtained a certificate for the first group.
2. Will be required to answer, in writing, a paper of questions on the elementary principles of ornament, and on the history and peculiarities of the ornamentation of the class chosen for illustration in the drawings set up in Stage 22*d*.
3. To sketch from memory elementary details of ornament, and, in a given time, to model a piece of ornament, in low relief, from a print or drawing.

For the fourth group, the following works are required, five in number: —

STAGE 18*a*. A modelled study of ornament from the cast.
" 18*b*. A modelled study of ornament from a drawing.
" 20. A modelled study of flowers or foliage from nature.
" 22. A modelled study of any one of the sections of this stage.

---

* Based on Lindley's "School Botany."

† It is intended by these studies to test the knowledge of ornament possessed by the candidate: he should therefore send a sheet or sheets of the most characteristic details of the best periods of the various styles, and should give the source from whence the examples are derived. Candidates from provincial schools must use for the same purpose the works circulated by the department, such as casts, electrotypes, photographs, books, prints, &c.

STAGE 22*a*. A sheet of studies of some plant or plants, botanically analyzed with a view to display their ornamental details, drawn or modelled.
" 22*d*. A set of studies executed during the period of training, from some one class of objects in the South Kensington Museum, sufficiently extensive to represent the history of the class selected.

FIFTH GROUP.

For the fifth group each candidate —
1. Must already have obtained a certificate for the first group.
2. Will be required to answer, in writing, a paper of questions on the anatomy of the human frame.
3. To answer, in writing, a paper on the history of ornament of the various periods and styles.
4. To make, in a given time, a sketch in low relief, from a print or drawing, of an antique figure; and to give the anatomical details from memory.
5. The living model will be posed for a time-study by each candidate.

From candidates who are, or have been, students of the Royal Academy, and there admitted to study from the living model, this last exercise will not be required.

For the fifth group, the following works are required, six in number: —

STAGE 8. An antique figure, shaded from the cast.
" 9. An anatomical rendering of an antique figure, modelled.
" 9*a*. A drawing of the skeleton placed within the outline of an antique figure.
" 19. A model of an antique figure in the round, rendered in relief.
" 20. A model of the human figure from nature, nude or draped.
" 20*d*.* Varied studies of the relief ornament, of historic styles, sketched from the casts, carvings, metal works, &c., in the Museum of the department, with written authorities for each, and sufficiently extensive to represent the history of the various classes selected.

SIXTH GROUP.

1. Certificates in the sixth group are granted, on proof of competency to teach (*a*) domestic architectural drawing, and (*b*) the special application of the ornament to plastic and surface decoration for various fabrics, manufactures, and architectural purposes.
2. The candidates for a certificate for architectural drawing must have already passed in Group 1; must send in a tinted drawing, from measurement of some architectural subject, and a design with plans and sections, for permission to compete: he will have to answer a paper on the details of architectural construction, and on the characteristics of the architectural ornament of various historic styles and periods,* and to make a design from specifications of some architectural subject in the presence of the examiner.
3. Candidates for a special certificate on ornament, who have been educated in the training-school, must have previously taken certificates for Groups 1, 2, and 3, or 1, 4 and 5. They will be required to send in, for permission to compete, two original works, painted or modelled, in order to show their technical skill as well as their power of designing; also a monograph, drawn up by themselves, of at least two historic styles, illustrated by sketches from works or drawings in the Museum. They will be examined by papers on the elements, history, and application of ornament, and will be required to design some work, in the presence of the examiners.
4. The character of the examinations in this group, for special certificates of technical knowledge will be determined by the nature of the applications for examination; and the conditions will be declared according to the circumstances of the case.

TRAINING-CLASS.

1. Students who have paid fees for two consecutive sessions are entitled, on passing the whole of the second-grade examinations, to an admission to their class for one year at a remission of half the usual fee. They are entitled to a continuance of the same privilege for a second year only, if they have obtained a "pass" for merit of work, or a prize or medal in the annual national competition.

Students who have paid fees as above are entitled, on passing satisfactory exam-

---

* It is intended by these studies to test the knowledge of ornament possessed by the candidate: he should therefore send the most characteristic details of the best periods of the various styles, and should give the source from whence the examples are derived. Candidates from provincial schools must use for the same purpose the works circulated by the department, such as casts, electrotypes, photographs, books, prints, &c.

† The text-books are Fergusson's "History of Architecture," and Parker's "Glossary of Terms used in Architecture."

inations in any three, or if females in two, of the subjects of the first certificate, to free admission, which will last for one year, and is renewable if the first certificate be fully taken within that time. After obtaining the first certificate, students will be continued to be admitted free, provided a "pass" for merit of work, or a prize or medal in the annual national competition be taken annually; or, in lieu of these, some more advanced studies of drawing from the antique, or painting. Students who have obtained the first certificate are also eligible to compete for weekly allowances, according to their progress in the school and the certificate obtained, of five shillings, ten shillings, or fifteen shillings, in return for which they have to perform certain duties as teachers, and must engage to accept the situations to which they are recommended.

MAINTENANCE ALLOWANCES.

1. A limited number only of students may compete with students of local schools of art, for maintenance allowances of twenty shillings, or twenty-five shillings weekly. No student will be eligible to receive such higher payments who has not taken one art certificate, or a science certificate in mechanical drawing, or building construction. Such allowances will be granted for one session only. They may be renewed at the discretion of the department, according to the progress and conduct of the student, and the demand for certificated teachers. No student in training will be allowed to remain as such after he has obtained five certificates. Besides their studies in the training-school, students in training will be required to give instruction in parochial and district schools as a part of their training.

Application for admission to the training-classes must be made the first Saturday in February, or the first Saturday in September.

2. With a view to assist female students in obtaining the necessary qualifications to become art teachers,* admission to the training-school for females is regulated by the rules stated above: they may then receive an allowance of from five shillings to fifteen shillings a week, according to vacancies on the list, for a period not exceeding two years, to enable them to obtain the certificate of the third grade. If their progress and promise justify it, they may (having obtained the second certificate within the two years) continue to receive an allowance for another year, while working for the third certificate.

III. — FRENCH.

ÉCOLE MUNICIPALE DE DESSIN ET DE SCULPTURE.

Dirigée par M. Lequien fils, Sculpteur, Rue de Chabrol, 18.

Cette École, fondée en 1835 et dirigée depuis 1854 par M. Lequien fils, est ouverte tous les soirs, pendant toute l'année, de 8 à 10 heures, et est frequentée par 180 élèves.

L'enseignement de l'École comprend: —

1. L'étude du dessin de la figure. D'après l'estampe, d'après la bosse, d'après le modèle vivant.
2. L'étude du dessin de l'ornement.
3. L'étude du dessin de fleurs. D'après l'estampe et d'après nature.
4. L'étude du modelage. Figure et ornement.
5. L'étude du dessin geometrique: —
   - 1°. Construction graphique de divers problemes de la géometrie plane. Applications; dallage, carrelage, bordure, etc.
   - 2°. Étude des proportions. Applications; divers assemblages des bois, pans de bois, combles, planchers, escaliers, plans de batiments epurés de coupes de pierre, decoupage de métaux en feuilles.
   - 3°. Élement d'architecture; lavis.

---

* Should opportunities offer for a female student in training to employ a portion of her time in teaching, she may accept engagements, with the concurrence of the head-master, and receive a reduced allowance, proportionate to the time remaining for studies connected with her certificate; it being understood that the duration of the allowances will in no case exceed three years. It must be distinctly understood, that, at the termination of the allowance, the department in no degree undertakes to provide or obtain employment as teachers for the male or female students so trained.

ÉCOLE MUNICIPALE DES BEAUX-ARTS ET DES SCIENCES INDUSTRIELLES DE TOULOUSE.

Dirigée par M. A. de Perpessac.

L'École Municipale des Beaux-Arts et des Sciences industrielles de Toulouse, dont l'origine remonte au-delà de 1720, est essentiellement gratuite.

Elle compte une vingtaine de professeurs et de cinq cents élèves à six cents (cette année 693).

Les élèves, presque tous de jeunes artisans, sont toujours externes, et même ils passent chaque jour alternativement de leurs ateliers dans l'école et de l'école dans leurs ateliers.

On y enseigne: dessin, peinture, architecture, dessin graphique, particulièrement des machines, perspective, chimie industrielle, mathématiques, arithmétique, algèbre, géometrie élementaire et descriptive, stéréotomie, mécanique, etc.

La dépense annuelle de la ville pour cette école est de 2,700 à 2,800 fr.; dont un prix de 4,500 fr. destiné à envoyer étudier à Paris pendant trois ans, un élève de peinture, sculpture, ou architecture.

OUVRAGES EXPOSÉS, 1863.

(1o.) 5 Ardoises. — Spécimen des premiers travaux des élèves, tracés à main lève, sans instruments.
3 Feuilles. — Tracés exécutés sans instruments, suite des précédents.
7 Dessins au trait, d'après des modèles en relief.
2 Têtes au crayon (copies).
7 Dessins ombrés, d'après des modèles en relief.
3 Têtes d'après la ronde bosse.
1 Portefeuille. — Dessins pour aider à l'intelligence de la méthode, d'après les reliefs.
2 Tableaux. — Compositions d'après un programme donné (Mort d'Eurayle). Deux prix *ex æque*, de 4,500 francs chacun.

(2o.) 2 Deus groupes composés d'une grande tête et de quelques fragments. — D'après la ronde bosse.
2 Académies. — D'après l'antique (ronde bosse).
3 Académies. — D'après le modèle vivant.
5 Épures de géometrie descriptive. — Coupé de pierres, etc. D'après les leçons orales du cours.
1 Album, specimen de ceux que font les élèves de sculpture.
11 Dessins divers, à la plume (copies).
8 Id. d'après nature.

(3o.) 1 Dessin d'après un croquis (placé à côté).
6 Dessins. — Projections diverses et coupés de corps géometriques d'après des croquis lèves, mesures et côtés par les élèves.
3 Dessins Lèves de batîments, d'après des croquis lèves, mesures et côtés par les élèves.
7 Dessins Lèves de machines, d'après des croquis lèves, mesures et côtés par les élèves sur les machines mêmes.
1 Épure de perspective (cube).
1 Id. Intérieur d'une chapelle, d'après un croquis lèves et mesure sur les lieux.
1 Id. Étude d'ombres.
1 Dessin. — Étude de dessin typographique.
2 Lavis d'architecture (copies).
1 Amplifie.
2 Dessins. — Projet d'après un programme donné.
4 Dessins. — Composition d'après un programme donné. Prix de 4,500 fr.

SCULPTURE.

1 Feuille d'achante, d'après nature.
1 Tête de Vitellius, d'après le buste.
1 Bas-relief, d'après l'antique.
1 Académie, d'après le modèle vivant.
1 Bas-relief. — Composition d'après un programme donné (Modon aux pieds de Télémaque), grand prix de 4,500 francs.

ÉCOLE SPÉCIALE DE DESSIN APPLIQUÉ AUX ARTS INDUSTRIELS POUR LES JEUNES PERSONNES.

Dirigée par Mademoiselle Henriette Lecluse, sous le patronage de M. le maire du XVIIe arrondissement. Impasse Saint Louis, 3 (*Batignolles, Paris*).

La figure, les fleurs, et l'ornement forment les bases principales des études qui sont suivies dans cette école. Les jeunes filles qui veulent devenir peintres, graveurs, lithographes, ornementistes, eventaillistes, celles aussi qui desirent colorier et corriger des photographies, dessiner et colorier des cartonnages, etc., peuvent acquérir dans cette, école l'instruction necessaire au but qu'elles se proposent.

Un certain nombre d'élèves sont admises gratuitement. Les autres le sont moyennant 3 franc par mois.

Les cours ont lieu les mardis, jeudis, et samedis, de 1 heure à 4 heurs.

ÉTUDES.

1. Élément du dessin.
2. Étude de la tête, d'après l'estampe.
3. Étude de la tête, d'après la ronde bosse.
4. Étude de l'ornement d'après l'estampe.
5. Étude d'ornement d'après la ronde bosse.
6. Étude de la figure drapée, d'après l'estampe et d'après l'antique.
7. Pastels, figures, fleurs, animaux.
8. Paysages d'après l'estampe.
9. Éléments de perspective.
10. Peinture à l'huile et mignature.

IV. — GERMAN SCHOOL.

INDUSTRIAL SCHOOL OF ART AT NUREMBERG, BAVARIA, GERMANY.

COURSE OF STUDIES.

DRAWING.
1. Ornamental drawing, from objects. Eighteen hours.
2. Drawing from the antiques. Twenty-four hours.
3. Drawing from life.

PAINTING.
1. From models in plaster.
2. From life.
3. Original compositions.

SCULPTURE.
1. Architectural and ornamental models, from drawings. Eighteen hours.
2. Finished objects from working drawings.
3. From antiques. Twelve hours.
4. From life. Twelve hours.
5. Objects of original design.
6. Wood-carving.
7. Engraving.
8. Modelling and casting in metal.

ARCHITECTURE.
1. Construction drawings.
2. Study of ancient construction.
3. Renaissance, architecture, and practical study of the same.
4. Gothic Architecture, and application to churches and civil architecture.

WORKING DRAWINGS OF DESIGNS.

COMPLETION OF ARTISTIC AND INDUSTRIAL DESIGNS.

THEORETICAL BRANCHES.
Perspective, and shades and shadows.
Anatomy.
History of art.

PHOTOGRAPHY.

CASTING IN PLASTER.

CABINET WORK.

Collections of objects connected with the several departments are contained in the building.

The school year is divided into two terms. The winter term is from November 1 to the last of February. The summer term is from April 1st to August 24th. Beside the vacation between the terms, there are the following: from Wednesday before until Tuesday after Easter; from Wednesday before until the Tuesday following Pentecost; Christmas holidays.

CONDITIONS OF ENTRANCE.

1. Each applicant must have reached the age of sixteen.
2. Must have a good moral character.
3. Must have attended a preparatory school in drawing and modelling.
4. Must exhibit specimens of his work.
5. Must have the permission of his parents or guardian.
7. He is allowed to enter at the commencement of the first term.
8. His acceptance by the school is shown by giving him a ticket of membership.
9. Listeners can be admitted on application to the director.
10. Each student is obliged to obey strictly the rules and regulations of the school.
11. No student will be allowed to pass into an advanced class until he is perfectly qualified to do so.
12. The student may enter the classes for which he is prepared.
13. The terms of tuition must be paid in advance. Residents, five fl.; Foreigners, ten fl.; Listeners, fifteen fl.
14. For the use of the materials used in instruction, an extra fee of twenty-four kreuzers per term is charged.
16. No student is allowed to be absent without sufficient excuse.
17. Any student violating the above rules, &c., shall be reprimanded by the professor. The third time he shall be reported to the director.
18. If he is absent *six* days in succession without a good excuse, he may be discharged from the school.
19. Ill-treatment of the professors, and ungentlemanly conduct, may also result in dismissal.
20. Copper-plate engravings, &c., may be used within the limits of the building on application to the proper authority.
21. Books without plates may be taken home with permission from the person in charge of such.
22. Any damage done to the collection must be paid for.
23. The students are marked at the end of each term as follows: —
    0, Extraordinary; 0/1, not quite so good; 1, very good; 1/2, pretty good; 2, good; 2/3, nearly good; 3, satisfactory; 3/4, nearly satisfactory; 4, middling.
24. A fee of twelve kreuzers will be charged for the mark. For special marks, and at the end of the course, a fee of thirty kreuzers will be charged.
25. A student must have visited the school at least one term to receive a mark.
26. An exhibition occurs every two years.
27. Each student is obliged to furnish works for this exhibition.
28. The students in the class of carving must take care that their work is properly finished.
29. A third part of the collection is selected by the professors for the collection of the school.
30. Students are obliged to leave part of their work as property of the school.
31. The best works are photographed. Each student is entitled to a copy of his work.
32. All plaster casts, carvings, castings in bronze, and engravings, done by the student, are to be considered as belonging to the school.
33. From the best works the student is entitled to one copy.
34. If the student does not fulfil the above conditions, his mark is withheld from him.
35. After the exhibition, the student shall receive those works not held by the school.

RULES AND REGULATIONS.

1. The chief management of the school, as regards discipline, &c., is in the hands of the director.
2. If, on account of absence or other cause, the director is prevented from attending to his duties, he is to appoint a director *pro tem.*, subject to the approval of the Minister of Education.
3. Each teacher is to perform his duties uninfluenced by any outside matters, and is to be governed by Article 9 of the By-Laws of May 26, 1818.
4. The acceptance of a position in any other school is to be allowed only by permission of the aforesaid minister.
5. Rooms are provided in the building for the use of the professors and teachers, that they may carry on their work undisturbed. The fruits of their labors

are to be placed before the students to serve as examples. All professors are obliged, when present, to see that the rules and regulations are obeyed.

6. It is not alone the duty of the school to see that the course of studies is carried out, but to see that finished works in its several departments are produced.
7. Every teacher is obliged to assist in the carrying-out of these works, and is to be reimbursed from the funds appropriated for that purpose.
8. All business of the school, such as contracts, &c., is to be referred to the director through his secretary.
9. All contracts are closed by the Board of Managers after an understanding is had with the professors interested: they are then handed to the guarantor, who is to see that they are properly executed.
10. All private business of the officers of the school is, of course, beyond control of the managers.
11. All works of the students which are to be exhibited are to be handed to the director at least two months before the exhibition.
12. Each teacher must report the progress of the students under his charge,—printed lists being furnished for this purpose. These reports assist in making up the annual report.
13. At the beginning and end of each term, the professors and teachers of the school are to come together to discuss matters relating to the same.
14. At the exhibition, all works of the exhibiter, and, if necessary, certificates as to the need of an examination, are to be furnished. The result of the examination, at the motion of the director, shall be determined by a vote of the faculty.
15. The secretary attends to all correspondence and business of the school, excepting that relating to the finances, under the direction of the director.
16. The finances are conducted according to regulations made by the Minister of Education.
17. The house inspector has charge of the order of the building in general, and of the collections in the same.
18. The materials, &c., used are to be provided according to the rules governing the same.
19. The photographic department copies, upon an order from the director, works of the students wh'ch have been selected by the professors for this purpose. The permission for the publication of all works of the students must be granted by the director.
20. The casting in plaster is done by a person employed for the purpose. The selection of the models is made by the professor having charge of the department. When the model is very large, permission must be obtained from the director.
21. In the cabinet-maker's department, meritorious works of the students in carving are reproduced. Objects are also constructed from drawings.
22. The house servant is to keep the building, &c., in order, subject to the order of his superiors.

INDEX.

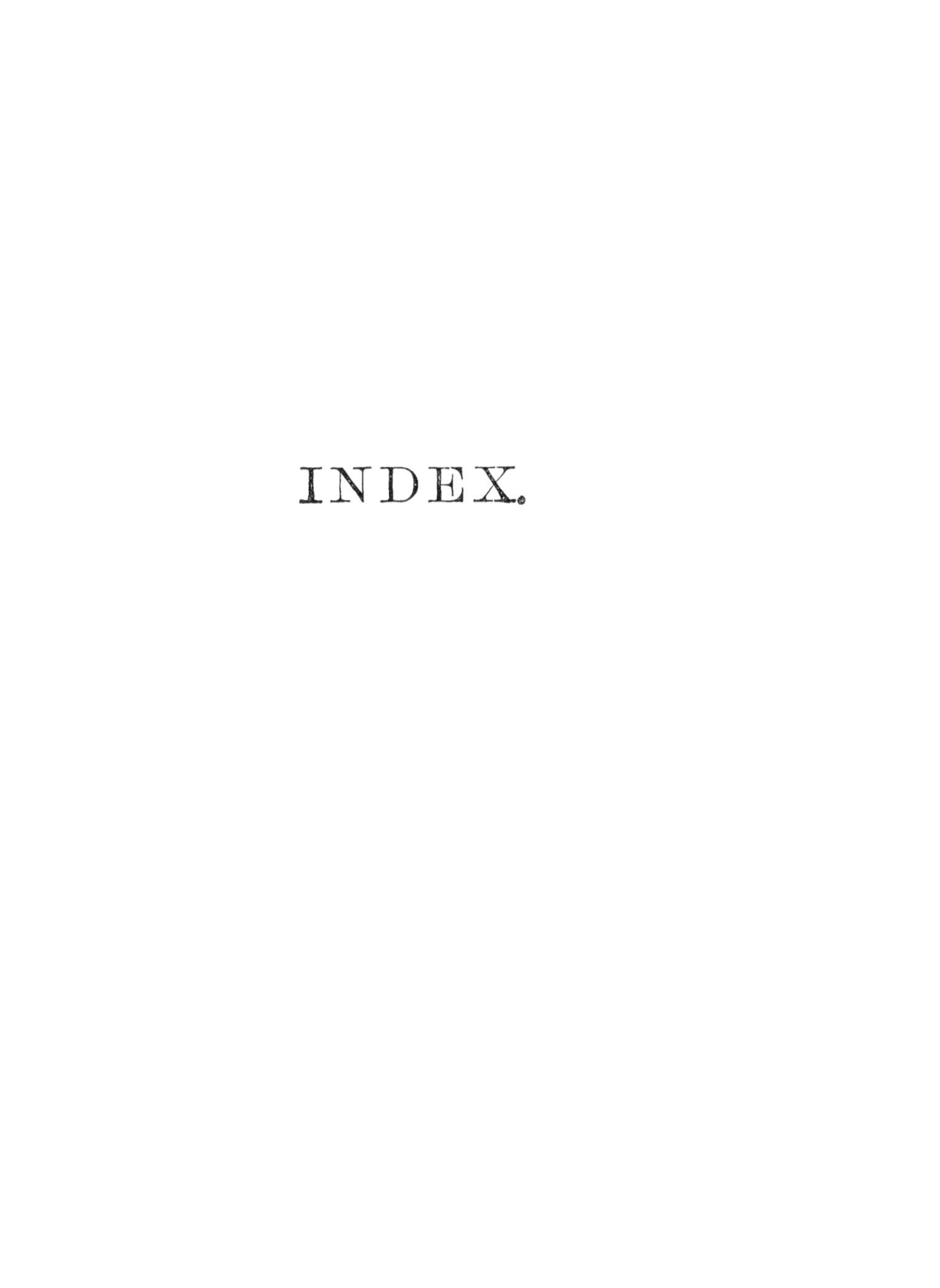

INDEX.

INDEX TO APPENDIX.

www.ingramcontent.com/pod-product-compliance
Lightning Source LLC
LaVergne TN
LVHW020925110826
845150LV00004B/775

* 9 7 8 1 4 2 5 5 5 3 1 4 2 *